Modern Afghanistan

Modern Afghanistan

A History of Struggle and Survival

Amin Saikal
with assistance from

Ravan Farhadi and Kirill Nourzhanov

I.B. TAURIS
LONDON · NEW YORK

Reprinted in 2006 by I.B. Tauris & Co Ltd
6 Salem Road, London W2 4BU
175 Fifth Avenue, New York NY 10010
www.ibtauris.com

In the United States of America and in Canada distributed by
Palgrave Macmillan, a division of St Martin's Press
175 Fifth Avenue, New York NY 10010

Published in 2004 by I.B. Tauris & Co Ltd
Copyright © Amin Saikal, 2004

ISBN 1 85043 437 9
EAN 978 1 85043 437 5

A full CIP record for this book is available from the British Library
A full CIP record for this book is available from the Library of Congress

Library of Congress catalog card: available

Typeset in Ehrhardt MT by Steve Tribe, Andover
Printed and bound in India by Replika Press Pvt. Ltd.

Contents

Preface

THE IDEA FOR THIS book first came to me in the early 1980s – not too long after the Soviet Union invaded Afghanistan in late December 1979. It was a time when the Soviet-backed communist regime was busy rewriting Afghan history to suit its ideological purposes, and Afghanistan had become the subject of more international focus than ever before. Whereas up to this point only a handful of western scholars had concentrated on Afghanistan as the main subject of their intellectual inquiry, suddenly many more established (and instant) scholars and observers of Afghan history, politics and society rushed to analyse the Afghan situation in both historical and contemporary terms. As I had recently completed a doctorate in Australia and was no longer able to return to Afghanistan, my home country, because of my opposition to the Soviet occupation, I was fortunate to have access to most of what was published about Afghanistan's past and present. While some works struck me as offering objective portrayals based on an in-depth historical understanding of the complexity of Afghan politics and society, as well as its region, in the context of broader world affairs, there were many works which were simply penned as a response to the call of the day for more focus on and publicity about Afghanistan. The concern which gripped me was that virtually all the western scholarly works overlooked some fundamental issues – most importantly the dynamic interactive relationship which had evolved between the factors of royal polygamy, major power rivalry and ideological extremism in heavily influencing the evolution of the modern Afghan state ever since its foundation in 1747. These were the issues which were quite plain to the eyes of many Afghan scholars and political practitioners, especially those who had a deep insight into the Afghan history or had been intimately involved in the operation of Afghan politics at some point in their lives, but could not be easily discerned by non-Afghan minds.

With this concern in mind, I visited Paris in early 1982 to speak with Dr Ravan Farhadi, who had recently escaped the Soviet occupation after having been jailed by the communist regime of Nur Mohammad Taraki and Hafizullah Amin for some 18 months. Dr Farhadi had been a mentor ever since I was a high school student in Kabul in the 1960s. He had impressed me as a powerful intellect and influential policymaker, with such personal integrity and social richness as to become (and to remain to the present day) a role model for me and many other Afghans like me. After having spent hours discussing the project, we agreed that I should proceed with this book. He kindly offered to serve as a source of information and criticism, and his wisdom was to prove indispensable, even as he assumed new responsibilities in the 1990s as Afghanistan's Ambassador and Permanent Representative at the United Nations. It was from that point that I commenced research for this book. However, since this was one of several projects which I had undertaken, it was to be a long-term project, to be completed over several stages as Afghanistan's turbulent historical journey took a bloody and uncertain direction over the next two decades. As I reached the final stages of the research and writing, I was very fortunate to find another valuable aid and at the same time colleague, Dr Kirill Nourzhanov, who provided much-needed and creative editorial help with the second half of the manuscript and the footnoting of the entire manuscript. His knowledge of Russian sources proved to be vital to the shape of the final product.

This book could not have been completed without the valuable assistance of Drs Farhadi and Nourzhanov. I owe both of them a world of gratitude, but dedicate the book to Dr Farhadi for all his selfless services to Afghanistan and world of scholarship, and to the people of Afghanistan for their love of freedom and human dignity.

Beyond this, over the long years of research, I conversed with many relevant Afghan and non-Afghan scholars, policymakers and activists, and benefited from support of many institutions. I am extremely thankful to all of them. Obviously, I cannot mention them all individually here, but there are a few I must name. The first and foremost are Professors William Maley and Robert McChesney. William acted not only as a reader and critic of the manuscript, but also as a very dear, loyal friend and source of encouragement throughout my years of research and writing. Robert, whose friendship has been inspirational, has enriched me so much as a source of intellectual influence through his writings and frequent personal interactions that I cannot thank him enough. I am also indebted to the former Afghan Deputy Prime Minister and Minister of Finance, the late Sayyed Qassem Rishtya, who in two long conversations provided me with more insight into the working of pre-communist Afghan governments than any source of literature could do. Further, I am very thankful to Carol Laslett for acting (often beyond the call of duty) to lighten my workload in the university so that I could devote a great deal of time to my research. Of the many institutions which supported this project either directly or indirectly, I owe a debt of gratitude to the Rockefeller Foundation, the Institute of Development Studies, University of Sussex, the Center of International Studies, Princeton University and above all the Australian National University, especially its Faculty of Arts, where I have held an academic position since 1983.

Of course, this book would have not originated had it not been for the inspiration and support of my extended and immediate families. I was and continue to be influenced by the dedication of my late parents, five brothers and two sisters to both the cause of Afghanistan's independence and wellbeing, and to what it takes to embrace many worlds as both proud Afghans and global citizens. Each one of them in their separate ways has had an impact on my knowledge about Afghanistan, but perhaps none of them more so than my youngest brother, Mahmoud Saikal, who has devoted most of his adult life to serving in whatever capacity necessary to preserve Afghanistan's independence and to alleviate the suffering of the Afghan people. My family has a story of its own in the struggle for a free, independent and forward-looking Afghanistan, which I hope will be told at another time. As for my immediate family, my wife, Mary-Lou Hickey, has given all the love and support that I have needed to get through this project and several more, though perhaps less daunting than this one. I also cannot thank her enough for reading and formatting the entire manuscript. Although my three daughters, Rahima, Samra and Amina were born at times when I had already become deeply immersed in this project, they had to endure my many moments of aloofness and long absences as I became more and more preoccupied with my research and writing. Yet despite my neglect of their many social and school occasions, they have continued to grow lovingly and delightfully, to manage to keep my feet on the ground, as much as an Australian as an Afghan. They are the pride and joy of my life.

Amin Saikal
Canberra

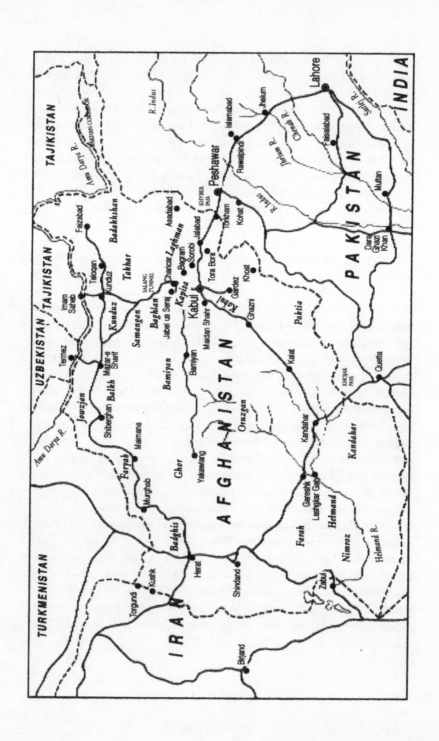

Introduction

RARE IS THE COUNTRY that has sustained as many blows, and such *hard* blows, as has Afghanistan since its foundation as a distinct political unit in 1747. Yet the country has managed to survive and to retain some form of sovereignty and territorial integrity, despite numerous wars and invasions and swings between extremist ideological dispositions, ranging from tribalist value-systems to Marxism-Leninism and Islamic medievalism. It is the only country in the world that has experienced military occupation or intervention by Great Britain (twice in the nineteenth century), the Soviet Union (in the 1980s) and the United States of America (since late 2001). Domestically, Afghanistan has witnessed periods of both remarkable stability and violent turbulence, which have succeeded one another in a seemingly haphazard manner. Mountstuart Elphinstone, writing in 1809, summarised exceptionally well the daunting task that an observer of Afghan politics could face: 'He would be surprised at the fluctuation and instability of the civil institutions. He would find it difficult to comprehend how a nation could subsist in such disorder.'[1] He would also find that 'Opportunism prevails in Afghanistan. The changing combination of forces is not based on any principle; they simply represent the unfolding of old rivalries and new clashes of interests.'[2] This is a judgement that is reaffirmed by many present-day analysts, who struggle to explain the recent cycle of fragmentation and renewal in Afghanistan in rational terms.

The horrific terrorist attacks on New York and Washington on 11 September 2001, masterminded from Afghanistan, shook the world and propelled Afghanistan once more to the forefront of world politics. The

United States government resolved to destroy the alleged perpetrators of those attacks – the Saudi dissident Osama bin Laden and his senior al-Qaeda activists, as well as their protectors, the extremist Islamic Taliban militia in Afghanistan. The traditionally divided Afghan people, who had been locked in warfare since the late 1970s, have once again found themselves under serious challenge for reform as a result. They are under unprecedented pressure, both domestic and external, to repackage their clash of interests and their disorder to regenerate a new polity and sense of national unity, although this time with a promise of extensive help from the international community, most importantly its most powerful member, the USA. Many Afghans despair at the thought of failing to rise to this challenge effectively, for the alternative would be Afghanistan remaining a dangerous source of perpetual devastation for its own people and instability in world politics for many more decades to come. This is the reason that all the world powers have promised, this time, not to turn their backs on the Afghans until they have achieved a stable political order and decent level of livelihood.

There is no way of predicting precisely what will happen in the future, given that uncertainty and unpredictability have been the hallmark of Afghanistan for most of its existence. However, what is possible is to look back critically at the evolution of the Afghan polity in order to answer three burning questions. Why has Afghanistan had such a turbulent historical course of development, remaining almost chronically vulnerable to domestic instability and foreign intervention as well as ideological extremism? Does the problem lie in the mosaic nature of the Afghan society, the country's landlocked geographical location and extensive cross-border ethnic ties with its neighbours and the interactive relations between these factors, or in something far less conventional which has eluded most analysts and historians of Afghanistan? Does Afghanistan have the capacity for rejuvenation and under what conditions?

Many seasoned analysts and observers of Afghan politics and society have made serious attempts at answering these questions. The result has been a number of significant works, which are rich in their content and reflective in their approaches. They range from Louis Duprée's seminal volume *Afghanistan* and *The Emergence of Modern Afghanistan* by Vartan Gregorian to Leon Poullada's *Reform and Rebellion in Afghanistan*, to *The Fragmentation of Afghanistan* by Barnett R. Rubin and *The Afghanistan Wars* by William Maley. These works and many more, some quite comprehensive and others very selective in their individual coverage and approach, have informed us well from various perspectives and ideological angles about a wide range of factors and dynamics influencing the Afghan polity and determining its fortunes and misfortunes in history. However, in general, either for reasons of convenience or lack of sufficient access to the inside working of the Afghan ruling elites and Afghanistan's social and cultural intricacies, their emphasis has been more on visible sociological and geo-strategic factors than on what may be viewed as a mixture of interactive relationships between elite behaviour and outside power rivalry, and the role of these in giving rise to ideological extremism in shaping today's Afghanistan. These relationships are regarded by the 'insiders' of Afghan politics and society – that is those who have had intimate access to the inner working of Afghan ruling elites and have often been key players in directing the polity – as absolutely critical to understanding and unpacking the social and political complexities of Afghanistan, and they stem from three main interrelated variables: *royal polygamy*, *foreign interference* and *ideological extremism*. Without engaging in reductionism, a close look at the relationships between these variables clearly demonstrates that, along with such other factors as social divisions, cultural mores and geographical location, they have been instrumental in determining the course of Afghan history and in laying the foundations for preventing the Afghans from developing the necessary attributes of a strong state with a lasting stable political order.

In a nutshell, the contention of this book is that it was largely the factor of polygamic rivalries within the successive royal families from the end of the eighteenth century to the pro-Soviet communist coup of April 1978 that substantially contributed to disabling the Afghans from developing solid domestic structures of statehood and stability. This interacted with major power rivalries, at first between Great Britain and Tsarist Russia (and, from 1917, Soviet Russia); then, following the Second World War, between the USA and the USSR; and, after the end of the Cold War and the collapse of the Soviet Union in 1991, between regional powers. Outside interventions ensured the weakening of already feeble domestic structures, generating a vicious cyclic interplay between the factors of polygamy and foreign interventions, with each feeding off the other. It was also mostly in the context of the interplay between these two factors and the failures of successive rulers and governments to harness national unity, institutionalise (as opposed to personalise) politics and establish a legitimate participatory political order, and bring about social-economic stability, that ideological extremism found space to gain hold among those who could seize state power in pursuit of radical political and social transformation. As rulers failed to incorporate moderate Islam – the traditional form in practice in Afghanistan – into a culturally relevant ideology of state-building and modernisation, there emerged sharp tensions between secular radical modernisation and traditional conservatism in the 1920s, communism and Islamism from the 1960s to the 1980s and moderate Islamism and regressive Islamic medievalism in the 1990s.

Naturally, for each historical period, the combination of political events, conditioning elite renewal, circulation and fragmentation in Afghanistan, has varied considerably. However, it is these three recurring themes, or hazardous forces, which consistently shaped and reshaped the Afghan politics and society. To elucidate this point, it is important to focus briefly on each of these variables individually.

Polygamy

Ahmad Shah Abdali, the founder of the independent Afghan state, came very close to the Weberian ideal of patrimonial rule, in that his power was fundamentally personal and independent of any objectively rational goal. This was also true of his immediate successors. Politics in Afghanistan was characterised by direct bargaining amongst clans, tribes, regional populations and other elementary solidarity groups. Rulers of the Sadozai (1747–1818) and Barakzai (1826–1929) dynasties were first and foremost leaders of the Durrani Pashtun tribal confederation, whose authority in the eyes of other communities in Afghanistan was tenuous at best. Sometimes they were able to exercise prescriptive and regulative functions in the Afghan polity, accumulating and distributing resources, and mediating between different contenders. Quite often, they simply struggled to survive in the mêlée of stronger political actors. At no point in time could they develop new common legal and political frameworks to transcend the traditional boundaries of various local units. Kinship, marriage and personal loyalty remained the only morphological elements of competing elite factions.

Even these traditional instruments of political exchange could not be successfully employed by Afghan monarchs until the 1930s to establish a stable dynastic rule – the necessary (but not sufficient) condition for an efficient centralised government.[3] Polygamic practices of the rulers were largely responsible for this failure.

Polygamous unions 'for politics and for pleasure'[4] were and still are noticeably spread throughout the Middle East.[5] In eighteenth- and nineteenth-century Afghanistan, the Durrani Pashtun leaders took excessive numbers of wives from other tribes and ethnic groups, often as a means of shoring up and asserting their privileged position. In addition to the four wives allowed by the Muslim holy book, the Qur'an, they could have an unlimited number of *surati*, or concubines. The sheer quantity of royal consorts and offspring, their fuzzy legal status and hierarchical order and the absence of primogeniture or any other canonised routine of succession and inheritance produced endless internecine conflicts and bloody feuds, mainly between half-blooded royal brothers and their relatives within the rival branches of the royal family.[6] Many Afghan historians have alluded to this when discussing their country's past from patrimonial positions, and have attributed much of the misfortunes of their homeland to the 'jealousy' of numerous princelings 'not content with their lot',[7] although the same cannot be said about their western counterparts. The polygamic-based inter-dynastic rivalries on the one hand made the weak or defeated power contenders vulnerable to dependence on outside rival powers, and on the other hand made it easier for these powers to intervene in Afghanistan with a considerable degree of impunity. This proved to be instrumental in preventing the Afghans from building appropriate domestic structures and processes for enduring political stability, social and economic development and national unity.

Beginning with the rule of Shah Zaman (1793–1799) individual, rival members of the ruling elite increasingly sought foreign support to overpower one another and their Durrani clansmen, and bring the rest of the population under control. This suited rival powers, as they wanted to manipulate such elements in pursuit of their conflicting regional interests. Although it is true that so long as a Pashtun prince depended on assistance from Persia, Bukhara, the Sikh State or any other traditional regional power, he could not have a decisive advantage over his opponents because their resources were limited and their alliances tended to be short-lived due to inherent instability in those countries, the advent of European actors in the Age of Imperialism changed the situation dramatically. From the reign of Dost Mohammad Khan (1826–1838, 1842–1863) onwards, the favourable disposition of Britain – and, to a lesser extent, Russia – became the overriding factor in the domestic struggle. It was Amir Abdur Rahman Khan (1880–1901) who 'decided to rise to the status of Afghan sovereign, and to become a genuine monarch from his position of a feudal leader of independent tribes using military hardware and financial help from across the British border'.[8] Having sacrificed Afghanistan's independence, he built a centralised state where the ruling elite consisted of his immediate family, affines and clients from amongst other Durrani clans. The forcible imposition of Durrani supremacy (or more specifically that of the Mohammedzai clan) put an end to the prospects of non-confrontational coexistence of diverse microsocieties in Afghanistan. Most successive regimes followed the pattern mapped out by Abdur Rahman Khan: a highly repressive administration operated by an exclusive elite upholding patrimonial codes and denying major groups and strata autonomous access to the sources of power.[9]

The patronage of a foreign power (or powers) proved akin to drug addiction. Throughout the nineteenth and twentieth centuries, no central government in Afghanistan could survive and maintain high levels of political and social control without support from abroad. The state's increasing economic and military dependence on external sources was complemented by the two-pronged threat posed by exogenous influences. First, a marginalised group in the Afghan polity could always appeal to an international sympathiser. Thus, after 1992, the Hazaras enjoyed a cordial relationship with Iran, whereas Uzbeks in northern Afghanistan built a good rapport with the leadership of Uzbekistan; similarly, the Pashtun Taliban exercised power, from 1996 to 2001, very much at the behest of Pakistan. Second, the dominant elites in Afghanistan have seldom been completely cohesive themselves. Members of ruling solidarity groups have often tried to promote their interests by securing foreign patronage. During the reign of Habibullah Khan (1901–1919), his brother, Nasrullah Khan, actively cooperated with the Germans, in contrast with the overall pro-British orientation of the state. During his premiership, from 1953 to 1963, Mohammad Daoud leaned towards greater cooperation with the Soviet Union, while his rival cousin and brother-in-law, King Zahir Shah, generally pursued a pro-American line. Foreign powers readily used their leverage over groups and individuals in Afghanistan to pursue their regional and global agendas. The patrimonial and non-representative nature of Afghan regimes had made such interference possible in the first place, but subsequently it was exogenous influences that facilitated and perpetuated neo-patrimonialism in Afghanistan. The evil circle proved impossible to break, particularly given the fact that Afghanistan has constantly been the focus of the geopolitical competition known as the 'Great Game' since the second half of the nineteenth century.

Major Power Rivalry

The attractiveness of Afghanistan for foreign powers has been variously attributed to its rich mineral resources,[10] its infrastructure development potential[11] and its ability to house military bases.[12] All these arguments were produced to portray the Soviet invasion of Afghanistan as a case of imperial territorial expansion, but by and large turned out to be irrelevant. It is rather the country's pivotal location in the heart of Central Asia that has made Afghanistan important in the eyes of foreign policymakers. In Malcolm Yapp's words: 'it is not imperial strategic interest which dictates developments, but the local border position… The imperial dimension confuses analysis and falsifies prediction.'[13] Afghanistan played the role of buffer state between the Russian and British empires, then between the USSR and British India and finally, until 1992, between the Soviet and western blocs. Richard Newell has come up with a laconic yet comprehensive characterisation of the country's status in all those years: 'Afghanistan is important enough – largely because of its strategic location – to try to influence, but it is not valuable enough to risk dominating';[14] those who have tried to dominate have lost out very badly.

The debate on the motives behind Moscow's decision to forego peaceful competition for influence in Afghanistan and undertake a military intervention has become a *cause célèbre* in specialist literature since 1979.[15] This book reiterates major arguments ranging from considerations of international prestige to costs miscalculation and argues that, although the occupation had been preceded by a long and complex period of Soviet involvement in Afghanistan, the invasion was hardly a logical culmination of this process. It attempts to shed light on a somewhat overlooked aspect of the Great Power rivalry, namely *insufficient information*, which time and again prompted international actors to undertake irrational steps which, in turn, served as a major source of uncertainty for political outcomes in Afghanistan. Dennis Smith has made an astute observation concerning the conceitedness of the British and Americans, which could have been easily extended to the Soviet Union as well:

> These two nations have, in turn, enjoyed the experience of global supremacy in the nineteenth and twentieth centuries. As a consequence they are known by the world far better than they, in turn, know that world. To use an analogy, the slave always has to know his or her master, in order to maximise the chances for survival. The master can enjoy the luxury of ignorance – at least until his throat is cut.[16]

Britain was 'burnt', although in varying degrees, in Afghanistan three times, during the wars of 1839–42, 1878–79 and 1919. The Soviet occupation of Afghanistan between 1979 and 1989 ended disastrously for the Kremlin. The USA is only beginning to reap the bitter harvest of its short-sighted strategy of making friends in the region. The 'Great Game', from its onset in the period after the Napoleonic wars, has been 'a tournament of shadows, a secret war of illusions',[17] costly to everyone involved, but Afghans in particular. The over- and underestimation of rival influences in Afghanistan, as well as sheer ignorance, as factors in great powers' decision-making are only now beginning to attract serious scholarly comment.[18] Documents emerging from Soviet archives point to the fact that the decision to invade Afghanistan was only one of the possible solutions mulled over by the Kremlin throughout 1979 amidst much controversy caused by conflicting reports from that country.[19]

In the post-Cold War era, competition over Afghanistan has continued with a greater number of participants, which have included Pakistan, Iran, India, the former Soviet Central Asian republics, Russia, Saudi Arabia, China, the USA and others: 'In fact any state that has any interest in Central Asia is interested in what happens in Afghanistan.'[20] As in the old days, major outside players have been busy cultivating clients amongst Afghan groups. As before, they often base their policies on insufficient information and/or poor cost-benefit analysis. Pakistan became directly involved in the conflict in Afghanistan, supporting the Taliban in the 1990s despite experts' warnings about the 'boomerang effect' this might have for the stability of Pakistan and the region.[21] As it turned out, the effect of the developments in Afghanistan finally became so great and touched the USA in such a disastrous way on 11 September 2001 that the US government was finally driven to intervene directly in Afghanistan to hunt down the perpetrators and to overthrow the Taliban regime.

Foreign interference enabled Durrani rulers to evolve a centralised quasi-modern state, which suppressed microsocieties and disguised the fragmented nature of the polity in Afghanistan. Great power rivalry in the twentieth century secured the continuity of this state under the guise of autocratic, 'liberal', authoritarian and Marxist regimes. After the collapse of the Soviet Union in late 1991, any semblance of functional central government evaporated in Afghanistan. At the same time it became clear that decades of state monopoly on coercion and distribution had undermined local communities and especially the essential horizontal linkages amongst them. Not just the polity but the entire society appeared to be fragmented. Presently, as Maley has noted, the core problem for Afghanistan is not reassembling a government but rebuilding a basic consensual framework in its society.[22] The difficulty of this task is proportional to the level of outside intervention in the country. Ahmad Shah Massoud, the only prominent figure in the Afghan resistance to the Soviet occupation and Pakistan-backed Taliban rule who did not have a powerful foreign patron (and who was assassinated by al-Qaeda/Taliban agents two days before the terrorist attack on the USA), observed in March 1998: 'The main scourge of our country is perennial foreign intervention… Only final cessation of foreign aggression will allow us to start solving all other problems of Afghanistan, economic and political.'[23]

Ideology

As the modern centralised state has been an artificial construct in Afghanistan, so too have been the elaborate ideologies employed by modern elites to justify relations of domination in society. Abdur Rahman Khan's ideas of absolute monarchy, the 'constitutionalism' of Amanullah Khan, the gradualism of the Musahiban rulers, the 'new democracy' of Zahir Shah, the 'socialism' of the *Khalqis* and *Parchamis*, the Islamism of the Mujahideen and the Islamic medievalism of the Taliban were all mere tools legitimating shifts in power and did not reflect fundamental changes in the systems of meaning across society. Most of the ideological shifts arose from rivalries within the ruling families and often free of any popular base. To borrow from Ernest Gellner, fluctuations in the configuration of social control:

> were produced by a transfer of the means of physical coercion from one set of hands to another... and *not* by some semantic transformation. What mattered was who held the gun, and who did not. To suppose the contrary is to indulge in an absurd form of idealism.[24]

Most political conflicts in modern Afghan history have not begun as disputes over such issues as the direction of development, religious belief, constitutional rights or social class. Rather, they have stemmed from the attempts of dominant communally based elites to accomplish a high degree of centralisation of power with the help of foreign patrons. Consciously elaborated, overt, systematic, institutionalised and dogmatic ideologies have been but a thin veneer on the traditional political culture constituted by largely implicit sets of beliefs, kinship norms, codes of accepted behaviour and hierarchies of identity.[25] The bearers of formal ideologies have been products of traditional society; they could never be divorced from their backgrounds. *Any* government or official political movement in Afghanistan, whatever its proclaimed goals and position on the left-right continuum, recruited, mobilised support and operated according to criteria of ethnic/tribal/clan solidarity. All prominent 'Constitutionalists' in the age of Habibullah and Amanullah were Durrani Pashtuns, linked by conjugal and patronage ties. Throughout the 'liberal' and 'democratic' periods in the post-Second World War era, the Mohammadzai clan never relinquished power. It was the power struggle between the two rival branches of the Mohammedzai ruling family that provided the foundation for the growth of pro-Soviet communism from the mid 1950s to the PDPA seizure of power in April 1978 and the Soviet-PDPA rule of Afghanistan in 1980s. The fact that PDPA rule was a story of rivalry between two major solidarity networks is common knowledge. The Islamic extremism of the Taliban rose essentially in pursuit of power, but as a reaction to the moderate Islamism of the Mujahideen, which had sought to fill the vacuum created by the failure of Soviet communism.

Nazif Shahrani has noted that:

> perhaps the most remarkable legacy of the policies of the old form of
> 'tribalised' state system in the contemporary political culture of
> Afghanistan may be their effect upon the rise and formation of many forms
> of political communities opposing the corrupt and oppressive state system
> itself.[26]

New opposition parties, alliances and groups shared three basic features:
(a) their continuous existence depended on external support;[27] (b) they
articulated formal ideologies which did not reflect their rootedness in
traditional disenfranchised communities;[28] and (c) the establishment of rigid
centralised government was invariably their ultimate goal. Clearly, none of
them was in a position to mobilise support from the majority of Afghan
microsocieties, with one notable exception: the Mujahideen movement, which
arose in response to the unprecedented displacement of traditional
communities under the Soviet-sponsored regimes of *Khalq* and *Parcham*.

Approach

In this book, we adopt an historical approach, that is, establishing the causal-
consequential dynamics of long-term political trends, reflected in the actions
of individuals, groups and institutions. We seek, as far as possible, to tell a
unified story and not to produce a new compendium of accounts of
traditionally important themes. At the same time, we do not strive to
undertake a *definitive* study of Afghanistan's past which would conform to
the ideal formula of 'history with the politics left out', as suggested by George
M. Trevelyan and upheld by social historians who concentrate 'on the sum
of persons, ways-of-doing things, and terrain'.[29] Perhaps in the future, an
attempt will be made to emulate Trevelyan's monumental *English Social
History* for Afghanistan,[30] but we explicitly confine the subject matter of
this book to processes associated with the polity, but grounded in three
interrelated themes of polygamy, major power rivalry and ideology.[31]

Anthony Giddens has remarked that there are no 'logical or even
methodological distinctions between the social sciences and history –
appropriately conceived'.[32] Indeed, anthropology, together with geography,
sociology, economics and other academic disciplines, has been successfully
employed in the systematic investigation of Afghanistan's political history.
In this sense, we follow the tradition of Vadim Masson and Vadim Romodin,[33]
Vartan Gregorian[34] and Louis Duprée.[35] However, there is always a danger
that the particularistic nature of such inquiries may leave the reader more
confused than informed about the dynamics of a given society.[36] To

paraphrase John Roberts, in the most recent period of history it is more than ever important to distinguish the wood from the trees and not to put emphasis on some concept simply because it is fashionable.[37] At the other extremity, the total absence of problem-oriented topicality may have a similar stultifying effect on the reader. Duprée's 'holistic' approach works because of his tremendous knowledge, wit, and life-long experience of Afghanistan. Others are not so fortunate.[38]

Three decades have passed since Duprée's definitive monograph was first published. The need for a new comprehensive political history of Afghanistan, given the immense changes in that country, in the region and in the world, is understandable. At the same time, this book is not a mere recapitulation of what has been said before with bits of new empirical evidence thrown in here and there. Most importantly, it offers a new theoretical perspective on politics in Afghanistan, disengaging from the Marxist perspective of Masson and Romodin, and the 'modernisationism' of Gregorian and Poullada,[39] as well as Duprée's claim of the irrelevance of political theory for an anthropologist ferreting out 'the patterns, functional and dysfunctional, in the total synchronic–ecological–cultural sense'.[40]

Structure

This book is divided into nine chapters, which are organised chronologically. Chapter 1 covers the period from 1747 to 1901 and provides an overview of social, geographic and ethnic conditions leading to the foundation of modern Afghanistan. The formation of the new state by Ahmad Shah Abdali (1747–73) was made possible by the collapse of the Safavid Empire and the weakening of the Mughal dynasty. The gestation of the new Afghan elite, which included Pashtun and non-Pashtun elements alike, was facilitated by territorial expansion and lavish war booty. When Ahmad Shah's son and successor, Timur Shah (1773–1793), was forced to go on the defensive, the elite cohesion collapsed. Until 1835, rival factions could agree on practically no issue and any political event, such as the death of a monarch or the arrival of a foreign mission, triggered instability in its most violent form. The succession of Dost Mohammad to the Kabul throne in 1826 signified a thorough renewal of the elite under the new Mohammadzai dynasty. A tenuous 'division of labour' emerged amongst the Pashtuns: Durranis formed the dominant faction enjoying massive economic benefits; Ghilzais and smaller tribes were forced to pay tax, albeit not excessively; and frontier tribes were largely left alone, only fielding militia units in times of peril. The king's role was to mediate and coordinate the Pashtuns' efforts at repelling foreign aggression and conquering new territories under the banner of Islam. The process of elite consolidation did not stop with Dost Mohammad's death in 1863 and continued under Amir Sher Ali (1863–1879). The First and Second Anglo-Afghan wars highlighted the growing dependence of the monarch on tribal leaders for defence – a dependence which was enhanced and strengthened by conjugal ties.

The reign of Abdur Rahman Khan (1880–1901) saw the emergence of a more or less monocratic elite for the first time in Afghanistan: predominantly Durrani in composition, Pashtun-centric in ideology and supported with British money, it succeeded in uniting Afghanistan within its present borders. Despite the creation of a central government and the introduction of elements of 'defensive modernisation', Abdur Rahman's rule had more in common with the rise of autocracy under Ivan the Terrible in sixteenth-century Russia than with modern nation-building: it 'was not accompanied by a change in political customs or goals, or by a new political consciousness. The political order had survived… with its traditional reliance on kinship, marriage, and consensus intact'.[41]

This consensus was based on the need to suppress the non-Pashtun minorities in the 'pacified' territories of Hazarajat, Afghan Turkestan and Nuristan; and to present an image of unity to the outside world in order to serve as a reliable buffer zone for British India in exchange for an annual subsidy. So long as Abdur Rahman continued to deliver on both issues, the elite professed support for the monarchy and was prepared to be tolerant.

Chapter 2 focuses on the reign of Amir Habibullah (1901–1919). This was a period of global upheaval, when accelerating processes of change in Turkey and Persia, followed by the First World War and the rise of the anti-colonial movement in India, threatened the status quo in Afghanistan. Habibullah proved to be a capable statesman who opted for a policy of gradual accommodation of change by opening up the elite through the incorporation and promotion of a handful of modern intellectuals. Limited factionalism was tolerated, which for the first time centred on ideological issues, such as constitutionalism and independence. The political system retained stability due to Habibullah's policies of neutrality, appeasement of ethnic minorities and maintaining good relations with the tribes. Habibullah's assassination under unclear circumstances violated the equilibrium.

Chapter 3 deals with the tumultuous rule of King Amanullah (1919–1929). His reformist zeal led to regime collapse, primarily because the coalition of national forces, which had hailed his ascendancy as a champion of independence, disintegrated soon after the end of the Third Anglo-Afghan war. Amanullah alienated tribal leaders by revoking their privileges; his modernisation schemes had depleted the treasury; and he could not secure adequate funding from external sources. The reformer-king had a forewarning of growing instability in 1924 when the Khost rebellion took place, but carried on regardless. His most notable failure was that he had not installed viable government structures, particularly coercive agencies, to ensure implementation of his plans. The crisis induced by Amanullah was so complete that for a brief period between January and October 1929 a Tajik, Habibullah Kalakani, proclaimed rule in the country. This immediate threat to Durrani supremacy made the leaders of the Pashtun elite factions quickly reach a compromise and, moreover, overhaul the entire political system inherited from Amanullah to avert similar occurrences in the future.

Chapter 4 covers the efforts of the new Nadiri dynasty of 1929–1953 to establish new rules for the political game. The elite was thoroughly overhauled and purged of liberal supporters of Amanullah. The government was run as a family business by the Musahiban brothers; at the same time, considerable autonomy was granted to private economic interests. The crisis associated with the Second World War showed that Afghanistan had acquired a somewhat ideologically unified elite once again, which was capable of preventing the country's occupation by Allied Forces, in contrast to neighbouring Iran. King Mohammad Nadir Shah (1929–1933), seeing the potential for rivalry between two polygamic-based rival branches in the ruling family, took the precaution of marrying two of his daughters off to his nephews. His son and successor, Zahir Shah (1933–1973), was largely relegated to a secondary role, due to the omnipotence of his uncles, Mohammad Hashim (Prime Minister, 1929–1946) and Shah Mahmud (Prime Minister, 1946–1953). In the post-war period, the new regime successfully forged ties with the USA, finally breaking away from the traditional pattern of balancing delicately between Russia and Britain.

Chapter 5 spans the period between 1953 and 1963, a period of increasing rivalry between King Zahir Shah and Prime Minister Mohammad Daoud – son of Mohammad Aziz (full blooded brother of Mohammad Hashim), but rival cousin and brother-in-law of King Zahir Shah. It was also a time of notable economic growth for Afghanistan, fuelled by generous financial assistance from the USSR, which was matched to some extent by the USA in the context of the Cold War rivalry. After 1955, Moscow became Afghanistan's key provider of military hardware and training. The bulk of Afghanistan's officer corps in the 1950s and 1960s was trained in the Soviet Union, whereas civilian specialists were sent to the West for education. For the first time, modern elite groups began to play a leading role in the political process, marginalising tribal leaders to an extent. The modern armed forces became an important instrument of social control. Although he enjoyed enormous support in military circles, Mohammad Daoud resigned peacefully in 1963 over policy differences with the king.

Chapter 6 analyses the most dynamic period in the modern history of Afghanistan (1963–1973), when an attempt was made to make a transition to a pluralistic, consensually unified elite operating a representative regime. This was deemed possible on the basis of the exponential growth of new elite groups, not necessarily Durrani or even Pashtun in origin. This experiment in liberalism failed, because elite factions representing the entire spectrum of political beliefs failed to act according to the norms of restrained partisanship. The pressures brought by the decrease in Soviet and American financial aid also contributed to the growing instability. However, ultimately the age-old power rivalry between Zahir Shah and Mohammad Daoud brought the period to a crushing end, with Daoud leading a successful coup against his cousin.

Chapter 7 is concerned with Daoud's presidency between 1973 and 1978, which saw Afghanistan slipping into a succession of ruthless inter-elite conflicts. The abolition of the monarchy removed an important source of ideological cohesion for Afghanistan's elite. The 1975 armed uprising of Islamists reflected a growing disunity amongst domestic political forces. When Daoud attempted to increase his personal power, partially in order to reduce his regime's dependence on and therefore vulnerability to the Soviet Union, and implemented a series of daring political initiatives in the region, he was brought down by a pro-Soviet communist coup, led by some of the very people that Daoud had protected and nurtured as a means to strengthen his own position in the rivalry within the royal family. As such, Daoud had played a critical role, though in many ways unwittingly, in the growth of ideological extremism, in this case of a Marxist-Leninist variety.

Chapter 8 covers the period of Marxist-Leninist rule in Afghanistan from 1978 to 1992. Although during this time all ruling elite groups professed the same communist ideology and were members of the same party, endemic factionalism, often coloured with ethnic overtones, incapacitated the new regime, which could not deal with the multiple threats to its existence. This was exacerbated by the rapid deployment of Islam as an ideology of resistance on the part of the opposition forces and their foreign supporters, most importantly the USA, against the imposition of Soviet communism on Afghanistan. The PDPA stayed in power for as long as it did only because of the Soviet occupation of Afghanistan in the 1980s and massive military and economic assistance from Moscow following the Soviet troop withdrawal. The moment this help stopped, the regime collapsed and an extremely violent process of elite renewal was triggered.

Chapter 9 explores inter-elite struggle in Afghanistan after 1992, characterised by the promotion of moderate Islamism as a replacement for Marxism-Leninism, and the absence of even elementary consensual activity aimed at creating a semblance of accommodation between various power and ethnic elites. Whatever alliances rival factions entered were of a purely opportunistic nature. The political system of Afghanistan suffers from chronic instability and virtually lost the ability to function independently of foreign influences. The chapter examines the fragmentation of the moderate Islamic government and its defeat by the Pakistan-backed Taliban, and the rule of the Taliban as yet another form of ideological extremism, as well as the consequence of this for Afghanistan and the international community.

The concluding chapter pulls together the major themes running through the book, to point out the direction of the future development of Afghanistan, based on the country's historical journey and the consequences of landmark events and changes which have affected its circumstances and those of the international community.

A Word on Sources

A general work of this sort is inevitably the product of the research of many people living in different countries in different times and writing in different languages. We have widely used chronicles and historiographies by Afghan and other Central Asian authors.[42] The aforementioned books of Gregorian, Poullada, Duprée and Masson and Romodin were always a source of inspiration as models of academic excellence. Rubin's monograph, although not strictly a work on history, should be also included in this list as an encyclopaedia of facts, concepts and ideas.[43]

Rawan Farhadi's amazing memory served as a very special source while we were writing this book. Dr Farhadi has made a splendid career in academia, the diplomatic service and high politics. Born in 1929 in Kabul, he received his Ph.D. from the Sorbonne in 1955 and entered Afghan public service. After a chain of diplomatic appointments, he served as Secretary to the Cabinet (1966–1971) and as Deputy Foreign Minister for Political Affairs (1970–1973). He was arrested by the *Khalqi* regime in 1978, released in 1980 and currently represents Afghanistan at the United Nations in New York. Rawan Farhadi's personal accounts of Afghanistan's political leaders and the inner workings of various regimes in the post-war period have proved invaluable. In addition, Dr Farhadi has generously shared the knowledge he received from his father about events in the times of Amanullah Khan, Habibullah Kalakani and Nadir Shah; the oral tradition still remains one of the significant mechanisms of narrative transmission in Afghan society.

At this point often comes the turn for self-serving criticism of special works relevant to the subject. As it happens, the corpus of literature on various aspects of Afghan history, society and culture is enormous, and most of its entries are first-rate studies. We confidently relied on the expert knowledge of Asta Olesen[44] and Olivier Roy[45] dealing with issues of Islam. Nancy Tapper[46] and Akbar Ahmed[47] provided exhaustive accounts of complex social phenomena governing the day-to-day lives of Pashtuns. A volume by Victor Korgun proved to be indispensable in dealing with the role of intellectuals in Afghanistan's politics.[48] A study on Afghanistan's foreign policy by Abdul Samad Ghaus was as comprehensive as it was elegantly written.[49] Finally, a number of recent volumes on the Taliban, including one written by Ahmed Rashid and one edited by William Maley, provided outstanding multidisciplinary accounts of the developments in that country in the past several years.[50]

Harold Bloom, lamenting the predominance of the School of Resentment in contemporary literary criticism, wrote: 'Reading a poem or a novel... is for them an exercise in contextualisation, but not in a merely reasonable sense of finding adequate backgrounds.'[51] We did not indulge in postmodernist discourse; our task is to seek adequate backgrounds in Afghanistan's past to help curious readers come closer to understanding its present. Such a story, it is hoped, will be popular, yet also scholarly, relevant and detached.

1

From Tribal Confederacy to National Coalescence

THE CREATION OF THE Durrani monarchy in 1747 triggered a dramatic turning point in the history of the vast region wedged between the rivers Oxus and Indus. After the Achaemenid period, multiple states rose and fell on the territory of what is now Afghanistan. New polities would emerge on the ruins of collapsed empires, build up to a critical size (sometimes briefly exceeding the limits of the parent entity), and then split up, as a result of succession disputes, external pressures, scarcity of resources or other reasons, into smaller principalities which would in turn expand, only to disintegrate again. In the middle of the eighteenth century, the Afghan state was quintessentially a loose confederation of chieftaincies, or 'localised autonomies that come to recognise the superior authority of one of their own in a grouping of small polities',[1] which emerged on the periphery of two great but moribund empires: the Safavids in Persia, and the Moghuls in India. In the century and a half that followed, this primitive construct, in contrast to so many similar and contemporaneous princedoms in northern India and Central Asia, not only failed to dissolve, but also evolved a governance system that possessed many of the trappings of the modern state. When King Amanullah proclaimed Afghanistan's complete independence in 1919, his country had internationally recognised boundaries, a standing army, a centralised bureaucracy and more or less regularised systems of justice and taxation. Moreover, Amanullah felt confident enough to declare that his mandate to rule stemmed from the 'Afghan nation'. Why did the Afghan monarchs succeed where their colleagues in Kashmir, Turkestan and Tibet failed? Did a modern 'nation-state' emerge in Afghanistan as a 'natural' result of social development? How far did its capacity to prescribe rules of social behaviour go? What were the grounds for its acceptance by the general populace? These are important questions to be addressed for the initial period of Afghanistan's existence as a distinct political entity.

The Land and People

Afghanistan has existed as a recognisable political unit since the middle of the eighteenth century. Prior to this, of course, the country did not have any national cohesion or a political identity as Afghanistan. The very names 'Afghan' and 'Afghanistan' were first chronicled as late as the tenth century AD;[2] some authors trace them as far down as the third century AD, although apparently without sufficient grounds.[3]

At the dawn of modern times, the territory of what is now Afghanistan was inhabited by a variety of ethnic groups which, apart from the Muslim faith, had little in common. In the period preceding the Durrani Pashtun ascendancy in 1747, the ethnonyms of 'Afghan' and 'Afghanistan' denoted a particular *ethnie*[4] – the predominantly nomadic Pashtuns – and a particular locality where they resided: the western frontier mountains of the Subcontinent (the Suleiman range).[5] They gradually moved to the valleys and plains, subjugating, assimilating and otherwise interacting with the ancient sedentary population – the Tajiks, concentrated in Kabulistan, Ghazna, Logar, Zabulistan and Helmand.[6] The morphological dichotomy between the Pashtuns and the Tajiks was and remains the most potent social divide in Afghanistan, while claims to the effect that 'the Pashtuns and Tajiks, who combined constitute most of the inhabitants of Afghanistan, have always shown a united front to all invaders and helped to preserve Afghanistan' are questionable.[7] Certainly, the two communities had never acted in unison before the emergence of the modern Afghan state in the last quarter of the nineteenth century.

Apart from Pashtuns and Tajiks, the Indo-European population of Afghanistan in pre-modern times also comprised Nuristanis, Baluchis, Heratis and other smaller ethnic groups. The major Turkic peoples of Afghanistan included Uzbeks, Turkmens and Qizilbash. Hazaras and Char-Aimaqs represented communities of mixed Turkic-Mongolian-Iranian stock, whereas Brahuis belonged to the subcontinental pre-Aryan anthropological type and spoke a Dravidian language. Small groups of Arabs, Jews, Armenians, Panjabis and others made the ethnic mosaic even more complex. The astounding ethnic diversity is reflected in the fact that as many as 30 languages may have been spoken in Afghanistan.[8] Babur Shah, describing the Kabul province in the beginning of the sixteenth century, commented that 'nowhere else does there exist such a variety of tribes and multiplicity of tongues'.[9] It was only in the eighteenth century that 'Afghanistan' transcended the confines of a purely ethno-cultural term, as the Pashtuns became what Asta Olesen has called the main state-supporting group.[10]

In the absence of a strong state or sense of nationhood, social regulation was performed at the level of microsocieties – tribes and other distinct localised communities[11] that had mainly been dominated by Safavid Persia in the west and Mughal India in the east. Meanwhile, they were separated from Tsarist Russia in the north by Khanates, or local princedoms, most importantly those of Bukhara, Kokand and Khiva in Central Asia; they were thus remote from Tsarist Russia and could not figure strongly in its growing imperial ambitions.[12] Nor could they be of much interest to Great Britain, for the latter had not as yet embarked on comprehensive colonisation of the Indian subcontinent.

Ahmad Shah's Confederal and Imperial Entity

This picture, however, changed with the rise of Ahmad Shah Abdali to rule the Afghans. Ahmad Shah was a leading figure of the prestigious Sadozai clan of the Pashtun Abdali Durrani tribe,[13] and a notable warrior and organiser, who had distinguished himself in the service of the Persian King, Nadir Shah Afshar. His Abdali tribal confederation, under the chieftainship of his father Zaman Khan, had ruled Herat prior to the conquest of the city by Nadir Afshar in the early part of the eighteenth century. In 1747, following Nadir Shah Afshar's assassination, Ahmad Shah came to Kandahar and successfully assembled the rival Abdali and Ghilzai chieftains from roughly within the boundaries of present Afghanistan in a *Jirga* (traditional tribal assembly), which pronounced him to be their paramount chief, and formed a grand Afghan ethno-tribal confederation, with Kandahar as its capital.[14] Despite the fact that Ahmad Shah's authority was not at once recognised throughout Afghanistan, and he had to rely on both conquest and diplomacy to achieve it, this event was momentous: it amounted to the declaration of Ahmad Shah as the first monarch of the Afghan people in modern history. After assuming the title of Durr-e Durran (Pearl of Pearls), Ahmad Shah during the 25 years of his rule rapidly managed to free divided Afghan tribes from Persian and Mughal domination, to consolidate them into a macrosociety and to distinguish them as an identifiable independent political unit within an expanded territory of present-day Afghanistan. This macrosociety also incorporated the Tajiks, Hazaras, Uzbeks, Baluchis and Khorasanis, with whom Ahmad Shah sought to maintain ethnic peace and political alliance. By the end of his rule he had not only established a powerful

Durrani conquest empire, stretching from its north-westernmost point at Khorasan to the Ganges plain in the Indian subcontinent, but had also laid the foundations for a lengthy period of Durrani dynastic rule. Although his empire faced disintegration within 30 years of his death in 1773, his Durrani descendants continued, at first under the Sadozai clan and from 1826 under the latter's kindred Mohammadzai clan of the Barakzai tribe, to hold the reins of power, in one form or another, for two centuries.

Ahmad Shah's rule was, by nature and practice, essentially a charismatic accretion on traditional authoritarian-tribal rule, with the political and military ascendancy of the Abdali Pashtuns revolving around the unchallenged position of Ahmad Shah as the paramount leader.[15] It had neither clear legal-constitutional bases nor an elaborate, institutionalised administrative and security apparatus which could provide for what could resemble a governmental system in the modern sense of the term. Nor did it have an ideological-philosophical commitment to the transformation of Ahmad Shah's confederation into a viable unit in the emergent system of nation-states, which had begun to take root in Europe following the Peace of Westphalia of 1648, and to proliferate elsewhere.

A fusion of the Islamic ideas of 'divine right' and 'divine rule' (as embedded in the tradition of the Sunni majority in Islam – the dominant sect in Afghanistan) with the hierarchical tribal codes of leadership and submissiveness of followers, backed by a multiethnic and tribal army that Ahmad Shah created, accounted for the core operative mechanisms of political legitimacy.[16] Whereas the Islamic idea that the leader is the main reflection or vice-regent of God and ought to be accordingly respected furnished the intangible but necessary theoretical grounds of justification for the leadership, tribal traditions and coexistence with major ethnic groups of the country provided the practical social framework within which the leadership could give concrete expression to its rule and actions.[17] The leadership utilised such ideas and codes, in combination with the use of several other variables, to legitimate its position and enforce the supremacy of the ruler. The other variables, most importantly, included: crude force as the prime factor in the acquisition of legitimacy in a traditional society; and inter- and intra-tribal consultations and cross-tribal marital linkages and alliances, governed by the principles of 'accommodation and rule' and 'reward and punishment'. In this respect, two other factors also figured very crucially. One concerned the skill of the ruler in managing his relationships with the other tribal chieftains, whose varying positions in the power structure of the confederation ultimately determined the ruler's success or failure. The other related to the ruler's shrewdness in pursuing methods of governance which helped ensure not only that the chieftains would remain content, in terms of both material gains and exercise of traditional authority, with their respective positions; but also that tribal followers of each chieftain would receive enough tangible benefits to secure their loyalty to their chief and through him to the central leadership.

Ahmad Shah, who has come to be recognised as wise and prudent,[18] provided for these factors largely through a two-dimensional policy of multiethnic-tribal accommodation, and military expeditions and conquests. His policy of accommodation turned on the formation of a fairly loose 'supra-tribal council' of the major Durrani Sadozai Khans (or chieftains), which acted as a consultative body to him; and an army, whose central command was mostly in the hands of Sadozais but whose units, divided along tribal and ethnic lines, were made up of both Pashtuns and non-Pashtuns such as Tajiks and Hazaras, with each unit assigned a specific fighting task.[19] It also involved the allocation of some of the important administrative posts to leading figures from other than his Abdali tribe. This was so despite the sectarian religious differences between the Pashtuns, who were mostly Sunnis, and a number of Shi'ite non-Pashtuns, particularly Khorasanis and Hazaras. Indeed, the inclusion of Khorasan in his domain, and the need to acquire the loyalty and obedience of its people, played a significant role in prompting Ahmad Shah to pursue a non-hostile accommodationist attitude towards not only the Khorasanis but all of his non-Pashtun subjects. For this and, of course, reasons of personal safety, he even went so far as to employ the Qizilbash ('Redheads'), who have historically functioned as a suppressed Shi'ite microsociety in Afghanistan, as his bodyguards – a practice which was continued by his successors, until the reign of Amir Sher Ali Khan (1863–1866).[20]

His policy of military expeditions, which gave a militaristic character to his rule and resulted in the rapid expansion of his confederation into a conquest empire, saw his army units continuously on the offensive, especially at a time when the Persians and Sikhs of West Punjab were weak and suffering from internal malaise and divisions. Two factors more than anything else motivated Ahmad Shah in this respect. One was his claim to be a defender of Islam and the constant urging from some Indian Muslim leaders, especially Shah Waliullah Dehlawi, that he defend the Muslims in the Indian subcontinent against Hindu hegemony.[21] Another was the consideration that the more the Afghan tribal militias were engaged in offensive operations, the greater the chances of their units and commanders becoming persistently preoccupied with warfare, proud of their conquests and, above all, engrossed in the pecuniary gains which war booty brought them. Hence, they remained divided as separate units, and void of the impetus needed to pose any real threat either individually or collectively to Ahmad Shah's central authority.

Thus, Ahmad Shah was able to establish an autocratic and yet reasonably charismatic popular imperial rule. While skirted by divine claims, his rule was in reality grounded in his unique personality, the supremacy of his own tribal Pashtuns and a skilful manipulation of flexible accommodation of non-Durrani Pashtuns and non-Pashtun ethnic groups and sub-groups, as well as offensive warfare. In this context, Ahmad Shah's rule was neither overtly 'Pashtunist' nor obviously discriminatory in its treatment of non-Pashtun subjects.[22] Consequently, it was in many ways consensual and mirrored to an appreciable extent the heterogeneous nature of his Afghan domain. Ahmad Shah's success in binding together different tribal and ethnic peoples, irrespective of their sectarian, linguistic, cultural and territorial differences, within an Afghanistan entity, and in leading them to coalesce within a collective framework under a single leadership and central authority, set the foundations for the emergence of modern Afghanistan.[23] As a result, this exalted Ahmad Shah to the position of *baba* (the father of the nation) and *Mu'assis* (founder) of present Afghanistan in history on the one hand, and left the stamp of personal rule imprinted on the Afghan psyche, giving rise to a recurring element in the development of Afghan politics on the other.[24]

Inter-Dynastic Power Struggle

The foundations laid by Ahmad Shah could not ensure the development of a viable process of political change and social stability in the long run. Three main factors and perpetual interactions between them undermined those foundations and came to influence the evolution of Afghan politics substantially over the next two centuries.

The first of these factors concerned the very structure of Ahmad Shah's rule and the nature of Afghan society. His confederation had, all along, a tenuous existence. It was very weak in its structure. Its core was made up of four major Abdali or Durrani tribes: Popalzai (to which Ahmad Shah's own Sadozai clan belonged), Barakzai (which produced the Mohammadzai clan that assumed the reins of power from the Sadozai from 1826), Alikozai and Achakzai.[25] On the periphery of the confederation was the Abdali's rival tribe, the Ghilzai, with which Ahmad Shah succeeded in forging an alliance that did not last for very long after his death, although this initial alliance proved instrumental in depriving the Ghilzais of any access to paramount leadership in the long run.[26] In the past, the Durrani clans had been engaged in intense rivalry and blood feuds, not only with the Ghilzais, but also among themselves. The central bond that held them together was Ahmad Shah's charisma and sensible policies in regulating and controlling tribal relationships within his confederation.

This made Ahmad Shah's style of rule highly personalised, with its durability and operational capacity dependent very much on *ad hoc* rather than institutionalised mechanisms for generating change or securing continuity. As a consequence, while Ahmad Shah succeeded in creating a central authority and an identifiable entity of 'Afghanistan', this was not the same as constructing a strong state based on the institutionalisation rather than personalisation of politics and horizontal integration rather than vertical federalisation of the microsocieties within a legal-rational framework. In other words, the kind of system of governance and political entity that he generated centred very much upon the existence of a charismatic, skilled leader like Ahmad Shah himself, and lacked the capacity to be institutionally self-generating and self-propelling in the absence of such a leader.

This meant that, at his death, Ahmad Shah's confederation lost its nerve centre, confronting it with a serious power vacuum. Ahmad Shah's successor, one of his older sons, Timur Shah, who was Governor of Herat in the later years of his father's rule, tried to fill the vacuum by largely continuing the policies that he inherited. He initially appeared successful in holding the Durrani Empire together to a considerable extent. However, he did not have the same leadership attributes as his father, which presented him with mounting difficulties in sustaining as firm a hold as his father on the levers of tribal authority and relationships. His rule was soon beset by challenges from within his own sub-clan, and revolts from other tribes and ethnic groups, particularly the Ghilzais, Khorasanis and Sistanis, forcing him to transfer the capital from Kandahar to Kabul during 1775–1776. Although he overcame most of the challenges and revolts, and concluded a treaty with the Emirate of Bukhara strengthening his authority south of the Oxus or Amu River, destabilising actions stemming largely from inter- and intra-tribal and ethnic rivalries continued to undermine his rule, especially from 1780 until his death in 1793.[27] This destabilisation increased under the rule of his son, Shah Zaman (1793–1800), despite his success in maintaining the Afghan Empire within more or less the same boundaries as he had inherited.

The second factor stemmed from the practice of unlimited polygamy within the ruling family. A deeply entrenched tradition in the Islamic world, the practice was based on a ruling in the Qur'an that a man is allowed a maximum of four wives and an unspecified number of what may be termed 'concubines' from among the women who are left 'unprotected' and need 'guardians'.[28] The practice had become widespread in the historically patriarchal Afghanistan[29] since the country's conversion to Islam in the eighth century. Before the reformist, monogamous King Amanullah (1919–1928) issued a decree against 'concubinage', limiting polygamy to only four lawful wives, the Qur'anic injunction had been abused among Afghans, especially by men of power and influence.[30] Rulers from Ahmad Shah to Amanullah's father, Amir Habibullah, as well as nobles, had allowed themselves to take into morganatic marriage, in addition to four wives, any woman whom the Afghans called *surati* or, more correctly, *suryati* ('bed-wife').

They entered into this type of marriage for a variety of reasons. Some of the more important ones related to the man's desire to have blood relations with another clan, tribe or ethnic group for the purpose of alliance or counter-alliance, or to secure a male heir or to obtain extra loved ones.[31] The position of the concubine, however, was essentially as legalised as that of the wife. Her children were neither illegitimate nor (particularly in the case of sons) automatically barred from inheriting the title, status and wealth of their father, although the extent to which this was enforced depended on the mother's shrewdness and the degree of influence that she carried with her husband in particular, and within the royal or clan power structure in general. The continuous pressure from the wife's tribe was also a factor to be counted.[32] The only thing differentiating a concubine's male offspring from a wife's son was that the latter, especially if he was from his father's first or favourite wife, conventionally took precedence over the former.[33]

Such polygamy, in the case of rulers and nobles, produced numerous brothers and half-brothers as well as power-brokers within and outside the royal family, with competing claims to the throne and other power positions.[34] This provided a perpetual and self-generating source of political and social tensions, conflicts and power struggles within successive ruling families and their supporting nobilities, which proved to have a lasting and devastating impact on the development of Afghan politics. Although Ahmad Shah prevented rivalry between his sons by promoting Timur Shah, from his first wife, as heir apparent, the same could not be said about the latter. While leaving behind many sons[35] who were full and half-brothers, most of them capable of claiming a right to the throne, Timur Shah failed to designate any one of them as his heir. In the absence of a clear leadership succession pro-cedure, the assumption of the throne by Zaman Shah, Timur Shah's fifth son by his favourite wife, who belonged to the East Pashtun tribe of Yusufzai,[36] with the help of a leading Barakzai figure of Kandahar, Payenda Mohammad Khan, set in motion a sequence of power struggles between him and his brothers that caused not only a series of turbulent royal successions among them, but also plunged Afghanistan into a long period of intra-ruling family and intra-tribal conflict which led to the ultimate demise of the Sadozai dynasty.

The third factor undermining political stability was the European powers' rivalry over Afghanistan. Germinated in the last years of the eighteenth century as part of the Anglo-French confrontation within the wider framework of the Napoleonic wars,[37] it gave way to Anglo-Russian competition by the 1830s. Even then geostrategic factors remained relatively marginal to the fortunes of Afghanistan. The country had first and foremost to face internal dissent. Fragmentation of power and civil wars ravaged Afghanistan almost incessantly between 1801 and 1834; the main external threats in this period came not from Russia and England, but from Afghanistan's immediate neighbours.

Major Power Rivalry

Until well into the second half of the nineteenth century, all the world powers' designs over Afghanistan were fuelled by paranoid considerations of 'security' without much substance behind them, as the country was still too remote from existing spheres of influence.[38] The rivalry with regard to Central Asia took off in earnest following the Crimean War of 1853–1856. Russia's Committee of Ministers, during its two sessions in November and December 1857, for the first time spelled out the importance of a policy of influence towards Bukhara, Khiva and Kokand, but did not mention Afghanistan.[39] The dogfight over that country between Russia and Britain made little sense until the age of mature imperialism, from the 1870s to 1890s. In the first half of the nineteenth century, the British were still preoccupied with the piecemeal subjugation of India, and Russia had just begun feeling its way through the steppes of Central Asia. Hundreds of miles still separated the two expanding empires. The spirit of rivalry and periodic outbursts of bellicose public opinion in the metropolises on the issue of Afghanistan were the result of misperception and general lack of information on both sides.[40]

Tsarist Russia's concerted drive southwards, launched in the mid 1860s, was justified by several sets of arguments, typical for any colonial power at the time: (1) geographical, that is, Russia must have safe borders preferably delineated by the ocean; (2) *Kulturträger*, or the civilising mission of the 'White Man';[41] and (3) economic – opening new markets for Russia's exports. Additionally, the Tsarist administration sought to counter rival colonial activities around its imperial domain.[42] As the British colonisation of the Indian subcontinent gained momentum and the British became assertive in protecting their new colonial outlay on a region-wide basis, and as the Russians sought safeguards partly against this development and partly in pursuit of their own ambitions, the growth of a serious Anglo-Russian rivalry in the region became inevitable.

In the meantime, the once powerful Durrani Empire lay in ruins. In 1818, it disintegrated into three major princedoms – Kabul, Kandahar and Herat – plus scores of lesser principalities. The Persians, under their new and assertive Qajar dynasty, were trying to remove Afghan control over part of Persia and Herat. The Sikhs, under their charismatic leader Ranjit Singh, threw off Afghan domination in the wake of the Battle of Nowshera in 1823, rapidly expanding influence in the traditional Afghan lands. In the evolving Anglo–Russian competition, the British supported the Sikhs, and the Russians encouraged and assisted the Persians to move against the Afghans as part of wider competition between the two imperial powers, placing Afghanistan in the midst of intense pressures from powers around it. This helped set in motion processes which eventually led Russia and Britain to regard Afghanistan as strategically vital in their confrontation. Whereas the British came to see the country as a defence line for their colonial interests, to the Russians it was considered a gate to British interests beyond Turkestan. The Anglo–Russian competition for political control of Central Asia, which before the end of the nineteenth century evolved incrementally into what Rudyard Kipling called the 'Great Game' between the two imperial powers,[43] developed three salient features.

First it unleashed an extraordinary chain of actions and reactions, unparalleled in modern history, aimed at the securing of regional domination. On the one hand, it prompted the British to manipulate the Afghans as a resisting force against possible Russian ambitions in the direction of the Indian subcontinent and the Persian Gulf. On the other, it motivated the Russians to become more assertive in their desire, first of all, to tighten their influence in the Central Asian territories lying between Russia proper and Afghanistan. This in turn increased British determination to do whatever possible to prevent the Russians from expanding *beyond* the Amu River and threatening British colonial interests. To this end, the British eventually developed what became known as the 'forward defence policy',[44] which was religiously advocated in the late nineteenth and early twentieth centuries by Lord George Curzon, the most resolute defender of British colonial power. To Curzon, Afghanistan, along with Persia, Transcaspia and Turkestan, had grown to be 'the pieces on a chessboard upon which… [was] being played out a game for the domination of the world'[45] – a game which survived the Bolshevik Revolution and continued even to influence Anglo–Soviet relations until the end of the Second World War.

Another salient feature was that neither Britain nor Russia thought it beneficial to colonise Afghanistan. This was for two reasons. First, total subjugation of the country by either side would have placed the two powers on a course of full military confrontation, which neither side seemed to wish to risk. Second, Afghanistan then had none of the *immediately exploitable* economic and mineral resources that might have made it sufficiently attractive to make colonisation worthwhile.

Third, the relative independence of central control and warlike nature of the tribes made conditions highly unfavourable to foreign invaders. In both the first and second Anglo-Afghan Wars, the British lost only one of the set-piece battles, but the writ of their puppet amir ran only, and even then not always, where their troops were, and they could occupy only main centres such as Kabul, Jalalabad and Kandahar. During each war, a British general election, in August 1841 and April 1880 respectively, resulted in replaceme.1t of a pro-'forward policy' government by one opposed to it. The new govern-ments, of Robert Peel in 1841 and William Gladstone in 1880, each dismissed the Governor-General/Viceroy who had ordered invasion, and after achiev-ing some face-saving victories, the Anglo-Indian forces returned to India.

These experiences eventually convinced both British and Russians that it was in their interests to transform the country into an effective 'buffer' zone, separating Russian imperial domain from British colonial possessions.[46] However, the only way the rival powers could enforce a buffer status on Afghanistan was for each one of them to make sure that it had sufficient influence in the country to pre-empt any moves by the other. This predictably led to their quest for individual spheres of influence in Afghanistan, with the British attempting to be dominant in the region south of the Hindu Kush range, which bisects Afghanistan in the middle from east to west, and the Russians trying to maintain influence in the region north of the range. At the same time, both sides endeavoured either to have a friendly government in Kabul or to check the power of the Kabul government by allying themselves with regional and tribal leaders in what they regarded as their respective zones of influence.[47] Needless to say, for the absolute majority of Afghans, regardless of their identification with a particular ethnic group, both the British and the Russians were first and foremost *kafirs* (unbelievers) against whom *jihad* (holy war) ought to be waged.

These factors of structural state fragility, polygamic animosities and major power rivalry interacted to the lasting detriment of the Afghan macrosociety. They precipitately created the type of internal conditions and external pressures that rapidly undid Ahmad Shah's confederation and plunged Afghanistan into a chronic state of disorder and violent conflicts which lasted intermittently for most of the nineteenth century. As in-fighting rooted in polygamy broke out among Timur Shah's numerous sons, particularly after Zaman Shah's rule, Afghans lost their confederative unity. They fractionalised once again into hostile microsocieties along the lines of their long-standing ethno-tribal, linguistic and sectarian divisions. These groups proclaimed individual autonomous or semi-autonomous territories in conjunction with the neighbouring countries. As a result, at times the domain of an Afghan ruler became confined either to Kabul or another major city, giving rise to city-state rule in the country.[48]

This was followed by a steady but forceful British campaign to limit and manipulate Afghan rulers. It had two objectives: to expand the security perimeter of their Indian colony and eventually confine Afghans within as limited a territorial base as possible; and to secure a foundation for *long-term* anti-Russian influence in the country. The British sought to achieve this by forging alliances and counter-alliances with competing southern tribes, their leading figures and various full and half ruling Durrani brothers and throne aspirants; and by acting as 'kingmaker' among them.[49]

Despite two major British military thrusts into Kabul, resulting in the famous Anglo–Afghan wars of 1838–1842 and 1878–1880, which both ended with British withdrawal, by late in the century the British had succeeded in fixing Afghanistan, by and large, within its present eastern and southern boundaries. To legitimise their actions, they forced several treaties and agreements upon weak and dependent Afghan rulers. Perhaps most damaging of all were two: the infamous Treaty of Gandamak, signed in 1879, under which British India gained practical control over Afghan fiscal, defence and foreign policies; and the demarcation of the 'Durand Line', concluded in 1893. The Durand Line, drawn by a British Commission and named after its head, the British Indian Foreign Secretary, Sir Mortimer Durand, was the line arbitrarily determining Afghanistan's present eastern and southern frontiers and it demarcated British and Afghan responsibilities in the Pashtun area. Since it ran through and split several Afghan Pashtun tribes, the Durand Line was rejected by most Afghans then and became the basis for what subsequently developed as a thorny border dispute between Afghanistan and British India and, after 1947, Pakistan.[50]

In the face of such British hegemonic activities, Tsarist Russia, whose own creeping ambitions were partly responsible for them, did not sit idle. It pursued a concurrent campaign of its own, not only to maximise its influence in Persia and pressure Ottoman Turkey, both of which had also become the subject of British designs, but also to strengthen its position from the north in the direction of Afghanistan as part of wider regional bargaining.[51] At a time when the Afghans were overwhelmed by domestic crises and British interventions, the Russians moved without much hindrance to nibble away virtually all of Central Asia between the 1830s and 1870s, thus extending the Russian borders effectively to the north of the Amu River.[52] The Anglo-Russian Agreement of 1873 reflected the changed strategic situation in the region: the two colonial powers had come to a direct contact and decided to settle their differences peacefully. British statesmen 'were willing to accept that Russian moves in Asia were guided by a legitimate desire to extend their commerce and to maintain the security of the Russian frontier',[53] whereas Russia explicitly stated that 'Afghanistan lay outside its zone of interest'.[54]

In the late nineteenth century, St. Petersburg found it appropriate to strengthen further its position by determining and securing its borders with Afghanistan. Russian troops took Panjdeh in 1885 after overcoming gallant resistance by the Afghan forces. In the east, they forced the Afghans to evacuate the principalities of Shughnan and Roshan in the Pamirs in 1894 after a ten-year occupation.[55] While raising the spectre of a war with the Afghans and the British, this development nonetheless prompted the appointment of a conciliatory Anglo-Russian Commission to defuse the problem. Following much bargaining, the Commission found it expedient to relinquish the Panjdeh Oasis to Russia and determine Afghanistan's northern boundary largely along its present lines.[56] Although the matter was thus settled for the time being, Russian designs did not cease in northern Afghanistan, where the Uzbek, Turkmen and Kirghiz ethnic groups shared a common ethnicity, language and religion with Russian-controlled Central Asian peoples north of the Amu River. Nor was the dispute over the Amu River itself resolved – a dispute which lasted until 1941 when finally on the basis of an Afghan-Soviet agreement the *thalweg* of the river was declared as the official border between the two countries. The brief Russian thrusts of the 1880s into Afghan territory were to be followed by two more: the limited and abortive Soviet intervention of 1929 and the massive Soviet invasion of late 1979.

The vicious cycles that the mutually aided domestic disorder and foreign interference and intervention produced fatally set back the Afghans from building and maintaining a national consensus. It is true that at times, despite all the odds, tribal Pashtuns exhibited considerable cohesion and resilience as a people in meeting foreign challenges, as they did successfully in the case of the two major British military expeditions.[57] But this was more on the basis of a unity generated by their common Islamic faith and tribal patriotism than anything else, and even then only in the face of a direct foreign intervention. Otherwise, for most of the nineteenth century, there was no national leader and modern governmental system or process of national integration and social-economic reform in the country. The Afghans existed very much within the bounds of their traditional microsocieties and sub-components of such societies, each revolving around a tribal, ethnic or religious leader or a local hero. These leaders functioned under various titles, ranging from Khan to Sardar to Mir and Pir, and entered all sorts of alliances and counter-alliances, some of which were forged at the behest of foreign powers, especially Britain, in order to ensure their survival. Leaving the small polycentric nobility aside, the bulk of the population led an austere, harsh and agriculture-based existence within confined geographical localities, and remained by and large not only separated from one another, but also detached from the nobility. There was neither an active entrepreneurial group nor an effective intelligentsia, whose activities could permeate the microsocieties on a nationwide basis. The authority of many Afghan rulers rested largely on the support of one or several factions of the divided nobility, one or more of the local leaders and heroes, on outside, mainly British, backing, or on some combination of these forces.[58] Major-General Sir Henry Rawlinson, arguably the most knowledgeable British expert on things Afghan of his age, wrote in 1874:

> Afghanistan never has had, and never can have, the cohesion and consistency of a regular monarchical government. The nation consists of a mere collection of tribes, of unequal power and with divergent habits, which are held together, more or less closely, according to the personal character of the chief who rules them. The feeling of patriotism, as known in Europe, cannot exist among the Afghans, for there is no common country... There is no natural or ethnical reason why Herat and Candahar should be attached to Cabul. Herat is inhabited by races entirely alien to the Afghans, by Jamshidis, Eymaks, and Hazarehs; while at Candahar, though the lands were parcelled out by Nadir Shah [Afshar] in the middle of the last century among the Durrani aristocracy, and their descendants still exist as a privileged class, the peasantry are everywhere of Persian, or Tajik, or Turkish descent, and have no community of feeling with the northern and eastern Afghans.[59]

From the reign of Zaman Shah's successor, his brother Shah Mahmud, in 1800 to Amir Abdur Rahman Khan's assumption of the throne in 1880, seven figures proclaimed their sovereignty over Afghanistan. Of these rulers, who held the throne on average for a period of seven years each, four of them assumed the throne twice. They were Shah Mahmud (1800–1803 and 1809–1818), Shah Shuja (1803–1809 and 1839–1842), Amir Dost Mohammad Khan (1826–1839 and 1843–1863) and Amir Sher Ali Khan (1863–1866 and 1868–1879). While Shah Shuja ruled both times completely at the behest of the British, the last two, whose reigns were the longest among all rulers, pursued policies towards the British that could be characterised as both accommodationist and mildly confrontationist. Sher Ali Khan at times even became receptive to Russian overtures against the British. Of the two, nonetheless, Amir Dost Mohammad Khan's rise to power marked a turning point in the Durrani rule.

Dost Mohammad Khan's Rule

In contrast to his predecessors, Dost Mohammad was a Barakzai Durrani. His father, Sardar Payenda Khan, was a notable Barakzai Kandahari who had served as a powerful official in the courts of Sadozais; and his mother was a Qizilbash Shi'ite concubine from Kabul. Although he was Payenda Khan's youngest son, because of his mother's influence he was favoured by his father more than any of his brothers. While two of his half-brothers, Rahmdel Khan and Sultan Mohammad Khan, headed powerful families in Kandahar and Peshawar respectively, Dost Mohammad Khan had become, in the company of his father, active in the Kabul political arena. When his father was assassinated by Sadozais in 1818 and a power struggle broke out between the latter and the Barakzais, resulting in a savage civil war, Dost Mohammad Khan succeeded in wresting the throne from the Sadozais. He thereby inaugurated the rule of Barakzai Durranis, in particular their Mohammadzai clan, named after his ancestral figure, Mohammad.

Dost Mohammad Khan in 1836 adopted the title of 'Amir al-Momineen' (Commander of the Faithful) – a title derived from the Islamic institution of Khalifate – to emphasise the predominantly Sunni character of Afghanistan. He urgently wanted to achieve the unity of Afghans. In pursuing this end, he initially appeared quite successful, partly because he adopted a policy of *modus vivendi* towards the British, whom he regarded as the ultimate power capable of determining the course of events in Afghanistan. However, he was soon faced with treachery and intrigues from his half-brothers who operated from their own autonomous centres of power in Kandahar and Peshawar; a serious challenge from one of Timur Shah's sons, Shah Shuja, who had earlier ruled from 1803 to 1809, and was backed by the British as most amenable to their interests; and related and independent tribal revolts. Amid all this, the Persians, with Russia's encouragement, challenged the Afghan control of Khorasan and laid siege to Herat, while the Sikhs, then allies of the British, overran many of the eastern parts of the Durrani Empire and exerted pressure towards the north-west beyond Peshawar. With this also came the gradual imposition of British hegemony over the Sikhs[60] and subsequent dominance over former Durrani territory as far as Quetta and Peshawar.[61] The British refusal to assist Dost Mohammad in recovering Peshawar from the Sikhs led him to receive a Russian officer in Kabul. The

British thereupon invaded in 1839, replacing Dost Mohammad with their client, Shah Shuja, and thus igniting the first Anglo-Afghan war. This foreign challenge provided a focus for the Afghans to unite, and their determined resistance was aided by three external factors to bring about British withdrawal.

The first was the ignominious failure of the first Russian expedition against the Khanate of Khiva in 1840. It reduced the British perception of a Russian threat to India and hence of Afghanistan's strategic importance for the time being. The second was that after Dost Mohammad's surrender in November 1840, his British captors gradually came to realise that deposing him had been a colossal error. The third was the change of government resulting from the British general election of August 1841. These factors combined to enable Amir Dost Mohammad Khan to regain the throne in 1842 and rule for another 20 years. The British intervention alarmed the Russians, prompting them to intensify their own hegemonic moves in Central Asia in the direction of Afghanistan.[62] This development in turn caused the British to revive their 'forward defence policy' during the 1870s, with the aim of gaining a durable foothold of influence in Afghanistan.

The second lengthy period of Amir Dost Mohammad Khan's reign saw a semblance of stability and the relative strengthening of central authority. However, this consolidation was a temporary phenomenon, not rooted in a genuine consociational pact amongst Afghanistan's microsocieties. The ruling elite remained exclusionist and continued to be dominated by the immediate family of the monarch and a handful of Durrani chieftains. Ethnic inequality, favouring Pashtuns over other ethnic groups, persisted. The tax base of the state was extremely limited, since most Pashtun tribes were exempt from contributing anything to the royal treasury. Dost Mohammad Khan succeeded in bringing together most territories which had formed the Durrani Empire in the mid eighteenth century, with the exception of Peshawar and other Pashtun lands on the right bank of the Indus. He held them together by force; it is impossible to talk about a solid authoritative national government for that time: 'The organisation of the Amir's government mirrored, and formed an extension of, the existing relationship of power which had become entrenched during the Sadozai period... Because of the chronic lack of funds the Amir's administration resembled a series of makeshift arrangements, constantly putting his negotiating skills and claims of leadership to test.'[63] Not surprisingly, the period of relative stability in Afghanistan was once more seriously disrupted with Dost Mohammad's death in 1863.

Although Amir Dost Mohammad Khan had designated one of his younger sons, Sher Ali Khan, as his successor, the inherent problems of polygamic life once again prevailed.[64] Sher Ali's rule was immediately challenged by his two older half-brothers, Mohammad Afzal and Mohammad Azam. In the ensuing power struggle Mohammad Afzal seized the throne and ruled from 1866 until his death in 1867, when he was succeeded by his brother Azam for one year before Sher Ali regained the throne in 1868.

Sher Ali Khan's Rule

During his second period of rule, Sher Ali, who assumed his father's title of Amir, proved more perceptive and innovative than any of his predecessors. He set out with vigour and zeal to create a professional army and organise a strong and effective central government based on what his father had left behind, somewhat along the lines of the modern meaning of the term; and to pursue such domestic and foreign policy steps as could both strengthen his authority and keep at bay the Anglo-Russian rivalry. His achievements were most notable in the following areas.

To a degree he revived the late Ahmad Shah's multiethnic accommodationist approach to government in an attempt to broaden his power base and create national cohesion. To this end, he not only set up a Council of Elders to advise him on state affairs, but also included people from diverse ethnic backgrounds in his administrative services. The Ghilzai tribesmen were particular beneficiaries from this policy change. He initiated a number of reformist measures, which at least on a modest scale provided some important bases for his successors in their efforts to achieve greater national unity and to modernise Afghanistan. They included the creation of a national army and a military school, which received students from different tribes and ethnic groups to be trained as an officer corps; the institution of a system for collecting land revenues in cash; a postal service; and the publication of a periodical, *Shams ul-Nahar* ('Morning Sun'). The latter came out irregularly and was different from the newspapers that had already begun to appear in Iran and Turkey: it served mainly as a forum for the government's policy announcements and views.[65] Furthermore, although favourably disposed towards Britain, he tried to avoid antagonising the Russians and played on Anglo-Russian rivalry to pursue what could be called a policy of 'mild neutrality' in his foreign relations.

Practically all Sher Ali's major innovations affected only Kabul and territories immediately adjacent to the capital city where he could project his power. Despite his vision and craving for reforms, the Amir remained hostage of traditional forces present in the country. He ultimately could not save his rule from the dangers inherent in the deep-rooted polygamic politics of the ruling family and Anglo-Russian rivalry. His decision to designate as successor his youngest son, Abdullah Jan, born from a favourite Kandahari wife but who died before the succession time, alienated his older sons, especially Mohammad Yaqub Khan and Mohammad Ayub Khan. Yaqub Khan revolted against his father's decision and was imprisoned. These rivalries among the royals, together with the tribal uprisings that they ignited, markedly hampered Amir Sher Ali Khan's efforts at reform.[66]

Sher Ali's conciliatory *realpolitik* attitude towards Russia, which was manifested in the conclusion of a defensive alliance between the two sides,[67] could not please the British, particularly at a time when the Russians had deftly reached the territory north of the Amu River and were in search of greater influence in Persia and Ottoman Turkey. This, combined with the decision of the hardline Benjamin Disraeli, who became Prime Minister of Great Britain in 1874, to make Britain more assertive against perceived 'Russian expansionism',[68] stirred the British to give practical expression to their 'forward defence policy'. When the British once again invaded Afghanistan in November 1878, external factors then again became dominant. Russia's successful war against Turkey in 1877–1878 appeared likely to give it access to the Mediterranean, astride Britain's west–east imperial line of communication. At the congress of Berlin in mid 1878, Disraeli succeeded in depriving Russia of most of its gains. The governor of Russian Turkestan, General Kaufman, meanwhile, assembled 30,000 troops, intending to invade India via Afghanistan in the event of war, and sent an envoy to Sher Ali, whom he convinced that Russia would come to his aid if the British invaded. When the British came, Sher Ali fled to the Russian border, intending to go to ask the Tsar personally for help. Had he done so, Kaufman would have faced at least dismissal for risking taking Russia to war with the British Empire, so Kaufman refused him entry. Sher Ali died in February 1879, and Yaqub Khan succeeded to the throne. To keep it, he signed the degrading Treaty of Gandamak in May, and a British residency was established in Kabul in July, whereupon the troops returned to India. In September the residency was sacked and its inhabitants massacred. A punitive force arrived in Kabul in October and inflicted a crushing defeat on tribal forces in December.

Ayub Khan also opposed Abdullah Jan's nomination as heir, but took a different path to his brother by fighting the British in the second Anglo-Afghan war. He emerged as a hero of the war, but was heavily defeated in August 1880. After the British left, Ayub seized Kandahar again, but was then defeated by Abdur Rahman's troops, and fled first to Persia, then to British India.

When the British punitive force arrived in Kabul in October 1879, Yaqub Khan was forced to abdicate. Britain's General Frederick Roberts took power in Kabul, hanged about 100 Afghans, including the mayor, for their part in

the massacre at the residency, smashed and dispersed tribal forces that
attacked in December, then in July 1880 marched his force to Kandahar and
heavily defeated Ayub Khan.

Abdur Rahman Khan's Rule

By then, the emergence of another Afghan ruler, who was to have an
unprecedented impact on the course of Afghanistan's state-building, had
provided the British with the necessary opportunity for a face-saving
withdrawal.[69] This was Sardar Abdur Rahman Khan, son of Mohammad
Afzal Khan and grandson of Dost Mohammad, who had lived in exile in
Samarkand and Tashkent for 12 years after his defeat by Sher Ali (half-
brother and arch-rival of his deceased father) in 1868. In February 1880,
General Kaufman, believing him to be pro-Russian and expecting him at
least to make trouble for the British, facilitated his return to Afghanistan.

He quickly marshalled the support of Afghanistan's northern Khans and
Begs (Uzbek and Turkmen leaders) and marched to Kabul. In the absence
of any other strong leader, the British found it advisable to support his claim
to the throne. This was less of a gamble than it appeared. Abdur Rahman
had seen Kaufman's incitement followed by betrayal of Sher Ali; 'the British,
however, reasoned that [he], like the afghan amirs before him would be neither
pro-Russian nor pro-British, but militantly pro-afghan.'[70] Following their
experience with Dost Mohammad, they found him acceptable, provided he
endorsed the most important point of the Treaty of Gandamak, namely that
Afghanistan have no relationship with any other country except Great Britain.
He agreed to this, became Amir, and the British left.

As it turned out, the British were not wrong in their reasoning. Abdur
Rahman proved not only an Afghan nationalist, with a special distaste for
the Russians, but also a man of great discipline, political will and foresight,
capable of establishing absolute rule and solidifying Afghanistan within the
structure of a modern nation-state. He identified the ethno-tribal
heterogeneity of Afghans and the Anglo-Russian rivalry as major sources of
Afghanistan's problems, and immediately sought refuge in Islam as the
common chord among the majority of Afghans to consolidate his rule,
centralise power and create national unity. He declared himself the Muslim
ruler of all Afghan people and claimed divine sanction for his rule, thus
becoming the first Afghan ruler strongly to invoke something akin to the
divine right of kings as a source of political legitimacy.

He described his mission as to work for 'the welfare of the nation and…
be devoted to the progress of [the Afghan people]… for the welfare and true
faith of the Holy Prophet Mohammad'.[71] While assuming the position of

champion of Islam and liberator of the Afghan lands, he attacked both internal divisions and foreign interventions. He accused local chieftains and landlords as well as religious leaders of using the people for their own individual purposes contrary to the true religious teachings and to the cause of national unity. He also scorned foreign powers as 'infidels' and aggressors, who constantly violated the faith, integrity and territory of the Afghan people.[72] However, he combined all this with extensive use of brutal force as the main instrument to achieve his objectives. He spared nothing in attempting to force his subjects' obedience, to break up the local centres of power, to eliminate most of his potential and actual opposition and to foster a patriotic xenophobia among the people vis-à-vis Anglo–Russian encroachments. Meanwhile, he played on the salient dynamics of the Anglo–Russian rivalry to obtain considerable financial aid and arms from the British under various old and new agreements, and to keep the Russians at bay. In his efforts at state-building, his achievements were unprecedentedly substantial in three areas.

First, he built a very disciplined and capable army, and engaged in a process of what subsequently became known as 'internal imperialism'.[73] As part of this process, he rapidly expanded his control beyond Kabul by conquering most of the areas in the country that were either insubordinate or independent and out of reach of the central government, including 'Kafiristan' (the land of infidels) which he converted to Islam and named 'Nooristan' (the land of light); and by smashing the power of local leaders, and bringing the religious establishment under his guidance and authority.[74] Gradually drawing on the loyalty of his mostly Pashtun and some non-Pashtun followers, who were discreetly placed in important military and administrative positions, he physically liquidated thousands of his opponents; and brutally banished and suppressed many more, whom he perceived as potentially troublesome. For example, he resettled a substantial number of southern Ghilzai families in the areas north of the Hindu Kush and repressed the Hazaras in order to gain full control over them in the central highlands of Afghanistan.[75]

Second, he initiated a number of substantive political, administrative, legal, economic and social reforms. Undoubtedly these reforms were limited in scope, and were in accordance with the Amir's perceived political needs and the resources available to him. Nonetheless, they did lay the basis for the institution of identifiable governmental, administrative and Islamic-legal systems.[76] Furthermore, they resulted in the introduction of some essential means of communications, light industry and commerce and in the strengthening of mechanisms for tax collection as well as of certain preliminary welfare services, health and education in particular. He employed some British technicians and experts to assist in establishing small industrial projects, medical and educational nuclei and a printing firm. His most important industrial show project was a small-arms factory, known as *masheen khana*, which he built in Kabul.[77]

Third, he concurrently managed to exhibit a great deal of caution and aloofness in his foreign relations and to assure both the British and the Russians that a strong central government under his leadership would be in the interest of both powers, as it would prevent either from using Afghanistan against the other. Despite his acceptance of British control of Afghan foreign relations under the revised Treaty of Gandamak, and his personal preference for the British, he trod a cautious tightrope with the Russians. While highly distrustful of Russians because of his direct experience of their advances into Central Asia during his long stay in the area and their subsequent thrust into Shughnan and Panjdeh, he was eager not to antagonise them. This partly explained his decision to give in, though very reluctantly, to the Anglo-Russian pressure and allow them to fix Afghanistan largely within its present borders.[78]

However, on the whole, as is evident from his autobiography – he was the first and last Afghan ruler to compile (or at least order) such a work – he neither felt easy about the Russian takeover of Panjdeh as a price for the Anglo-Russian Commission to demarcate the Afghan-Russian border, nor ever accepted the Durand Line as more than a line delineating the Afghan and British responsibilities in the Pashtun tribal areas. He contended that the line could not constitute a permanent border between Afghanistan and British India.[79] At the same time, he was convinced that many of Afghanistan's problems with the British could not be solved through dealings with the government of British India, but only through direct relations with London. However, he could not make London accept this conviction. The best he could ultimately achieve was to keep his government as distant as possible from the Russians and as restrained towards British India as permissible, for he saw this as a minimum requirement for ensuring the survival of his rule and of Afghanistan at least as a semi-independent state. Consequently, he even refused to boost his modernisation efforts by inviting either of the powers to help Afghanistan in exploiting its natural resources and participate in developing its economic infrastructure, even though British India was keen to extend its railway from Qalat and Quetta into Afghanistan.[80]

Amir Abdur Rahman Khan's rule was brutal and absolute, based primarily on coercion and backed by an elaborate spy network, which earned him the title of 'Iron Amir'.[81] Similarly, his reforms were largely *ad hoc*, confined mainly to Kabul, and did not constitute a countrywide programme for change and development. And his foreign policy efforts could not counter the Anglo-Russian rivalry, in particular the creeping British advances, sufficiently to enable him to achieve full sovereignty for Afghanistan in its domestic and foreign affairs. This still cannot deny the fact that he contributed more than any one but Ahmad Shah Durrani to the development and consolidation of the Afghan state. By the time of his death, the Iron Amir had 'created an Afghanistan that had recognised international boundaries, was politically unified, and governed directly by a centralised authority, within the framework of fairly well-defined and universally applied administrative and judiciary rules and regulations'.[82] Ahmad Shah created the fundamentals for the modern evolution of Afghanistan as a political unit. Amir Abdur Rahman Khan took serious steps towards building the first modern state in that country. But how and at what price? A modicum of 'national cohesion' was maintained by instituting a single group (Pashtuns) as an overlord vis-à-vis all others, and not only in the political and military aspects; such issues as the sense of ethnic superiority amongst Pashtuns (promoted, *inter alia*, through marital praxis) and economic oppression[83] were great obstacles on the road to genuine national consolidation of Afghanistan, yet they formed the backbone of every Afghan monarch's policy, Abdur Rahman's in particular.

The problem of territories to the north of the Hindu Kush has been carefully avoided by Pashtun and western authors.[84] The Uzbek khanates of Balkh, Sheberghan, Andkhoi, Qunduz, Maimana, Khulm and other smaller principalities had very little to do with Durrani monarchs. If anything, they were linked to the territories on the right bank of the Amu Darya, where rulers were of the same Chingizid stock. Ahmad Shah conquered Uzbek principalities between 1750 and 1752, but by 1756 they had already rebelled, and under Timur Shah they regained complete independence. Dost Mohammad and the ruler of Qunduz exchanged embassies, being peers, until the former launched a treacherous attack in the mid 1850s. The final showdown occurred under Abdur Rahman:

> The military occupation of Uzbek-populated lands of today's Afghanistan by the Afghan troops, the atrocities committed by the conquerors, led not only to passive resistance of the local population (not just Uzbeks, but also Turkmens and Tajiks) which resulted in mass migration to the northern, right bank of the Amu-Darya, but also to numerous attempts at rebellions whose aim was to get rid of the enslavers' yoke through armed struggle.[85]

Abdur Rahman practised methods just short of genocide. In the course of pacification of Kafiristan, 10,000 were killed and 16,000 forcibly resettled throughout the country, reducing the local population by half.[86] To make way for Taraki Pashtun settlers in Bamiyan, the indigenous Hazara population was deported – 'so thorough was this "ethnic cleansing" that not even the dogs remained behind'.[87] The *Powinda* allies of the Amir were encouraged to seize lands and pastures of the Hazaras, dooming the latter to poverty and starvation.[88] Thanks to Abdur Rahman, the anti-Pashtun elements in the historic memory of the indigenous population of Afghan Turkestan were greatly reinforced.[89]

Despite its narrow popular base, the Afghan monarchy managed to survive and consolidate its gains. The only reason for that was, of course, the Great Game. While the British were annexing traditional Pashtun territories in the south, they were pushing the Amirs to pursue an expansionist policy in the north to deter the Russians. Abdur Rahman's victorious campaigns in Turkestan were blessed, financed and equipped by the government of British India. When local resistance leaders (for example, Ishaq Khan in 1888) approached Russia and Bukhara for help, they were invariably denied on the basis of the 1873 Anglo-Russian agreement.[90]

Abdur Rahman died of natural causes in 1901; but despite his having taken several wives, his death did not bring as turbulent a leadership succession crisis as the deaths of his predecessors had caused. He had established sufficient governmental structure and mechanisms of control to enable his heir and elder son, Habibullah Khan, though born of a Samarkandi concubine mother, to succeed him with relative ease and rule for the next 18 years. Generally, unqualified glorification of Abdur Rahman is hardly warranted. True, he was an outstanding personality, but he was a ruthless ruler, and it was only by terror that he managed to keep such a heterogeneous and conflict-ridden entity as Afghanistan together. Repression, isolation and reliance on financial assistance from abroad at the cost of sovereignty were his trademarks, not comprehensive modernisation and nation-building. The legacy of Abdur Rahman was an ethnically polarised Afghanistan. When it comes to the introduction of modernity to the Afghan society, Habibullah Khan was a much more successful, yet underrated, figure.

2

National Awakening
and Nationalism

HABIBULLAH KHAN'S SUCCESSION TO the throne in October 1901 inaugurated
a formative, eventful and interesting period in the evolution of Afghan
politics. His rule was distinguished not so much for what it achieved but for
what it unleashed. In conjunction with shifting polygamic rivalries in the
royal household and favourable fluctuations in Anglo-Russian competition,
it helped generate a nationalist reformist movement that put Afghanistan on
a speedy course of change to modernise and achieve full independence. In
fact, the genesis of the decade of political radicalism that followed Habibullah's
assassination in 1919 lay in the very intellectual and nationalist resources
spawned during Habibullah's rule. The aim of this chapter is to evaluate Habibullah's rule as a significant phase in the Afghans' attempts at state-building.

Habibullah did not have an altogether smooth start.[1] Upon ascending the
throne, he was initially discomfited by the leadership aspirations exhibited
by his brother, Nasrullah Khan, who was deeply religious and had a potential
power base in the religious establishment. Given Amir Abdur Rahman Khan's
brutal suppression of opposition, and his consequent restrictions on the
powers of the religious establishment, Nasrullah Khan became a rallying
point for such opposition.[2] This contributed to the outbreak of a series of
religious and tribal intrigues against the new Amir. However, Habibullah
Khan was able to consolidate his leadership quickly and force the opposition
into acquiescence.[3]

Influences on Habibullah Khan's Rule

Four main variables dominated Habibullah Khan's rule and set the parameters within which it steered Afghanistan towards radical domestic modernisation and national independence.

The first variable concerned the personality of Habibullah Khan himself. Despite being in many ways as autocratic as his father, he proved more politically astute, socio-culturally open-minded, and amenable to modern changes. His taste for a glittering and luxurious existence and admiration for technological innovations, particularly when they could aid his own royal comfort, as well as his desire to preside over a strong, united and modernised Afghanistan made him a great deal more receptive than his father to modernist and nationalist changes.[4] After securing his leadership, he set out eagerly to continue and build on his father's reforms.[5] He assumed power at a time when Afghanistan could no longer remain aloof from certain reformist and nationalist waves that were deeply affecting a number of regional Muslim states. Two developments were especially important. One was the pan-Islamic efforts of the celebrated Muslim thinker and activist, Sayyed Jamaluddin al-Afghani (1839–1897), which called for the reformation and unity of the Muslim world, particularly against British colonial domination; this had made an inroad into the psyche of many Muslims and inspired the growth of several nationalist groups in the region.[6] Another concerned the fact that a number of regional Muslim countries, especially Persia, Ottoman Turkey and Egypt, were experiencing growing demands for internal reforms and for resistance to outside intervention and subjugation. These demands, which resulted in major national and regional changes in the succeeding decades, were also to have an impact, in one way or another, on the rise of modernist and nationalist thinking in Afghanistan.

The second variable was related to the growing reformist movements in the region: the emergence in Afghanistan by the turn of the century of a tiny but effective cluster of intellectuals and nobles with ambitions for reform and independence. Evolving from this cluster was the rapid development of a group known as the 'Young Afghans', modelled after the 'Young Turks', existing concurrently in Ottoman Turkey.[7] The group was by no means homogeneous, but rather a collection of individuals from different social backgrounds.[8] It neither had an identifiable organisation, nor did it operate as a political party in the modern sense of the term. More than anything, the fledgling reformist movement in Afghanistan resembled a club of intellectuals centred on the first modern educational facility in the country – the *Habibiyya* lycée, which opened in Kabul in 1904. The ideas of anti-colonialism and enlightenment espoused by Dr Abdul Ghani, the Indian director of the lycée, and his staff clearly influenced the Young Afghans. In January 1906, they managed to publish the first and only issue of the newspaper *Siraj al-Akhbar*

Afghaniyah, edited by a *Habibiyya* teacher, Abdur Rauf Khan Kandahari. It called upon 'all scholars and enlighteners of our country to help society... and to show people the way to get rid of the malaise [of backwardness] and map out measures necessary for the blossoming of the Fatherland and the increase in people's standards of living'.[9]

Generally, what connected the Young Afghans and brought them together within an informal network was their common position as faithful Muslims and Afghans, a shared yearning for national cohesion, stability, progress and independence. They believed in a blend between Islam as a dynamic force for national unity, reassertion and salvation and in certain western liberal concepts and scientific-technological achievements as the most appropriate way to help Afghans achieve modernisation and independence. Their views and aspirations were very similar to those upheld by a number of leading Muslim thinkers and activists of the time, in particular al-Afghani, whose ideas they published and circulated. They revolved largely around the personality of Mahmud Tarzi, a prominent modernist and nationalist, who served as instigator and mentor for the Young Afghans. Tarzi's appearance on the Afghan scene was sudden, but essentially a result of Amir Habibullah Khan's readiness to adopt some progressive views.

As one of his first acts, Habibullah Khan decreed a general amnesty for all who had been imprisoned or exiled by his father for no other reason than that they had appeared potentially powerful and influential, and were therefore a threat to his rule. They included two notable families: the Tarzis, and the Yahya Khel, also known as the Musahiban. Both of these had been forced into exile in the early 1880s on charges of conspiracy against the state, and had consequently taken refuge in the Ottoman Empire and British India respectively. However, after their return, both families were destined to play pivotal roles in shaping and directing Afghan politics in the coming decades. We should first turn briefly to the Tarzi family, to which Mahmud Tarzi belonged.

This family was descended from the relatively powerful Sardar Rahmdel Khan of Kandahar, a half-brother of Amir Dost Mohammad Khan, and was headed, until his death in exile in 1901, by a distinguished noble, Ghulam Mohammad Khan Tarzi. After falling into disgrace with Abdur Rahman Khan, Ghulam Mohammad Tarzi and his family left in 1882 for the Ottoman Empire and lived mostly in Damascus for the next 20 years. This gave the family's eldest son, Mahmud Tarzi, an opportunity to receive a modern education in Damascus and Constantinople. While in exile, the young Tarzi's learning process and life experience enriched him with a good knowledge not only of western ideas, governmental systems and scientific-technological progress, but also of the emergent Islamic and modern type of nationalist ideas and movements, exemplified in the teachings of al-Afghani and the activities of the Young Turks.[10] Thus, by 1902, when the family returned from exile, he had been deeply impressed by what a careful marriage between the dynamics of Islam and certain western ideas and practices could produce, holding out the possibility of putting Afghanistan on a viable path to modernity and full independence.

It was basically along these lines that he initially made a favourable impression on Amir Habibullah. As the latter's personality rapidly interacted with Tarzi's brand of nationalism, despite the opposition from some elements in the Royal Court, Tarzi began his career as a distinguished thinker and reformer in Afghanistan. Given his command of several languages and high literary calibre, he was appointed within a few years as Chief of the Bureau of Translation for the Royal Court, enabling him to inform and advise the Amir directly about events in the Muslim world and Europe. Deeply impressed by the role of the press in the West in general, and certain nationalist newspapers that had come into operation in Turkey and Persia in particular, Tarzi achieved one of his most highly desired objectives in 1911 by founding *Siraj al-Akhbar Afghaniyah* ('The Lamp of the News of Afghanistan') – the first successful bi-weekly newspaper in Afghanistan. Although officially sanctioned, the paper, which became known simply as *Siraj al-Akhbar*, rapidly developed under Tarzi's editorship into a fairly independent and effective news medium, earning Tarzi subsequently the title of 'father of modernisation and journalism of Afghanistan'.[11] The paper, which survived until 1919, not only published government, national and regional news, but also served as a mouthpiece for Tarzi and some of his prominent Young Afghan followers and their associates to disseminate views, policy recommendations and prescriptions on a wide range of issues.[12] These ranged from the role of Islam and monarchy and the relationship of the two, to fundamental questions of Afghan nationalism, modernisation and independence.

Since a full discussion of Tarzi's views and formulations falls outside the scope of this work,[13] it suffices here to state that in general he propounded an Islamic-based but liberally inclined nationalist ideology of change and development and freedom for Afghanistan. As can be discerned from his writings in *Siraj al-Akhbar* and elsewhere, he essentially argued that Islam was not necessarily incompatible with either a system of constitutional monarchy or a process of national social-economic reform that sought help from certain appropriate western ideas, practices and achievements, provided they were guided by the principle of 'the common good'. At that special juncture of Afghan history, 'the common good' to him meant first and foremost the necessity to improve the Afghan people's living conditions in relation to an organic notion of unity, freedom, justice and equality. Thus, the good of the individual is fulfilled through the happiness of the community as a whole – a notion that tallies with the Islamic concept of 'brotherhood' – within a Muslim society. He considered all this a prelude to creating a positive national consciousness among the Afghans, to gaining full independence and building an Afghan nation-state that would be part of the Muslim world, but at the same time capable of adapting to modern changes, withstanding internal and external pressures, and ensuring its long-term survival in a competitively changing world.

As first steps in this direction, while appealing to the Afghans' common sense of Islamic brotherhood and historical pride, he attached urgent priority to the growth of literacy, scientific and vocational training, health care and means of communications within a western-inclined framework of modernisation; and demanded gradual political reforms in conformity with changes in these areas. His order of priorities was understandable, for at the time of Habibullah's ascendancy over 98 per cent of Afghans were illiterate,[14] incapable of understanding his ideas of nation-statehood and national reforms, and of providing for the institution of such ideas, while an equal number lacked even basic medical care. There were no effective communication links, nor sufficiently broad interactions between central authority and the country at large. The people in general constituted little more than a very heterogeneous, divided and xenophobic Afghan ethnos.

In his fundamental ideological dispositions, Tarzi was certainly not all that original, in some ways echoing the stance of not only al-Afghani but also several contemporary nationalist reformers in the region. Such reformers were most successful in Ottoman Turkey, where the Young Turks had managed to secure a series of democratic-nationalist reforms that ultimately led to the abdication of Sultan Abdul Hamid in 1909, and in Iran, where a divided but forceful Constitutionalist Movement had prompted the Qajar monarchy to acquiesce to certain populist limitations on its powers under a new constitution adopted in 1906. Nonetheless, Tarzi was unique in his dispositions in relation to the prevailing circumstances in Afghanistan.[15] He provided an ideological stimulus and direction which helped many of his Young Afghan followers to pioneer the rise of a modernist and nationalist trend that dominated Amir Habibullah's rule. However, neither Tarzi nor the trend that he generated would have proved terribly effective had it not been for Tarzi's profound influence on one of Amir Habibullah's sons, Amanullah Khan.[16] Amanullah, who was also married to a daughter of Tarzi's, was involved with the Young Afghans from the early days. Before turning to this central issue, it is appropriate to complete our discussion of the third and fourth variables dominating Amir Habibullah's rule.

The third variable was related to a replay of ongoing polygamic rivalry within the ruling family. As mentioned earlier, Amir Habibullah originally succeeded in consolidating his leadership against the political aspirations of his brother, Sardar Nasrullah Khan and opposition by other elements. But this did not mean either that Nasrullah privately gave up all his ambitions, or that other forms of opposition ceased altogether. The way that Amir Habibullah initially retarded his brother's aspirations was by sharing power with him in some ways. He appointed Nasrullah, who was known for his close links with some leading figures in the 'independent' tribal territory on the British India side of the border, as Commander-in-Chief of the Army and President of the State Council – an institution that Amir Abdur Rahman had created for the purpose of legislative legitimacy. This, together with his control of most of the Afghan finances during 1910–1913, enabled him to enjoy considerable power. Although later in the second decade of Amir Habibullah's rule he relinquished his position as Commander-in-Chief and concentrated on civil affairs, he was a potential source of threat against which the Amir had to be constantly on guard.

However, another real source of trouble eventually undermining Habibullah's rule arose from his own polygamic practice. His taking of four wives and some 35 concubines, who bore him about 50 offspring,[17] caused the usual simmering tensions and rivalries between different wives and sons in the royal household. Among his wives, two proved politically very influential: his second wife, the ambitious Ulya Hazrat; and his fourth and younger wife, Ulya Janab.[18] Both were descended from the powerful Mohammadzai clan, but from two different lineages. The first was from an important family called the Loynabs of Kandahar – direct descendants of Amir Dost Mohammad – who belonged to the same 'Dil' group of clans in Kandahar with the Tarzis, and was the mother of Amanullah; the second belonged to another emerging influential family, the Musahiban, and was a sister of Mohammad Nadir.

It is appropriate at this juncture to shed more light on the Musahiban family. The Musahiban (a lineage name, the origin of which will be explained shortly) were descended from a once-powerful Barakzai Sardar, Sultan Mohammad Khan, nicknamed Tela'i ('possessor of gold'), who was a rival brother of Amir Dost Mohammad. As mentioned before, during the successful Barakzai campaign against the Sadozais for the throne between 1818 and 1823, Sultan Mohammad assumed control of the government of Peshawar, but soon, in a power struggle with his brothers, he befriended

Ranjit Singh and surrendered Peshawar to the Sikhs, opening the way for its eventual annexation by the British. This consequently contributed to border disputes, first with British India, later with Pakistan.[19] Nonetheless, it was Sardar Mohammad Yusuf Khan, a grandson of Sultan Mohammad through his son, Yahya, who founded the Yahya-*khel* clan, later known as the Musahiban family. Upon falling out of favour with Amir Abdur Rahman, Yahya, together with his family, went to India, where they 'lived under British influence and protection' until 1900.[20]

However, under Amir Habibullah's amnesty, they returned to Afghanistan to become yet another important force in the Amir's rule. Yusuf Khan had taken several wives, but only the siblings from his first two wives came to play leading roles in Afghan politics. From the first wife were Ulya Janab and her brothers, Mohammad Nadir, Shah Wali and Shah Mahmud; and from the second wife, a Sadozai, were Mohammad Aziz and Mohammad Hashem. Yusuf and these of his children constituted the Musahiban family. As Amir Habibullah grew fond of Yusuf, he married his daughter, Ulya Janab, simply because she was nubile and from the 'right' family.[21] Meanwhile, Yusuf and his sons achieved rapid official prominence. By 1905, Yusuf and his brother, Asef, became the Amir's Musahiban-e Khas (Attendants par Excellence), from which originated the family name Musahiban.[22] With this grew Yusuf's influence on the Amir and his elder son, Sardar Enayatullah (who, like his younger brother, Amanullah, had married another daughter of Mahmud Tarzi).

Yusuf's sons also made similar progress in different military and civilian capacities. During the second decade of Amir Habibullah's rule, Mohammad Nadir, the eldest son, achieved the position of Commander-in-Chief, Shah Wali and Shah Mahmud reached the ranks of Commander and General respectively and their two half-brothers, Mohammad Hashem and Mohammad Aziz, rose to the positions of Deputy Commander of Herat and Secretary at the Foreign Office respectively. Thus, Yusuf and most of his sons were in positions that figured prominently in Amir Habibullah's entourage.

Tarzi's Group Versus the Musahiban Family

The Musahiban family was thus able to develop a strong power base within Amir Habibullah's administration, and a wide range of contacts especially among the border Pashtun tribes. However, the family's ideological stance on the whole was one of nationalist conservatism. On the one hand, Yusuf, his brother, and their sons, desired the development and greater independence of Afghanistan, but on the other, they wished these objectives to be achieved through a cautious, evolutionary process of change and accommodation with the British. This stemmed largely from their special understanding of the ethno-tribal nature of Afghan society, but also from their being basically pro-British, given their military careers, British-influenced education and the protection given to them by the British during their exile in Dehra Dun, India. As such, their stance ran contrary to the process of accelerated modernist and nationalist changes concurrently being advocated by Mahmud Tarzi and his Young Afghan followers. As a result, by the second decade of the twentieth century, two informal but conflicting political trends appeared to be at work in Amir Habibullah's administration: one revolving around Tarzi; and another around the Musahiban family, especially its increasingly most influential member, Mohammad Nadir.

Essentially, the rivalry between the two groupings at court was a competition between two approaches to reform and modernisation in Afghanistan, namely the Middle Eastern and Indian Muslim ones. The Musahiban brothers never openly challenged Tarzi and his group and mostly maintained a public calm in the face of their activities. But this does not mean that there was no rivalry between the two sides. The Musahiban brothers neither joined the Young Afghans nor lent much appreciable support to them, at least during the movement's formative years. Moreover, they privately worked hard to influence Amir Habibullah in their favour and restrain him from moving in a radically innovative direction; and quietly developed their own ambitions for leadership. In this, Ulya Janab became a tool in the hands of her full brothers. She was constantly urged by Mohammad Nadir to compete with Ulya Hazrat, so as to enable her own son, Asadullah, to succeed eventually as Amir. However, Ulya Hazrat was not the type to lose to her rival. Given her status as chief queen, her powerful family background, domineering character and political knack, she had the necessary determination and influence to ensure that the Amir promoted his third and favourite son, Amanullah, 18 years senior to Asadullah, to inherit the throne. In the meantime, Amanullah grew to be the type of politically extroverted character who could fulfil his mother's ambitions – an issue which now needs to be detailed.

Born in 1892, Amanullah in his early life was undoubtedly very much dominated by his mother. It was she to whom he owed much of his initial political drive and his acquaintance with the politics of royal survival. But this was not all, for he proved highly intelligent and ambitious in his own right, with a refreshingly inquiring mind and wide political concerns. Whilst educated in the military school, *Harbiya*, set up by his father for young Afghan aristocrats in 1906, he went enthusiastically beyond such an education to learn about human conditions inside and outside Afghanistan. In pursuit of this, he exhibited more political acuity, social courage and accessibility than any other members of the royal family, including his elder brother, Enayatullah, who under normal circumstances might have been considered rightful heir to the throne.[23] He was prepared, at a great deal of personal risk, to inquire directly into the people's living conditions, and give tentative hearing to others' views, prescriptions, demands and complaints – a quality which subsequently became one of the hallmarks of his rule.[24] Although he did not travel abroad until 1927, he acquired most of his understanding of events and movements in the outside world through reading foreign publications widely and listening to those whom he found best informed.

Meanwhile, his rather gentle, unassuming and receptive personality allowed progressive individuals from within and outside the court to confide in and influence him. He reportedly nurtured, as early as the age of 15, considerable pro-modernisation and anti-British feelings. He admitted that 'he was deeply ashamed of the backwardness of his country' and blamed this on 'the ignorance of the Afghan people and the deliberate imperialist policies of Britain', which he held primarily responsible for denying Afghanistan 'the greatness it deserved'.[25]

This led him to develop strong reformist and nationalist convictions, as well as an impatient political drive in pursuit of two intertwined goals: to modernise Afghanistan and free it from the British colonial yoke. This brought him into line with what Tarzi and his Young Afghans aspired to achieve, leading him into an early association with Tarzi and a particular faction of the Young Afghans called *Mashrutakhwahan*, or Constitutionalists.[26] Although this faction took off about the same time as the Constitutionalist Movement in Persia, it was not connected in any way to the Persian phenomenon, as there were very few cultural ties or exchanges between the two countries at the time. Amanullah's association with Tarzi, whom he came to respect and admire, also resulted in a direct family union between them. In 1913, following two previous consecutive but unhappy marriages, one of which ended in divorce and the other with his wife's death in childbirth, Amanullah married one of Tarzi's daughters. She was Soraya, a beautiful and talented woman born of Tarzi's only wife, Asma Rasmiya (a Syrian). Both daughter and mother subsequently played a key role in pioneering the cause of women's rights and freedoms in Afghanistan. It is worth stressing here that, in spite of the deeply rooted tradition of polygamy, both Tarzi and Amanullah had grown opposed to the tradition in view of its negative social and political consequences. They desired its reform, with an urge also to improve the status of Afghan women.

Thus, the palace feud between Ulya Hazrat and Ulya Janab grew in many ways to be a symptom of an undeclared simmering tussle played out in the wider arena between two competing groups of Mohammadzai aristocracy: one led by Tarzi and Amanullah, the other headed by General Mohammad Nadir. Seemingly, the circumstances could work only in favour of the first group, for two main reasons. First, above everything else, Amanullah was gaining political ascendancy, as Amir Habibullah increasingly preferred him over his brothers and installed him as Regent during the Amir's frequent absences from the capital on long hunting trips. Second, Amanullah's and Tarzi's nationalist-reformist attitudes were indicative of a changing mood which was gaining strength within the Kabul intelligentsia. However, on one occasion the Amir came very close to putting Amanullah and his mother behind bars for intriguing against him and, ironically, it was the intercession of Nasrullah that saved the future king.[27] Meanwhile, Mohammad Nadir's star was not doing too badly. His fortunes took an upward turn following the 'pacification' of the Southern Province tribes in 1909.[28]

Habibullah Khan and Anglo-Russian Rivalry

The nascent reformist sentiments in the Afghan elite were neither divorced from the growing impetus for change in the region, nor disrupted by the outbreak of the First World War. In fact, the war, and such subsequent momentous events as the Turkish Revolution under Mustafa Kamal Ataturk and the Bolshevik Revolution under Vladimir Lenin, served as further sources of encouragement rather than distraction for the Afghan nationalist-reformers. From the start the British not only failed to recognise and show sensitivity to this changing mood in Afghanistan, but also rather hardened their attitudes towards the country; and this in turn contributed substantially to the shape and direction that the reform movement took in Afghanistan. This brings us to the final variable dominating Amir Habibullah's rule.

In the past, as discussed before, under various forced treaties the British had recognised Abdur Rahman as Amir of a 'semi-independent' Afghanistan, accorded him an annual subsidy and pledged to defend his realm against possible Russian attack, in return for extensive control of Afghan foreign affairs. However, when Habibullah assumed the throne, Lord Curzon, the hardline Viceroy of India after 1898, suddenly changed tack. As a staunch defender of British imperial power, Curzon reactivated the 'forward defence policy' as absolutely imperative for India's security, or what he called Britain's 'inalienable badge of sovereignty in the Eastern Hemisphere'.[29] Consequently, he withheld extending the same recognition to Habibullah as the British had done to his father. Curzon's objective was to extract further concessions from the new Amir, and reinforce control over Afghan foreign relations.

However, he underestimated the strength of the Amir's character and national pride. When Habibullah refused any more concessions, Curzon in 1901 created a Pashtun Province, the North-West Frontier Province (NWFP), out of Punjab at the cost of increasing cross-border tribal disturbances, and also began preparations for a third British invasion of Afghanistan among other measures. The only thing that averted Curzon's war efforts was London's opposition, and the whole project was abandoned following Curzon's resignation in 1905. His successor, the more levelheaded Lord Minto, found it expedient to sign an agreement with Habibullah, according him full recognition as Amir on a basis similar to that which had governed his father's relationship with British India. He also invited the Amir to India in 1907 to a fully fledged royal reception. While a third Anglo-Afghan war was thus averted for the time being, Habibullah did not start off on friendly terms with the British and neither did the British relinquish their forward policy pressures on Afghanistan.

In fact, Lord Minto's expedient behaviour came at a time of fresh challenges and opportunities for British imperial power. The most important challenges included Wilhelmine Germany's growing assertiveness in world politics and vigorous search for colonies in Africa and Asia, where Persia and Afghanistan also appeared to be targets for German influence; the US acquisition, despite America's low-key involvement in world affairs, of territories in the Caribbean and Pacific; and Japanese expansionist ambitions, particularly in the wake of Japan's humiliating defeat of Russia in their war of 1904–1905. These, coupled with the rise of modernist and nationalist groups in Turkey and Persia as well as al-Afghani-inspired pan-Islamist movements in the region – all of which were receptive to a German idea of nationalism – occasioned increasing concern for the British and their Russian allies.[30] At the same time, there were certain emerging opportunities which the British could exploit against the challenges. They prominently involved the sustained slide of the Ottoman Empire, for long regarded as the 'sick man' of Europe; and the Tsarist regime's growing internal and external difficulties, which manifested themselves in the abortive revolution of 1905–1907 and the serious damage that Russia's defeat at the hands of the Japanese inflicted on the regime's stature and credibility in the eyes of most of Russia's Asian neighbours, including the Afghans.[31]

In the matrix of these challenges and opportunities, the British in general found it useful to persevere with a policy of exploitation and assertiveness towards Afghanistan, irrespective of the wishes of Afghan nationalists and Amir Habibullah, and the heightening anti-British mood in the country. They continued to oppose or obstruct those of the Amir's domestic and foreign policy initiatives which they considered detrimental to either Britain's hold on Afghanistan or its broader interests in the region. They opposed the Amir's wish to establish broader direct foreign relations, in particular with countries other than British India, such as Britain, Turkey, Germany, Japan and the USA.[32] Nor did they want him to be receptive to the types of reforms advocated by Tarzi and his followers.[33] The only major problem that they willingly helped to resolve, in response to mutual dissatisfaction on the part of Afghans and Persians, concerned the Sistan boundary drawn between the two countries by a British Commission in 1872. Even then, they redrew the border very much on its previous line along the course of the Helmand River in south-west Afghanistan, and failed to resolve the two sides' dispute over equitable distribution of the river's waters.[34] Otherwise, they pressed the Amir to undertake only those projects that could foster Afghanistan's links with and dependence on British India. One of them was construction of an extension of the British India railway system from the border to Kabul; the Amir, like his father, carefully avoided this.

Moreover, while rejecting Amir Habibullah's requests for more military aid to recover some of the Afghan lands lost to the Russians in the late nineteenth century, the British found it opportune to gain international recognition for their grip on Afghanistan within the country's existing boundaries. To this end, at a time when the Tsarist regime was both internally and externally very vulnerable, they opened negotiations with the Russians that culminated in the infamous St. Petersburg Agreement of 1907. Under this Agreement, the parties agreed to divide Persia into northern Russian and southern and south-eastern British zones of influence, separated by a central Persian-controlled buffer zone. Moreover, Russia again acknowledged Afghanistan as lying outside its sphere of influence, and undertook to conduct its relations with it through the British, in return for a nominal British pledge not to occupy or annex any part of Afghanistan nor interfere in the country's internal affairs. The British had no intention of annexing all or part of Afghanistan, because, after decades of political setbacks and two wars, they saw no benefit in incurring the political and material costs of doing so. Of course, to make their Agreement binding, both signatories initially sought to obtain Amir Habibullah's endorsement; but when he rejected the whole enterprise as illegal, on the grounds that the Afghans had had no part in formulating it, they simply ignored his rejection and declared the Agreement legal and binding anyway.[35]

Furthermore, the British vigorously sought to check the direction of Amir Habibullah's rule from within through not only a degree of reliance on the Musahiban family, but also by secretly planting their agents in the Afghan government. For many years allegations persisted in Afghanistan that these agents were headed by Dr Abdul Ghani, who achieved a prominent position in the Amir's administration and sought to overthrow him by infiltrating the *Mashruta* cell of the Young Afghans.[36] Although the Afghan government uncovered the 'plot', imprisoned Ghani and executed many of his collaborators, popular myth had it that the British involvement continued to haunt the Amir and the Afghan nationalist-modernists.[37] They felt besieged by the British and Russians on the one hand, and deeply offended by the deliberate designs of the British to dampen their legitimate aspirations on the other. Explaining the position of Afghanistan at the time, one historian wrote: 'Between the Russian Dominions in Asia and the Indian Empire of Great Britain, Afghanistan is placed, like a nut between the levers of a cracker. The notoriously unwholesome quality of the kernel, however, will perhaps continue to preserve it from being shared by its powerful neighbours.'[38]

As unwholesome as the kernel may have been, the British attitude ultimately contributed much to causing its most politically active section, the Young Afghans, to harden against Anglo-Russian encroachments in general and British designs in particular. In a solid nationalist step towards an independent foreign policy, Mahmud Tarzi and Amanullah at the outbreak of the First World War advocated that Afghanistan enter the war on the German-Turkish side, principally out of opposition to Britain. In this, they had the support of Nasrullah Khan and many religious leaders, whose religious piety and political views had over the years inclined them favourably towards the Ottomans, against what they perceived as continued infidel assaults on Islam. Their position also concurred with that of Enayatullah, Amanullah's older half-brother from Amir Habibullah's first wife, Ulya Jah.[39] Although Habibullah initially appeared amenable to the idea, in the final analysis he and several other Mohammadzai leaders around him, including General Mohammad Nadir, found little point in joining the Central Powers, concluding realistically that Afghanistan was too poor and weak to gain anything from entering the war, and would only provide its now allied imperial neighbours with a pretext for joint invasion.[40] As a result, the Amir declared Afghanistan's neutrality, causing much dismay and frustration to the Tarzi-Amanullah group and consequently something of a rift between it and the Amir.

The declaration of neutrality, nonetheless, was not intended to stop either the Amir or the Tarzi-Amanullah group from flirting with both Germans and Turks to strengthen their bargaining position vis-à-vis the Russians and British, especially the latter, and to cover themselves against possible German-Turkish victory. Despite mounting British objections, the Amir concurred with Tarzi and Amanullah and received a Turko-German mission in Kabul in September 1915. The result was a treaty 'under which the Germans agreed to give Afghans 100,000 rifles, 300 cannon and 20 million [pounds] in gold',[41] but without any Afghan commitment to the mission's immediate goal, namely persuading Afghanistan to attack British India and help stimulate anti-British uprisings in the border areas before an expected Turko-German triumph in the war.

Indeed, the treaty was ludicrous, for it was extremely doubtful that the Germans could fulfil its provisions. Nonetheless, the development enabled Amir Habibullah to send a signal to the British that he expected to be properly rewarded for his neutrality, in the form of the acquisition of complete political independence and territorial concessions, the most important of which was access to the Indian Ocean.[42] As such, the Amir's dealings with the Germans and Turks were mainly a balancing act – something marking most of his rule, as he attempted to preserve his own position by promoting parity between different forces with varying and often conflicting demands and pressures. Although his balancing diplomacy did not pay off immediately, given British opposition in wartime to any concession that could benefit the Central Powers, the war's end changed the situation in favour of nationalist-reformist demands in Afghanistan.

Even before the Allies' victory, the correlation of forces at both regional and international levels had begun to alter substantially. In Russia, the Bolshevik Revolution of 1917 resulted in the replacement of Tsarist rule by the world's first Marxist-Leninist regime, and in that regime's withdrawal of Russia from the war and, in many ways, the international equation.[43] This created unprecedented long-term ideological and practical challenges to the prevailing capitalist position in the world order, but in the short run it made Soviet Russia very inward-looking, as the Bolshevik regime's need for domestic consolidation took precedence over its Tsarist predecessor's foreign policy ambitions, making it expedient for the Bolshevik leaders to adopt a non-confrontationist foreign policy. Thus, despite initial British concerns about the expansionism inherent in communist ideology, in reality Soviet Russia temporarily ceased to be the threat to British regional interests that it had been perceived to be under the Tsars. This led to an apparent British reassessment of its international role, especially in relation to two main questions. These were first, how to respond to the communist takeover of Russia and the possible stimuli that its wider intertwined revolutionary appeal and peaceful overtures might provide to nationalist-reformist movements in the region; and second, how best to ensure the security of Britain's India-centred colonial interests.

In general, of course, the British adopted a hostile attitude towards the

Bolshevik regime, and provided substantial help to the White Russian opposition, particularly through Persia.[44] However, with regard to Afghanistan, it was seemingly concluded that, while it must be maintained as a frontline post for anti-Bolshevik designs, in the absence of an immediate threat British India could afford to relax its hold on the country, and allow Habibullah's regime to exercise greater foreign policy freedom, though still within the British sphere of influence.[45] In this way, it was intended to divert the Afghan nationalist reformers from seeking inspiration from the Bolshevik Revolution, and avoid providing impetus to nationalist groups, especially Muslim ones, which had become active on the Indian political scene in pursuit of national independence.[46]

This opened the way for the first round of talks in 1918 between British India and Afghanistan on an 'independence' settlement. While the Young Afghans approached the development with great enthusiasm and urgency, the British did not; they appear to have wanted the talks to proceed in accordance with their gradual assessment of the changing situation in Soviet Russia in particular, and in the region in general. Moreover, whilst the Young Afghans were predisposed to the ideal of full independence, the British had indicated their acquiescence only to limited independence, conditioned upon Afghanistan's remaining a British ally through special ties with British India. As a result, the talks faced serious difficulties from the start. In order to wear down the Afghans, the British adopted a negotiating approach characterised by procrastination and delaying tactics.[47]

This accorded with Amir Habibullah's personal preference for a gradual approach to Afghanistan's national development and independence,[48] but annoyed the Tarzi-Amanullah group and many other nationalists who, for historical reasons, perceived cynical motives behind the British procrastination. These elements had already grown very impatient with the Amir's persistent reluctance to accelerate the pace of social and economic change, to which he had initially proved amenable, and to accompany them with substantial political reforms towards a constitutional monarchy. In fact, serious differences on such issues between the Amir and Mahmud Tarzi, finally led Tarzi in 1918 to cease publishing *Siraj al-Akhbar,* largely in protest.[49] As a consequence, some of these elements, supported by a number of either benefactors or self-motivated individuals, plotted against the Amir, who was assassinated in mysterious circumstances on 20 February 1919 while asleep in his tent during a hunting trip near Jalalabad.

Habibullah Khan's Assassination

There has been a great deal of debate as to who precisely the plotters were and who exactly was the triggerman.[50] Those named as plotters have ranged from Amanullah and Tarzi, who were both in Kabul at the time of the assassination, to Ahmad Shah (a subsequent Minister of Court) and General Mohammad Nadir, who were with the Amir. Both Amanullah and General Nadir were most probably involved, though in varying degrees, as principals in the plot, for different reasons.[51] They had formed an alliance of convenience, which, as will be seen later, did not last long, for different objectives. Whereas Amanullah was driven by his passion for accelerated modernisation and national independence, General Nadir saw, in all probability, an opportunity in the plot either to assume the reins of power or to act as a kingmaker in the chaos the assassination was expected to create.

However, as it turned out, post-assassination events did not fulfil General Nadir's expectations. Initially, Nasrullah, who was also in Jalalabad at the time of the killing, declared himself his brother's lawful successor.[52] But the fact that he was out of the capital enabled Amanullah, who appeared well prepared for the event, to seize the seat of power, the Royal Palace (Arg) in Kabul, which also housed the royal treasury, and to mobilise the support of the most effective army units in the capital. He swiftly overpowered his uncle, imprisoned him in the Palace;[53] and for good measure placed under virtual house arrest in the Palace his elder half-brother and potential rival, Enayatullah, who was also in Jalalabad at the time of the assassination and was believed to have supported Nasrullah. While proclaiming his own rule, he also implicated the British in the plot, and imprisoned a number of other people, including General Nadir and his brother Shah Wali. He executed some of those arrested but, ironically, soon released General Nadir and his brother. Whereas the Musahiban's choice of royal successor, Asadullah, was too young to be any serious threat, Amanullah appointed Nadir and most of the other suspected key participants in the plot to important governmental posts.[54] Mahmud Tarzi was made Foreign Minister; General Nadir was appointed Minister of War, leaving him little choice but to cooperate with Amanullah for the time being. The other freed people elevated to important positions included Abdul Hadi Dawi, a close assistant of Tarzi and a prominent political figure over the next five decades, and Abdul Rahman Lodin, also a major associate of the Young Afghans.

As for the identity of the assassin who actually shot Amir Habibullah, it is now credibly suspected that it was Shuja-ud-Dawla, the Amir's Chief Chamberlain since 1917.[55] In the early 1930s, living in exile in Germany, Shuja-ud-Dawla confessed as much to Ghulam Siddiq Charkhi, the former Deputy and Foreign Minister of Amanullah, and produced the murder weapon, a pistol. He acted partly because of personal animosity towards the

Amir and partly because he was encouraged by the plotters. Following the killing, he too was promoted by Amanullah to several high positions, first as Chief of Kabul Police, later as Commander of the Second Army Division in Kabul and Head of the Ministry of Security respectively. His last post, to which he was appointed in 1925, was as Afghan Minister to London. However, after his unsuccessful bid in the last days of Amanullah's rule to govern Herat on Amanullah's behalf, he went into exile in Germany, where he died in 1945.

In a sense, Amir Habibullah's assassination could be partly attributed to a clash between his politics of gradual change and the Young Afghans' drive for speedy national modernisation and independence. But this would be an oversimplification, for the event was also grounded in the deeper problems which had come to mark the evolution of Afghan politics since the early nineteenth century: the age-old and complex interplay between the polygamic rivalries within the ruling family and the fluctuating Anglo-Russian competition. Although there is no documentary evidence, it is clear from orally transmitted reports that one issue which may have motivated the plotters to act concerned Amanullah's impatient drive to assume the throne and General Mohammad Nadir's momentary support for this drive to achieve a double-edged objective: at best eventually to win the throne for himself, and at worst to become part of Amanullah's team to achieve later what he failed to accomplish this time.[56] The discreet support of the British for General Mohammad Nadir, their continued insensitivity to the nationalist-reformist aspirations of the Young Afghans and consequent failure to move faster on independence negotiations with Amir Habibullah, created a climate conducive to the plotted killing of the Amir. Had the British acted otherwise, particularly in the face of the emergent non-confrontationist posture adopted by Russia under the Bolsheviks, there would have been fewer grounds for the plotters to act as they did at the time when negotiations for possible independence were in progress.

Whatever the reasons for Amir Habibullah's assassination, his rule opened up Afghanistan to a considerable extent to the intertwined internal and regional reformist and nationalist trends.[57] Although he himself could not substantially deviate from the traditional absolutist approach to the exercise of power and authority, and was a gradualist in his desire for change and reform, these trends were instigated and upheld by individuals who singularly or collectively were capable of influencing the potentially politically-active segments of the Afghan people in Kabul. The activities of these individuals, many of whom could be identified with the Young Afghans, cut to some extent across the boundaries of at least the urbanised elements of Afghan microsocieties on a national basis. They provided a Kabul-based ideological guidance and motivation for a national mobilisation to pursue by radical means their two interrelated goals of modernisation and independence. The assassination of Amir Habibullah opened the way for them to make greater strides in this direction.

3

Independence and Radical Modernisation

The advent of Amanullah's rule inaugurated an extraordinary and arguably long overdue stage, marking a watershed in the quest by Amanullah, Mahmud Tarzi and their 'Young Afghan' followers for reform, independence and statehood. The politics of gradual change and development pursued in fits and starts by earlier Afghan rulers gave way to sustained efforts to initiate a radical process of change, so as to place Afghanistan in the ranks of modern states as quickly as possible. By the same token, Amanullah's rule ushered in changes which seriously disturbed the delicate balance among rival families in the Afghan power elite, on the one hand, and between these, the religious establishment and microsocieties, on the other; and consequently undermined the relative stability and order the Afghans had come to enjoy over the previous 40 years. Thus, Amanullah's radical approach to building a strong unitary state produced a period of both intense reform and social revolts, leading to the collapse of his rule within a decade. Yet whatever the degree of his failure, his rule still set a yardstick for reform by which the efforts of future Afghan leaders and political groups could be measured. This chapter examines the most salient features of Amanullah's rule and their wider implications for the development of Afghan politics. However, this cannot be done without also allowing for the ongoing themes of polygamic rivalry and major power competition.

Amanullah's Power Consolidation

Despite the initial disturbances caused by Amir Habibullah's assassination, Amanullah was able to consolidate his leadership very quickly. Once he had imprisoned Nasrullah, placed under surveillance Enayatullah, who was also declared to have forfeited all claim to the throne, and coopted some of his other potential rivals, including General Mohammad Nadir, Amanullah skilfully managed to mute any immediate challenges to his rule. He used a subtle policy of manipulation through royal pardon, reward and trade-offs to avoid disturbing further the interests of his Mohammadzai sub-clan – the power elite of successive Afghan rulers for almost a century. While appointing several Mohammadzai notables to important court and cabinet positions, he drew primarily on two sources, though in varying degrees, to pursue his predefined goals of independence and radical reform. One was the intellectual and innovative strength of Mahmud Tarzi and a number of other liberal-minded Young Afghan supporters. The other was the potential of those who were not necessarily in full concord with the Young Afghans but had the capacity, through control or influence over the administrative and traditional instrumentalities of power, to help implement his policies. These most noticeably included the Musahiban brothers and their descendants.

Not only was General Mohammad Nadir given the post of Minister of War, including responsibility for all dealings with frontier tribes, but his brothers were also promoted to important military and civilian positions in the next few years. Shah Wali was given command of the troops on the Kandahar Front; as a result of his excellent services he was made a full General by the end of 1919 and subsequently went on to occupy other prominent positions until his departure for Paris in 1926. Shah Mahmud, whom Amanullah valued highly for his bravery, was assigned to command the troops at the Paiwar Pass and was elevated within a few months to the position of Civil and Military Governor of the Southern Region, again a prelude to other significant military posts. Mohammad Hashim was promoted to the Governorship of Jalalabad in December 1919 and of the Eastern Province a year later – a position followed by service as Acting Minister of War in 1922 during General Mohammad Nadir's absence from the capital and by his final appointment as Minister to Moscow in 1924. On the other hand, Mohammad Aziz was allowed to continue his civilian career, and was put in charge of education of the first batch of Afghan students sent to Europe; he remained there with them until 1926. The importance that Amanullah attached to the Musahiban brothers reflected their military and administrative ability, and the professional and border-tribal loyalty that they had acquired over the years. Despite the pro-British conservative leanings of some of them, Amanullah seems to have found them sufficiently powerful and patriotic to keep them within his power structure.[1] He even consented to the marriage of two of his sisters to the Musahiban brothers,[2] to strengthen ties further with this influential family.

Independence

Amanullah was therefore quickly able to turn to his long-cherished goals of national freedom and modernisation. These required immediate and unconditional independence from Britain; and inter-related structural changes in the political and social-economic conditions of Afghan microsocieties under the authority of a powerful but popularly sanctioned government. He appeared to have wanted nothing short of a revolutionary process of change, necessarily instigated from above. In this, he had something in common with a contemporary revolutionary, Ataturk, who had simultaneously embarked, though in a different manner and for a different ideological end, on a course of radical change in Turkey. There is no doubt that both Amanullah and Tarzi gained some inspiration and courage from Ataturk;[3] however, this is where the comparison really ends.

As convinced Muslims, Amanullah and Tarzi could not altogether approve of Ataturk's secularist approaches to change and reform. Ideologically, they wanted an Islamic-based, western-inclined transformation of Afghanistan into a viable modern, sovereign nation-state. Meanwhile, Amanullah's leadership was far less equipped than that of Ataturk for the task it set itself to achieve. It started from the palace, with little grass-roots involvement in the formulation of its goals. It lacked revolutionary experience and structural organisation.[4] Nor did it have a strong professional army and a sufficient intellectual pool and politicised public on which it could rely for law enforcement and better policy deliberation, or the trained manpower it critically needed for revolutionary change. It was also operating in a country far poorer and more insulated from the outside world's ideas and changes than either Turkey or Russia.

However, all this did not seem to matter to Amanullah and Tarzi. What appeared most important to them was the firmness of their moral and political convictions, and their will to act to realise these convictions in pursuit of what they considered best for Afghanistan at that particular historical juncture. While they were accused of being idealistic, they seemed to believe in idealism as a potentially positive means of stimulating the Afghan people towards unity, freedom, structural change and a participatory political and social order. They were convinced of the mutually reinforcing nature of the goals of independence and modernisation. The Royal Manifesto published on the day of Amanullah's coronation (28 February 1919) is a revealing document in this sense:

> O nation, proud through the realisation of its dignity! In the minute when
> my great people has placed this crown on my head, I announce with a loud

voice to you that I shall accept the crown and throne only on the condition that you render me support in the realisation of my plans and intentions. I have explained my ideas to you already, and I shall reiterate only the most important of them now:

1. Afghanistan must become free and independent, it must enjoy all rights that all other sovereign states possess.

2. You will help me with all your strength to avenge the blood of the martyr – my deceased father.[5]

3. The nation must become free: no man should be an object of oppression and tyranny.[6]

This was the first time ever that an Afghan ruler claimed to seek legitimacy not so much in tribal politics or Islam, but in broad public acceptance. Nationalism, elements of populism,[7] respect for the traditional Pashtun values (the oath to punish his father's killers) undoubtedly constituted important parts of the new king's credo. However, it was independence, and, more specifically, independence intertwined with modernisation, that became the cornerstone of his platform. This basically meant that Afghanistan could not modernise without first of all being freed from British domination and therefore 'Great Game' interference, and could not preserve its independence without being modernised. Thus, from the start, the Young Afghans' domestic reforms became inextricably linked to foreign policy and vice versa; and by extension, failure in one domain would have serious implications for the other.

Given British procrastination over the question of independence,[8] Amanullah's leadership quickly reached the conclusion that the best way to secure unconditional independence was through a military confrontation. Although it was not said at the time, this confrontation was intended to be limited in both scope and results and therefore necessarily in proportion to the available resources. It was to pressure the British to speed up the ongoing diplomatic negotiations and to agree to Kabul's demand for full and unconditional independence. In late April 1919, during a mass meeting in one of Kabul's main mosques, Masjid-e Eidgah, Amanullah appealed to the Afghan people's religious and nationalist sentiment and honour, and declared a *jihad* against Britain, launching the Afghan War of Independence or the Third Anglo-Afghan War. The use of the term *jihad* instantly proved effective, not only boosting popular support, but also establishing his position as the supreme political-religious leader.[9] The war lasted only a month, from 3 May to 3 June 1919, and produced mixed results.

Initially, the three columns of Afghan troops – one of them commanded by General Mohammad Nadir – achieved considerable success, raising the passion of Afghans as great holy warriors, especially when they were on the offensive. But with the exception of General Nadir's forces at the Khost-Ghazni Front, they soon ran out of steam, resulting in a military stalemate.[10] Nevertheless, the initial success helped open the way for serious diplomatic negotiations and eventual Afghan political victory. On 24 May 1919, Amanullah despatched a letter to the Viceroy of British India, suggesting the cessation of bloodshed and, on 3 June 1919, an armistice was proclaimed.[11] The road to final settlement, however, was still to be long and full of frustration for the Afghan negotiators. The negotiations, conducted in several stages at Rawalpindi, Mussoorie and Kabul, were often bogged down, largely due to continued British determination to accept only a settlement that retained Afghanistan within the sphere of British colonial interests.[12]

On the whole, three factors coloured this British approach to Afghanistan's independence. One was their dislike of Amanullah, which seemingly equalled their aversion to the Bolsheviks. They found in Amanullah's nationalist militancy serious vulnerability to Bolshevik influence.[13] Another British concern related to Amanullah's Islamist rhetoric that permeated his anti-British campaign, adding to, and amplifying, the broad anti-colonial and pro-independence agitation then gaining momentum in India and, indeed, the region as a whole.[14] The third was British pride and self-righteousness as an imperial power, which often inhibited their developing more realistic perceptions of the position of the other side with which they had to deal.[15] These factors initially led the British to agree to an independence settlement whose written provisions were open to equivocal interpretation. The Treaty of Peace between the Illustrious British Government and the Independent Afghan Government signed at Rawalpindi on 8 August 1919 was precisely along these lines. Its wording was so ambiguous as to allow the Afghans to read in it British acknowledgment of their full independence; and the British to find grounds in it still to make 'sphere of influence' claims on the country.[16] Indeed, soon after the conclusion of the Treaty, Lord Curzon, by then Foreign Secretary, made such a claim, and refused to deal with the Afghan government through any other channel than the British India Office.[17]

When Amanullah and Mahmud Tarzi demanded renewed negotiations to clarify some of the terms of the Treaty, and further settle the problems associated with the Durand Line, the British showed great reluctance. They sought not only to sabotage or prolong such negotiations, but also to undermine Amanullah's rule, engaging in a barrage of anti-Amanullah propaganda and encouraging border tribal uprisings against him, to prompt him to moderate his position on the question of total independence.[18] However, Amanullah's intransigence finally left the British with little realistic choice but to sign a new Anglo-Afghan Treaty on 22 November 1921 in Kabul, superseding that of Rawalpindi.

Of course, from the Afghan point of view, the new Treaty was not altogether satisfactory, for it failed to address some of the major border and territorial problems. The Afghan leadership initially wanted the Durand Line determination abrogated, and the entire Waziristan and adjacent frontier territories returned to Kabul's fold. Habibullah had been promised that during the First World War, and it was a major issue at Rawalpindi and Mussoorie, too.[19] But Amanullah's leadership found its abandonment acceptable in return for those provisions of the Treaty which explicitly recognised Afghanistan as an independent and sovereign state.[20] For *realpolitik* reasons at least, Amanullah, and Mahmud Tarzi who had headed the Afghan negotiating team, wanted the Treaty to form a solid basis for the development of a sound and equitable relationship between Kabul and London. To this end, they promptly agreed to direct diplomatic relations, which were formally established in 1922.

However, the British did not react with similar equanimity. They could neither embrace the Treaty, nor tolerate the Afghans' treatment of it as a major political victory. They ended their annual subsidy and all other assistance to Kabul, in a display of heightened disdain for Amanullah. They resented the upsurge that Amanullah's success caused, not merely in his prestige and popularity at home, but in his reputation as a Muslim nationalist and anti-colonial figure in the eyes of many nationalist-reformist forces in the region, especially in the Indian subcontinent.[21] They also resented the Bolshevik leaders' prompt offer of support and friendship to Amanullah for what was termed his 'anti-colonial struggle' – an issue which will be covered in detail shortly. In official British Indian circles, he was seen as an unscrupulous militant, and dangerous for wider British regional interests. In contrast to Amanullah's and Tarzi's initial openness to good relations with London, the British evidently resolved to use their diplomatic muscle in whatever way possible to keep the Afghan leadership weak and incapable of having any regional impact. This was manifested most sharply in Britain's efforts to frustrate Kabul's urgent search for wider international recognition of Afghanistan's independence and alternative sources of foreign aid, partly to make up for the loss of British support and partly to counter what it perceived as the persistent British menace.[22]

To effect their plan to accompany independence moves with substantial modernisation steps, Amanullah and Tarzi needed to gain as much international recognition and support as possible. Immediately following the signing of the Treaty of Rawalpindi, they dispatched missions, mostly headed by Mohammad Wali, a liberal Tajik associate of the Young Afghans and a leading figure in the negotiations with the British, to Soviet Russia, Iran, Turkey, Europe and the USA. Soviet Russia was the first to recognise Afghanistan's sovereignty, make friendly overtures and establish diplomatic relations in 1919; Turkey, Iran, Italy, France and Germany followed suit. But Amanullah's leadership could not persuade its main target, the USA, to do the same.

Balancing Foreign Relations

Haunted by continued British pressure, and cautioned by historical Russian ambitions, Amanullah desperately wanted to forge close ties with the USA, for two important reasons. First, the USA was a physically distant great power, capable of helping a country like Afghanistan without acquiring the geographical leverage which had enabled British India and Tsarist Russia to intimidate it. Second, the USA had a relatively unblemished colonial image, which protected Kabul from criticism for dealing with a 'colonial power'. Indeed, initially Washington showed some receptiveness. President Warren G. Harding received Wali's mission on 26 July 1921, which some Afghans construed as US recognition of both Amanullah's government and Afghanistan's independence, and promised to consider seriously the question of US diplomatic representation in Afghanistan. But unfortunately nothing more happened for many years.[23]

It appears this was as far as Washington at that stage was prepared to go – something which seriously puzzled Amanullah's leadership. The USA astonishingly displayed as much insensitivity as the British to Afghan needs. The American position was influenced by: Washington's ambivalence towards the communist regime in Russia; its perception of Afghanistan as unimportant to the USA; its treatment of Afghanistan as part of the British sphere of influence and therefore British responsibility; and, more importantly, as some informed Afghan sources believe, London's constant advice to Washington not to help Amanullah get off the British hook[24] – advice the British continued to give until the mid 1930s.[25]

This American position was a great setback for Amanullah and Mahmud Tarzi. They felt not only terribly let down, but also deprived of an appropriate and significant international source of support, which they considered crucial to their efforts to free Afghanistan from being a cockpit of traditional Anglo-Russian rivalry and to enlist outside capital, economic-technological assistance and expertise for their modernisation drive. The USA neither officially declared support for Afghan independence for another decade nor established full diplomatic relations with Afghanistan until 1942. It was to repeat this degree of insensitivity in the 1950s, but this time at much greater eventual cost, as will be detailed in Chapter 5.

America's lack of interest was paralleled by Amanullah's similar failure to attract the support of another emerging power, namely Japan, also mainly due to British diplomacy, which actively discouraged Tokyo from helping Kabul out. The situation created a serious foreign policy vacuum for Amanullah's regime. To fill this vacuum, it had little choice but to pursue a foreign policy that would not only underline its commitment to 'pan-Islamism' but also allow it urgently to develop bilateral relations with whatever other powers happened to be receptive.[26]

In the Muslim world, Kabul immediately sought close ties and concluded treaties of friendship and cooperation with Turkey and Persia,[27] and subsequently with Egypt. While neither Persia nor Egypt could offer much more than diplomatic support, since their predicament was similar to that of Afghanistan, relations with Turkey proved most rewarding. Given Amanullah's and Tarzi's special admiration for Ataturk, and the latter's appreciation of the Afghan leader's nationalist-reformist stance, Afghan-Turkish relations quickly became close. Turkey not only voiced strong political support for Amanullah's regime, but also made a marked contribution to its programme of modernisation, supplying many teachers and civilian and military advisors, who played an important role in Amanullah's educational, administrative and military reforms. Turkey also received the first batch of Afghan students, male and female, for training in medical, scientific and military fields in order to provide much-needed trained manpower. Nevertheless, Turkish support was insufficient either to underpin the modernisation programme or to be used as an effective lever against Britain.

For this, Amanullah's regime had to look elsewhere. Given its limited options, it naturally turned to certain European powers, especially Italy, Germany and France. As mentioned earlier, Kabul's approach to them proved successful, particularly as their individual responses were influenced by shared dislike of Britain. Between 1921 and 1922, they all recognised Afghan independence and signed separate agreements for full diplomatic relations and economic-scientific and educational cooperation. Their political support and material assistance, involving supply of teachers, technical expertise, capital goods and some financial aid, proved helpful. However, they, too, were limited in what they could contribute to offset Anglo-Soviet pressures on a landlocked Afghanistan, whose foreign transit was very much at the mercy of British India. Germany for a long time appeared to be Amanullah's main hope: as early as spring 1920, he 'sought to impress on the Germans the difficulty of Afghanistan's strategic position between Russian and British imperialism, and his desire to counterbalance that reality with close ties to Germany', and on many occasions thereafter he 'reiterated his preference for Germany and all things German, and his continuing desire to see Germany play the leading role in the development of Afghanistan'.[28]

However, the Weimar Republic, 'torn by internal German conflicts, was unable and unwilling to conduct a foreign policy that might lead the German government to difficulties with her former enemies'.[29] This meant that the only major power to which Amanullah and Tarzi could turn for friendship and effective assistance to counterbalance the British and help the reform programme was Soviet Russia. Yet it was the development of this friendship that proved the most sensitive and controversial.

Afghan-Soviet Relations

The sudden upturn in Afghan–Soviet relations was as much a product of the extraordinary circumstances under which the Amanullah leadership operated as it was of the Bolsheviks' clever and timely exploitation of Amanullah's vulnerability in the face of Britain's insensitivity and misconceived policies. Whereas in the past, Tsarist behaviour had made the Afghans generally distrustful, and often prompted them to rely on Britain as a counterforce, there was now a dramatic change in both Afghan and Russian circumstances, which made the development of close ties between the two sides not merely possible but desirable. As Amanullah's leadership found the British attitude unacceptable and threatening, it deemed it necessary to overlook, at least temporarily, historical fears of Russian ambitions for the sake of better ties with Soviet Russia. On the other hand, the Bolsheviks, who had just overthrown the Provisional Government, were facing growing internal opposition and external resentment.[30] They were therefore obliged to promote a foreign policy which could help them to achieve rapid power consolidation, without sacrificing any of their revolutionary principles or foregoing any opportunity to enhance the security of their domain.[31] This meant that both Amanullah and Lenin had reasons to forge close ties.[32]

As Amanullah requested recognition and support, the Bolsheviks saw in this, and in Britain's hostile behaviour towards him, an important opportunity to reverse the historical balance of power, with a view to achieving several objectives. They were: to fuel the Afghans' growing anti-British yearning for total independence; to provide an example of harmonious Afghan-Soviet relations as a way to encourage other countries, particularly neighbouring Muslim ones, to enter similar relations; to establish in Afghanistan an espionage network for the spread of communism into India; and to deter the Afghans from providing any active support for their Muslim counterparts in Central Asia, particularly in Bukhara and Khiva, previously Tsarist 'protectorates' that in early 1918 had reclaimed their independence.[33] By 1920, the Kremlin had by and large laid the foundations for its own regional 'forward policy': first, Sovietising the Muslims of Central Asia; afterwards, with their help, Sovietising their brethren in Afghanistan, Iran and India. In this context, Afghanistan was often described as 'the Suez Canal of the Revolution' leading to India.[34]

Lenin's government offered its support as part of a general peace offensive, particularly towards Soviet Russia's neighbours. Following Amanullah's prompt recognition of the Bolshevik regime and call for friendly relations, the Kremlin in May 1919 recognised Amanullah's declaration of independence, and went much further. It renounced past Tsarist claims against Afghanistan, and also against Iran, and praised Amanullah's regime as an anti-colonial anti-imperialist force in the region.[35] Furthermore, it promised all-round political and material support, free of any strings. In so doing, it played down Bolshevik international revolutionary ambitions and highlighted neighbourly friendship, governed by principles of mutual respect and non-interference, grounding this in a view expressed by the Soviet Ambassador to Iran, one of Lenin's closest associates, F.A. Rothstein, that 'any attempt on... [the Soviet] part... to start revolution in any part of Persia [or the region] would immediately throw it [Persia] into the arms of the British, who would be received as Saviours of the Fatherland'.[36] The instruction prepared by the People's Commissariat of Foreign Affairs for Soviet Ambassador Ia. Z. Surits departing for Kabul, read:

> You are advised to pay special attention to the reformist programme of the Amir. In the current stage of Afghanistan's development, the enlightened absolutism similar to our XVIII century constitutes a serious progressive phenomenon for it... Not for a minute do we become monarchists or adherents of absolutism. This has to be clear to everyone. But we render all possible assistance to the reformist endeavours of the progressive-minded Amir. In every conceivable way you must avoid the fatal mistake of planting Communism in that country... Not for a minute are we inclined to impose upon your people a programme which is alien to it at this stage of its development.[37]

Amanullah's leadership found in these gestures a substantial shift from the past Russian attitude and a strong source of anti-British leverage, as well as a foundation of support for its modernisation programme. Of course, at

first neither Amanullah nor Tarzi could be terribly relaxed about accepting
Soviet offers of assistance; they had enough historical knowledge to realise
the possible wider implications of such action. While interested in playing
the 'Russia card', they seemingly wanted to play it as judiciously as possible,
so as to avoid giving any impression of ideological affinity with the Soviets,
and to make sure that Afghanistan reaped maximum benefit from it. At first,
they forbore to rush into any substantial deal with Moscow, as they waited
for their initial approach to it to provoke favourable responses from Britain
and, eventually, the USA.[38] However, when such responses did not
materialise, and instead the British continued to cause pain and frustration
during the independence negotiations, they ultimately accepted the Soviet
gestures in good faith, and raised Afghan-Soviet ties to a higher level.

After many careful bilateral discussions, the first Afghan-Soviet Treaty
of Friendship and Good Neighbourly Relations was concluded in February
1921. This Treaty by all accounts favoured Afghanistan.[39] Each side
undertook to respect the other's independence and territorial integrity and
to refrain from any military and political agreement with a third power 'which
might prejudice one of the contracting parties' (Article II). Moreover, the
Soviets pledged not only to aid Afghanistan's national development (Article
X), but also to return the disputed territories 'on the basis of free expression
of will' of their population, mainly Turkmens and Baluchis (Article IX),[40]
and to respect 'the actual freedom and independence of Bukhara and Khiva,
regardless of the form of government there, according to the wishes of their
peoples' (Article VIII).

While inaugurating the first phase of Soviet economic and military aid to
Afghanistan, the signing of the Treaty produced mixed results for the Afghan-
British relationship. On the one hand, it provoked the British to show more
flexibility towards the Afghan demand for full independence, for fear that
failure to do so could push Amanullah further towards the Soviets. This
sped up the process of negotiation, culminating in the Anglo-Afghan Treaty
of November 1921.[41] On the other, it made the British more worried than
ever about possible Soviet ulterior motives behind friendship with
Afghanistan. In fact, the British Minister, Colonel Humphrys, who arrived
in Kabul in March 1922 to advise London how to combat the Bolsheviks in
Central Asia, interpreted Moscow's assistance as part of a Soviet design to
dominate northern Afghanistan,[42] and at the same time several British officials
began accusing Amanullah of pro-Soviet leanings.[43]

However, the British understanding was based largely on misperceptions
rather than any sober assessment of Amanullah's objectives. In reality, close
scrutiny clearly establishes that his leadership wished only to pursue a

balanced and neutral foreign policy, which would tally with its Islamic-based ideological disposition and liberal-inclined goal of modernisation. Friendship with Soviet Russia was intended to aid the promotion of this policy, which was expected to provide Afghanistan with an anti-British lever, and, by the same token, to induce Britain and other western powers to put their relations with Afghanistan on a similar footing. This is why, despite all the British discouragement, Amanullah's leadership never abandoned its efforts to seek American and German friendship. Nor did it ever waver in its staunch ideological opposition to 'Godless Communism', thus setting limits on the extent to which relations with Moscow could develop. It never envisaged friendship with Soviet Russia as an end in itself, but merely as a means to strengthen a neutral and balanced independent foreign policy for Afghanistan in a zone of sustained great power rivalry.[44] In this respect, Amanullah's leadership reflected the desire of a small and weak state to retain its independence and modernise through a policy of playing off the very major powers which had limited it in the past.

Even so, the Soviets were soon to disappoint Amanullah and become a major source of irritation to his rule, once the traditional British support for the Afghans as a deterrent to Russian ambitions had been removed from the regional power equation. They proved strong in rhetoric and promises, but weak, self-serving, evasive and conniving in deeds. On the one hand, under the Afghan-Soviet Treaty of 1921 and a few other subsequent accords, they promised generous aid and political-territorial concessions. For example, they pledged to provide yearly a free financial subsidy of up to one million gold or silver roubles to replace Afghanistan's loss of the similar subsidy from Britain, substantial economic, technical and vocational aid and expertise and some military assistance. On the other hand, they were neither capable of fulfilling all their aid promises, nor willing to deliver the political-territorial concessions.[45] Throughout Amanullah's rule, the promised Soviet aid was undercut by Soviet industrial and military weakness, deep preoccupation with domestic power struggles and a consequent need to eschew entanglement in any foreign situations, in Afghanistan or elsewhere, that could risk confrontation with the British. Nor could their promised political-territorial concessions be reconciled with the expansionist agenda that they secretly entertained. Moreover, to have a ready lever of political pressure on Amanullah's regime, the Bolsheviks sponsored the creation in Bukhara in late 1921 of the 'Central Committee of Young Afghan Revolutionaries', whose aim was 'to liquidate the existing capitalist order, to establish, according to the people's will, a Republican Government and thus liberate the Afghan people from the despotism of the Amir and *beks*'.[46]

The results were manifold. First, while raising the Afghan leadership's expectations, and helping it accept the costs of gaining independence in the hope that such costs would be at least partly met by Soviet aid, Moscow could give only a very limited amount of economic and military assistance to Afghanistan. During the whole Amanullah period, Soviet assistance came most importantly to include construction of a telegraph line between Kabul, Kandahar, Herat and Kushk; a few small industrial and commercial projects; the dispatch of an insignificant number of engineers, mostly employed to survey the Salang-Aibak-Mazar route; and some pilots and advisors to train Afghan pilots and assist in flying six German and five Soviet fighter aircraft Amanullah purchased to form the nucleus of an Afghan air force; and the delivery of some small arms.[47] This sufficed to give the Soviets a symbolic presence in Afghanistan, but not enough either to play a major role in Amanullah's modernisation drive, or enable him to pose any threat to British interests in the region.

Meanwhile, the Soviets reneged on some of their important pledges under the Treaty of 1921 and several Memoranda of Mutual Understanding. They embarked on a path of blatant expansion in Muslim Central Asia, in the clear knowledge that a weak, unprotected and necessarily friendly Afghanistan would be unable to pose any impediment. First, they failed to return the most important border district, which, from the Afghan point of view, was Panjdeh. The only piece of land they finally and reluctantly conceded, under an Afghan-Soviet protocol in 1926, was a small island, called Urta Toghai, which had developed in the middle of Amu River as a result of a gradual change in the river's course.[48] Second, they reneged on their pledge to respect the freedom and independence of Bukhara and Khiva. By the mid 1920s, they had crushed these two small Muslim emirates, first by aiding 'revolutionary' groups of 'Young Bukharans' and 'Young Khivans' to seize power, then by officially annexing them to the USSR.[49] Third, as these actions stimulated the growth of an anti-Soviet Islamic nationalist guerrilla resistance, which became known as the Basmachi Movement, the Soviets launched a bloody, brutal drive to 'pacify' the Muslims of Central Asia.[50] During the 1920s, they succeeded in subordinating the Basmachis and all other forms of nationalist movement; in doing so, they also violated Afghan territory several times in the mid 1920s, only to withdraw in the face of stiff Afghan reaction.[51] Thus, they were able effectively to expand Russia's actual control for the first time to the current border between Afghanistan and the Central Asian Republics.

This had multiple effects on Afghanistan. The Amir of Bukhara and several of his ministers, together with about 80,000 Muslim people of Tajik,

Uzbek, Turkmen and Kyrgyz origins, fled to Afghanistan in the spring of 1921.[52] They joined many more Muslims who had previously crossed the border in the wake of the Bolshevik revolution.[53] While the Amir and his ministers sought refuge in Kabul, with one of the ministers even seeking to maintain a Bukharan government-in-exile there,[54] most of the others settled among their ethnic kin in northern Afghanistan, bringing with them endless tales about the horrors of 'Godless', 'anti-Islamic' Soviet communism.[55] Such tales, rapidly disseminated by word of mouth, prompted the devout Muslim Afghans to develop an intense distaste for the Soviets and their ideology, with many religious leaders calling on the government to act in support of the Central Asian Muslims.[56]

This development seriously perturbed the Afghan government, which rapidly became disillusioned with and distrustful of the Soviets. It became clear to Amanullah and his supporters that all along the Soviets' gestures of friendship and goodwill had not really been meant to facilitate Afghan independence and modernisation, but to assist themselves in domestic consolidation and socialist empire building, with a special imperative to avoid British opposition through Afghanistan. Meanwhile, the Afghan leaders were in no position to change the situation radically. To confront the Soviets, they needed substantial western support. They made some efforts to secure it, but to little avail. Ironically, even then neither the British nor the Americans were prepared to respond positively to Kabul's call for more cooperative relations. In order again to attract American friendship and ensure equilibrium in Afghan relations with Moscow, Kabul in 1925 even went as far as to forward to the US State Department through the Afghan Minister in Paris (then General Mohammad Nadir), a draft treaty of friendship with the USA; but Washington never responded.[57]

It is worth stressing that, by the 1920s, British preoccupation with growing nationalist agitations in British colonies and protectorates had deepened, and there was intensifying debate in London on Britain's handling of its colonial affairs and on the wisdom of its initial belligerence towards Soviet Russia. On the one hand, Hindu and Muslim nationalist opposition to British rule was sharply on the increase in India, and administrative and security operations against it were becoming costly. On the other, despite their expansion into Central Asia, the Soviets appeared to the British, at least in the short run, less of a threat than their predecessors, particularly given the heightening divisions and power struggles in the Soviet Communist Party after Lenin's death in 1924. These factors, in separate ways, put pressure on London to rationalise, in any way possible, its 'forward defence policy' in the Afghan region.[58] This may not only have prompted Britain to soften its initial belligerence and formally recognise Afghanistan's independence under the Treaty of 1921, but may also have affected the eventual British decision to abandon much of its active opposition to Soviet Russia from the mid 1920s.

The failure of Amanullah's government to attract substantial western support was accompanied by lack of interest from two other regional actors, Ataturk in Turkey and Reza Shah in Persia, in the fate of the Central Asian Muslims. At a time when both had deployed most of their resources to support domestic power consolidation, they did not find it expedient to risk entanglement in any foreign problem that did not affect them directly. Their fear of a British threat and reluctance to antagonise the Soviets left Amanullah's government with little choice but to confine its opposition to Soviet expansionism to diplomatic protests, attempt to reduce its own acceptance of Soviet aid and accommodate those who fled to Afghanistan.[59] Of course, its protests cut no ice with Moscow. In response to one of them, Moscow assured Kabul that only a 'limited contingent' of troops had been dispatched to the Emirates of Bukhara and Khiva, at the request of their governments, and would be withdrawn when no longer needed.[60] The language of this Soviet response would be redeployed six decades later to justify the Soviet invasion of Afghanistan. Signing of the Pact on Neutrality and Non-Aggression between the USSR and Afghanistan in August 1926 consolidated Soviet gains in Central Asia, and destroyed any hopes of success the Islamic resistance in the region might have had.[61]

Amanullah's inability to provide active support for the Central Asian Muslims, in particular the Basmachi Movement, markedly undermined his credibility. From the start, one of his main pillars of legitimacy was a claim to be, above everything else, an Islamic ruler; but when the real test came to substantiate this claim in the face of Soviet actions, he could not do so. This highlighted a serious tension between Amanullah's stance on 'pan-Islamism' and the general course of foreign policy that he could pursue. Thus, instead of helping Amanullah out of his predicament, the Soviets contributed substantially to it.[62] Their behaviour could not but demean Amanullah as a weak Muslim in the eyes of many Afghans, some of whom accused him of 'sacrilegious' behaviour. As a result, his position rapidly deteriorated to the point where he was disliked by the British, ignored by the Americans, deceived by the Soviets and incapable of giving much credibility to his pan-Islamic stance. This played into the hands not only of those foreign forces which wanted him replaced by a more receptive figure, but also of the domestic opposition which was gaining strength on the basis of the flaws in his policies of reform. Before discussing the nature and sources of this opposition, let us first briefly look at the reforms and their objectives.

Modernisation

As mentioned earlier, Amanullah and Tarzi saw independence and modernisation as indissolubly linked and mutually reinforcing. As soon as the Treaty of Rawalpindi was signed, they set out on what proved a very difficult and complex course of modernisation in a traditional, Islamic ethno-tribal society, where in the Pashtun areas the clergy espoused ideas in line with the ultra-conservative Deobandi school of Islam.[63] On the whole, the reform programme had its origins in the ideological vision that Amanullah and Tarzi had come to share by the time they came to power. It envisaged comprehensive and radical structural transformation of Afghanistan. Originating from an unlikely source – a normally conservative monarchical institution – the reforms rapidly came to be far more vigorous, bold and innovative than could initially have been expected. They focused immediately on four interlinked structural objectives, for which only a modest and *ad hoc* start had been made under Amanullah's father and grandfather. The objectives were: to develop a formal-legal system of constitutional monarchical government; institute an Islamically defensible but liberal process of social-cultural change and economic infrastructural development; build professional and efficient armed forces; and enforce an appropriate method of mobilising and integrating the Afghan microsocieties into a viable sovereign macrosociety and nation-state.[64]

During the initial stages of reform, up to 1924, a number of important steps were taken in all areas. In the realm of political reforms, for the first time in the history of Afghanistan a well-structured Cabinet, the Council of Ministers, headed by Amanullah himself, was established. A number of urgent measures were adopted to reform and reorganise the administration in order to make governmental functions more responsible and efficient at central, provincial and local levels. New rules and regulations, defining ministerial administrative structures, duties and responsibilities were enacted. These reforms were envisaged as laying the bases for developing a modern bureaucratic system along what could be described as Weberian lines. In the sphere of participatory legislation, a national Legislative Council (*Mahfal-e Qanun*), partly appointed and partly elected, was set up, and steps were taken to establish provincial councils in the same vein. The Legislative Council was the precursor of a more representative legislative body, called the National Council (*Shura-ye Melli*), which came into existence under the first Afghan Constitution promulgated in 1923, a document to which we shall turn shortly.

In the legal arena, a serious attempt was made to create an independent and comprehensive judiciary. The old judicial system, governed, in principle, by Islamic prescriptions but in fact drawn from the old traditional canon, had proved of limited value in dealing with changing conditions, and was subjected to a rigorous review. Much of it was replaced by new formulations, in which secular codes based on Turkish codes, in turn derived from French codes, were adopted within the bounds of wider interpretations of the Islamic law (*Sharia*) for penal, civil and commercial cases. A General Law on Courts was enacted, in order to organise a new set of courts, ranging from trial courts to appellate tribunals.

These reforms were accompanied by numerous decrees intended to make their implementation as streamlined and routine as possible. No doubt, in the first instance, the reforms were designed to strengthen rather than diminish the powers of the central authority, with the monarch capable of initiating and enforcing his desired changes without serious disruption to the maintenance of order and stability. However, in the long run, the intentions were to institutionalise the reforms in such a way as to provide for evolution of a fully fledged constitutional monarchical system of governance, based on the rule of law and western democratic notions of separation of powers and 'checks and balances', under which the rights and duties of both governor and governed would be defined and protected within a legal-rational framework.[65]

In the economic and financial sphere, the reforms in general focused on laying solid foundations for infrastructural development, focused on reorganising and rationalising the taxation and fiscal systems. This resulted among other things in the abolition of numerous arbitrary taxes; and the introduction of the first national budget, marking for the first time a clear distinction between the public treasury (*bait ul-mal*) and the monarch's private funds (*'ain ul-mal*). Also, a new unit of currency, the afghani, was introduced to replace the old and generally valueless rupee, with a view to boosting Afghan foreign exchange.[66] The reforms also aimed at broadening and diversifying foreign trade, rationalising the system of commerce and developing small industries, with emphasis on import-substitution, as well as growth of hydro-electricity. Moreover, they provided for building communications networks, like roads (although the roads constructed were gravelled; no asphalted ones were built until 1957), telegraphic, telephone and postal services and civil aviation, which was inaugurated by the mid 1920s.[67] One of Amanullah's cherished dreams in this respect was to construct an all-weather road linking southern and northern Afghanistan through the Hindu Kush – a project not realised until 1964. Special attention was paid to agriculture, with stress on new methods of cultivation, increased productivity, and building model farms and agricultural exhibitions.[68]

Amanullah's land reforms were particularly important, and had a long-lasting effect. Theoretically, since the time of Ahmad Shah Durrani, the

Afghan monarch had been the ultimate owner of all lands within his realm. In practice, however, there existed four major categories of land ownership: private (*mulk*),[69] communal (*shamilat*), crown (*diwani* or *sultani*), and religious endowments (*waqf*). The Amir received all income from crown holdings, which were concentrated mainly in northern Afghanistan; his supreme ownership right on other lands was realised through rent or tax. Most Pashtun chieftains were exempted from taxation for a variety of reasons; still, their possession of land remained what it was for centuries – purely feudal occupancy rights granted in fee by the monarch. As Abdur Rahman had demonstrated, those rights could be withdrawn by a strong sovereign at any time. Generally, land allotments could be sold or otherwise alienated according to the routine practised elsewhere in the Muslim world, but the non-recognition of private property in land had precluded the development of modern capitalist forms of land tenancy and cultivation.[70] Obsolescent agriculture could no longer absorb the surplus rural population: in the early 1920s, only 20 per cent of peasants ran their own properties.[71] Beginning in 1920, Amanullah issued a number of edicts which institutionalised transferable private property in land, provided for a comprehensive cadastral surveys of all lands and rationalised and monetised land taxes. Most importantly, he tried to alleviate the plight of landless peasants by selling large chunks of crown lands for extremely low prices.[72] As Amalendu Guha has noted:

> Large-scale sales of Crown lands alongside establishment of private landed property led to the growth of a new class of landowners. They received their title to land from the State, but their authority of ownership had no tribal sanction. Anyway, the process of transformation of communal property into individual private property was strengthened by this measure.[73]

To complement the political and economic reforms, a promising start was also made in the fields of educational and cultural-social changes. In addition to Islamic subjects, which were reinforced as permanent components of teaching at all levels, secular curricula were introduced and numerous new schools at primary and secondary levels and night literacy classes were opened.[74] Amanullah and his wife actively participated in teaching, the King attending one of the night classes, while Soraya taught in the first girls' school. In fact, Soraya and her mother pioneered the cause of women in demanding not only education, but also equal rights and opportunities in the traditionally male-controlled Afghan society. Their efforts gained saliency, particularly when in the later years of Amanullah's rule greater emphasis was given to women's education, virtually non-existent prior to 1920. These initial educational measures were to be followed by more ambitious reforms, which significantly involved the dispatch of the first batch of Afghan students, including a number of women, for tertiary training to Turkey and Europe,[75] opening of vocational colleges and a proposed medical school.

The social reforms also put much stress on any traditions pertinent to the phenomenon of slavery. Although slavery had never been widespread in Afghanistan, it had nonetheless been practised by some, particularly those in positions of power and influence, for the promotion of luxury and for polygamic purposes. One ethnic group historically subjected more than others to this practice was the Hazara minority. Although the reforms fell far short of substantially improving their lot – they remained the most underprivileged group in Afghan society – Amanullah still set the pace for some among them to strive for a more liberated and just life.[76] Moreover, in what was considered one of the most controversial moves, women were granted the right to freedom of choice in marriage and equal inheritance rights with their brothers and sons.[77] Forced and child labour were also outlawed. Although polygamy was not outlawed, an informal anti-polygamy campaign was launched, which stressed the importance of monogamy as admirable in Islamic terms; and Amanullah personally set the example by taking only one wife at a time.[78]

These measures were to be further refined with active encouragement of women to unveil within the bounds permissible in Islam. Queen Soraya personally took the lead.[79] Although the practice of unveiling initially remained limited to a few within the royal household, it was considered a first step towards full female emancipation.[80] People were also required, though only in the later phase of Amanullah's rule, to wear western dress at court functions and in certain parts of the capital.[81] Further, decrees were issued to curb extravagant expenses in formal and ritual ceremonies, such as marriage and burial,[82] and emphasis was laid on the construction of welfare projects, such as homes for orphans, medical clinics and general hospitals and development of medical training and preventive medicine.[83] Special attention was also paid to general sanitary conditions and municipalities were directed by law to keep the cities clean. Many Kabul citizens were provided with purified drinking water from Paghman, with more water supply projects planned.

In respect of religion, measures were enacted to nationalise those religious holdings (*waqfs*) which had not already been claimed by Amir Abdur Rahman. Moreover, special care was taken to improve the general educational standard of religious judges and local religious leaders, the mullahs. This was to be a precursor to weakening the influence of the religious establishment at all levels, a formidable task, given that in 1913 there were 200,000 mullahs, *ishans* and other Muslim clerics in Afghanistan, compared, for example, to 154,000 clergy of various kinds in Russia.[84] Another important element in this direction was the prohibition of *pir – murid* (Sufi teacher – disciple) links in the Afghan army, which had seriously undermined military discipline. Amanullah could not and did not wage outright war against Islamic circles; he tried to bring them into line with the state's reformist needs in general.[85] Similar restrictive measures were adopted against tribal chiefs, courtiers, hangers-on and distant members of the royal family by abolishing the privileges, decorations and gifts from the palace that they had traditionally received, including such honorary titles as *sardar* and *khan*.

In order to instil a sense of nationhood through exploring (and inventing) common history and propagating the notion of belonging to one polity, a museum was established and archeological research on the origins of Afghans encouraged. A special archaeological agreement was concluded with France in 1922.[86] Above all, the press was given extra impetus. Immediately after Amanullah's assumption of the throne a new newspaper, called *Aman-e Afghan*, replacing *Siraj al-Akhbar*, was established; its first editor was one of Tarzi's disciples, Abdul Hadi Dawi. While this paper served as the central government's main organ,[87] several other small journals – some published by different ministries, others, including *Anis*, by private individuals – appeared, and were soon followed by a number of provincial publications.[88] This, together, with the opening of the first Afghan radio station in 1925, inaugurated a new age in the development of mass media in Afghanistan.

Meanwhile, a cautious but vigorous reorganisation and modernisation of the military was undertaken. Of course, the development and strengthening of this vital mechanism of state control, which mainly consisted of the Royal Guard, had been a central concern of all previous Afghan rulers, given its utility as the most potent force for leadership protection, acquisition of political power and rule enforcement. The initial support Amanullah received from this source was instrumental in his ability not only to assume power, but also to launch Afghanistan's war of independence. It is even more surprising, then, that in subsequent years 'he did not make the army's strength and loyalty his top priority, as had Abdul Rahman'.[89] At the suggestion of Mahmud Tarzi and Turkish military advisors, in 1921, Amanullah set out to transform Afghanistan's armed forces into a small but professional and efficient entity. Soldiers' pay was reduced four-fold in order to get rid of older rankers; veteran units were disbanded and replaced with younger recruits; the Military Academy, where Amanullah himself had received training, was restructured; a model battalions (*qit'a-ye namuna*) programme was launched, with a concerted effort to equip the army with modern arms from

wherever possible; and the foundation was laid for development of an air
force with the purchase, mentioned earlier, of a few German and Soviet
aircraft. Subsequently, in 1924, the draft system was also changed from one
of local selection to a universal lottery (*peshk*) system, requiring two years'
service period for males from the age of 21. The ultimate objective was to
create professional armed forces which could participate in the modernisation
programme in peacetime and, in the event of domestic disturbances or foreign
aggression, could fulfil an effective law enforcement and deterrent-defensive
role. In reality the military reform proved a colossal disaster:

> The condition of the army was worse still. They were ill-kept and ill-fed.
> Under the laws of conscription every Afghan was required to serve in the
> army for two years. But in practice the rule applied to the poor only; the
> rich could easily bribe the officials and stay at home. The sanitary
> arrangements of the cantonments were very bad. The soldiers were paid
> only Rs.4 a month, with which to maintain themselves, and in most cases
> their families as well. Some of these wretched people were obliged to get
> leave from their officers and to engage in some private work with which to
> eke out their meagre allowance. Others deserted the army but since their
> salaries continued to be drawn and went into the pockets of officers, nobody
> cared to bring the offenders to book. Thus when the time came for active
> service, not even one-tenth of the enrolled strength could be mustered;
> nor was this small percentage quite willing to fight on the side of its
> oppressors.[90]

Generally, Amanullah begrudged funds for his army, believing diplomacy
would be more efficient in deterring aggression from abroad, and education
would avert internal strife.[91] The motley equipment procured from half a
dozen European countries could not be used efficiently, for lack of trained
personnel. Foreign instructors, mostly Turkish, 'showed more interest in
enjoying their handsome salaries than in improving the morale or efficiency
of the soldiers'.[92] The top military leadership was paralysed by a schism
between pro-Turkish reformers (including Tarzi and Mohammad Wali) and
champions of more gradual and independent modernisation (Mohammad
Nadir). Similarly, the officer corps witnessed a growing alienation between
older servicemen and 'young upstarts' – graduates of the *Harbiya* Military
College and foreign training facilities.[93] One has to agree with Leon Poullada,
who, analysing the weaknesses of Amanullah's administration, wrote:

> Finally and probably most significant, Amanullah's military policy was
> disastrous under the circumstances. In the absence of national political
> unity which was implicit in the tribal situation, a strong and independent

army seemed to be essential to any attempt to introduce the kind of changes Amanullah envisioned.[94]

The Young Afghans were convinced that corruption constituted the major impediment to reform.[95] An unprecedented anti-corruption campaign was launched in 1921, with the objective of stamping out all forms of bribery, nepotism and other malpractices endemic among Afghans in positions of authority at all levels. It climaxed in 1928, when all public servants were ordered to produce income declarations and were warned that conspicuous spending would henceforth be treated as evidence of corruption. The drive's results, however, were negligible.[96]

In order to institutionalise the reforms and provide an overall legal-rational framework for the future development of the Afghan state, Amanullah swiftly formulated and adopted a national charter. He held a *Loya Jirgah* in 1921, to consider the reform proposals. As a result, the Basic Codes of the High State of Afghanistan (*Nizam-Namah-ye Asasi-ye Aliyah-ye Afghanistan*) were drafted with the help of Turkish experts, and promulgated on 9 April 1923. There is no doubt that this document was in essence a Constitution. It was called the 'Basic Codes' primarily to avoid giving the impression that it was a substitute for the Sharia. For their time, the Basic Codes were very elaborate in their western-type democratic dispositions, providing for the structure and responsibilities of a constitutional monarchical system, a liberal relationship between state and society, and individual rights and freedoms. Their underlying ultimate goal was 'to lead to an autonomous development of secular law-making and to show the way to the separation of secular and canonical jurisprudence'.[97]

Amanullah's reforms aimed at system reconstruction, not merely cosmetic changes. While Islam was upheld as the central unifying nerve among the Afghans, the reforms were multi-structural in nature and fairly secularist in purpose. They were intended eventually to cut deep through the fabrics of Afghan microsocieties and change their traditional values and practices. Government's and citizens' rights and responsibilities would be institutionalised, and the needs of modern political and social-economic existence vis-à-vis traditions regulated in terms of some clear distinction between the political and religious spheres. The objective was not to subordinate religion to politics, but to curb or modify those values and practices which stemmed from either outdated ancient traditions or selfish and sectarian interpretations of religious dictates on which these traditions had been based, so as to remove those impediments which had historically prevented Afghans from achieving modern statehood.

Backlashes

Of course, to institute such a type of modernisation has historically been difficult even in a domestically ordered and externally secured society, let alone Afghanistan. Conditions in Afghanistan were such that no measure undermining the status quo could easily be implemented, or widely understood and accepted. As could have been expected and as is usually the case in any modernising society, the reforms rapidly generated a degree of debate, uncertainty, confusion and reaction, particularly among those who either perceived or found their interests threatened. However, Amanullah's leadership should have been able to cope with this, for a number of reasons.

First of all, throughout Amanullah's rule the reforms never reached a point where they widely permeated Afghan society. Given the central government's limited resources and basic infrastructural difficulties, which severely hindered contacts between Kabul and the rest of Afghanistan, most of the reforms had very limited application, primarily affecting Kabul province and only touching some other provincial centres. What did reach the predominantly rural microsocieties, or more accurately their centres, was word of the implementation of reforms in Kabul and the rumour and gossip that this generated about what the Amanullah leadership was all about and the ways its reforms could affect the rural areas.[98] Only in this way was a link created between what was happening in Kabul and what could possibly happen elsewhere.

However, this linkage between Kabul and the rest of the country lacked the strength and dynamism necessary to cut across the deeply entrenched social divisions within the uneducated, rural population and to generate widespread popular discontent towards the central government. Therefore, it could play little role in the process of engendering systematic or spontaneous mass uprisings that Amanullah could not handle as his father and grandfather had. For the link to prove effective in precipitating a crisis, it had to be exploited extensively by those elements inside and outside the microsocieties whose interests were potentially affected by the reforms and who were in a position to manipulate rural cleavages against the reforms either for self-preservation or wider ambitions.

Certainly, there was no shortage of such elements. Some of the prominent members included religious, ethnic-tribal, military, administrative and professional notables, who grasped the reforms' objectives and found them threatening to their individual interests in one way or another. The religious figures resented the secularist objectives of some of the reforms, and the continued state efforts to undercut what was left of their power-base in the wake of Amir Abdur Rahman's suppressive measures. The ethnic-tribal leaders shunned both government intrusion into their traditional realm of power and attempts to reduce their traditional entitlements, including hereditary titles. Many in the top and middle echelons of the military could not approve those aspects of the military reforms that resulted in dislocation and pay cuts for themselves. Administrators and professionals ordered to curb malpractices could not embrace the administrative reforms. Thus, these elements all had something against Amanullah's regime and consequently seized upon not so much the substance but rather some exterior symbols of reform that were easily discernible by the predominantly illiterate public, to incite anti-government agitation.

The first organised revolt against Amanullah's reforms broke out in the south-eastern city of Khost in March 1924. It was touched off by a number of traditionalist mullahs, who reacted especially against those reforms that aimed at liberalising the position of women and placing certain family problems beyond their local control, as well as the new conscription system. Religious figures such as Abdullah Kharoti, alias *Mullah-ye Lang* ('the Lame Mullah'), and Abdur Rashid of Sahak wielded enormous influence amongst the Mangal and Jadran tribes of Khost and had no trouble persuading tribal chiefs that Amanullah's efforts had the potential of undermining their authority.[99] The religious and tribal leaders' combined forces managed to continue the revolt, or what became known as 'the Khost rebellion', for about nine months, before government forces gained full control,[100] and the rebellion proved quite damaging in several respects. It shattered the people's faith in the strength and infallibility of Amanullah's rule and opened the way for more public agitation. It also smeared Amanullah's reforms as anti-Islamic, a characterisation upon which the monarch's opponents in the wider political arena could rely to generate more uprisings. Furthermore, in effect, it set the early parameters for Amanullah's leadership in terms of how far and how fast it could go with its reformist policies. In fact, as a consequence of this rebellion and several others that followed, Amanullah had no choice but to revise many of his reforms and slow their implementation. Eventually, his reform programme entered a period of relative remission, lasting some four years.

However, the Khost rebellion raises a number of important questions: why was the incident, which started as a local event, allowed to develop into a rebellion, and why did it last as long as it did? Why, after this rebellion, did further uprisings take place, particularly given that the reform programme was put in remission and therefore its impact on the microsocieties lessened even further? Why was the government unable to suppress these uprisings, as it had the Khost one, and thus avert Amanullah's eventual downfall?

Naturally several scholars of Afghan history and society have attempted to answer these questions. Their efforts, couched in different approaches and ideological perspectives, have certainly resulted in a number of credible works which competently reveal a great deal about Amanullah's rule in general and the factors that contributed to failure of his reforms and his downfall in particular. This has been done with a focus primarily on the nature of his reforms,[101] the relationship between them and the human and institutional capacity of his regime to deliver them and of Afghan society to absorb them,[102] as well as the relationship between Amanullah's domestic and foreign policy objectives.[103] Indeed, they provide substantial answers within a rational analytical framework. Nevertheless, they fail for one reason or another to highlight some of the determining factors which incapacitated Amanullah's leadership from within and fatally interacted with certain of its foreign policy failures. These factors were grounded not so much in what went wrong with the reforms, and whether Amanullah's leadership had the necessary resources to implement them effectively, as in the changes which engulfed Amanullah himself, and in the rivalries within the Afghan power elite that had traditionally kept central governments weak and influenced the course of political development in Afghanistan.

There were at least four such factors. They stemmed from a growing self-confidence and self-centredness which came to beset Amanullah's own personality and behaviour in the wake of his initial successes; his encirclement by contradictory power groups, which could not reconcile their fundamental differences in support of a united approach to Amanullah's goal of modernisation; his susceptibility to a number of figures who emerged as opportunists and found it both possible and compelling, in the context of contradictory power groups, to put self-enrichment above the dedication that successful implementation of Amanullah's reforms required; and the interaction between these factors and Amanullah's failure to achieve his foreign policy goals in such a way as to reinforce his process of domestic modernisation.

Initially Amanullah and Tarzi, supported by the Young Afghans, shared common goals and set out in considerable harmony in pursuit of them.[104] Although Amanullah appeared as the mover of the reform programme, it was nonetheless Tarzi who was the main intellectual force behind it. But unfortunately this harmony could not be sustained for very long. In the wake of independence and initiation of reforms, Amanullah's popularity reached an all-time high. This bolstered his self-confidence; and he rapidly developed a sense of self-righteousness, which led him to become too single-minded and, in many ways, unrealistically hasty in pursuit of his objectives. Until the very end of his rule he remained honourable and quite modest within the bounds of his strong moral convictions and liberal-inclined views, but from the early 1920s he began to exhibit the traits of an increasingly impatient and autocratic moderniser.

These traits could not please Tarzi and some of his followers. In view of the adverse national conditions, Tarzi preferred a gentler and steadier approach to implementing the reforms. He wanted the social and economic reforms firstly to be instituted at a pace suited to the absorbing capacity of Afghans; and, secondly, accompanied by certain appropriate liberal-oriented political changes, so as to widen political participation and create a constitutional monarchy in support of socio-economic reforms. He believed that the achievement of one without the other could result in creating an unstable political environment that could imperil the chances of success in both areas.[105]

These different approaches laid the grounds for disagreement between Amanullah and Tarzi from as early as 1922. Meanwhile, Amanullah became susceptible to certain individuals, whom Tarzi regarded as opportunist, unreliable and incompetent. Amanullah's promotion of such individuals to positions of power and influence caused Tarzi more anguish and pain than he was ever prepared to admit publicly. One of them, for example, was Sher Ahmad, a son of Sardar Fateh Mohammad, and therefore a Mohammadzai of the Zikria clan. While by 1917 he had reached the position of Military Chamberlain in the court of Amir Habibullah, under Amanullah he climbed fast in the power hierarchy. Following his dispatch as Minister to Rome in 1922, he was appointed Deputy Foreign Minister in 1923 and President of the National Council (*Shura-ye Melli*) in 1924. This position gave him access to and influence with Amanullah to the extent that he became a major player in court politics. He was even appointed Prime Minister in mid 1928, but could not form a government when Amanullah's fall became imminent. From Tarzi's perspective, Sher Ahmad had neither serious commitment to Amanullah's reforms, nor the necessary qualifications and intellect to manage an important policy role; he was essentially a self-centred individual, interested in power as an end in itself.

In addition, perhaps what further disturbed Tarzi was Sher Ahmad's close relationship with General Mohammad Nadir and his brothers, whose cooptation by Amanullah did little to remove Tarzi's suspicion of them as ambitious, political players.[106] Of course, Sher Ahmad was well rewarded for his loyalty to the Musahiban brothers when, shortly after Amanullah's downfall, General Mohammad Nadir succeeded in establishing his own family rule. In December 1929, he was appointed as Privy Councillor to Nadir, followed by an appointment a year later as Ambassador to Tehran. Although after 1934 he held no more official positions, he still managed to exercise considerable political influence until his death in the 1960s. He was helped in this respect, at first through the marriage of his nephew to one of King Zahir's sisters, and then through his son, Ghulam Mohammad Sherzad, who served consecutively as Acting Minister of Mines, Minister of Communications, Ambassador in Rome and Paris, and Minister of Commerce between 1946 and 1963; and assumed the role of a powerful mediator similar to that of his father in the cobweb of inter-royal family relationships.[107]

Meanwhile, after conducting difficult negotiations for independence with the British and giving a reasonable direction to Afghan foreign policy under very trying circumstances, Tarzi faced mental exhaustion. He used this as an excuse – rather than invoking the differences between him and Amanullah – to ask for a change of portfolio in 1922 from Foreign Affairs to Finance, and then in the same year to take up the post of Afghan Minister in Paris. He became Foreign Minister once more in 1924, but only to leave Kabul again – this time for 'medical treatment' in Europe – in January 1927, amid reports of widening differences with Amanullah. Upon his return to Kabul the following year, Tarzi assumed no more official positions and left Afghanistan once again a few months later, when Amanullah's rule crumbled. The downturn in the Tarzi-Amanullah relationship had two fundamental effects. It deprived Amanullah of the full support of an initial mentor, who in many ways was regarded as an irreplaceable source of wisdom and prudence. It also increasingly forced Amanullah to depend on individuals and families, many of them of questionable loyalty and administrative capacity.[108]

The second effect was precisely related to this where the role of General Mohammad Nadir was concerned. As discussed earlier, Amanullah initially bought off General Nadir and his brothers largely through a policy of cooptation and family intermarriages. But this did not mean that either the old differences between the Young Afghans and the Musahiban family had been resolved, or that General Nadir had dropped his leadership aspirations. As Amanullah embarked on radical reform and as this caused some dislocations and affected the position of some with vested interests, new opportunities were opened up for old competitors to raise their individual stakes in the power structure. No person was better placed than General Nadir to manipulate the disruption to his advantage. His appointment as War Minister, responsible for all dealings with the frontier tribes, where he and his brothers had already built a substantial following, enabled him not only to strengthen his tribal power-base further, but also to establish a print medium to disseminate his views among the frontier tribes and possibly other segments of the Afghan population about the direction the country's development should take.

While maintaining clandestine contacts with the British, particularly in the face of what he considered the Amanullah-Tarzi reliance on the 'Russian card', General Nadir started a newspaper, the *Ittihad-e Mashriqi* (Eastern Unity), in Jalalabad in February 1920.[109] In this paper he cautioned Amanullah against rapid modernisation and close ties with Soviet Russia. When faced with an intransigent Amanullah and an uncompromising Tarzi, he found it expedient to use the military reforms as a pretext to focus opposition to Amanullah's rule along the traditional pattern of polygamic and power rivalries between members of powerful families. He apparently decided as early as 1922 to oppose Amanullah's military reforms and to sabotage his rule through what may be described as a 'go slow' policy. He avoided discharging effectively the responsibilities of his portfolio, and sought to induce major military commanders and noted civilian figures to behave similarly.

Although he was cautious and calculating in his moves, and did not want them to be seen as a direct challenge, his opposition to the military reforms was most disturbing in one way: it gave sharp impetus to officers who were urged by certain tribal leaders and sections of the religious establishment into common opposition to Amanullah. Meanwhile, it became evident to Amanullah that he could no longer rely on General Nadir to strengthen the loyalty of the armed forces and contain the growth of the opposition.[110] In a careful move, he appointed Nadir as Minister to Paris in January 1924 – a position from which he resigned in early 1926 because of ill health, after which he remained in France for the next three years. His departure caused much anguish among his brothers, and in reaction to it, possibly on Nadir's instructions, they followed their older brother's hands-off approach to their official responsibilities.

The cumulative effect of all this was three-fold. First, despite their differences, Amanullah had found the Musahiban brothers very efficient administrators, and their alienation robbed him of energy and support that he needed very badly. Second, the slowing of his reforms disillusioned many of his Young Afghan supporters who were keen to see the reform programme retain its radical course. Third, as these developments were accompanied with growing public disquiet and agitation, Amanullah not only increasingly turned to less trustworthy individuals, but also developed a siege mentality. This, together with Kabul's perception of British threat, American indifference and Soviet deception, placed Amanullah in such a state of internal and external uncertainty that he could neither proceed with most of his reforms nor be confident of the security of his throne. The more he felt pressured, the more he foreswore his liberalist tendencies, and sought refuge in autocratic self-assertion and self-preservation. This played into the hands of his domestic and foreign opponents, who depicted him as nothing more than a self-centred and sacrilegious despot.[111]

The Second Phase of Modernisation

Nonetheless, he still made a final attempt to rescue and accelerate the pace of his reform programme. To underscore his seriousness about this, present the 'civilised' face of his modernisation to the outside world and gain wider foreign recognition and support for his efforts, he set out in December 1927 on his first trip (or what was described as a 'grand tour') abroad, lasting until July of the following year. He visited, with all the style befitting a modernising and independent monarch, India, Egypt, several European countries (including Britain), the Soviet Union, Turkey and Iran. The trip was by and large successful; he received a warm reception from all the host governments, except the British. In India and Egypt he attracted enthusiastic reception as an Islamic nationalist reformer; in many European states he was hailed as a liberal moderniser; and the Soviet Union warmly welcomed him as an anti-colonial and anti-imperialist leader. During the last leg of his trip, he was enthusiastically received in Turkey, where Ataturk not only expressed a great sense of comradeship with him and praised the Afghan spirit of independence, but also reportedly gave Amanullah valuable advice, based on his own experiences.[112] He enjoined Amanullah that to modernise a country like Afghanistan, first of all, he needed a very strong, centralised army[113] as well as a vanguard party, a nationalist ideology and a popular movement as the best means to mobilise the Afghan people behind his leadership and policies, and thus marginalise any opposition which his reforms might cause. In Iran, Reza Shah upheld with him common goals of independence and modernisation and promised goodwill and cooperation.[114]

The trip provided Amanullah with a unique opportunity to gain first-hand knowledge of industrially advanced democratic states and familiarity with several other countries at varying stages of development. He had considerable success in generating greater German, Italian and French interest in his modernisation programme and enlisting more technical and expertise support.[115] He was also able to purchase a noted amount of defence material. However, he failed to achieve much in Britain. In London, he was not only refused military aid, but also treated very discourteously by the British leaders. This was subsequently reported by Amanullah's chief translator during the tour, Ali Mohammad (who himself was to hold key positions in Afghan politics over the next four decades).[116] The British behaviour stemmed partly from their residual grudge against Amanullah and partly from his insistence on settlement of the border problems with British India. His raising of the border issue was quite untimely. Tarzi had cautioned him against it, and was offended by his refusal to listen.

Deeply impressed by western advances in general, and Turkey's progress under Ataturk in particular, and encouraged by his international reception, upon his return Amanullah launched the most intensive phase of his reforms. This phase aimed at wholesale modernisation, not only to strengthen and expand the structural reforms already under way, but also to improve the status of women and bring about symbolic changes in people's dress as Ataturk had done in Turkey. These changes, which, like many of his reforms, remained confined to the main cities, especially Kabul, ranged from imposition of western dress to requiring mullahs to make themselves more agreeable to the changes.

The Decline

No doubt his support for the emancipation of women and the symbolic changes caused greater dissatisfaction and provided his opponents with more effective ammunition to fuel agitations in Afghan microsocieties against what they termed his 'infidel' rule.[117] They spread all sorts of rumours to the effect that during his trip he had engaged in un-Islamic activities, including eating pork, allowing his wife to appear in western clothes in public while abroad, and paying homage to statues – a reference to several presents given to him by other heads of state.[118] On 2 October 1928, violent anti-government demonstrations took place in Kabul, which, although suppressed, were soon followed by provincial rebellions, starting with Shinwaris in the east, who were joined by a number of other southern and south-eastern tribes.[119] Initially, the uprisings appeared to have mainly local impetus, but they rapidly snowballed and became national, spreading into areas adjacent to the capital. In early November, Amanullah entered negotiations with the Pashtun chieftains and *ulama*, who gave him an ultimatum, with the following provisions:

divorce from Queen Soraya;[120]

expulsion of the Tarzi family from Afghanistan, with the exception of Mahmud Tarzi, who was to be tried;

closure of all schools for girls;

recalling of the girls sent abroad for education;

abolition of all foreign legations except the British;

abolition of new reformist laws;

reduction of taxes;

restoration of the veil;

restoration of the Shari'at laws and the Ulama to their previous positions
of eminence.[121]

Amanullah was prepared to acquiesce in many of these demands and to seek
a compromise in order to stay in power. The situation became critical for
him, however, when the continuous uprisings and general decay of central
government provided an opportunity for a former army non-commissioned
officer and subsequent highwayman by the name of Habibullah (called by
the nickname of Bacha-ye Saqao or 'Water-Carrier's son') from the Kalakan
district of Kohdaman, north of Kabul, to attack the capital.[122] As a British
diplomat reported in early 1929:

> For the last few months the activities of Bacha-i-Saqao have been reported
> from time to time in the weekly diaries of the military attaché and secretary.
> On the outbreak of the Shinwari rebellion, the operations of this bandit
> not unnaturally became bolder and more extensive. There was no reason
> to connect him with the rebels, but he was considered an opportunist ready
> to make the most of the chances that fortune might throw in his way... He
> practically blocked the main road to the north between Kabul and Charikar,
> but his efforts seemed directed only against the King and his government,
> ordinary individuals and traffic being allowed to go free. This distinction
> was so marked that the Bacha quickly earned for himself a sobriquet akin
> to that of Robin Hood.[123]

While Habibullah's initial raids were repulsed,[124] his attack of 14 January
1929 proved successful. Amid mounting disorder and bloodshed, Amanullah
found himself with little choice but to abdicate in order to end the fratricide,
which he said was due to 'a general hatred of me'.[125] Having placed his brother,
Enayatullah, on the throne as his successor, Amanullah fled to Kandahar.
However, Enayatullah's rule lasted no more than three days. As Habibullah's
forces surrounded Kabul, on 17 January 1929 Enayatullah surrendered and
pledged allegiance to Bacha-ye Saqao, who ten days later proclaimed himself
Amir and assumed the titles of *Ghazi* ('victor') and *Khadem-e Din-e Rasulullah*
('Servant of the Messenger of God').[126]

Amanullah, still in Kandahar, was terribly disturbed by the turn of events.
Indeed, in response to what he called the wishes of the people of Kandahar
and several other provinces, he rescinded his abdication and called on the
people to defeat Habibullah.[127] However, neither this nor several attempts
on his behalf by some influential figures could enable him to regain the

throne. Of the attempts declared to be in his support, one proved most controversial. It was headed by Amanullah's ambassador to Moscow, Ghulam Nabi Charkhi, a member of the powerful Charkhi family, whose father was one of Amir Abdur Rahman's favourite generals. It involved a group of young Afghan officers, who were being trained at a Turkish military academy, and a Soviet 'strike force' of 800 well-trained soldiers with machine guns and artillery,[128] in only the second Russian military intervention in Afghanistan since the 1885 Panjdeh incident. Before detailing the issue further, the Soviet role must be placed in its wider context.

At first, the Soviets displayed great ambivalence towards developments in Afghanistan. Moscow's position was influenced primarily by two considerations. The first was its perception that the British were behind the southern tribal uprisings against Amanullah and therefore his downfall, simply because they disapproved of his radicalism in general and close ties with the Soviet Union in particular.[129] The second was the view of some senior Soviet policymakers that Habibullah's successful uprising was the culmination of a revolution against what they perceived as essentially aristocratic and bourgeois rule and pro-capitalist reforms.[130] Consequently, during the first few weeks of Habibullah's rule, Moscow seemed to be edging towards recognising the bandit as a revolutionary anti-imperialist ruler.[131]

On the other hand, the British, concerned about the possibility of the Soviets using Habibullah for their own hegemonic and anti-British aspirations, and keen to retain the Anglo-Afghan Treaty of 1921, could not treat the Soviet ambivalence light-heartedly. This, together with their general unhappiness with Amanullah, led Britain to give Habibullah's rule a cautious de facto recognition, the first European state to do so.[132] However, the fact that Habibullah was a Tajik prevented London and Moscow from officially endorsing his regime. Stalin reached the conclusion that Habibullah not only would never gain the support of the dominant Pashtun tribes in Afghanistan, but also could become a source of nationalist inspiration and assistance to the Soviet Tajiks.[133] Similarly, the British understood that any support for Habibullah could easily alienate the southern tribes and plunge Afghanistan into a civil war, which could enable the Soviets to seek advancement for their own interests, and, more importantly, reduce their own chances of helping to replace Habibullah's rule with a pro-British one with the support of the border Pashtun tribes.[134] As a result, whereas the Soviets found it expedient to decide on a non-committal policy towards Habibullah, and even to attempt to help Amanullah to be reinstated, the British withdrew their diplomatic mission from Kabul and adopted a wait-and-see approach.

It was in this context that the Soviets offered military support to Charkhi's mission – a development naturally resented by the British. Initially, Charkhi and his party crossed the Amu River and made solid advances in the north, occupying Tashqurghan, Balkh and Mazar-e Sharif. Reportedly, the way to Kabul was wide open, but the party's advance came to a sudden halt at Aybak (Samangan) before crossing the Hindu Kush, and it retreated, apparently for no convincing reason. Soviet sources have attributed the retreat to Amanullah's abandonment of his struggle to regain the throne, as in late April he left Kandahar for permanent exile abroad.[135]

However, Afghan sources give a different reason. According to a reliable source with access to the leading figures involved in the Charkhi adventure and to Afghan foreign office files, the retreat came about as a result of a secret deal the British struck with the Soviets.[136] This required the Soviets to cease their support for Charkhi in return for a British pledge not to cause any further security problem for the USSR from Afghanistan. The exact content of the deal has never become known, but it was this deal more than anything else that brought Charkhi's expedition to an end. In fact, the expedition's retreat substantially contributed to Amanullah's and Tarzi's decision to leave for exile rather than the other way around. Amanullah went via India into permanent exile in Italy, where he died on 26 April 1960; and Tarzi left for Iran, from where he sought permanent refuge in Turkey until his death on 23 November 1933.[137]

Amanullah's Legacy

In exile, both Amanullah and Tarzi lived and died as frustrated nationalist modernisers. In retrospect, they may have rejoiced over the promising start they made to their grand vision of transforming Afghanistan into a progressive, modern, independent nation-state, but at the end they must have wondered what went wrong. Amanullah's period has produced so many controversial and contradictory assessments that it is very difficult to identify a clear set of factors responsible for his failure. However, as has emerged in this study, the reasons for the tragedy can be found primarily in a combination of four variables: Amanullah's own impatience and inexperience as a moderniser; the fact that his modernisation programme was more *ad hoc* than well planned and systematic in accordance with the national needs and means; the traditional intra-clan polygamic-based power rivalries, which made Amanullah dependent on a number of disloyal, opportunistic and incompetent figures on the one hand, and provided serious impetus for internal reaction to his reforms on the other; and the age-old Anglo-Russian rivalry, which in one form or another prompted Britain and Soviet Russia as well as some possible counterbalancing forces, like the USA, to display markedly selfish and insensitive attitudes towards Amanullah's grand design. The last two were the very variables that had also imperilled the rule of his predecessors. It was also these that now opened the way for General Nadir, joined by his brothers and backed by the British, to defeat Habibullah Kalakani and establish the rule of the Musahiban family within less than a year of Amanullah's abdication.

Whatever the judgements and conclusions of historians from differing perspectives about Amanullah's rule, it laid certain durable foundations for Afghanistan's evolution, and opened the way for different directions that evolution could take. Of these foundations, perhaps, the five most important were the following.

The first was the entrenchment of both national and international recognition of Afghanistan as an independent state with a formal-legal monarchical system of government. The second was the introduction of a radical process of modernisation and the exposure of what such a process could entail. The third was the awakening and growth of an urban-based and politically active intelligentsia which rapidly embraced the ideas and values of a modern way of life. Although still very small, this intelligentsia was more non-royal in character and composition than ever before and was capable of interacting with the educated members of the small aristocracy in the post-Amanullah period. The fourth was the creation of a limited but viable administrative and economic infrastructure, upon which the Afghans could rely to strengthen their chronically fragile political and social structures, despite the fact that much of this infrastructure was temporarily paralysed during the brief rule of Habibullah Kalakani. The fifth was the assertion that, while it was imperative for the Afghans to be part of the Muslim world for reasons of both religious identity and cultural links, they had to come to terms with the demands of their geographic location and progress. This required them to strive for a foreign policy of neutrality, based on no military alliance with any power or bloc of powers, but rather cooperation and friendship with all non-hostile receptive states, especially the neighbouring ones, as the only way to ensure Afghanistan's place as a modern independent state in the face of the traditional Anglo–Russian rivalry.

In all, Amanullah left behind a model for subsequent Afghan reformers. While the rural population generally remained ignorant of his aspirations and reforms, the Kabul-based intelligentsia and indeed many residents of the capital who directly experienced his changes could not help but look back at his rule with mixed feelings of nostalgia and frustration in the coming decades. There were those who came to admire his courage, bravery and reforms; and those who came to take stock of his inexperience, excesses and exasperation in modernising a society which could not accommodate revolutionary change. While the first view embraced a popular image of him as a nationalist and moderniser *par excellence*, providing a model against which they could judge the performances of post-Amanullah leaders, the second view cherished his ideals but could not agree with his radical approach to implementing them. In the prevailing circumstances, it was this second category that gained political ascendancy, with the advent of Yahya Khel Musahiban rule (1929–1978).

4

The Nadiri Dynasty:
Politics of National Gradualism
and 'Royal Dualism'

THE FALL OF AMANULLAH marked the end of the most radical reformative period to that date in Afghan history. This was followed by the short tenure of Habibullah Kalakani, which lasted from 17 January to 13 October 1929. The occupation of the throne in Kabul by a Tajik was unprecedented in the country's history.[1] This was indeed an aberration from the political practice that had developed since the mid eighteenth century, and that treated Durrani Pashtuns alone as entitled to rule the country. It produced a severe legitimacy crisis and shattered the social order that Afghan microsocieties had been painstakingly led to accept from the times of Abdur Rahman Khan.

Habibullah Kalakani's Rule

Habibullah Kalakani's authority did not extend far beyond the limits of Kabul and a handful of other urban centres – Ghazni, Kandahar, Mazar-e Sharif and Herat – and was sustained by coercion. His rule unravelled most of Amanullah's reforms in the name of what Habibullah Kalakani crudely perceived to be Islamic values. Although supported by some of Amanullah's former administrators and officers, as well as the ex-king's ultra-conservative religio-political opponents, it was clear from the outset that Habibullah Kalakani's regime could gain neither much domestic legitimacy nor external recognition. The mere fact that he was a Tajik and lacked a verifiable record of statesmanship made him totally unacceptable to the Durrani Pashtuns and, for that matter, a dark horse to whom neither of Afghanistan's powerful neighbours, British India and the USSR, could give *de jure* recognition without incurring substantial political risk. As his authority remained extremely fragile in the face of growing tribal revolts and hostility from the progressive elements of the intelligentsia, a window of opportunity opened for the well-established Musahiban family, led by General Mohammad Nadir, to bid for power. This chapter will examine the events leading to the establishment of the new dynasty by Nadir, and the peculiar features of the political regime that it ushered in. Special attention will be paid to the re-emergence of polygamic royal dualism as a major factor in Afghan politics.

Afghan historians have been split in their attitude towards Habibullah Kalakani's nine months at the helm of the Afghan state. Many have depicted him as a mere simpleton, an illiterate bandit with a traditionalist rustic upbringing, who essentially represented the forces of darkness and reaction.[2] They have attributed his success in taking over Kabul to a combination of good luck, external support and treacherous behaviour by Amanullah's highest officials.[3] A much smaller proportion of authors, mostly non-Pashtuns, attempted a more sympathetic analysis. One of them was Khalilullah Khalili, arguably Afghanistan's most celebrated poet of the twentieth century.

Khalili, himself a Tajik and a contemporary of Habibullah Kalakani, originated from the same area as the new ruler. His father, Mohammad Husain, had served as a financial secretary to Amirs Abdur Rahman and Habibullah. After holding a variety of positions, including Cabinet posts, in successive Afghan governments between the 1920s and 1970s, Khalili embraced the anti-communist cause of the Mujahideen following the Soviet invasion. He died in Pakistan in 1987. According to Khalili, Habibullah Kalakani was no ordinary villain, no bloodthirsty bandit with a penchant for unlimited power.[4] Rather, he portrayed the image of an Afghan Robin Hood, who fought evil in his own way and with considerable popular support. While not denying Habibullah Kalakani's reputation as a highwayman, he concentrated on the fact that in later years Habibullah Kalakani was motivated by sincere concerns about social and economic injustices and ethnic inequalities in Afghanistan. Dispelling the myth about Habibullah Kalakani's intellectual inadequacy, Khalili praised him as a good soldier who excelled fighting against the Red Army in Bukhara in the early 1920s, and was later decorated for exemplary service in the model battalion of the Afghan army. As to his illiteracy, Khalili argued that it was more than compensated for by his abundance of common sense.[5]

Khalili advanced a potent argument to the effect that although Habibullah Kalakani had not come to power through a popular elective process, he could have claimed as much support as any of the previous monarchs, who had not been voted into office either. His power base consisted of different social and ethnic strata, though: Tajik peasant masses rather than nomadic and semi-nomadic Pashtun tribes of the Mohammadzai. The new Amir also had the support of the bulk of the mullahs in the country who even bestowed the title of 'Servant of the Messenger of God' upon him. Thus, it was no coincidence that initially he managed to spread his rule to most of the cities – a success which confused European powers and forced them to refrain from large-scale intervention against him. In summary, Khalili believed that Habibullah Kalakani was elevated to the exalted position not simply through a combination of good fortune and favourable circumstances, but as a result of a logical alignment of forces in Afghan society, at a time when many ordinary people readily identified with his cause after years of Amanullah's haphazard experimentation.

Finally, Khalili stressed that Habibullah Kalakani's regime had been brought down not by a nationwide revolt, but by tribal upheavals. Most importantly, he had been betrayed by members of his own court – a fate that hardly any Afghan ruler had managed to avoid since 1747. Being a Tajik, he fell victim to intense detestation not so much amongst the Pashtuns as a whole, but in the milieu of the Durrani chieftains who claimed to be the natural-born leaders of Afghanistan. Additionally, his xenophobic brand of Islam was ultimately seen as a threat by the USSR and British India.

Whatever the degree of objectivity versus sentimentality in Khalili's analysis, Habibullah Kalakani's ascendancy was not just an accident. It signified the failure of Amanullah's decade-long efforts to establish a viable process of change and continuity in Afghan politics.[6] His forced modernisation backfired, and the thin veneer of national statehood over the predominantly traditional society ruptured under the pressure, allowing one man to seize power in the name of the defence of Islam and Afghanistan.[7]

In his coronation speech to several thousand Kabulis on 17 January 1929, Habibullah Kalakani said:

> I have declared the holy war in the name of protection of the true faith and in order to save you, brothers, from ungodliness and penury, in order to stop wasting state treasury on school construction but to distribute it amongst the soldiers, to quash their hunger, and the mullahs, so that they preach.[8]

The next day, he published a proclamation where the usual assortment of accusations aimed at Amanullah's multiple violations of the *Shari'a* was followed by what amounted to the new Amir's political programme. Habibullah Kalakani promised to abolish all of his predecessor's reforms deemed anti-Islamic; cancel compulsory military service; introduce voluntary

armed forces; shut all modern schools; and liquidate taxes imposed by
Amanullah.[9] In February 1929, regular payments by the state to Islamic clerics
were resumed, and a number of new *madrasas* were opened. A campaign of
terror and intimidation against all those who sympathised with western-
oriented modernisation of Afghanistan was unleashed.[10] Intellectuals were
purged and newspapers were closed.[11] Courts and schools were brought back
under the *ulama*'s jurisdiction. All modest changes in the direction of women's
emancipation were reversed.

Habibullah Kalakani was said to have captured some £750,000 in the
royal palace, which helped him consolidate his power temporarily.[12] He
exploited the differences between various Pashtun tribes: 'I am generally
not too worried about the Pashtuns because I can make them obey like
monkeys, by giving them a few rupees.'[13] Indeed, until the summer of 1929,
the Tajik core of Habibullah Kalakani's forces was supplemented by tribal
militias of the Solaiman Khel, Ali Khel, Kharuti and Dari Khel, which
inflicted a series of defeats upon the anti-Habibullah Kalakani coalition
headed by General Mohammad Nadir in the Eastern Province. Similarly,
the powerful Ghilzais, although not compromising themselves by a formal
union with Habibullah Kalakani, frustrated Amanullah's efforts to organise
resistance around Kandahar simply because of their centuries-long dislike
of Durrani supremacy.

However, it soon became clear that the new regime was bound to face
serious financial difficulties. The treasury had been largely depleted by
Amanullah's excessive spending on modernisation projects. The rapid
contraction of domestic and foreign trade, as well as decay in agricultural
and industrial production caused by civil unrest, had undermined the state's
fiscal base. Habibullah Kalakani was forced to renege upon his promise and
not only retain the taxes introduced by the Young Afghans during 1927 and
1928,[14] but also eventually introduce new ones, which cost him the support
of the peasant masses and merchants. Moreover, he was forced to resort to
massive confiscatory measures to finance the functioning of the government
and army.[15] In a sign of desperation, Habibullah Kalakani started issuing
paper and even leather money, as well as coins of inferior quality.[16] In Leon
Poullada's words: 'The tribesmen now realised he was squeezed dry and
they began to look for other sources of gain.'[17] With domestic support quickly
evaporating, it was only a matter of time before Habibullah Kalakani would
be deposed by a concerted action of Afghan Pashtuns. That it was General
Mohammad Nadir who spearheaded this action was by no means an accident
but rather the logical culmination of his long-standing power ambitions veiled
under patriotic and nationalist slogans.

The Nadiri Dynasty

Ending his self-imposed exile in the south of France, where he had retired primarily because of his differences with Amanullah, Nadir Khan left for Afghanistan shortly after the fall of Kabul to Habibullah Kalakani's forces. Nadir Khan's aim was to overthrow Habibullah Kalakani; aided and encouraged by the British, he succeeded in raising cross- and trans-border Pashtuns and ultimately defeated Habibullah in a string of battles.[18] The Tajik Amir retreated from Kabul to his patrimony on 12 October but later surrendered to Nadir, who promised him a complete pardon and his life.[19] He should have known better the value of such an oath: on 2 November 1929, he was executed.

Upon capturing and ransacking Kabul on 15 October 1929, the leaders of the 12,000-strong tribal army held a *jirgah* and elected General Nadir as the King. Although Nadir had initially shown a degree of reluctance, particularly in the face of Amanullah's expressed willingness to resume the throne if invited to do so,[20] he now found it appropriate and legitimate to accept the crown on 17 October 1929. His accession, subsequently endorsed by a *Loya Jirgah* convened the following September, inaugurated the rule of the Nadir Shah (or Nadiri) dynasty of the Mohammadzai branch of the Barakzai Durranis. The advent of King Nadir signalled a return to the politics of gradual national change and development, and the rise of yet another period of 'royal dualism', that is, of two rival branches within the same ruling family. While the strategy of gradualism came to frustrate radical nationalist-modernists inspired by Amanullah, the 'royal dualism' set the scene for the growth of an initially low-intensity but ultimately disastrous power struggle inside the royal family. It was this power struggle that facilitated the development of communism in Afghanistan in the context of western insensitivity towards the country's needs, leading eventually to the Soviet invasion of December 1979.

As mentioned in Chapter 3, Nadir was not particularly sympathetic to the Young Afghans.[21] He did not share his predecessor's flamboyant nationalism, and scorned Amanullah's erratic methods of modernisation. Given his empathy with Britain, as well as his keener understanding of the prevailing conditions in Afghanistan, he had become a pragmatic moderate, favouring a concept of sober nationalism, that is, a commitment to nation-building without unduly alienating Afghanistan's neighbours, and a gradual process of change and development, based on peaceful coexistence with conservative forces, as most appropriate for Afghanistan at the time. This, together with his firm convictions and ruthlessness in leadership, augmented by shrewdness and flexibility when necessary, placed him conveniently between the radical reformist and conservative forces.

It was on this basis that, although opposing Amanullah on several counts, he had managed to cooperate with him for many years before and after he rose to the throne. At the same time, Nadir maintained a good reputation amongst moderate and conservative elements of the elite, most importantly tribal chiefs and the Islamic establishment. Even when no room was left for productive collaboration with Amanullah, Nadir retired to France quietly and gracefully, with a largely unblemished image inside and outside Afghanistan.[22] In this manner, he kept his options open to bid for power at an opportune time. The years of retirement enabled him to gain a first-hand knowledge of what was happening in the West, and also gave him time to reflect on the changing situation in Afghanistan and consolidate his ideas pertaining to its future. His brothers, who deeply respected Nadir because he was a senior member of the family and because they shared his political vision, were instrumental in keeping him in close touch with the progress of events in Afghanistan and liaising with its various strongmen.

When Amanullah's fall and Habibullah Kalakani's harsh reign plunged Afghanistan into turmoil, Nadir did not hesitate to terminate his exile and fight for the throne in Kabul. His campaign lasted for six months; he was fully assisted by his brothers, particularly his two full brothers Shah Wali and Shah Mahmud. He was also backed, discreetly, by the British, who allowed him to mobilise trans-border tribes and assisted him with money and weapons.[23] Another factor that proved crucial to the success of Nadir's struggle was a substantial change in the positions of both Soviet Russia and Britain vis-à-vis Afghanistan.

Although still rivals, at this stage both powers had compelling reasons to rescind their competition over Afghanistan, provided there would be a government in Kabul that could ensure its stability and neutrality. These reasons related mostly to domestic developments in the USSR and tensions in Britain's colonies. The Soviets were coping with the strains of the early stages of industrialisation and collectivisation; Stalin had largely given up Bolshevik proselytism on a global scale. The British were increasingly troubled by rising nationalist agitations in India and other overseas possessions. As a result, it was in the best interests of both powers to have a benign foreign environment and avoid dissipating precious resources.[24]

Initially, the Soviet leadership was not favourably disposed towards Nadir, given his long history of association with Britain and support for the Basmachi.[25] They would have liked to see Amanullah return to power or, better still, an unequivocally pro-Soviet regime in Kabul. With this in mind, they backed Gholam Nabi Charkhi's expedition against Habibullah Kalakani. However, as the chances for Amanullah's restoration faded away, and following British protestations against Charkhi's activities, Moscow was obliged, as was noted in Chapter 3, to reach a secret understanding with London and withdraw from northern Afghanistan in June 1929.[26] The USSR eventually came to view Nadir as a better bet than Habibullah Kalakani, for two main reasons. First, Habibullah Kalakani was a renowned supporter of militant Islam in Soviet Central Asia, and on several occasions called for a *jihad* to liberate Bukhara.[27] Second, the Kremlin had realised that the Musahiban held more sway than anybody else with the Durrani Pashtuns and, by implication, with the rest of the Afghan people. Since Moscow's major objective in Afghanistan at the time was to have a stable and friendly government that would honour the provisions of the 1921 and 1926 treaties, the Soviets apparently came to believe Nadir most likely to fit the bill. They proved right in this calculation: Nadir in due course reconfirmed all the treaties concluded with the Kremlin in the preceding decade.

Similarly, the British could not identify a better person than Nadir for the task of normalising Afghanistan. Although he had fought the British during the Third Anglo–Afghan war, and had made it clear that he would not compromise on Afghanistan's sovereignty and integrity, London could still count on the Musahibans' understanding of British vested interests. The British saw in Nadir a leader who could avert a Soviet threat in the region by strict neutrality and end the destabilising escapades of Habibullah Kalakani in Central Asia that might provoke a harsh Soviet response.[28]

The Politics of 'Gradualism' and Neutrality

It was in the context of these policy changes and perceptions on the part of the two powers that Nadir fought his way successfully to the throne. Whereas the Soviets did not seek to create obstacles for Nadir's military efforts, the British helped him gain and consolidate power. Both countries recognised the Nadiri regime, although the Soviets did so only after some hesitation. London also provided 10,000 rifles, 5,000,000 cartridges and £180,000 in aid to Nadir in 1931.[29] The new king did not disappoint his two mighty neighbours' expectations. He immediately declared his priorities as being to rebuild Afghanistan and

> to rule according to the *Shariat* of Muhammad... and the fundamental rules of the country [and to strive] for the protection of the glorious religion of Islam, the independence of Afghanistan and the rights of the nation, and for the defence, progress and prosperity of the country.[30]

In criticism of Amanullah, he stressed that while Afghanistan needed to be reformed, he could not agree with the radical process through which the former monarch pushed his reforms. 'I am for a certain progress and for cultural reforms in the western sense, but I want such reforms to be introduced with a slower pace than those adopted by Amanullah.'[31] He further intimated that it was not within the functions of government to impose new ideas and institutions on the Afghan people; new programmes ought to evolve naturally, and should develop within the boundaries set by Islam and the socio-cultural realities of Afghanistan. Nadir proclaimed that religion and progress should not be perceived as incompatible, for he believed that they could coexist and march side by side.[32]

He declared neutrality the best course for Afghanistan's foreign policy, believing the country's future was linked to its two powerful neighbours' continuous stake in preserving its independence: 'It was obviously a return to the foreign policy of Abdul Rahman Khan, minus, of course, its strict isolationism, which had become both untenable and harmful because of changed conditions and shifts in Afghan attitudes.'[33]

These domestic and foreign policy pronouncements formed the cornerstones of the conduct of the Nadiri regime. In their pursuit, Nadir Shah embarked upon establishment of an administrative system that would centralise power to the extent of securing his absolute rule and allowing him to silence or eliminate all opposition, and to coopt those forces that had dethroned Amanullah. While essentially introducing family rule, with himself as King and Commander-in-Chief of the armed forces, and two of his brothers, Mohammad Hashim and Shah Mahmud, appointed Prime Minister and Minister of Defence respectively, Nadir Shah allocated other governmental positions in such a way as to buy the support of the religious establishment and tribes.[34] He scrapped most of Amanullah's reforms and restored many pre-existing social and cultural practices in deference to the conservative strata in society.

To make these legally binding, in 1931 he endorsed a new constitution, which in form resembled Amanullah's instruments of rapid political institutionalisation and modernisation, based on the separation (though incomplete) of state and religion. In theory, the constitution provided for the creation of a constitutional monarchy, based on the principles of separation of powers and functional checks and balances, as well as guarantees of some basic individual rights and freedoms. It prescribed a bicameral parliament, comprising the National Consultative Assembly (*Majles-e Shura-ye Melli*) and House of Elders (*Majles-e A'yan*), and an Islamic-dominated judiciary.[35] It upheld the rights of citizens to enjoy legal immunity and civil liberties against forced imposition, oppression and tyranny, irrespective of their race, colour and creed. In practice, however, all these provisions were subordinated to the political needs of absolutism and the continuous political domination of the Durrani Pashtuns.[36] Since only a limited number of intellectuals could firmly grasp the dichotomy between the theory and the practice, it was all too easy for the new royal family to present its initiatives to the public as being what suited Afghanistan best at that historical juncture. Meanwhile, the government undertook a thorough reorganisation and reconstruction of the armed forces, primarily with reliance on existing resources, military hardware ordered by Amanullah, limited foreign credits and British aid.[37] Gradually, as the regime achieved consolidation and confidence, some of the saner economic, social and cultural reforms contemplated by Amanullah were reinstituted in a non-controversial way.

Thus, Nadir Shah effectively sought political legitimation and mass – most importantly, Pashtun – acquiescence through a policy of enlightened absolutism and fostering the centre's supremacy over the periphery through an alliance with Islamic and tribal leaders. He subsequently proceeded to carry out his ideas of modernisation within the framework of this alliance, which required an exceedingly cautious process of change and development. Nadir's rule essentially amounted to a return to the policy of 'national gradualism', in many ways similar to the policies pursued by Amir Habibullah in the first two decades of the century. To some, in the radical wing of the intelligentsia and ardent supporters of Amanullah, this meant nothing but the commencement of yet another 'reactionary' period in Afghan history.[38] However, Nadir Shah and his co-thinkers presented it as the most realistic embodiment of what needed to be done in Afghanistan at the time.

To tackle the domestic opposition, and allay any possible fears of regional powers, Nadir found it imperative to combine his politics of national gradualism with heavy-handed reprisals at home and a foreign policy of 'positive neutrality' and friendship. The domestic suppression involved physical elimination, deception, discrediting and cooptation of the opposition. In the case of his most dangerous opponents such as Habibullah Kalakani and Gholam Nabi Charkhi, Nadir at first promised them forgiveness if they surrendered, then had them executed. He employed a carrot-and-stick approach to drive the rest of the opposition into silence, and, generally, succeeded in this endeavour: there was no organised resistance to his reign; however, the regime's adversaries resorted to individual terror.[39]

One of the important pillars of the regime's stability was its reinvigorated reliance on the Pashtun elements in all spheres of public administration, especially the army.[40] Nadir Shah tried to avoid any more foreign military aid beyond what he had initially received from the British and what had been secured under Amanullah; he allocated a greater proportion of GDP to the defence sector, having scaled down substantially expenditure in the areas of social and cultural reforms.

Nadir's foreign policy of 'positive neutrality' and reciprocal friendship with all states sought to achieve two immediate objectives: non-provocative, balanced relationships with both Britain and the USSR, and acceptance by the Muslim states, to prevent any possibility of their aiding Amanullah and his supporters. The feverish diplomatic search for foreign assistance for development projects, so characteristic of the previous decade, subsided almost to a standstill. Under Nadir, the budget was financed exclusively from domestic sources.[41] This enabled him to wield a considerable grip over the domestic environment, while remaining immune from outside pressures. Moreover, he tried to allay the concerns of the two regional powers by abandoning all border claims, and withdrawing support for the Basmachi and tribal insurgents in the NWFP, as well as for various nationalist groupings in India and throughout the region.

Nadir Shah sent two of his brothers, Shah Wali and Mohammad Aziz, as his envoys to London and Moscow. In May 1930, the Anglo-Afghan Treaty of 1921 and the Trade Convention of 1923 were confirmed. He opted to distance himself from events in the tribal belt, where Wazirs, Afridis and Mahsuds started a major anti-British uprising in May 1930.[42] The most prominent anti-British movement on the Indian side of the Durand Line at the time was the *Khudai Khidmatgaran* ('Servants of God'), also known as the Red Shirts. Their leader was Abdul Ghaffar Khan, known as 'the Frontier Gandhi', who had enjoyed Amanullah's support and combined Islamic rhetoric with the Gandhian principle of non-violence as the only method of achieving freedom and progress.[43] Nadir did his best to dissociate his government from this movement's activities, and used his authority to prevent mass involvement of the Pashtuns with the Red Shirts. For all practical purposes, Nadir Shah recognised the Durand Line as an international border between Afghanistan and British India, which was surely appreciated in India and the United Kingdom.[44]

Nadir Shah and his brother, Prime Minister Hashim, who had served as Amanullah's envoy to Moscow for several years and had developed a special distaste for Bolshevism, could never feel particularly comfortable in dealing with the Kremlin. However, Nadir found it expedient to confirm all Amanullah's treaties with Moscow, concluded a new Treaty of Mutual Neutrality and Non-Aggression with the Soviet Union in 1931, and supported Soviet initiatives at a number of international conferences. One of the clauses of the non-aggression pact stipulated a ban on the activities of organisations hostile to one of the contracting parties on the other's territory.[45]

In adherence to this provision, Nadir defaulted on the traditional solidarity with the Muslims of Central Asia, and recognised Bukhara as an inalienable part of the USSR.[46] He was instrumental in eliminating the remaining Basmachi resistance groups: they were denied material support, and eventually Afghan troops commanded by Shah Mahmud disarmed and expelled all guerrilla units.[47] Meanwhile, the relationship between the two sides was largely confined to diplomatic links, which basically suited the Kremlin, embroiled in all sorts of internal problems. The border between the two countries was virtually closed, and only a handful of Comintern agents stayed in Afghanistan to propagate the virtues of the Bolshevik cause.[48]

Nadir Shah maintained the good relations that Amanullah had forged with Iran and Turkey,[49] but refrained from any action that might be interpreted as support for nationalist and democratic forces in the region. Treaties of friendship and cooperation were signed with Iraq and Saudi Arabia in 1932. With regard to other countries, Nadir deemed it necessary to follow Amanullah's example and strengthen Afghanistan's independence and international profile by wooing European powers such as France and Germany. The idea of rapprochement with Berlin was particularly attractive to him, given that German-Soviet relations were at their peak, and Afghanistan could count on favourable treatment by the Kremlin of transit trade with Germany. However, the Germans' ongoing flirtation with Amanullah precluded Nadir from pursuing this aggressively.[50]

By the same token, he was interested in establishing ties with the USA. While serving as Ambassador in France, he had floated the idea of a treaty of friendship with America. However, not until 1934 did the USA recognise the Nadiri dynasty, and even then it did not find it feasible to create a mission in Kabul, because, in the State Department's opinion, Afghanistan 'is doubtless the most frantic, hostile country in the world today. There are no capitulatory or extra-territorial rights to protect foreigners... and though Nadir Shah (the Afghan king) is sound, he cannot control the tribes and will soon fall.'[51] Nonetheless, US recognition was definitely a boost to Nadir's regime, as Washington had not deigned to so 'honour' Amanullah due to British pressure. The flurry of recognition of Afghanistan's new administration by foreign partners was topped by conclusion of a friendship treaty with Japan in 1930, and the development of limited trade and educational ties between them: 'The Japanese ran into the same reservations and difficulties that faced the United States.'[52]

In summary, Nadir's policies of national gradualism and positive neutrality and friendship were rather effective, and enabled him to establish control over the domestic environment. He traded the lofty ideals of a radical national ideology and comprehensive reformation of Afghanistan for the *realpolitik* of self-preservation for himself and his dynasty. The silencing of the most vocal part of the intelligentsia did not mean the Amanullah-bred adherents of headlong modernisation had renounced their plans and grievances. Nadir Shah's oppression and elimination of certain powerful opposition figures eventually proved very costly to him and his family. His brother, Mohammad Aziz, who had been transferred from Moscow to Berlin as Envoy in March 1933, was assassinated by an Afghan student named Sayed Kemal, and Nadir Shah himself was murdered on 8 November 1933 by Mohammad Khaliq, an adopted son of the ill-fated Gholam Nabi Charkhi, who simply acted to avenge Charkhi's killing by the Musahiban brothers a year earlier. In reprisals, Prime Minister Hashim and Defence Minister Shah Mahmud not only executed Mohammad Khaliq and his entire family and eliminated or imprisoned for life whoever was suspected of collaboration with Khaliq, but also tightened their dynastical suppression of all forms of opposition.[53] The King's assassination, and his succession by his 19-year-old son, Mohammad Zahir, was to confirm the pattern of 'royal dualism' in the politics of Afghanistan.

The Politics of 'Royal Dualism' and Change

As outlined in Chapter 2, the Musahiban brothers, in order of age, were: Mohammad Aziz (b. 1877), Mohammad Nadir (b. 1883), Shah Wali (b. 1885), Mohammad Hashim (b. 1886) and Shah Mahmud (b. 1887). They, however, belonged to two different and potentially competing branches of the same family. Mohammad Nadir, Shah Wali and Shah Mahmud were sons of Mohammad Yusuf's first wife, a Sadozai, whereas Mohammad Aziz and Mohammad Hashim were borne by his second wife, a Mohammadzai. Nadir Shah was fully aware of the potential for rivalry and conflict within the family. He used his seniority,[54] discretion in allocating positions of power and the international factor to strengthen unity inside the ruling clan. Upon his accession, he appointed Hashim and Shah Mahmud to top Cabinet positions and sent Aziz and Shah Wali to head the most sensitive diplomatic missions in London and Moscow. At the same time, he encouraged intermarriages within and between the two branches, though Hashim remained a bachelor all his life, and Nadir and his other brothers all were monogamous.

Nadir had two sons – Mohammad Tahir, who died in Paris at the age of 18, and Mohammad Zahir – and five daughters, of whom the eldest died at the age of 16. Shah Wali fathered three sons and a daughter (who died at a young age). Shah Mahmud's offspring comprised five sons and five daughters. As to the other branch of the royal family, Mohammad Aziz had eight children, some of whom died young, but was survived by two sons who were to play a central role in Afghan politics – Mohammad Daoud and Mohammad Naim. Numerous agnatic marriages took place within the clan in the decades to follow, usually between first and second cousins. Perhaps, the most significant of these were matrimonial unions of Nadir's daughters, Zainab and Zohra, to Daoud and Naim respectively, in 1934 and 1935. Interestingly, when some years previously Nadir was arranging these engagements, Naim was to marry Zainab, but he became enamoured of the older Zohra. When the matter was put to Daoud, he resigned to Naim's choice and reportedly did not care which sister he married, claiming he did so only out of respect for his uncle.

Nevertheless, once Nadir had gone, the split within the royal clan was inexorable. The competition between the two branches continued, with a varying degree of intensity, for over 40 years, with Daoud, initially supported by his uncle Hashim, emerging as the ultimate victor. These internecine squabbles led not only to the demise of Durrani Sadozai rule, but also had devastating repercussions for Afghanistan as a whole. The conflict commenced with the swift proclamation of Mohammad Zahir by Shah Mahmud as successor to the throne. Shah Mahmud's objective was clear: to ensure the continuity of his branch at the helm of royal power and to dispel any confusion and uncertainty that Afghans and foreign powers might entertain concerning the regime's stability. Indeed, this time around Afghanistan was spared the chaos that accompanied succession struggles throughout the nineteenth century. Hashim, who at the time of Nadir's assassination was on a tour of the Northern Province, had little choice but to endorse Shah Mahmud's nomination, and he pledged his allegiance to the new King. The news of the smooth succession was made public just two hours after Nadir's death on 8 November 1933.

Zahir was then 19. He had had part of his schooling in Kabul, but was mainly educated at the Lycées Jeanson de Sailly and Pasteur in France, returning after seven years to Afghanistan in October 1930. He enrolled in the Infantry Officers' School in Kabul and subsequently served briefly as Assistant War Minister and Education Minister. Meanwhile, he married Humayra – the eldest daughter of Court Minister and Nadir Shah's cousin, Ahmad Shah. This nuptial arrangement had been finalised by his family and turned out to be an unhappy one, as will be discussed later. At his accession, he was young and inexperienced in the art of governance. His years in Europe had accustomed him to the western way of life, but he did not know his own people well. Well read and intelligent, the new monarch possessed a soft and introverted character. These features made him more suitable for living in an ordered society rather than carrying the burden of leadership and dealing resolutely with the harsh political realities of a country like Afghanistan. That the throne was actually thrust on him at the behest of his powerful uncle added nothing to Zahir's self-confidence: he realised that he was very much at the mercy of the members of the royal clan, and that he sat on the throne more for symbolic reasons than anything else.[55]

Indeed, the domineering and dictatorial Mohammad Hashim, who remained Prime Minister, made sure that Zahir remained a figurehead for a long time to come. Hashim's endorsement of Zahir's succession by no means meant that he was prepared to forget that the new King was, after all, from the rival branch of the clan. He took precautions to deny Zahir the opportunity to realise his potential, beyond fulfilling the symbolic and ceremonial role of a weak monarch, so as to allow himself and his associates to rule Afghanistan. He treated Zahir as an immature boy, and did everything possible to confine him to the palace and concentrate as much power as possible in his own hands and those of his favourite nephews, Daoud and Naim. His efforts at isolating Zahir were so successful that at one stage the King had to seek his uncle's permission and advice for almost everything, including when and where to hunt and what to eat. During Hashim's premiership which lasted until his retirement through ill health in 1946, Zahir was completely excluded from the decision making process. The monarch was so bored that he spent most of his time painting miniatures on the ceilings of four rooms in the royal palace, with the help of an artist named Ali Mohammad Chendawali. This isolation and subordination created incredible docility in Zahir, with a lasting impact on his psychology and ability to govern Afghanistan after he finally assumed the reins of power in 1963.

Meanwhile, Mohammad Hashim used the legitimacy provided by the figurehead King to entrench his own personal rule, and pursue domestic and foreign policies that mainly continued what Nadir had initiated. While maintaining the alliance with the tribal and religious leaders, he pressed on with the strategy of gradual political centralisation and suppression of opposition, modest modernisation, and neutrality in external relations. Hashim's efforts led to controlled implementation of some of Amanullah's economic and social reforms. Afghanistan experienced a degree of 'pocket growth', as opposed to comprehensive modernisation hinging on industrialisation and import substitution – the fundamentals of Amanullah's design. Between 1929 and 1953, the Musahiban concentrated mainly on establishing the economic and social infrastructure for future industrial development. Their primary tasks were to expand the state's fiscal base and create a bourgeoisie which would support the regime against traditional contenders for power.

In late 1929, Nadir Shah had announced a programme of economic revival based on the idea of all-round encouragement of Afghan private entrepreneurship:

> Today we see in our country export, import, transportation, brokerage and everything else are all done by foreigners; only shopkeeping is left for our people. This situation is intolerable and we must have our own nationals engaged in all these activities throughout the country. We must find a way to cut off the hands of the foreigners.[56]

The first steps in this direction were the formation of a banking system, the introduction of credit and universally accepted paper money, state-sponsored investments, the spread of joint-stock companies and the provision of necessary legislation. The first bank in Afghanistan was set up in 1931, with the state controlling 90 per cent of its capital.[57] It was followed by some 30 private companies, usually based on a trade monopoly (sugar, petrol, Karakul lambskins, etc.), whose combined capital rose from 1 to 90 million afghanis between 1931 and 1937.[58] Trading businesses of this kind proved very lucrative: profit margins of shareholders in a monopoly rarely fell below 30 to 50 per cent per annum, and quite often reached 500 per cent.[59] This meant that the distribution of monopoly trading rights became an important element of political exchange, which inexorably took the form of patronage networks.

One of the most formidable groupings of this kind was associated with the name of Abdul Majid Zabuli, the founder and Managing Director of the Afghan National Bank. Born in 1896, he originated from the Pashtun Tarakis who had resettled in Herat in the late nineteenth century. After studying in Tashkent in the second decade of the century, he spent three years in Berlin before returning to Afghanistan at the Nadir government's request, to play a central role in directing Afghan economic development. Royal patronage and the monopoly system enabled Zabuli to attract the bulk of the private capital in the country between 1933 and 1946, and to invest in some 50 trading and industrial companies.[60] As members of the ruling elite, particularly younger ones, were shareholders in these companies, Zabuli gradually acquired substantial political clout. His support was instrumental in the rise of Nadir's nephew, Mohammad Daoud, in the 1940s and early 1950s. The entire generation of post-war politicians, including those of Marxist persuasions, grew up under Zabuli's influence.[61] Still, cordial ties with the royal family remained vital to his privileged position, and when he fell out with Shah Mahmud in 1951, he had no choice but to leave the country.

On the whole, the government succeeded in accumulating capital to launch a modest modernisation programme.[62] However, whatever new social and economic groups came into existence as a result, they invariably revolved around the royal family and remained subordinated to its political requirements. Those elements wishing to operate beyond this rigid framework were treated harshly by the government as actual or potential opposition.

In the sphere of foreign relations, Hashim could still count on Soviet and British preoccupation with their domestic and colonial affairs. Stalin was busy further consolidating his personal power, and the Sovietisation of Central Asia was not proceeding as smoothly as envisaged by the planners in the Kremlin. Britain was hit hard by the Great Depression, and was having difficulties coping with the nationalist tides in India and elsewhere in the imperial realm. Hashim had all grounds to anticipate a protracted passive power parity between London and Moscow in relation to Afghanistan, so long as he observed neutrality, maintained law and order, and generally did nothing to provoke suspicions of preferential treatment of one at the expense of the other. The Prime Minister proved shrewd and perceptive in this respect, although not unnaturally, he was deeply distrustful of communism and everything associated with it.[63]

As part of Soviet consolidation in Central Asia, Moscow tightened security along the border with Afghanistan, in order to prevent the flight of Tajik, Uzbek or Turkmen peasants escaping collectivisation. Although the Afghan government could not approve of the rough handling of its ethnic brethren across the Amu Darya, there was little it could or would do. In 1930, the Soviets staged a series of shows of force on the border, firing into Afghan territory, so as to reinforce their warning not to meddle in what they perceived as their internal affairs.[64] When the Afghan leadership told the British about this, they were coolly advised to maintain good relations with the Soviet Union.

As Europe entered the post-Weimar period, Afghanistan's international situation began to change, too. Hashim had to react to Hitler's increasingly enticing overtures. That the reaction was favourable could be explained by a long history of Afghan-German association and by the USA's continued disregard of Afghanistan. The Third Reich planned to create a coalition with Turkey, Iran and Afghanistan in order to challenge British supremacy in the region, with the complicity and possible participation of the Soviet Union, as epitomised in the German-Soviet Non-Aggression Pact of 1939.

In 1937, Afghanistan joined Turkey, Iran and Iraq in the Saadabad Pact – the first regional security organisation of its kind, which, however, was unlikely to be useful in the event of aggression by a major western power or the USSR.[65] Originally, Moscow did not appear disturbed by Afghanistan's dealings with Germany and pro-German leaders of Turkey and Iran, so long as the Soviet-German Pact held. However, when, on 22 June 1941, the

Nazis attacked the USSR, Stalin entered into an alliance of necessity with the old rival, Britain, against the common enemy. For both powers, close Afghan-German ties became unacceptable, and they demanded expulsion of all Axis citizens from Afghanistan, despite Hashim's hasty proclamation of complete neutrality in the World War.[66] Iran's refusal to obey a similar order led to its occupation by the Soviet and British forces in August 1941. To avoid a similar fate, Hashim convened a *Loya Jirgah* on 5 November 1941, which acquiesced to the Soviet-British pressure on condition of providing safe conduct to Germans, Italians and Japanese to their countries.[67]

The leverage against Anglo-Soviet encroachment that Afghanistan had so painstakingly built was no more. Moscow stepped up its demands while tightening the security regime at the border even further, and it required Kabul to renounce officially all types of solidarity with the Muslims of Central Asia. According to Ali Mohammad, Foreign Minister of Afghanistan between 1939 and 1952, and Deputy Prime Minister and Court Minister until the early 1970s, the Cabinet had to go to extremes to placate its northern neighbour. In 1942, Hashim's security service, *Zabt-e Akhbarat* ('Record of News'), established permanent surveillance over Central Asian refugees suspected of anti-Soviet activities, and in 1943 a number of those were incarcerated. One of them was Sayed Mobashir Tarazi, who taught at the Istiqlal lycée in Kabul. His entire family was put behind bars. The Afghans also closed the self-styled Bukharan Embassy in Kabul, which operated under the former Minister of Education of the People's Soviet Republic of Bukhara (PSRB), Hashim Shayeq 'Afandi'. The PSRB had been proclaimed in September 1920, only to be dissolved in 1924 into the national republics of Uzbekistan, Tajikistan and Turkmenistan within the USSR. Hashim Shayeq, upon emigration, was employed by the Afghan Ministry of Education and published a journal entitled *Erfan* ('Knowledge').

Soviet pressure on Afghanistan was also exerted through the two socialist republics proclaimed in northern Iran, which were under the nominal control of the *Tudeh*, the pro-Soviet Iranian Communist Party, but of which, in reality, the Red Army was the master.[68] London, which had already withdrawn its occupation troops from Iran at the war's end, joined Washington in calling for immediate and unconditional Soviet withdrawal. Stalin had to yield to the combined protest of the western powers, and in March 1946 the Red Army left the so-called Socialist Republics of Azerbaijan and Kurdistan, which shortly thereafter were re-subordinated to the authority of Tehran.[69]

At the same time, two major developments resulted in a temporary decrease in Soviet pressure on Afghanistan. One was the imminent demise of the British colonial empire and independence of India. The other was the emergence of the USA as the Soviet Union's main adversary. This prompted the Afghan government to require its ambassador in Moscow, Sultan Ahmad, to discuss Afghanistan's grievances with the US Ambassador in the USSR, Averell Harriman, who had good communications with Stalin and his Foreign Minister, Vyacheslav Molotov. Harriman conveyed the message concerning the plight of neutral, powerless and non-threatening Afghanistan, and this appeared to have some results, as Moscow ceased demanding further concessions from Mohammad Hashim.

An Afghan cultural delegation was invited to visit Tajikistan in 1948 on the 20th anniversary of the formation of the Tajik Soviet Socialist Republic. The noted Afghan historian, Abdul Hai Habibi, and the future Minister of Culture and Information, Dr Mohammad Anas, were amongst its members. As reported by Habibi, despite red-carpet treatment, this visit did not make a good impression on the Afghan delegation. Amongst the people they met was the famous Tajik poet Sadriddin Aini, whom the Soviet authorities held in high esteem as the father of modern Tajik literature. According to Habibi and Anas, even 'Aini, who spoke Persian fluently, was so much in fear of the Soviets that he refused to speak to them in Persian, and the little that he said was in Russian'.[70] The delegation came back with reinforced distrust of communism and Soviet power. It must be noted that so far, there was neither any interest of Afghan leaders in the ideas of socialism, nor a communist party in Afghanistan. Moscow, however, did not have to wait too long for such a party to emerge. Three factors proved instrumental in this respect: the growing rivalry within the Afghan royal family; the transformation of the traditional Anglo-Soviet competition into the post-Second World War Soviet-American confrontation epitomised in the Cold War; and the continued US insensitivity towards Afghanistan, which matched that of Britain in the past.

As pointed out earlier, in the wake of Nadir's assassination, Hashim deemed it necessary and expedient to strengthen the position of his own branch in the royal power hierarchy. In the process, while reducing Zahir Shah to a figurehead, he vigorously promoted his two nephews, Daoud and Naim, whom he treated as sons after the assassination of their father – a custom widespread amongst Afghans. Daoud and Naim were older than Zahir by five and three years respectively. Thus, Daoud had a certain edge of seniority amongst all Musahiban siblings. This was further strengthened when Daoud married Zahir's sister, which made Daoud *Agha-Lala* (Senior Brother-in-law) to the King – a term of kinship carrying substantial weight in the Pashtun code of consanguinal relations. Moreover, while Naim received all his education in Kabul, visiting India only once, in 1929, Daoud had largely followed Zahir's path, with one fundamental difference. Zahir attended the French-run Istiqlal lycée before going to France, but Daoud went to the Amaniya college, which ran a German curriculum, before spending nine years in France and returning to Kabul simultaneously with Zahir in 1930.

Thus, in contrast to Zahir's pronounced Francophone education and tastes, Daoud had a somewhat wider cultural exposure. He developed a keen interest in reading German publications regularly, and kept in touch with developments in Germany even while in France. Not surprisingly, he became susceptible to certain ideas and practices prevailing in contemporary Germany, one of which was the peculiar vision of nationalism. Hitler's national socialism, which promised the emergence of a powerful and progressive Germany built on the principle of 'One People, One Nation, One Leader', impressed Daoud, as it did many other educated Afghans, and statesmen and intellectuals in Iran, Turkey, and the Arab world. While Hitler's ideology and his success in elevating Germany to the heights of power provided an impetus for the resurrection of nationalist pan-Iranism and pan-Turkism in Iran and Turkey, and helped Arab politicians to hammer out a concept of Arab nationalism, Daoud and many like-minded Afghans began to regard the application of nationalism as the best means to achieve what Amanullah had unsuccessfully attempted to do in Afghanistan. This, together with the fact that Daoud felt ashamed of his ancestors, especially Sultan Mohammad, who had surrendered Peshawar and other Pashtun lands to the British (allowing the Durand Line to emerge), contributed to his reformist zeal, political ambitions and intense nationalist appetite.

In the mid 1930s, the political atmosphere in Afghanistan favoured Daoud's attempts at building his own power base and promoting his German-influenced nationalist ideas, although in public he supported his uncle's policy of gradual reform and restrained nationalism. After attending the Infantry Officers' School for a year, he was given the rank of Major-General in November 1932, and appointed General Officer Commanding in the Eastern Province, while, at the same time, Naim was appointed Director-General of Political Affairs and Under-Secretary of the Foreign Office, then Minister (Head of Mission) in Rome in December 1932. However, when Mohammad Hashim acquired supreme power, he immediately entrusted his nephews with even more important jobs. In February 1934, in addition to his military duties, Daoud was given charge of civil administration in the Eastern Province and, in July 1935, officially made Civilian and Military Governor of Kandahar as well as of Farah and Chakhansur Divisions, which gave him control over most of southern Afghanistan. Similarly, Naim was promoted to Deputy Foreign Minister, then Acting Foreign Minister whenever the Minister, Faiz

Mohammad Zikria, was abroad. Given his royal connections, this allowed Naim virtually to conduct Afghan external affairs. In 1936, Naim also acted as Head of the Afghan National Bank – an important institution, an achievement of the Nadir and Hashim era – in the absence of Abdul Majid Zabuli.

Although still mindful of his uncle Hashim's political and social conservatism, Daoud worked very discreetly to build a coterie of devoted followers and a patronage web during his tenure as Governor of Kandahar between 1935 and 1938. As is evident from his private conversations, as well as his policy initiatives over the next three decades, not unlike Hitler he saw national progress as inseparably intertwined with a type of chauvinist nationalism under a centralised, determined, charismatic leadership. Daoud staunchly believed that the best way to tackle Afghanistan's problems was to embrace the notion of supremacy and unity of Pashtuns, based on their common ethnicity, language, culture and religion, and aimed, amongst other things, against pan-Iranism. Thus, his brand of nationalism was synonymous with 'Pashtunism' and called for the 'Pashtunification' of Afghanistan and reunification of all Pashtuns on both sides of the Durand Line.

To achieve this, he cultivated a number of influential Pashtun leaders from the Kandahar region who came to act as torchbearers for his ideas. These were mainly Durrani and Ghilzai tribal chiefs, some of them dedicated racists, who saw an opportunity in Daoud's stance to gain more political clout and privileges.[71] Their ideology was formulated through the efforts of such people as Abdul Hai Habibi, Faiz Mohammad Angar, Mohammad Din Zhwak and Abdur Rahman Pazhwak.[72] Encouraged and protected by Daoud, these Pashtunists embarked on a campaign to promote the Pashtu language as the universal medium of communication, and the Pashtun culture as the dominant culture in Afghanistan.[73] Similar groups mushroomed across the country. In the Eastern Province, the campaign was headed by Gholam Mohammad Safi and, in the zone of the border tribes, Siddiqullah Rishtin emerged as the central figure. Daoud surreptitiously built working relationships with Pashtun nationalists, who eventually formed the backbone of his supporters in later years.

In 1936, Mohammad Hashim issued a decree which envisaged the gradual replacement of Dari by Pashtu in the schools at all levels.[74] It was prompted by another prominent Pashtunist, Nadir's first Foreign Minister, Faiz Mohammad Zikriya, who harboured a pathological fear of the growth of pan-Iranism. Although the decree was subsequently amended, because Pashtu still had not evolved a universally recognised literary canon, and due to vehement protests by speakers of the Afghan Farsi dialect (or what was named from the early 1960s as Dari – 'the language of the court'), preferential treatment of Pashtu and Pashtun culture remained a salient feature of Hashim's domestic politics and persisted long after him.

When Hashim finally brought Daoud to the hub of central government, appointing him Commander of the Central Forces in Kabul in 1939 (Naim was made Minister of Education in the same year), Daoud brought many of his Pashtunist sympathisers with him to the capital, and placed them in sensitive government positions. For example, Abdul Hai Habibi became Vice-Chairman of the newly established Department of Press and Information in 1939. From that time on, the number of Pashtunists in the state administration and educational institutions was constantly on the rise; the foundation of the Pashtu Academy (*Pashtu Tolana*) in 1937 gave this process a tremendous boost. Abdur Rahman Pazhwak was the Academy's first President. He was succeeded by Habibi, whose tenure spanned 1945–60, and then Rishtin, who stayed in charge until 1973. Understandably, Daoud spared no efforts to strengthen the Pashtun core of the army; most high-ranking positions in the Central Forces in Kabul were occupied by his protégés.[75]

Thus, by the outbreak of the Second World War, Daoud was well placed in the royal power structure, and, indeed, within the country as a whole. Using Pashtunist intellectuals and their publications, he and his supporters could now make inflammatory pronouncements in support of the right of Pashtuns on the British side of the Durand Line to self-determination. According to numerous articles in Kabul newspapers at that time, self-determination meant either joining Afghanistan or creating an independent Pashtun state, friendly to Afghanistan, on the territory of British India.[76] It was argued that either of these eventualities would give Afghanistan direct access to the sea, freeing it from dependence on transit arrangements with neighbours. Territorial gains featured prominently during a series of private meetings from March to June 1941 between Zabuli and German officials, who discussed the possibility of Afghanistan's entry into the war as an Axis ally in return for 'British possessions in the south-east and south, to Karachi, and the Indus as the new Afghan border'[77] after the victory. Although the meetings failed to produce any concrete results, because Hashim clung to the principle of strict neutrality, the substance of discussion clearly demonstrated that the Afghan Pashtunists had far-reaching plans pertaining to the problem of Pashtuns in British India.

As long as Hashim was Prime Minister, Daoud and his supporters had to camouflage their aspirations, verbalising their position through media and publications rather than as policy directives. However, when Hashim resigned in 1946, one year before the end of British rule in the subcontinent and its partition into the two independent states of India and Pakistan, Daoud acquired freedom of action to push for creation of a sovereign territorial unit for Pashtuns across the border, and to bid openly for power in Kabul.

Royal Factionalism Peaks

Hashim's resignation occasioned no immediate power struggle. According to seniority in the Musahiban family, Shah Wali should have succeeded to the premiership. However, Shah Wali, who served as Minister in Paris from 1931 and returned to Kabul in 1935 to assume the posts of Minister of Defence and Acting Prime Minister, was not prepared to carry the burden of full leadership. His reluctance may have been explained by his past disagreement with Mohammad Nadir over whether Amanullah should be given a second chance to prove himself as monarch. Consequently, it was agreed amongst the remaining brothers that Shah Mahmud would lead the Cabinet. Shah Wali went to Pakistan as Ambassador, and served in this capacity in 1947 and 1948. Hashim had to agree to this arrangement, believing, in all probability, that it could not jeopardise the positions of his branch, given the degree of authority his two nephews had accumulated. As it happened, Shah Mahmud's candidature satisfied everyone in the Musahiban clan except Daoud. After Hashim's death in 1953, Daoud felt there was no compelling reason for him not to challenge his half-uncle, exploiting favourable developments inside Afghanistan and abroad.

As a politician, Shah Mahmud held convictions essentially similar to those of Nadir Shah and Mohammad Hashim. He believed in strong centralised government, gradual social and economic change and a cautious and restrained foreign policy. He avoided introducing structural reforms that would undermine the precarious stability inside the country, and tried to conform to the *modus vivendi* which Britain and the USSR had reached over Afghanistan. In other words, Shah Mahmud, a soldier-turned-politician moulded in the Habibullah era, fitted nicely into the canon of political behaviour set by his brothers. He was also favourably viewed by the USA, whose importance in Afghanistan's foreign relations was growing exponentially in the post-war period. In the second half of the 1940s the first wave of American-educated Afghans, such as Drs Abdul Zahir, Abdul Qayum, Abdul Majid and Abdul Majid Ansari, was incorporated into the governing elite.

In his personal qualities Shah Mahmud was more outgoing than his predecessor. His hedonistic tendencies, choleric temperament and a spirit of camaraderie made him more amenable to instituting policy changes. Daoud exploited these features masterfully. He set out to undermine Shah Mahmud's positions from several directions, but first he institutionalised and consolidated his power base in the form of the *Wikh-i Zalmayan* ('Awakened

Youth') movement founded in 1947.[78] The degree of Daoud's actual commitment to *Wikh-i Zalmayan's* programmatic goals is hard to gauge. Most likely, he employed it as a tool in his machinations. Its members were invited to join the National Club, which was set up in 1950 and quickly became the favourite gathering spot for Kabul's power elite, including the Minister of the Interior. Daoud was the Club's founding president, and Zabuli bankrolled its activities. According to Victor Korgun, Daoud was successful in his designs over *Wikh-i Zalmayan*, 'the goals and objectives of which boiled down to the weakening and discreditation of Shah Mahmud Khan in order to clear way to the summit of power for Mohammad Daoud'.[79]

Under pressure from the growing strata of merchant capitalists, liberal-minded intellectuals, western-educated state officials and other professionals, the government gradually began to open up the political system. In 1949, relatively free elections to the local and national legislatures took place and, in 1951, the Law on the Press was passed, sanctioning the creation of privately owned newspapers and abolishing preliminary censorship. In 1951, *Wikh-i Zalmayan* was joined by two other political organisations centred around the newly established *Watan* ('Motherland') and *Nida-ye khalq* ('People's Voice') newspapers. *Watan*'s liberal, anti-monarchist objectives resembled those of *Wikh-i Zalmayan*; however, its ethnic composition was characterised by predominance of non-Pashtun elements.[80] *Nida-ye khalq* was also a Tajik party *par exellence*, but with a pronounced left-wing agenda, including an undertaking 'to incite the people to use and defend their rights, to direct the people, and to fight against the exploitation of the people'.[81]

The emergence of organised opposition crowned the domestic processes during what Louis Dupree called 'the avuncular period' in Afghanistan's history, yet it basically ran contrary to the spirit of the existing political order, based on traditional control by the royal family. The policy of gradualism in social reforms combined with the laissez-faire attitude to the national economy under Zahir Shah's uncles guaranteed internal stability, but was hardly conducive to a quantum leap in Afghanistan's development: in the years since 1930

> a new structural mould – with its system of banking, paper currency, exchange control, capitalistic enterprises and new legal concepts was coming into existence. But such changes did not yet involve any radical transformation of the traditional society, nor could they yet imbibe the spirit of individualism which is the very basis of modern capitalism.[82]

Political development lagged behind even those modest economic achievements.

The regime's flirtation with liberal ideas and institutions proved short-lived. When the term of the *Wolosi Jirgah* expired in October 1951, one of its leftist deputies noted with satisfaction:

> This convocation of the People's Council was not like the previous ones. It broke the graveyard silence. The deputies of this convocation opened the floodgates and paved the way for those who will succeed them. They could not liquidate the arbitrary rule, but they threw a stone at it.[83]

According to some calculations, as many as 40 or 50 out of 120 parliamentarians sympathised with the People's Front (*Jabhi-e Mardum*) faction, comprising *Wikh-i Zalmayan*, *Watan* and *Nida-ye khalq* leaders.[84] The royal family and its entourage had become seriously disgruntled with the nascent opposition's activities and, before the new parliament was elected in April 1952, Shah Mahmud banned all political organisations, disbanded the Kabul University's Students' Union and closed down practically all independent newspapers. Dozens of prominent and young politicians were imprisoned, including General Fateh Mohammad, Mir Gholam Mohammad Ghobar, Abdurrahman Mahmudi and Babrak Karmal; Abdul Hai Habibi chose to leave the country, and scores more were dismissed from government service or demoted and fined, and rescinded political activity forever.[85]

There was not a single opposition member in the new parliament, but it was clear that urban-educated elements, young officers and successful entrepreneurs were developing a taste for politics, and Daoud, 'an enlightened, forward-looking man, realised that something had to be done to bridge the growing chasm between economic and infrastructural development and political stagnation'.[86] Meanwhile, Zahir Shah, who had gained some political maturity but had grown very unhappy about being persistently run by his uncles, now wanted an opportunity to play a more active role. This motivated him, despite whatever trepidation he may have harboured towards Daoud, to share the latter's sentiment that the time had come for the younger generation in the royal family to become more assertive. When Daoud approached Zahir Shah for such a change, he found Zahir Shah receptive and willing to throw in his lot with Daoud in opposition to Shah Mahmud. However, he did so based on a 'gentleman's agreement', whereby Daoud would become Prime Minister on the proviso that Zahir Shah would be allowed to exercise his Constitutional powers as central to the operation of Afghan politics. It was against this backdrop that the King finally supported Daoud's bid for power, forcing Shah Mahmud to resign on 20 September 1953.

5

The Cold War and
the Rise of a Rentier State

DAOUD'S RISE TO THE prime ministership marked a major shift in the politics of gradual domestic change and balanced foreign relations which had thus far characterised the rule of the Nadiri dynasty. He reached the summit of authority by persuading King Zahir Shah to collude with him to bring about a generational change and wider role for the King in both domestic and foreign affairs. Once in office, however, Daoud found it expedient not to honour his informal commitment to the King: he rapidly concentrated power in his own hands and those of his brother, Mohammad Naim, largely relegating the King to his previous ceremonial position.[1] This badly bruised the King, sharpening power differences between the two rival branches of the royal family. While Daoud maintained his ascendency, the King and his supporters continued to keep a close watch on Daoud and political developments in the country, with a view to strengthening their power base. Although it took a decade before the circumstances changed in their favour, the subtle but bitter polygamic-based power struggle during this time was waged against the backdrop of major changes in regional and global politics. Daoud's skilful manipulation of the internal settings and the growing American-Soviet Cold War rivalry enabled him to put Afghanistan on an accelerated course of modernisation, but at the cost of transforming the country into a 'rentier state',[2] with close ties with, and ideological vulnerability to, the Soviet Union. To understand this, it is first of all important to establish the critical nexus that emerged between what he sought to achieve domestically and the external opportunities that he could exploit in support of his policies inside Afghanistan.

Domestic and International Imperatives

After the Second World War, the domestic status quo established under Nadir Shah and Hashem Khan came under increasing pressure from both internal and external sources. Two domestic groupings, which incorporated many of Daoud's supporters, proved to be critical in this respect: the western-educated intellectuals and national bourgeoisie, which were numerically small but nonetheless a growing source of pressure for reform, called for liberalisation of politics and devolution of authority. Prime Minister Shah Mahmud was not averse to some reform, but he wanted to manage it in such a way as to preserve the oligarchic foundations of government and dramatically expand the capability of the dynastic state to exercise social control. Daoud drew on the paradoxes inherent in Afghanistan's established political system to advance his own power ambitions as a senior member of the conservative royal family on the one hand, and as a radical Pashtunist reformer, dedicated to the goal of creating a strong state, with an ability to determine the fate of the Pashtuns on the Pakistani side of the border, on the other. It was in this context that he forged an informal alliance with the King, and set out to chart his own policy objectives. Yet it was clear that he could not maintain his royal legitimacy and at the same time engage in radical modernisation and Pashtunisation without outside economic, technical and financial help, as well as military assistance. He found it imperative to link his domestic initiatives to the profound changes in the system of international relations which had arisen following the collapse of the British colonial empire and the onset of the American-Soviet Cold War rivalry.

As was pointed out earlier, Britain's departure from the subcontinent resulted not only in the creation of the two hostile independent states of predominantly Hindu India and Muslim Pakistan, but also in a serious power vacuum in the region – a vacuum which neither the West, nor indeed the Soviet Union, could ignore. The USA moved swiftly to fill the void. It forged close political, economic and military ties with Pakistan, Iran and Turkey, which eventually led to these states being incorporated into western-sponsored regional alliances, such as the Baghdad Pact in 1955 and its successor the Central Treaty Organisation (CENTO) in 1958. In the process, the USA gained wider influence over the oil riches of the Gulf. Washington now seemed determined to extend its policy of containment to West Asia. The objective was to deny the Soviet Union any opportunity to take advantage of the end of British colonial rule to gain a strategic and 'subversive' foothold in the region.

This policy, together with a perception, based on Stalin's reluctance to end its wartime occupation of northern Iran,[3] that the Soviets were keen to expand in the direction of the Persian Gulf, figured strongly in Washington's urgent moves. Moscow in turn regarded this US behaviour as part of an elaborate attempt to turn the whole of South Asia and the Middle East into a bastion for anti-Soviet activities, denying the USSR the degree of security and economic interests which that country should naturally and reasonably have had in the area.[4]

The Kremlin viewed with growing suspicion the US involvement in building a strategic highway from the Pakistan border to Kandahar in 1947, and especially an Afghan invitation of western, mainly French, experts to explore oil deposits in northern Afghanistan. A stiff aide-memoire delivered by the Soviet representative to the Afghan government on 7 August 1952 vehemently objected to the presence of specialists 'belonging to the aggressive North Atlantic bloc' near the Soviet border and intimated that it could lead to the aggravation of the 'good neighbourly relations' between the two countries.[5] Moscow's démarche, the first manifestation of political pressure on Afghanistan in the post-war period, sent panic waves across the Kabul government, which, on 8 September 1952, assured Stalin that all westerners would be removed from border zones and, generally, Afghan territory would not be used for anti-Soviet purposes.[6] Interestingly, when Shah Mahmud Khan turned for support on this issue to the USA, State Secretary Dean Acheson failed to allay his apprehensions, expressing the view that the Soviet demand 'considered in historical perspective does not pose any substantially new political problem for the Government of Afghanistan.'[7] At that juncture, partly because of serious commitments in Korea, Greece, Pakistan and elsewhere, Washington was not prepared to make the unequivocal commitment to defend Afghanistan vis-à-vis a Communist threat. It rather preferred to entangle Kabul into various regional blocs – an inadequate palliative in the eyes of the Afghans.

Afghanistan, whose leaders had claimed in 1948 that 'properly armed and convinced of US backing... [Afghanistan] would stand in the Hindu Kush and hold the Soviets back to give the United States and its allies time to defend the Middle East and South Asia',[8] refused to join the proposed Middle East Defence Organisation (MEDO) in 1953 that would encompass a number of Arab states, Turkey, Iran and Pakistan. Similarly, it rejected the western-sponsored Baghdad Pact (1955) and its successor CENTO, for two important reasons. First, the Afghan government deemed it to be in the general interests of Afghanistan to persevere with its traditional policy of neutrality in world politics; and thus avoid any complication in its relations with the Soviet Union in the absence of all-round goodwill on the part of the USA.[9] Second, the regional alliances ran contrary to Kabul's quest for a resolution of its significant border dispute with Pakistan concerning the

Durand Line and the tribes of the North-West Frontier Province (NWFP), and also a lesser border problem with Iran.

While successive Afghan governments had rejected the validity of the Durand Line, on the partition of India the trans-border Pashtuns in the NWFP and Tribal Agencies were given the option of selecting between India and Pakistan. The plebiscite was held on 20 July 1947; 289,244 of those who participated voted for union with Pakistan and 2,074 for union with India.[10] However, the Afghan government protested against the results of the poll, pointing to the fact that, firstly, the choice had been limited only to India and Pakistan and did not include the option of acceding to Afghanistan or forming an independent state, and, secondly, only 55.5 per cent of the eligible voters took part in the plebiscite.[11] By 1948, separatist tendencies were afoot amongst Pakistani Pashtuns and, in August 1949, Afridi tribesmen formally announced the birth of an independent Pashtunistan. Although the term Pashtunistan had originally been coined by All India Radio,[12] 'Afghanistan was perhaps the first and the only country to extend recognition to this new state, and since then the issue has become a major irritant between Pakistan and Afghanistan.'[13] In 1949 and 1950, there were a number of border clashes between Afghan and Pakistani regular army units; Pakistani planes bombed civilian dwellings in Afghanistan, and eventually all fuel supplies to Afghanistan were cut.[14]

By the end of 1949, it had become clear that the USA, which had initially adopted a neutral stance, was inclined to support Pakistan on the Pashtunistan issue. Then Assistant Secretary of State, George C. McGhee, wrote:

> An independent Pashtunistan would not, in our view, have been a viable state, and there was no one to pay for it except us. US relations with Pakistan were at this time on the upswing. Pakistan, particularly because of the pressure of its rivalry with India, was courting us assiduously. In seeking aid, particularly arms aid, Pakistan took pains to dissociate itself from Indian neutralism, and promised that its forces would be at our side in the event of Communist incursions into South Asia. They offered for us an attractive alternative to the somewhat truculent Indian neutralism.[15]

Afghanistan, not unnaturally, found sympathy for its cause among Indian leaders, who were keen to see Pakistan entangled in hostility with Afghanistan as a means to serving India's conflict with Pakistan, especially over Kashmir. However, New Delhi tended to confine itself to moral support of the Pashtuns' right for self-determination, always keeping in mind parallels with the irredentist situation in Kashmir. In 1949, Prime Minister Nehru stoutly denied any Indian involvement:

> We are continuously being charged with having intrigues with Afghanistan and bringing pressure upon her to adopt a policy in regard to Pakistan which she might not otherwise have done… That, of course, I regret to say is one of the numerous things without foundation which emanate from Pakistan.[16]

All the same, American diplomacy operated on the premise that India rendered Afghanistan all-round support, thus contributing to the unsettled situation between the latter and Pakistan.[17] Consequently, it was only a matter of time before Afghanistan would seek rapprochement with Moscow to be, *inter alia*, in a stronger bargaining position over the Pashtunistan question.

The friction with Iran revolved around the sharing of Helmand River water and dated from literally centuries before. However, with the implementation of massive irrigation projects in Afghanistan by an American firm, Morrison-Knudsen, the problem became somewhat more acute. In 1951, an international commission comprising US, Canadian and Chilean nationals offered a temporary amicable solution based on the proportional usage of the flow and, generally, 'Iranian-Afghan relations did not suffer any major setback.'[18] The Afghan government even ardently supported Prime Minister Mohammad Mossadeq's nationalisation of the Anglo-Iranian Oil Company in defiance of Britain.[19] Even so, traditional rivalry between the Iranian and Afghan monarchies for reasons of history, culture and self-identity continued to preclude close relations between Kabul and Tehran.[20]

Daoud's Modernisation and Soviet Aid

Chapter 4 discussed at some length how upbringing, education and early military and civil career had instilled in Daoud an autocratic approach to politics, a strong sense of Pashtun chauvinism and a burning desire for a centralised mode of accelerated modernisation. Upon assuming the premiership, he opted for three interrelated policy goals: to centralise power as comprehensively as possible under his leadership; to institute a command-based process of speedy social and economic change; and to promote Pashtunism as the foundation for an Afghan nationalism, involving a resolve to help the creation of 'Pashtunistan'. Yet he wanted to accomplish these goals without either abandoning or compromising his predecessors' foreign policy of neutrality – a policy which he continued to regard as absolutely imperative for the long-term well-being of Afghanistan.[21] In 1955, Afghanistan participated in the Bandung Conference of the Afro-Asian Movement, and in September 1961 Daoud led the Afghan delegation to the Belgrade Conference, where he joined the Non-Aligned Movement.

However, to achieve his goals, Daoud needed substantial foreign technical-economic and military aid. Although personally impressed by Soviet technical and industrial achievements, in deference to his own ideological apprehension, to Afghans' historical distrust of the Soviets and dislike of communism and to the fact that Moscow carried little leverage with Pakistan, Daoud initially wanted to secure the USA as the prime source of such aid. He thought he could do this, given the appeal of his policy of neutrality to Moscow and of his opposition to communist ideology to Washington. In 1953–1954, he approached Washington at least twice with a request for arms and economic assistance, and for an equitable resolution of the Afghan-Pakistan dispute. However, Washington was particularly uninterested in providing military aid and in mediating actively and impartially between Kabul and Karachi.[22] It regarded Afghanistan as strategically less important than its two neighbours.[23] Its formal decline of Daoud's requests led the latter and his brother, Deputy Prime Minister and Foreign Minister Mohammad Naim, not only to feel insulted, but also to interpret the rejection as an ominous sign of Washington's growing commitment to Pakistan against Afghanistan (as well as India). A US diplomatic observer noted in April 1954 that: 'a belief is growing in Afghan governmental circles that the US has turned its back on Afghanistan.'[24]

Daoud and Naim now found it imperative to play their 'Soviet card' by turning to Moscow for aid.[25] In essence, Daoud's neutrality in foreign policy clashed with Washington's global resolve to help only those states which were prepared to embrace the United States anti-Soviet stance. The outcome reflected an acute strategic short-sightedness on Washington's part, closely resembling its rejection of Amanullah's request for close friendship in the 1920s. On both occasions the US refusal prompted Afghan leaders instead to seek political leverage through a relationship with Moscow. Washington's spurning of Daoud entailed serious consequences, leading eventually to the Soviet invasion of Afghanistan more than two decades later.

The rapid American penetration of the region and yet the American failure to embrace the neutral positions of a number of countries, most relevantly and importantly Afghanistan and India, provided the Soviets with a serious challenge and a pretext for 'responsive' regional initiatives. The Soviets simply could not forego the opportunity that the USA's rejection of military aid to Afghanistan had created in the region. From the Kremlin's perspective the South-west Asian region mattered more to the Soviet Union than to its western adversaries, given its proximity to the USSR and the long frontiers and cross border-Islamic ethno-linguistic groups that the USSR shared with the region's main constituent states.

Thus, it could not give up its traditional consideration of the region as potentially part of the Soviet 'sphere of influence'.[26] Nor could Stalin's successors, especially Nikita S. Khrushchev, fail to use Afghanistan as a test case for a new policy approach to win support in the Third World and to bust containment at its weakest points. To achieve this, the Khrushchev leadership realistically had to water down Soviet ideological pronouncements, which hitherto had emphasised a conviction that the newly independent Afro-Asian and Latin American states would inevitably follow a non-capitalist path of development. Instead, it began to stress the role that the Soviet Union could play in helping these states towards a socialist path of development, through a foreign policy of 'peaceful coexistence', 'non-interference' and 'mutual respect', in parallel with greater economic, trade and military ties with certain key units among these states, in accordance with Soviet mears and interests.[27]

While fearing US encirclement and the probability of Washington's establishing strategic military bases in Iran and Pakistan, the Khrushchev leadership welcomed Afghanistan's request for support in 1955. In a remarkable display of skill in power politics, the Soviet Union moved swiftly – but (as indicated in Khrushchev's memoirs and confirmed in Oleg Penkovsky's secret reports to the West) purposefully and with a long-term view of Soviet interests – to exploit the window of opportunity presented by the developments in Afghanistan.[28] Moscow not only began a generous programme of economic and military aid to Afghanistan,[29] but also supported Kabul in its claims against Pakistan.[30] It accompanied this by a similar aid programme for the newly independent, non-aligned India, which had also been embroiled in serious border and political disputes with Pakistan, something which set the basis for possible development of a Moscow-Kabul-New Delhi axis.[31]

The underlying Soviet aims were clear: to counterbalance the American penetration of the region; to exert pressure on the regional states not to allow the USA to establish missile bases on their soil; and to discourage any western-sponsored regional cooperation. But the long-term goal, potently demonstrated by subsequent Soviet actions, was to secure a bridgehead in Afghanistan in an attempt to strengthen Moscow's bargaining position in the event of fortuitous developments in the region. Such developments were a distinct possibility in view of the regional states' fragile social and political structures, historical disputes with each other, and involvement with the USA.

Soviet Penetration

The Soviets achieved rapid success in Afghanistan. The aid programme enabled them progressively to penetrate the Afghan armed forces, which within a decade became mostly Soviet trained and equipped,[32] as well as the country's economic and administrative infrastructures: by 1979, some 6,000 civilian specialists, and 4,000 military officers had been trained in the Soviet Union.[33] Still, the Soviet domination in the military sphere was of the utmost importance. Whereas in education, economic planning, communications, justice, and fiscal management Afghanistan relied on and actually encouraged participation of experts from different countries, 'almost the only area of government not subject to such cross currents has been in the military. In that field the Russians have maintained a monopoly.'[34] With the aid came a large number of Soviet military[35] and civilian advisors, who by 1964 totalled 520.[36] Further, under a 1955 agreement, Kabul each year dispatched 100 students (non-military) to the Soviet Union for short and long-term training.[37] In the course of their education, a large number of these students, who, interestingly enough, always completed their studies with the highest grades in the Soviet system, were also required to attend weekly classes in Marxism-Leninism, as part of their curriculum. They came from both urban and rural backgrounds, and not all of them upon their return embraced Soviet ideology. However, some of them rapidly fell into the normal trap of Soviet hospitality and what impressed them as Soviet progress and achievements within the communist framework.

Daoud tried to introduce a modicum of diversification in training the country's professionals. He sent military cadets to the USSR, but future doctors, engineers and other civilian specialists were schooled elsewhere. In 1964, for example, 1,000 Afghans were studying in the West, as compared to some 250 in the Soviet bloc.[38] Inside Afghanistan, the majority of faculties at Kabul University had strong affiliation with the US institutions, the Soviets built and were running the Polytechnic, but the French were involved in training lawyers and medical practitioners, and the Germans were put in charge of the Police Academy. However, given the role of the Afghan army as the mainstay of the regime and the only organised force capable of bringing about structural changes, Moscow had a better chance of pushing its line in Kabul through the Soviet-trained officer corps.

Afghan students in the USSR became easy targets for KGB recruitment and after their return to Afghanistan acted as clandestine agents under the discreet direction of both the Soviet Embassy, which soon emerged as the largest foreign mission in Kabul, and of its agencies, including its consulates and trading companies. Given the severe shortage of trained manpower and Daoud's desire for rapid military and social-economic modernisation, some of these students were swiftly promoted to important policy-making and policy implementation positions. This enabled them to work closely with Soviet advisors, in conjunction with whom they influenced policies and through whom they kept the Soviet embassy informed of what was going on inside the government bodies. In return they were supplied with the embassy's instructions. The result was the rapid development of an informal, underground Soviet-Afghan network, whose effectiveness in enabling the Soviets to play a determining role in the future direction of Afghan politics was beyond the Afghan leaders' expectation.

This network was complemented by two other factors: the frequency of exchange visits by officials, and the growth of commercial and cultural ties (in the fields of education, sport, and the arts) between the two sides; and the character of the projects into which the Soviets chose to channel their aid.[39] The first factor helped the Soviets to impress a wider circle of Afghans by their hospitality, which always seemed lavish to people who had rarely experienced such treatment, and to familiarise them with their ways of life. It also allowed the Soviets to make offers of generous help, in terms of supply of grants-in-aid, low-interest loans, free-of-charge personnel and infrastructural assistance in both cultural and commercial spheres.

Consequently, the Soviets succeeded in gaining a firm foothold in certain Afghan cultural fields, including some institutions of higher education, which in turn allowed a limited amount of their ideological and propaganda literature, with the help of their Afghan agents, to infiltrate Afghanistan. Also, the volume of Afghan-Soviet trade increased dramatically, making the USSR by 1960 the largest of Afghanistan's trading partners.[40] Further, the Soviets managed to be of valuable assistance in facilitating an alternative transit route for Afghanistan, particularly when Daoud's 'Pashtunistan' policy led to growing tensions and serious border skirmishes with Pakistan and a breakdown of diplomatic relations between the two sides during the period 1961–1963.[41] Some Afghan businessmen, especially grape exporters, had every reason to be happy with the Soviets during this period.[42]

The second factor made it possible for the Soviets not only to participate substantially in Daoud's drive for infrastructural development, but also practically to direct the course of economic reforms at later stages. The government of Afghanistan planned to finance its ambitious programme of capital-intensive projects through mobilising internal resources and foreign aid. As it constantly failed to tap domestic sources of revenue by improving taxation, its dependence on grants and loans from abroad became more and more pronounced. Thus, during the first Five-Year Development Plan (1956–1961) fiscal savings contributed less than half the planned level of investible funds, but the anticipated development investment was actually surpassed, due to a greater aid inflow.[43] Naturally, the Soviet Union, which contributed the lion's share of the money,[44] had a say as to how this money ought to be spent. The very fact that economic development was conceived in five-year periods, similar to the Soviet practice, denoted Moscow's growing influence. Daoud was profoundly influenced by the idea of a centralised, planned economy. He combined the Premiership with the portfolio of the Minister of Planning, and, like General Abdul Nasser in Egypt, tried to manage his country as a factory in the military-industrial complex.

Parallels with Nasserism can be extended further. The Egyptian leader also cunningly exploited the US-Soviet rivalry, having secured a staggering US$1,023 million in credits and grants (excluding military aid) from Moscow between 1958 and 1970, without making serious political commitments.[45] Nasser's departure from a market in favour of a regulated economy after 1960 can be regarded as an attempt at augmenting state control over investment flows in order to facilitate the process of modernisation: 'If the bourgeoisie neither could nor would lead development, that task became the duty of the state'[46] – the kind of étatist policy that Daoud eagerly embraced. And, like Nasser, Daoud viewed a comprehensive land reform as a key element for the success of modernisation.[47]

To paraphrase John Waterbury, the weight given to the economy in literature on post-war Afghanistan, particularly in Soviet studies, does not reflect the priority of the Afghan elite itself, which was absorbed almost entirely in the hurly-burly of domestic and international politics and had to deal on a daily basis with real and perceived threats to their own survival.[48] Even for Daoud, 'the country's goals are ranked in this order of preference: nationalism, neutrality, and development… with nationalism including social stability and national unity by the consolidation of the central power over the tribal and regional interests.'[49] Daoud was the first Afghan leader ever who managed to elevate the state to the heights of a relatively autonomous institution capable of imposing its rules of behaviour on the bulk of the populace. The existence of the modern standing army was the cornerstone of this achievement. The national leader was no longer obliged to summon tribal levies to quell even a minor rebellion. In 1959, the fierce and belligerent Mangals preferred to flee across the border to Pakistan rather than confront regular government units – an unprecedented occurrence in Afghanistan's modern history theretofore. It all became possible 'as a result of the air and armoured equipment and extensive military training provided by the Soviet Union. Government control over the population thus came at the cost of an open-ended political relationship with a neighbouring global power.'[50]

In summary, substantial Soviet investment in Afghanistan, growing Soviet influence, and a muting of the traditional resentment of the USSR existing within the Afghan power elite marked Daoud's tenure as Prime Minister from 1953 to 1963. The fact that many of Daoud's foreign policy interests and verdicts – for example, his opposition to colonialism, imperialism and Zionism and support of non-alignment and liberationist movements – also coincided with those of the Kremlin,[51] meant that Afghanistan fell in line with the Soviet Union to the extent that by the turn of the 1960s many in the West hastily identified the country as an increasingly dependent state falling within the Soviet sphere of influence.[52]

However, this was not how the Afghan leadership saw it. Daoud was undoubtedly aware of some of the negative consequences that close ties with Moscow involved. Given the absolute nature of his rule, he was able to assess through his secret police, *Riyasat-e Zabt-e Ahwalat* (Department of the Record of Information), which was an important instrument of his rule, the nature of Soviet ideological activities among certain Afghan circles. However, individuals with direct access to him have reported that he was unperturbed by it for several reasons. First, he persistently believed in the infallibility of his personal friendship with Khrushchev and the Soviets' respect for Afghanistan's independence and non-alignment, and assurances that they had no other design than to have a friendly regime in Kabul and maintain exemplary neighbourly relations with a country like Afghanistan.[53] Second, he could foresee no change in national conditions which would facilitate a Soviet takeover of Afghanistan. Third, he remained convinced of the integrity of his policy of positive neutrality, to which he gave wider credibility by actively participating in the Non-Alignment Movement meetings. In fact, from his and his brother's vantage point, one of their central purposes in close friendship with the Soviet Union was to induce a reluctant Washington to attach greater importance to Afghanistan, with due respect to its non-alignment; to accord it substantial aid as it had requested; and to play a constructive role in prompting Pakistan to negotiate open-mindedly with Afghanistan in settling the two sides' disputes.[54] In this sense his motivation in pursuing friendship with the Soviet Union was similar to that of Amanullah Khan in the early 1920s.

If this was indeed a consideration, it worked to some extent. Alarmed by the speed of Soviet involvement in Afghanistan, Washington attempted to counter it by expanding its economic aid to the country, which by 1979 amounted to $520 million in total. Much of the money was spent on infrastructural projects. However, as it turned out, not all of the projects proved to be beneficial to the Afghans, and nor did they enable the USA to secure enduring leverage in Afghanistan. The two American show projects – an international airport in Kandahar and an agro-irrigational venture in Helmand – turned out to be prohibitively expensive white elephants.[55]

Washington's relative parsimony, and failure to provide military aid and to mediate actively in the Afghan-Pakistan dispute – the very two areas that Moscow had deftly used to penetrate Afghanistan – denied it the necessary basis to counter Soviet influence effectively. This was despite at least two opportunities, after Daoud's initial approaches, that became available to Washington for securing such a foundation. One of these opportunities arose during the 1961–1963 crisis in Afghan-Pakistan relations; and the other followed Daoud's resignation in March 1963. While the second of these opportunities will be detailed in the next chapter, it is important to discuss the first one here.

Rupture with Pakistan

As mentioned earlier, the unqualified Soviet support for Daoud against Pakistan enabled him to become increasingly vocal about the 'Pashtunistan' issue. Pakistan's refusal, backed by the USA, to discuss the issue on the grounds that Kabul's stance constituted a direct interference in Pakistan's internal affairs, led to the frustration of Daoud's 'Pashtunistan' policy, on which he had relied to justify, among other things, his close friendship with the Soviet Union. The consequence was a build-up of border tensions, resulting in September 1961 in a break of diplomatic ties and closure of the border between the two sides. Although Pakistan, via which most Afghan foreign trade was conducted[56] did not directly prohibit the transit of Afghan goods, Daoud decided that the closure of Afghan consulates in Pakistan, which were largely responsible for handling Afghan transit, in effect amounted to the establishment of an economic blockade.[57]

Daoud expected this development to exert pressure on Washington to soften Pakistan's opposition on 'Pashtunistan'.[58] As Washington remained reluctant to mediate, Daoud's 'tough' approach backfired. Not only did the export to the outside world of Afghan goods, particularly fresh and dried fruit (the main source of foreign exchange) come to a halt, but also all capital goods destined for western, and most notably American, aid projects in Afghanistan piled up in Pakistan.[59] The result was an escalation in the war of words between Kabul and Karachi, with Daoud calling for military mobilisation. This brought the two sides very close to a major war, on the one hand, and plunged Afghanistan into a serious economic crisis, on the other. Meanwhile, Daoud quickly realised that while Moscow was prepared to side with him on the crisis and to provide him an expensive alternative air transit route, it was disinclined to support him in a war, for two main reasons. First, Pakistan by now was militarily far more powerful than Afghanistan and an Afghan defeat could land the Soviets in a major regional conflict, from which the USA, as an ally of Pakistan, could not remain aloof. Second, as the Afghan-Pakistan crisis peaked, with no solution in sight despite an offer of mediation by the Shah of Iran,[60] Moscow found itself embroiled in a more dangerous confrontation with the USA (the Cuban Missile Crisis), the fallout from which prompted Soviet caution over the ensuing months. In neither case did Moscow want to engage in a confrontation with the USA.

Ultimately, Daoud found himself caught in a situation of no war and no peace with Pakistan, and, more importantly, severe national economic depression, accompanied by greater logistic dependence on the Soviet Union and its uneconomical air transit route.[61] In order to find a way out, his brother once again approached Washington with a specific proposal. He appealed 'o President Kennedy for help in quickly developing an overland route through Iran, connecting Afghanistan to the Iranian port of Khorramshahr on the Persian Gulf. The Kennedy administration considered such a route too expensive as a replacement for access through Pakistan.[62] The US President urged Kabul to adjust its policy for a resolution of its problem with Pakistan and thus safeguard its independence by avoiding total dependence on the Soviet Union. He personally met with Pakistani leader Ayub Khan and Mohammad Naim during the United Nations session in September 1962 and prompted them to reach a workable compromise.[63] Thus, instead of making an alternative proposal, which could have involved positive American mediation in the Afghan-Pakistan crisis, Washington once again reduced its chances of luring Afghanistan from the USSR. Of course, the American motive in this may have been to force the demise of Daoud in favour of a new leadership, with less inclination towards Moscow.[64] This is precisely what happened.

As the crisis dragged on, it created a suitable opportunity for elements of the rival branch of the royal family, headed by Zahir Shah, to question the wisdom of Daoud's 'Pashtunistan' policy and close friendship with the Soviet Union. The King, who by now had gained sufficient experience in the arts of politics and had established close links with a number of key figures in the government, intellectual circles, and armed forces, decided that it was time for him to rule.[65] Daoud also realised that he had no other way out of the crisis but to resign gracefully. He did so on 9 March 1963 on the basis of yet another 'gentleman's agreement' with the King: Daoud undertook not to do anything to undermine the King's rule in return for the King's pledge to accord the fullest respect to Daoud in his retirement and to incorporate a proposal for political reforms that Daoud had just handed to the King into the working programme of his successor.[66] The proposal essentially called for the establishment of a constitutional monarchy and a parliamentary form of government. Daoud favoured a system whereby two political parties would contest seats in the national legislature, and the King would ask the winner of the majority of seats to form the Cabinet. However, he had advised that the creation of such a system should be preceded by a transitional period of four years, during which a one-party-system should be in operation in order to teach the people the basics of party politics and prepare them for full democracy in Afghanistan. Daoud claimed that it was time for such a reform and if he had not had to resign he would have implemented it himself.[67] Yet according to a source close to Daoud, the latter in his proposal was also driven by a personal desire to regain the Prime Ministership by forming his own party at a later date.

Daoud's Achievements

The decade of Daoud's rule was a time of unprecedented socio–economic progress for Afghanistan. Generally, 'in the short period of a decade, Afghanistan moved from relative inaction to relative action'.[68] In the economic sphere, whole new industries, such as electric power generation, chemical and building materials industries were created, and import-substitution branches were developed as well.[69] Daoud's government paid exceptional attention to the improvement of infrastructure: investments in transport and communications made up 54.2 per cent of all government allocations during the first Five-Year Plan.[70] By 1963, the country had been covered by a growing network of roads, banks, warehouses, telephone and radio stations, which not only laid a good foundation for future economic development, but also enhanced substantially the state's penetrative capacity.

Writing on the configuration of Afghanistan's political system under the Musahiban brothers, Barnett Rubin has singled out the grown economic base of the rentier state as the most important factor behind its stability: 'Because the state did not depend directly on the khans, it needed neither to confront them (as Abdul Rahman or Amanullah had) nor to mobilise them for conquest (as Ahmad Shah Durrani had). Instead both khans and *ulama* were given symbolic roles and allowed considerable autonomy in their local affairs, a strategy called encapsulation.'[71] Yet during the decade of Daoud's premiership the state itself, or, more precisely, the governing elite changed little compared to the preceding periods. The summit of power continued to be dominated by an exclusionist circle of people who operated according to the principles of group solidarity: 'First, there has been the royal family, secondly, families related to the royal family and, thirdly, families who have been important through belonging to the same tribe as the royal family. Finally, some influence on the centre has also been exercised by heads of federated tribal families.'[72] Wherever possible, the state did not hesitate to substitute the policy of 'encapsulation' for suppression and destruction of autonomous microsocieties. This particularly affected non-Pashtun ethnic communities: the process of resettlement of Pashtuns in northern Afghanistan went on in much the same fashion as in the times of Abdur Rahman.[73] Yet at the same time, while maintaining the Pashtuns' political and military dominance, Daoud managed to co-opt some non-Pashtun figures into his administration, which opened the way for wider participation in the government by non-Pashtuns, especially Tajiks, who provided the bulk of the Afghan intelligentsia.

The increased state authority allowed Daoud to proceed with the social reforms that cost Amanullah the throne three decades before. In 1959, the compulsory wearing of the veil was abolished, women started to be employed in state-owned enterprises, and by 1962, 500 women were working in executive capacities in various government agencies.[74] Between 1955 and 1963, the number of students in primary and secondary schools nearly tripled, while the college population increased more than four-fold.[75] Learning institutions in Kabul and later in Herat and Mazar-e Sharif introduced co-education of men and women. The power of tribal chiefs and the *ulama* was eroded, and the state civil and military bureaucracy, reasonably educated and brought up on the principles of nationalism, came to the fore as the most formidable force in the Afghan power elite.

In foreign policy, Daoud could claim some success, with the one glaring exception of Pakistan. The two world superpowers had to confine their rivalry to the economic realm in Afghanistan, while respecting its independence and neutrality – the phenomenon which was sometimes referred to as the 'Competitive Peaceful Coexistence'.[76] One of the stalwarts of Soviet foreign policy, Anatoly Dobrynin, has written that in those years Afghanistan:

> was respected by many nations for a policy of nonalignment that kept it out of great power conflicts even though it shared a border of almost a thousand miles with the Soviet Union. Even the great powers themselves reached a modus vivendi within the country... In Moscow, the Afghan department of our foreign ministry was one of the quietest places in the Soviet diplomatic service.[77]

Daoud's successful balancing act meant that Afghanistan could finance three-quarters of its development programmes from external sources[78] without tilting towards any of the Cold War blocs.

Fiery patriotism was one of Daoud's major features as a politician. He once proclaimed that:

our whole lives, our whole existence, revolved round one single focal point – freedom. Should we ever get the feeling that our freedom is in the slightest danger, from whatever quarter, then we should prefer to live on dry bread, or even starve, sooner than accept help that would restrict our freedom.[79]

Daoud stood by his words unswervingly: when, in 1960, Khrushchev offered to finance the *whole* Afghan second Five-Year Plan (to the tune of US$1 billion!), subject to the presence of Soviet advisors in all Afghan ministries, this offer was instantly rejected.[80] The second, less agreeable feature of Daoud as a statesman was his unbounded Pashtun nationalism, manifested in his clinging to the absolutely untenable stance on Pashtunistan. His policy of constant brinkmanship damaged the economic interests of Afghanistan and inadvertently pushed it closer to the Soviet Union. By 1963, various strata in Afghan society had come to favour a settlement with Pakistan, and it became clear to the ruling elite that the main obstacle to a settlement was Daoud, who had developed intense interpersonal problems with President Ayub Khan of Pakistan.[81] In the light of the subsequent developments, one has to agree with Louis Duprée's opinion that:

Sardar Daoud stepped down for the good of the nation, a most remarkable feat for a strong man in a developing society. He fully realised that his presence made normal relations with Pakistan difficult if not impossible. In addition, I think he actually thought he would be brought back to power by means of the free elections he envisioned for Afghanistan eventually.[82]

Thus ended the first tenure of Mohammad Daoud, the reformer and state leader who enjoyed considerable popularity inside the country and commanded respect of contemporary superpowers and the global community at large. However, the methods he employed to implement his agenda opened Afghanistan to Soviet influence to an unprecedented degree, strengthened rentierism of the state, and preserved and encouraged the politics of polygamic-based rivalry within the royal family. This last factor remained in play beyond his retirement, enabling Daoud to stay politically active behind the scenes and engineer his return to power.

6

Experiment with Democracy, 1963–1973

THE SUDDEN RESIGNATION OF Prime Minister Daoud ushered in a complex phase in Afghan politics. While King Zahir Shah and his family branch assumed full power, this phase, which lasted a decade, witnessed a series of changes in pursuit of controlled democratisation of politics, liberalisation of social and economic life and rationalisation of foreign relations. For the first time since the accession of the Nadiri dynasty, the premiership and key Cabinet positions were not delegated to members of the royal family, and thus a *nominal* separation was made between the royal family and government. Although the general thrust of Daoud's approach to national development and foreign policy was maintained, an 'experiment with democracy' was unfolded to transform the political system into a 'constitutional monarchy'. A reform programme was initiated to broaden public participation in policy formulation and implementation, to foster the growth of a relatively liberal education and freer social and economic environment, and to conduct foreign relations with a closer eye on changing domestic needs and regional-international imperatives. It was also during this phase that fringe ideological extremism, nurtured largely in the context of an intensified polygamic-based power rivalry within the royal family, found root in Afghan politics.

The reforms, however, ultimately did not amount to a comprehensive process of structural changes. They were greatly strained in three ways. First, they were poorly planned and implemented in an ideological vacuum, apart from a broad patriotic discourse and neutralist stance in foreign affairs which had come to characterise the Nadiri rule since its inception. Second, on the one hand, Zahir Shah proved to be an indecisive personality, with a poor understanding of what a transition from traditional to constitutional rule required, and on the other, Daoud retained his power ambitions to realise his own vision for Afghanistan. Third, in the context of growing Afghan-Soviet friendship in the 1950s, and America's neglect of the changing Afghan situation, many pro-Soviet Marxist elements, some of whom were protected by Daoud as instruments in his rivalry with the King, succeeded in penetrating the administration and armed forces. This provided Moscow with increasing influence in Afghanistan's domestic affairs, and eventually enabled Daoud to lead a successful republican *coup d'état* on 18 July 1973, terminating Zahir Shah's rule and the decade of the 'experiment with democracy'.

Change of Government

As was noted in Chapter 5, towards the end of Daoud's premiership the Afghan ruling elite had concluded that the time was ripe for constitutional changes[1] and a reasonable accommodation with Pakistan if the Nadiri dynasty were to continue its rule effectively, and Afghanistan were to reap greater benefits from Daoud's modernisation drive. Upon accepting Daoud's resignation and assuming the leadership, King Zahir Shah took the boldest decision of his career so far by appointing a non-Mohammadzai, Dr Mohammad Yusuf, to form a new government.[2] Yusuf was a German-educated scientist, who had served as Minister of Mines and Industry between 1953 and 1963 under Daoud.

The composition of Yusuf's Cabinet, which was confirmed by the King on 14 March 1963, and its initial policy pronouncements testified to a firm resolve on the part of the King that henceforth no member of the royal family would be allowed to limit his power, as had his uncles and Daoud in the past. They also indicated that he would seek to build popular legitimacy for his rule, and to modify foreign policy according to the changing national conditions, with a measured accommodation with Pakistan. The new 19-member Cabinet, although retaining six ministers from the Daoud period, was distinct from its predecessor in two ways: it included no members of the royal family, and was generally dominated by young technocrats. The key post of Defence Minister went to General Khan Mohammad Khan, who, although a Durrani Pashtun, did not have close affiliation by blood or marriage with the ruling family. He owed his promotion to the fact that he was a confidant of the King and had excelled himself, as commander of Kandahar province, in suppressing riots caused largely by the government's removal of the veil from Afghan women in 1959.[3]

In his first policy statement, while paying high tribute to Daoud for outstanding services to the nation, 'admirable energy, competence and patriotism',[4] Yusuf inaugurated what he called the phase of 'new democracy', so as not to appear to denigrate his predecessor's period as 'undemocratic', but rather to stress the need for constitutional reforms and a more representative government. He announced that whereas the past planned and guided approach to national development and the traditional foreign policy of positive neutrality would continue, the private sector would be encouraged to play a greater role in national development. He stressed that every effort would be made to strengthen Afghanistan's position as an independent non-aligned actor in global politics.[5] Unable to repudiate Daoud's Pashtunistan policy,[6] Yusuf moderated his pronouncements on it in pursuit of improved ties with Pakistan. Meanwhile, he praised the Soviet Union for its assistance in Afghanistan's development, and called for continued cooperation and friendship between the two countries,[7] but with an emphasis on broadening links with other neighbours such as Iran and India, as well as the Muslim world and the West, the USA in particular. King Zahir visited Washington in September 1963, to dispel whatever doubts the USA may have had regarding the pro-Soviet leaning of the Afghan leadership, and to secure further economic support.[8]

The new government's early policy statements clearly reflected a new mode of leadership thinking, and provided important indicators about the imminent changes in the ruling elite's priorities and long-term objectives. They foretold greater political institutionalisation, broader public participation, and a freer social and economic life, with an emphasis on expansion of individual freedoms and initiatives, in conformity with the political needs under the King's leadership.[9] The government's immediate priorities included finding a negotiated solution for the rupture with Pakistan; adopting a new constitution; and stimulating economic growth and attracting more foreign aid to continue the process of modernisation that Daoud had begun.

Afghan-Pakistani Relations

The Yusuf government swiftly extended an olive branch to Pakistan's President, Field Marshal Ayub Khan, and signalled its willingness to accept outside mediation. The Shah of Iran had sought to play a mediating role when he visited Kabul and Karachi in the summer of 1961, but his mission had failed given the personal feud between Ayub Khan and Mohammad Daoud and their extreme obduracy.[10] The Shah now renewed his attempts at brokering a settlement. In May 1963, Afghan and Pakistani delegations met in Tehran, and reached an agreement to normalise relations between the two countries. Diplomatic, trade and transit links were restored; both sides pledged to conduct their duties in accordance with international law and to respect each other's sovereignty. In general, this impressed upon the world community that Afghanistan was willing 'to put into cold storage the "Pushtoonistan" demand, which has so poisoned the relations of the two countries and proved so detrimental to the peace and security of the Middle East'.[11]

During the Tehran negotiations, the Afghan government kept both Moscow and Washington informed of its position and the progress of the talks. The superpowers were pleased by this attention, but on the whole they viewed the Pashtunistan issue largely within the broader context of their global competition. In the words of a senior US State Department official:

> We attempted... to dissuade the Afghans from pressing this issue, since it could have led to a war with Pakistan and created opportunities for Soviet intervention in both countries. Apart from these considerations the disposition of the Pathans has little strategic interest to us.[12]

In a similar manner, the Soviet leaders, who had at first interpreted the Tehran talks as an attempt by the West, or more importantly the USA, to manipulate Afghanistan,[13] eventually welcomed the opportunity to distance themselves from Khrushchev's effusive and belligerent statements in support of Daoud's position. This was especially true after Khrushchev was removed from the helm in October 1964,[14] for several reasons.

First, the Kremlin had gained some trust in King Zahir, who had professed to maintain friendship and cooperation with the USSR. Second, after Daoud's resignation, Moscow had reached a view that it might not be able to influence Afghan politics very much, and that the continued confrontation between Afghanistan and Pakistan could have unpredictable ramifications for the USSR. Third, the regional and international situation had taken a direction that made Moscow's overt support of Pashtunistan counterproductive to its interests. In the wake of the Cuban Missile Crisis, the Soviet leaders had become fully aware of the country's weaknesses, prompting them to adopt a more moderate stance towards the West.

The growing Sino-Soviet split also was not conducive to pursuing an adventurist regional policy. The Sino-Indian border war of 1962 facilitated a degree of Soviet-Pakistani rapprochement. India's acceptance of military assistance from the West created an impression in Moscow 'as if India and Pakistan were changing places, India seeming to be coming under American domination while Pakistan was slipping out of it'.[15] In June 1963, the Pakistani Ambassador to the United Nations reported: 'The Soviets were very responsive to any move by Pakistan to establish better relations with USSR in economic or any other field.'[16] The post-Khrushchev Soviet leadership doubled its efforts to woo Pakistan, by moderating its view that Kashmir formed an integral part of India. In April 1965, President Ayub Khan visited the Soviet Union and was promised substantial Soviet loans as well as military cooperation. Undoubtedly, 'the two countries... travelled a long way since that fateful day in May 1960 when Khrushchev singled out Peshawar [in Pakistan] and threatened to wipe it off the world map'.[17]

Furthermore, the Indo–Pakistani war of 1965 objectively strengthened the Soviet position in the region. The CENTO military alliance was crumbling: even the Shah of Iran, the staunchest US ally in the region, had become disillusioned with it, and dismayed at Washington's lack of support for Pakistan, another CENTO member, during the hostilities.[18] Meanwhile, Moscow adopted an effectively double-edged posture. On the one hand, it continued its all-round assistance to India; on the other, it called for unconditional cessation of combat activities and offered mediation for a peaceful settlement.[19] The Kremlin also despatched a message to the Afghan leadership, urging it to remain neutral in the Indo-Pakistani armed confrontation and behave in a manner conducive to the cessation of hostilities. Of course this advice was heeded, as it corresponded with Kabul's own changed attitude towards Pakistan.[20] But it did surprise many in the Yusuf Cabinet, most of all those like Dr Ali Ahmad Popal, Second Deputy Prime Minister and Minister of Education, who had been an ardent champion of the Pashtunistan cause in Daoud's government. While some of these 'old faithful' tried to impress on their ethnic brethren across the border that had they been enfolded by Afghanistan they would have been spared the excesses of the war,[21] the Afghan government as a whole assured Pakistan that it harboured no evil intentions whatsoever. Moreover, it did nothing to discourage the frontier tribes who 'tried to join the Pakistan armed forces to fight the infidel Hindu enemy'.[22] As a result, Pakistan was able to redeploy its military resources from the Afghan border to the eastern front.

The warming of bilateral relations received a further boost during President Ayub's state visit to Kabul in January 1966. In the course of negotiations, both sides expressed the intent to strengthen the spirit of mutual understanding and undertook 'to create further conditions for friendship and cooperation', with the Afghan side reaffirming its hope for the 'fair resolution of the Pashtunistan problem which remains the sole source of differences between Afghanistan and Pakistan'.[23] In 1966, Afghanistan's relations with Pakistan had 'never been better. Pakistan, content with Afghanistan's playing down the "Pashtunistan" issue, pushes for more economic co-operation and trade, and trade has increased considerably since 1963'.[24] The atmosphere of rapprochement reached its high point in early 1967, when King Zahir visited Pakistan on an unofficial tour.[25]

In the 1960s, many analysts pinned great expectations on the regional economic partnership known as the Regional Cooperation for Development (RCD). Officially launched by Turkey, Pakistan and Iran on 22 July 1964, it was an offspring of the CENTO member-states' desire to foster economic, technical and cultural ties along the lines of the European Economic Community, and quite independently of the bloc's decaying military activities.[26] The idea of the RCD was floated by Ayub Khan on 12 June 1963: 'We feel great need of all-around collaboration and co-operation between Iran, Turkey, Afghanistan and Pakistan, and wish that the traders of these countries may also feel like us so that this strong combination may become invincible.'[27] It was argued that Afghanistan would be a major beneficiary if it joined the RCD, in terms of gaining economic, educational and administrative assistance without annoying the Soviet Union:

> since increased Turkish, Iranian or Pakistani influence in Kabul no longer need to be interpreted by the Russians as American inspired or supported. In fact, it would seem unlikely that the Russians would wish to risk harming their recently improved relations with all of them by showing resentment over their increased presence in Afghanistan.[28]

Yet the Afghan government consistently declined to accede to the RCD out of fear of compromising Afghanistan's neutrality; ostensibly, it had 'the unjustifiable suspicion that RCD is just a reincarnation of the western-inspired CENTO'.[29]

In 1966, the Soviet Union reached the peak of its influence in the subcontinent. The USA, by then deeply involved in Vietnam, lost interest in performing the role of arbiter between India and Pakistan and even encouraged Soviet mediation at Tashkent: 'The two superpowers found themselves at one in denying the People's Republic of China any role in the region's affairs.'[30] The Tashkent Agreement, signed on 10 January 1966 to contain the Kashmir dispute, was no little feat.[31] No country or international institution had proved able to persuade India and Pakistan to negotiate successfully before. Both parties withdrew armed units to the positions held before 5 August 1964, and created mechanisms to continue a dialogue over Kashmir. However, of the three participants in the talks at Tashkent:

> the Soviet Union was the only one to emerge with unqualified satisfaction... Soviet diplomacy, long successfully excluded from the subcontinent... had made a dramatic breakthrough and proved itself a major factor in the power politics of South Asia. Finally, Russia, hitherto often labeled a potential aggressor by the West, was able dramatically to project herself as a peacemaker at a time when the US was escalating the war in Vietnam.[32]

The Afghan leadership was particularly pleased in assessing Soviet peacemaking efforts.[33]

The USSR continued its 'special relationship' with New Delhi and simultaneously tried to draw Pakistan into its orbit. President Ayub Khan visited the Soviet Union in 1965, 1966 and 1967, and Soviet Premier Alexei Kosygin was accorded a warm welcome in Rawalpindi in April 1968. Kosygin agreed to finance the US$100 million steel plant at Kalabagh, a nuclear power station at Rooppur, a radio link between Karachi and Moscow, a fishery and other industrial and agricultural projects. The Pakistani side, in a gesture of appreciation, discontinued the US lease of a communications base near Peshawar and recorded the 'closeness of views of the two governments on a number of international problems', including the war in Vietnam, the Middle East conflict and non-proliferation of nuclear weapons.[34] While Soviet commitments to the development programmes in Pakistan were substantial, they still fell far short of the massive US aid which, according to experts in Moscow, prevented that country 'from conducting an independent foreign policy'.[35]

In July 1968, delivery of Soviet arms to Pakistan commenced. India's and Afghanistan's loud protests subsided once it was revealed that Pakistan would not receive sophisticated weapons such as supersonic jet aircraft. At any rate, total Soviet military assistance to Pakistan remained negligible: up to 1979 it totalled only $20 million, compared to $450 million to Afghanistan and $1,800 million to India.[36]

The Soviet Union attempted to consolidate its gains in the region in 1969, when Leonid Brezhnev advanced the idea of collective security in Asia open to all Asian countries, including the Soviet Union, which emphasised its position as 'simultaneously a European and an Asian power', and its interest 'in having all the peoples in Asia live in peace'.[37] India and Pakistan quickly signalled that they were not interested in this proposal because of their unresolved disputes. Pakistan tilted towards the USA again and even provided its good offices in Sino–American relations in mid 1971 – a move which was objectively against its own interests, for it compelled the Soviet Union hastily to conclude an alliance treaty with India. This ultimately made possible Mrs Gandhi's victory in the 1971 Indo-Pakistan war, [38] resulting in the birth of the independent state of Bangladesh out of East Pakistan, which destabilised the situation in the region and further polarised all major players' positions.

Afghanistan's position vis-à-vis the Soviet-sponsored idea of collective security was more subtle. Its leaders, eager to maintain the country's neutral and non-aligned status, could not bluntly reject Moscow's proposal, given their vested interests in continuous Soviet economic and military support and the friendly atmosphere that characterised the contacts between the two countries' leaders, but at the same time had no wish to offend China, against which the Soviet proposal was generally considered aimed. Consequently, they either evaded the question, or pointed to the unresolved problem of Pashtunistan and unsettled differences with Iran over distribution of the Helmand River waters in Sistan. Alexei Kosygin, who visited Kabul in May 1969, appreciated Zahir Shah's guarded position more than any other Soviet leader[39] and considerably relaxed the Soviet pressure. The joint Afghan-Soviet Declaration of 30 May 1969 stated:

> the Soviet side praises Afghanistan's line of neutrality and non-alignment which creates important conditions for the achievement of tasks related to Afghanistan's progress and development, and whose earnest observation has earned Afghanistan respect of the peace-loving countries throughout the world[40]

But the Declaration made no reference to collective security in Asia. For the time being Moscow decided not to pressure Afghanistan, which sympathised with the Soviet position on the war in Vietnam, nuclear disarmament, the Indo-Pakistani and Arab-Israeli conflicts and other international issues, and remained a major client in terms of economic aid, into an alliance with vague goals and an uncertain future. One has to agree with Morris McCain's assessment:

> Events in Kabul went well from the Soviet standpoint through most of the postwar era. With the possible exception of Finland, Afghanistan represented the best-disposed and least threatening of Moscow's neighbours until the 1970s. Its friendship was maintained at little cost, the Americans seeming to accept tacitly that the country was both insignificant and firmly in the Soviet sphere of influence.[41]

Although the Soviet Union periodically resuscitated the idea of an Asian security system until 1975, and actually won the Shah of Iran's approval,[42] the Kremlin accepted that caution, patience and prudence had to be exercised to achieve the best results in Afghanistan.

Reforms

The initial easing of tensions between Afghanistan and Pakistan led towards a normalisation of relations, resulting by 1965 in the full reopening of the Afghan-Pakistan border, with Afghanistan regaining its valuable transit route. Against a backdrop of certain regional changes and somewhat improved US-Soviet relations, this created a favourable climate for the post-Daoud leadership to intensify its domestic reform efforts, without initially dramatically impacting on the monarchy's power or causing undue concern to Afghanistan's neighbours, especially the Soviet Union. Yet the changes during the period of 'experiment with democracy', and the Afghan management of them, produced some inescapable fresh challenges and opportunities for the USSR and its allies. To understand this fully, it is now imperative to turn to those changes and their consequences, Daoud's use of them to regain power, and the USSR's manipulation of them to maintain its interests in Afghanistan and the region.

As mentioned earlier, Daoud himself, at the time of his resignation as Prime Minister, had proposed to the King certain constitutional reforms. But he had expected the reforms to be implemented according to his vision and not to block his return to politics at an appropriate time in the future. As Louis Duprée observed within two months of Daoud's retirement:

> the step down... did not destroy the power potential of either Sardar Daoud or his equally capable brother, Sardar Mohammad Naim Khan. Actually, the move is politically adroit... I personally cannot conceive of either Sardar Daoud or Sardar Naim remaining in the background very long.[43]

Daoud had all along intended, as subsequently became clear, to relinquish power only for a limited period, to provide the King and his supporters with an opportunity to improve relations with Pakistan and initiate the reforms. His medium-run aim was that once the reforms were in place he would be able to declare himself detached from the royal family, create his own political party and assume power again, but this time in his own right and on a more popular legitimate basis. It was in this context that Daoud not only consented to the King's appointment of a commoner, Mohammad Yusuf, to replace him, but also refrained from objecting to some of his senior ministers joining Yusuf's Cabinet, and from engaging in any action that could possibly encourage his numerous supporters in the administration and armed and security forces to undermine either the King's newly assumed powers or the functioning of the Yusuf government.[44] Although immediately after his resignation he made several public appearances and met with various influential figures, sparking rumours in Kabul of a comeback, possibly during a parliamentary session in September 1964,[45] he soon assumed a reclusive lifestyle, after the King and other members of the royal family urged him to do so for the sake of political continuity and stability.

In return, nonetheless, Daoud expected the King to honour their 'gentlemen's agreement' and proceed with reforms according to the blueprint that he had submitted. But this did not happen. The kind of changes, and the manner in which the King and his supporters began to unfold them, rapidly caused Daoud immense personal political damage, prompting him to resume his power ambitions and rivalry with the King sooner rather than later. His quest for political redemption commenced shortly after the King set the constitutional reforms in motion.[46]

Although Zahir Shah had developed a personal taste for democratic reforms,[47] the substance and direction of the reforms came to be prominently influenced by three forces. The first comprised members of the royal family. It revolved around the King's full-blooded uncle, Marshal Shah Wali Khan, who was retired but acted as an influential advisor to him, and Shah Wali Khan's son and the King's son-in-law, General Abdul Wali.[48] Daoud's resignation had finally provided both father and son with the opportunity to elevate their own branch of the family vis-à-vis Daoud. The second force consisted of a number of seasoned and ambitious political figures, such as Sayed Qassem Reshtia,[49] who had served under Daoud in various capacities but resented his immense personal power and dictatorial behaviour. The third force comprised a number of bright aspiring young Afghans who had received modern education in the West, perceived themselves well qualified to assume an active role in formulating and directing democratic reforms, and managed to link up in one form or another to the pro-Zahir Shah camp within the royal family. Mohammad Musa Shafiq, Dr Abdul Samad Hamid and, for a short time, Hamidullah were most prominent figures in that grouping. Although these three forces differed in their approach to democratic reforms, they were united in one goal: to avert Daoud's return to power.[50]

The constitutional reforms proposed by Daoud had envisaged a strong, neo-patrimonial, one-party regime, where the King would retain only a ceremonial role, and the traditional *Loya Jirgah* would serve as a booster for an all-powerful head of Cabinet. Zahir Shah and other members of his royal branch perceived that:

> Such a Constitution would perpetuate the de facto rule of Daoud Khan. His leadership had become too autocratic, disregarding the traditional collective decision-making of the royal family. A future prime-minister could use these powers… to completely alter the political system, even including abolishing the monarchy.[51]

The reformist elements in the power elite insisted on implementation of what Mohammad Yusuf termed 'Afghan democracy', based on retention of the monarchy, incorporation of traditional tribal institutions, strong parliamentarism, and 'cooperation of all classes of the nation, especially the educated people and the youth'.[52]

It was in deference to the advice of these elements and to his resolve to rule in his own right that the King endorsed the process of reform. In the absence of a historical tradition, this was all to be a 'King's gift' to the nation, to be arranged by Yusuf's government at the monarch's behest. On 28 March 1963, Zahir Shah appointed a seven-member committee to draft a new Constitution to replace that of 1931, adopted by his father. Although he placed one of Daoud's allies, Sayyid Shamsuddin Majrooh (then Minister of Justice in Yusuf's Cabinet), to chair the committee, the remaining members came from the King's entourage. They were: Sayed Qassem Reshtia (Yusuf's Minister of Press and Information until December 1963 and Minister of Finance, July 1964–October 1965); Reshtia's radical liberalist brother, Mir Mohammad Siddiq Farhang (Head of Planning, Ministry of Mines and Industries); Mohammad Musa Shafiq (Director of the Law Department, Ministry of Justice); Dr Abdul Samad Hamid (Head of Secondary Education, Ministry of Education); Hamidullah (Professor of Law and Political Science, Kabul University and son of the veteran politician, now Minister of the Royal Court, Ali Ahmad Khan); and Dr Mir Najmuddin Ansari (Advisor to the Ministry of Education). Thus, the committee was dominated by people who either detested Daoud or were indifferent to him, but professed loyalty to the King for reasons of personal power ambitions and political aspirations. During its first meeting, on 31 March 1963, the committee assigned Shafiq, Hamid, Hamidullah and Farhang to research and draw up the new basic law of the country. Assisted by a French expert, M. Louis Fougère (who had had past experience with constitutional reform in Morocco), they authored the first draft of the Constitution, which was approved by the full committee in February 1964.

The draft was by no means finalised independently of the King. While it may have been an exaggeration to call Zahir Shah 'chief innovator of the 1964 constitution',[53] there is little doubt that the committee members, although not immediately controlled by the royal family, were sensitive to the monarch's views and preferences.[54] In order to put the draft Constitution to a wider test, and secure public legitimacy for it, Zahir Shah convened the Constitutional Advisory Commission (CAC), which worked between 1 March and 1 May 1964, to be followed by a *Loya Jirgah*. The 29-strong CAC, which claimed to represent different Afghan social strata and ethnic groups, was carefully hand-picked by the King in such a way as to give both liberal and conservative opinions utterance, without risking substantial changes to the draft. Dr Abdul Zahir, President of the National Assembly, Zahir Shah's personal physician and confidant, and later Prime Minister (1971–1972), chaired the CAC. In addition to a handful of intellectuals and religious scholars, the Commission included several collateral members of the royal clan, including Noor Ahmad Etemadi, a Mohammadzai protégé of Mohammad Naim, then Director-General of Political Affairs in the Foreign Ministry, and subsequently Prime Minister (1967–1971).

The commission's deliberations on one constitutional issue proved less harmonious than might have been expected. It was the controversial question of the royal family's future participation in politics. The reform advocates, ostensibly with the King's consent, argued that:

> the removal of royal family members from the government benefited the monarchy by placing responsibility for policy and its implementation on the officials of the civil government. This would leave the royal house less exposed to attack and to the vicissitudes of politics.[55]

Some others, most notably Noor Ahmad Etemadi, protested vehemently, sensing that this provision would be offensive to Daoud and Naim, and could become a source of conflict between them and the King.[56] At the end of the day, Zahir Shah's version prevailed: the King's supreme power was preserved, while the immediate members of the royal family were barred from the highest positions in the legislative, executive and judicial branches of power. Incorporated as Article 24 into the Constitution, it read:

> The Royal House is composed of the sons, daughters, brothers, and sisters of the King and their husbands, wives, sons, and daughters; and the paternal uncles and the sons of the paternal uncles of the King... Members of the Royal House shall not participate in political parties, and shall not hold the following offices: Prime Minister or Minister; Member of Parliament; Justice of the Supreme Court.[57]

The ninth *Loya Jirgah* in Afghanistan's history was convened in Kabul on 9 September 1964, in order to endorse the Constitution. Its 452 delegates (103 of them appointed by the King) 'appeared to represent the full range of social, political, and religious opinion'[58] and treated their duties seriously, discussing each provision of the new fundamental law with great vigour and skill. The debate generally centred on three main issues: the Constitution's compatibility with Islam; the equitable representation of diverse ethnic interests; and the role of the Royal House in politics. Although at times the exchange of opinions was quite heated, since the *Loya Jirgah* had historically functioned not as a decision-making but as a legitimising body, the *Jirgah*'s work went smoothly for ten days. The delegates approved the essential framework of the draft Constitution, albeit with some additions.

In the finalised document, Article 2 read: 'Islam is the sacred religion of

Afghanistan. Religious rites performed by the state shall be according to the provisions of the *Hanafi* doctrine [sic].' Otherwise, in comparison with the 1931 Constitution, which contained numerous substantive references to Islam, the new codex was 'a frankly secular document because of Article 69, that establishes the supremacy of secular law over religious law, and Article 102, that establishes the supremacy of secular over religious courts'.[59] Most importantly, deviation from the canonical Islamic doctrine that sovereignty belongs to Allah was evident: Article 1 identified the locus of sovereignty in the nation as 'composed of all those individuals who possess the citizenship of the State of Afghanistan in accordance with the provisions of the law', and Article 6 proclaimed that the King personified sovereignty in Afghanistan. Thus, the new Constitution failed to support the concept of Islamic *'umma*, but subscribed to the modern notion of a nation-state.[60] By and large, the religious leaders who took part in the *Loya Jirgah* did not seriously challenge the government's position. According to Asta Olesen, the roots of this situation can be found 'firstly, in former Prime Minister Daoud's harsh treatment of the religious opposition and, secondly, because of the well-qualified, religious-trained but liberal-minded members of the constitutional Committee.'[61] On a more general level, the increased capacity of the state to exert social control must have induced religious and other traditionalist elements to compromise with the central authorities and to seek representation of their interests through institutionalised procedures, rather than by directly confronting the modernising government, as had been the case in 1928–1929.

Article 3, which identified Pashtu and Dari (a dialect of Persian) as Afghanistan's two official languages, raised objections from Uzbeks, Hazaras, Baluchis and representatives of other ethnic minorities. The edited version, which read 'From amongst the languages of Afghanistan, Pashtu and Dari shall be the official languages', was acceptable to them only because it implicitly recognised the existence of other languages.[62] Encouragement of the use of Pashtu, a consistent policy of all Musahiban rulers since the early 1930s, was reflected in Article 35, which obliged the state to carry out a special programme to develop and strengthen Pashtu as the 'national' language.[63] In the mid 1960s, feverish attempts were made to hammer out a literary Pashtu based on its southern (Paktiya) dialect.[64] A flurry of publications in the influential journal of the Afghan Academy, *Kabul*, authored mainly by an inveterate Pashtun chauvinist Rishtin, extolled Pashtu as the language that had matured on the territory of Afghanistan long before the advent of Islam, but was subsequently suppressed by various conquerors and despots.[65] According to a Soviet author:

In the conditions of multiethnic Afghanistan, establishment of Pashtu as the official language was used as a means towards strengthening the political hegemony of the Pashtuns, which led to the exacerbation of ethnic tension. The policy of Pashtunisation… gave definite advantages first of all to Pashtuns, and then to those who had mastered the language.[66]

By the mid 1970s, Pashtuns occupied up to 70 per cent of top and middle-level positions in Afghanistan's civil and military hierarchies.[67]

Article 24, contrary to many expectations, was passed with relative ease. Since its main purpose was to neutralise Daoud and Naim, all factions – the royal party, the liberal modernisers, and the traditionalists – reached a consensus on this issue. Only ten members opposed the prohibition of royal family membership in a political party.[68] When, on 19 September 1964, the *Loya Jirgah* ended its deliberations and the delegates individually endorsed the draft, Noor Ahmad Etemadi added next to his signature that he accepted all its provisions, except Article 24.[69] The King initialled the final instrument on 1 October 1964, and Afghanistan acquired a new constitution.

Thus, Zahir Shah and his advisors delivered to the nation a new legal-rational framework, within which Afghanistan would be steered towards some kind of democratic polity. It was touted as 'possibly the finest Constitution in the Muslim world',[70] and led observers in the West to declare that:

Afghanistan may offer… an example of a peaceful transition. There the western-educated 'new men' were invited into responsible government positions and encouraged to use their energies peacefully to create a new political synthesis. Under royal patronage and within the framework of the existing political structure, the modernisers are carrying forward tasks of what has been called 'nation building' with what appears to be a satisfactory level of participation in responsibility.[71]

The new Constitution borrowed many ideas from French, British and American legal documents, particularly in what concerned the individual rights of citizens.[72] Yet it was fraught with potential authoritarian strains. Article 1 proclaimed Afghanistan 'a constitutional monarchy, independent, unitary and indivisible state', but in reality the King had more powers than any other head of a constitutional monarchy could dream of enjoying. He stood above any institution of government, acted as supreme commander of the armed forces, and had the right to declare war, conclude peace, and enter treaties at his discretion. He was also entitled to summon the *Loya Jirgah*, dissolve Parliament and appoint the prime minister, the chief justice and judges of the Supreme Court and half the members of the upper chamber of Parliament at will (Article 9). Article 15 added that 'The King is not accountable to anyone and shall be respected by all.' Article 113 empowered him to declare a state of emergency for a period of up to three months. Although Article 14 imposed formal restraints on the royal powers, to be exercised 'within the limits prescribed by the provisions of this constitution', in real life the monarch had a free hand in controlling the government, which was clearly divided into three branches.

The new legislative body, the *Shura* (Parliament), consisted of the *Wolosi Jirgah* (House of the People) and the *Meshrano Jirgah* (House of the Elders). Whereas the lower house was to be elected by the citizens of Afghanistan in a 'free universal, secret, and direct election' for four years (Articles 43 and 44), the *Meshrano Jirgah* was to have one third of its members appointed by the King from wise and experienced persons for five years, another third nominated by provincial *Jirgahs* for three years and the rest elected by popular vote for four years (Article 45). The lower house was entrusted with overseeing the conduct of the executive branch; it could move a vote of no confidence in the Cabinet and set up inquiry commissions to investigate the administration's actions (Articles 65 and 66).

The executive branch consisted of the Council of Ministers and various ministries; it was headed by the Prime Minister and functioned as the Cabinet.[73] The Constitution proved rather contradictory in defining the Cabinet's jurisdiction and accountability. On the one hand, the King could appoint and dismiss all its members whenever he deemed it necessary (Article 9). On the other hand, Articles 89–93 subjected the Cabinet to approval by the *Wolosi Jirgah*, which could demand its resignation by a two-thirds majority vote. Moreover, the Prime Minister and his ministers were responsible to the lower house for actions undertaken by them while implementing the King's decrees (Article 96). Thus, the chair of the government was wedged between the monarch and the legislature, and his/her functions were largely confined to being the go-between for those two actors.

The judiciary was made a separate branch of the state for the first time, independent of the executive, headed by a Supreme Court appointed by the King. Article 98 stipulated that no case could be adjudicated by 'other authorities': previously the Office of the Prime Minister, and the Ministries of Commerce, Communications and the Interior had had their own special courts.[74] Article 102 read:

> The courts in the cases under their consideration shall apply the provisions of this Constitution and the laws of the state. Whenever no provision exists in this Constitution or the laws for a case under consideration, the courts shall, by following the basic principles of the *Hanafi* jurisprudence of the *Shariah* of Islam and within the limitations

set forth in this constitution, render a decision that in their opinion secures justice in the best possible way.

In Duprée's opinion:

> Article 102 is the most important Article in the Constitution... Note that Article 102 enjoins the courts to consider cases in the light of the 'Constitution and the laws of the state', and mentions the *Hanafi Shariah* as a last resort. In effect, Article 102 (plus Article 69, which deals with legislation) makes Afghanistan a secular state, even while paying lip service to Islam throughout.[75]

The *Loya Jirgah*, the tribal institution with no legal framing which had been convened eight times in the twentieth century prior to 1964 to resolve matters of paramount national importance, was integrated into the fabric of the national legislature in a special Title V of the Constitution. According to Article 78, it was to comprise all members of the national Parliament and leaders of the provincial *Jirgahs*. The *Loya Jirgah*, to be assembled on the King's request, was to serve as an instrument for testing popular attitudes and also as an additional means for the King to secure wider political support for his initiatives.[76]

The final part of the Constitution rendered the Yusuf government transitional until the election of the first *Shura* to be held on 14 October 1965, and entrusted it with preparing new laws on elections, press, courts and political parties for the Parliament's consideration (Article 126).

However, for a document of this type to take root and prove effective and binding, it was imperative that, first of all, it enshrined the values shared by the politically active segments of the society, most of all those power and interest groups which competed with the state for influence over the populace. Second, these groups should have been prepared to accept the new rules of the game, and uphold the legal-rational authority stemming from the constitutional document, as well as to contribute constructively to the evolution of common conventions of political behaviour. Third, the public in general should have had the necessary level of political and social awareness to understand the need for the constitutional changes, and thus be prepared to trade some of their traditional rules and practices for innovations at both individual and societal level which might, or might not, lead to a better life.

The problem was that none of these imperatives was taken into account in the formulation of the new Afghan Constitution. It reflected mainly what the King and his western-educated advisors considered feasible in terms of their political needs and aspirations, rather than corresponding to the realities of Afghanistan. In its prescriptions, the Constitution was hardly indigenous; it was based on borrowings from different western documents which were presented, with some contradictory modifications, as applicable to Afghanistan. Put to the test, they did not necessarily work as intended. For instance, the principle of legality adopted from the 1791 French Constitution and the 1948 Universal Declaration of Human Rights, which professed presumption of innocence and prohibition of retrospective enforcement of the penal law (Article 26), was proclaimed in Afghanistan:

> at a time when statutory law had remained underdeveloped and legal practice in the country was largely governed by Shari'a law... It soon became evident that the constitutional principle of legality could not be implemented without the existence of a body of statutes to guide the legal practice and the on-going activities of the courts... Indeed, the legislative record of the four-year term of the first parliament following the 1964 Constitution 'can only be described as abysmal'.[77]

Even a decade later, traditional courts based on the Hanafi *fiqh* continued to dominate Afghanistan, although in appearance they may have become statutory courts.[78]

The fact that the Constitution was hastily approved by a largely hand-picked *Loya Jirgah* by no means signified that a satisfactory compromise had been achieved between Islamic, traditional and customary values on the one hand, and modern liberal codes on the other. The traditional elite, no longer able openly to challenge the centralised state, elected to defend its interests by constitutional means, through the Parliament, local elections, mass demonstrations and the press, with some success.[79] At any rate, the Constitution and the whole experiment with democracy rapidly proved of little relevance to the vast majority of the Afghan people. The best indication of this was the 1965 parliamentary election ('as fair as any... in Asia, or in some parts of Alabama, or in Cook County, Illinois'), where only roughly one out of every six eligible citizens bothered to vote.[80] During this poll and the next, in 1969, people voted according to ethnic or kinship ties and at the behest of powerful individuals, propelling the true power elite, rural 'khans, begs, boyars, maliks, and mullahs',[81] to parliamentary seats in Kabul.

To whom, then, was the Constitution relevant? It is possible to identify three major groups whose interests were served by its promulgation. They were: the ruling branch of the royal family; the senior government officials, in particular those close to the King; and the politically active segments of the small urbanised intelligentsia and their 'benefactors', who thrived on the activities of these segments in one form or another. They had been brought together by hostility to one man and his policies and thus could be dubbed 'the anti-Daoud coalition':

> So long as its elements feared that Daoud Khan might regain power, they saw a need for unity. But by the time the Constitution had been drafted, reviewed, and ratified it appeared that Daoud Khan had withdrawn from the political system that had rejected his leadership. The elements of the coalition then began to compete for power, and to fracture internally.[82]

The King was by far the most central figure in this coalition. Indeed, with all the powers vested in him under the new constitution, the country's efforts to modernise and reform were 'almost entirely dependent upon the goodwill and farsightedness of the king'.[83] However, Zahir Shah, who had finally tasted real power after three decades on the throne, turned out to be exceedingly preoccupied with strengthening his own leadership. Although the first *Shura* passed the Political Parties Bill according to the letter and spirit of the Constitution, he never signed it into law. In the words of an Afghan expert:

> Zaher Shah was not sincere in his support of democracy. He did not realise that a little bit of democracy was dangerous like a little bit of learning. He could not believe any one around him. While there were several parties existing, he ignored them and kept the law of parties under his knee. Therefore, every party remained in its cocoon and did not experience competition, nor did they gain political awareness by working together and forming coalitions and alliances.[84]

The King failed to promote national issues capable of overriding traditional divisions and petty personal interests. Nazif Shahrani has argued that, apart from Pashtun nationalism, Zahir Shah's regime did not have *any* commonly held ideological purpose, and indulged in 'nothing more than the public exhibition of a few hollow "democratic" procedures, such as voting, parliamentary elections, parliamentary debates, "free" press, and so forth'.[85] The general feelings of optimism so characteristic of spring 1963 had given way to tidings of discontent and pessimism amongst the educated stratum of Afghanistan, reflected in political group agitations and student demonstrations that began in October 1965 and recurred periodically until 1973.

Lacking the political will to reverse the situation, and wary as ever of Daoud's spectre, Zahir Shah invoked his absolutist prerogatives to secure his own political survival. Since the Constitution had not barred him from appointing immediate and distant members of the royal family to secondary positions in the army and civil administration, he created personal patronage networks in these structures. In this he relied heavily on General Abdul

Wali, Daoud's bitter opponent, who did not hesitate to use troops under his command to quell dissent, even without the Prime Minister's agreement.[86] Zahir Shah made army affairs and all military dealings with the Soviet Union an exclusively royal domain, to the extent that Cabinet could not even discuss military matters during its weekly meetings, nor extract any relevant information from the Minister of Defence, who reported directly to the King. In fact, no government of the 'New Democracy' era was seriously concerned with any military issue, be it armed forces' reorganisation, equipment purchases, recruitment procedures, or the growing dependence on the Soviet Union for personnel training and weapons maintenance. By 1973, the USSR had succeeded in placing an estimated 550 advisors at all levels in the Afghan armed forces, with a substantial number of them attached to the Armoured Corps and the Air Force.[87] In the early 1970s, American diplomats reported that: 'There is... no effective organisation within the military to counter or even catalog the long-term, possibly subversive effects of Soviet training of the many military officers who go to the USSR for stints as long as six years.'[88]

There existed the Afghan intelligence organisation, the Department of Record of Information under the auspices of the Office of the Prime Minister, but its reports dealt largely with disciplinary and ethical issues in the armed forces. Apparently the King had instructed its senior officers not to delve too deeply into ideological beliefs of army personnel and their Soviet mentors' activities. He falsely believed that his control over the army and air force was absolute, since he personally made every appointment to the rank of captain and above.[89]

Zahir Shah worked vigorously to create ramified patronage networks of marginal members of the royal family and senior public servants who owed their offices directly to him. For example, the King's first cousins from Shah Mahmud Khan, Sultan Mahmud Ghazi and Zalmai Mahmud Ghazi, were assigned to chair the Aviation Authority and represent Afghanistan in various West European countries respectively. At the level of deputy ministers and heads of departments, the government was dominated by Zahir Shah's associates, who by virtue of their royal backing wielded more power than their superiors. Shafiq and Hamid, the constitutional advisors, were amongst the most important of them.[90]

Zahir Shah acted as patron for all four prime ministers during the whole period of the experiment with democracy: Mohammad Hashim Maiwandwal (November 1965–October 1967), Noor Ahmad Etemadi (November 1967–December 1969, December 1969–May 1971), Dr Abdul Zahir (July 1971–November 1972) and Mohammad Musa Shafiq (December 1972–July 1973). Rather than selecting the head of the Cabinet from amongst influential members of *Wolosi Jirgah*, the King preferred to appoint old cronies, whose political fortunes depended not so much on the efficiency of the government's performance, but more on the behind-the-scenes deals that Zahir Shah cut with leaders inside and outside the parliament.[91] He had always privately promised the position of Prime Minister to his favourites well ahead of time, by intimating to them that one day they would be appointed the head of the government. This, indeed, made a mockery of the constitutional process.

In short, the Constitution helped the King to seek modern legitimacy for his traditional leadership, and also regulated the relationship between him and the royal family, muting any challenge which had historically come from his own royal rivals – in the present situation from Daoud. However, Daoud was not a man to sit idle indefinitely. When it became clear that Zahir Shah was not inclined to implement the reforms that Daoud had suggested, Daoud had no reason to keep his end of the bargain. As Hasan Kakar has observed:

> Da'ud, in whose blood politics had mixed… was waiting for the right moment to strike… Da'ud was free to call on friends. He received visitors in Cheltan, his suburban estate… He was personally supervising construction of the hospital which was to be contributed to the government upon completion. It is generally assumed that he met there with his 'friends' or with the emissaries disguised as masons or workers.[92]

Daoud set out to use the constitutional process to create a political environment that would allow him to regain power. He had many sincere supporters, as well as opportunists both inside and outside government agencies, to help him in his endeavour.

Daoud's Intrigues

In the administration, some former ministers of the Daoud regime, such as Dr Ali Ahmad Popal and Abdullah Malikyar, who served in Yusuf's Cabinet, maintained close informal ties with Daoud. However, it was Abdul Razaq Ziayee, a Vice-Minister in the Administrative Department of the Ministry of Foreign Affairs, who constantly encouraged Daoud's power ambitions, and around whom a potent Daoudist network coalesced.[93] Abdul Razaq Ziayee, a graduate of Kabul University in Law and Political Science, had been a protégé of Prime Minister Mohammad Hashim, who had put him in charge of administering part of his personal wealth in the USA, subsequently inherited by Daoud and Naim. This had enabled Ziayee to develop close ties with, and eventually great personal devotion to, the two brothers. Daoud's resignation in 1963, at which time Ziayee already held a senior administrative position at the Foreign Ministry, deeply shocked Ziayee. In private conversations with close friends, he made disparaging remarks about Mohammad Yusuf, calling him a 'commoner, Kashmiri', as well as about Yusuf's deputy, Sayed Qassem Reshtia, regarding them both as traitors to Daoud and unworthy of their positions. Ziayee's circle of contacts encompassed many politicians and bureaucrats, including Mir Akbar Khaibar, a pro-Soviet Marxist.

In his efforts to launch a campaign for Daoud's return to power, Ziayee craftily exploited traditional inter-clan rivalries, patronage allegiances and personal grievances of government officers. In this respect, for example, his recruitment of Sayyid Wahid Abdullah and Massoud Pohanyar, both working at the Foreign Ministry, was important. Wahid Abdullah, a Mohammadzai on his mother's side, had dropped out of high school, but entertained great political ambitions. He was formerly married to Reshtia's daughter, but since the breakup of his marriage, had fallen out with Reshtia, whom he suspected of having used his influence to deny him custody of his children. On the other hand, Pohanyar's pro-Daoud leanings stemmed from Nadir Shah's discrimination against his family because of its leanings towards former King Amanullah and aversion to Nadir Shah's assumption of his throne.

Ziayee also used Mohammad Hasan Sharq, a well-educated and diligent former head of the Prime Minister's secretariat during 1953–1963. Sharq harboured deep resentment towards the King's branch of the Musahiban family, because his father, Mir Sayyid Qasem, Minister of Education in the early 1930s, had been imprisoned for many years on suspicion of having had a hand in King Nadir Shah's assassination. Sharq considered that his father had been made a scapegoat, and much misery thereby inflicted upon his family.

Ziayee, Abdullah and Pohanyar formed the core of what can be termed a Daoudist solidarity network, which launched a sub rosa propaganda campaign and started to establish links with like-minded individuals in other ministries, even before the new Constitution was ratified and the experiment with democracy had begun in earnest. Dr Yusuf, who was also acting as Foreign Minister, deemed it necessary to send Ziayee away as Minister to Tehran in mid 1964. However, he returned to Kabul in 1967 to become Director-General of Administrative Services. By that time a new government was in power, with Yusuf replaced by his Minister of Information and Culture, Mohammad Hashim Maiwandwal, on 2 November 1965. Maiwandwal and his successor, Noor Ahmad Etemadi, strove to maintain better relations with Daoud's clique, for they had become increasingly aware of Daoud's unhappiness with the constitutional process and his potential to torpedo their governments' policies. As a sop to Daoud's branch of the royal family, Etemadi included Pohanyar in his Cabinet as Minister of Tribal Affairs in his two consecutive governments (November 1967–July 1971). Yet this appointment gave the Daoudist network direct access to all Cabinet discussions and decisions. Pohanyar reported to Ziayee on every weekly Cabinet meeting, and Ziayee unfailingly passed this information to Daoud.

The Daoudist circle in the executive branch was supplemented by a group of deputies in the first and second *Shuras*. Small in numbers, but highly active and vocal, Daoud's protégés and admirers, such as Ishaq Osman and Azizullah Wasifi quickly organised a Daoudist parliamentary core to pressure the executive through the *Wolosi Jirgah*. Quietly guided by Daoud, this core unleashed a campaign to make life extremely difficult for the constitutional governments. The lack of regular political parties, and absenteeism in the national legislature:

> encouraged an active minority of *wakils* [deputies] in the twelfth Parliament [1965–1969] (about 50 out of 216) to control (perhaps stultify would be a better word) government activity in all branches by launching a series of investigations of government activities by various committees of the House.[94]

The Daoudists colluded with a variety of anti-monarchy groups, most of all the leftist pro-Moscow elements, led by Babrak Karmal,[95] whose identity and role in Afghan politics will be discussed shortly. Beginning in 1966, Daoud regularly but secretly conferred with Babrak and his comrades, trying to elaborate a strategy for a new regime; young military officers loyal to Daoud also took part in those discussions, which were attended by some 50 people at various times.[96] Successive constitutional governments knew of Daoud's clandestine activities, but preferred not to interfere, for three reasons. First, they did not believe that Daoud would do anything to undermine Mohammadzai dynastic rule. Second, they underestimated Daoud's power and influence after several years of retirement, and overestimated the strength of the new constitutional framework of political competition, and third, they regarded Daoud's activities as an issue better left to the King.

The Malfunctioning of the Executive

In the meantime, the alliance between the royal court and reformist and traditionalist elements was rapidly proving temporary and opportunistic. The case of the King and his family has already been discussed: they ultimately refused to be moved from the apex of the ruling hierarchy to share power with reformist technocrats and/or traditional strongmen. Educated liberals who had been so enthusiastic about the prospects of building democracy in Afghanistan were tamed:

Prime ministers and ministers known for their dynamism and determination to push the country along the road to parliamentary democracy were soon frustrated, owing partly to the lack of royal support, the only basis of their power... the king's style of rule remained basically the same: to seek advice from a few closest to him and to give instructions to his ministers, treating them as individual officials rather than as members of a collective team. Except for a few Cabinet members who were bold enough to initiate policies of their own in their departments, the bulk of the Ministers looked for implicit or explicit royal instructions. On the whole, the executives of the constitutional period functioned dependently, being closely associated with the monarch.[97]

The King's failure to sign into law the Political Parties Bill proved a fatal mistake. On the one hand, the already informally existing, mainly leftist, political organisations could not be silenced. On the other hand, the failure denied the executive vital partisan support and dramatically weakened the government, making it a hostage to the monarch's goodwill and the *Shura*'s politicking. Thus, relations with the King rather than seniority in Cabinet determined how much power prime ministers and ministers wielded. It became routine for individual ministers to go to great lengths to outdo not only one another, but also the Prime Minister in pursuit of their ambitions. Two such ministers in the Yusuf Cabinet were Sayed Qassem Reshtia and Mohammad Hashim Maiwandwal.

Reshtia's well-known opposition to Daoud had endeared him to the King, who deliberately selected him to work on the new constitution. While in Yusuf's government, Reshtia worked diligently to set up a patronage network of his own, with a view to replacing Yusuf. He also tried to strengthen his position in the parliament by helping his brother and sister to be elected to the first constitutional *Wolosi Jirgah*. Maiwandwal, on the other hand, was at loggerheads with both Yusuf and Reshtia. A self-educated man, son of a preacher originally from Bukhara, Maiwandwal replaced Reshtia as Minister of Information and Culture in December 1964, having previously served as Ambassador in Washington, President of the Department of Press and Information in Daoud's Cabinet between 1955 and 1956 and Press Advisor to the King. While initially regarded as a protégé of Mohammad Naim, and having played no part in creating the new constitution, Maiwandwal's loyalty, political skills and especially his great eloquence had earned him the King's favour. Dr Yusuf tendered his resignation on 29 October 1965, following large-scale student demonstrations in Kabul, instigated by Karmal and other leftist politicians. On 4 November Maiwandwal, newly appointed as Prime Minister, staged a dramatic appearance at Kabul University, where he made a brilliant speech promising to consider the students' demands in due course.[98] Maiwandwal's premiership, from November 1965 to October 1967, was marked by attempts to set up an efficient executive and make the constitutional process irreversible.

Despite the Political Parties Bill remaining unratified, Maiwandwal informally set up a political organisation behind his government in August 1966. Called *Democrat-i Mutaraqi* (Progressive Democracy – PD),[99] it set out to 'create a free and progressive society on the basis of national unity... the predominance of law, equality and social assistance'.[100] Calling for a 'Quiet Revolution', Maiwandwal mapped out a strategy that was potentially attractive to a broad stratum of political forces:

> Islam is the backbone of our outlook, constitutional monarchy guarantees our national sovereignty, democracy is our path of development, nationalism is the reflection of the country's historical face, our goal is socialism, ie building a flourishing society living by common interests.[101]

Multi-party parliamentarism, a mixed economy, an anti-corruption drive and strict neutrality in foreign affairs were the hallmarks of the PD programme, which drew a number of politicians across the political spectrum to Maiwandwal, including poet Abdur Rauf Benawa, one of the founders of the *Wikh-i Zalmayan*; Abdul Hai Habibi, a well-known Pashtun historian; Mohammad Siddiq Tarzi (Mahmoud Tarzi's cousin); moderate Marxist Fazl Rahim Mohmand;[102] and Pashtun nationalist Professor Abdul Shakur Rashad. To reassure the Soviets and Afghan leftists that his ambassadorship in Washington had not led him to anti-Soviet leanings, Maiwandwal even appointed Ehsan Taraki, a 'part-time Marxist', as Minister of Justice.

Zahir Shah, however, soon became alarmed by the PD's growing influence and popularity. He resorted to his usual technique to get rid of Maiwandwal, by beginning to encourage the ambitions of individual Cabinet members, particularly Maiwandwal's First Deputy and Foreign Minister, Noor Ahmad Etemadi. After Maiwandwal resigned because of ill health, Zahir Shah did everything possible to expunge him from the political landscape. The PD's newspaper, *Mosawat*, was periodically suspended, its supporters were placed under constant police surveillance, and Maiwandwal's attempt to run for parliament in 1969 was frustrated.[103]

The same pattern recurred throughout the constitutional period: the monarch devised methods to keep premiers in check. Etemadi soon not only became an object of palace intrigues, but also was constantly harassed by scathing criticisms in the Afghan press, abetted by the King,[104] and this finally prompted him to resign. In the Cabinet of his successor, Dr Abdul Zahir, the Foreign Minister and King's favourite advisor, Musa Shafiq, stirred up much trouble in pursuit of the premiership, promised to him by the monarch. All this caused internecine fighting, dissension and back-stabbing within successive governments, resulting in precipitous erosion of government power, emasculation of the office of Prime Minister, and inability of the executive branch to act collegially and effectively.

In the meantime, the legislative branch, *Wolosi Jirgah*, malfunctioned. In the absence of political parties and provincial election laws, the parliament was dominated by *Wakils* who had no institutional commitment but retained strong tribal/parochial loyalties, were not qualified to make judgments on issues of national importance, and in most cases were mainly preoccupied in reaping as many material benefits as possible from their positions as intermediaries between the centre and the periphery.[105] *Wakils* of the second *Wolosi Jirgah*, elected in October 1969, had inherited 31 items of unfinished legislation, including normal and development budgets, laws on taxation, banking and government disputes, and judiciary statutes; a year later, they all still awaited a vote, and were topped by a backlog of pressing new issues.[106] In order to get approval for its activities, the executive was forced 'to settle for fickle ad-hoc legislative alliances', bribing or otherwise persuading individual deputies.[107]

Afghanistan had finally been given a political system that was a parody of Westminster democracy: the doctrine of separation of powers was pushed beyond the limits acceptable in a traditional society, where the executive's predominance had been a given for centuries. Creation of a potent legislature and an independent judiciary was not accompanied by establishment of a working mechanism to ensure proper coordination amongst all branches of power. The only force that could make the state machine work at all was the monarch. However, although he ushered in the era of constitutionalism, he proved incapable of following its course unswervingly. Apart from putting the Political Parties Bill on hold, Zahir Shah also refused to sign the vital Municipal Councils Act and Provincial Councils Bill, thus missing a chance to create an institutional infrastructure that might have provided for the polity's greater stability. This lack of courage (or vision) stemmed from the Mohammadzai dynasty's politics of survival, which took precedence over the nation's interests, as well as from Zahir Shah's personal traits.[108]

The 'New Democracy' was also undermined by deteriorating economic conditions. Afghanistan continued to depend heavily on foreign aid to implement its development programmes. Yet after 1964, for a variety of reasons, financial and commodity assistance from abroad decreased dramatically. Foreign project aid obtained for the second Five-Year Plan (1962–1967) was only 58.9 per cent of the planned level, and dropped even further, to 49.1 per cent of the planned level during the third Five-Year Plan (1967–1972) despite its more modest scope.[109] The US government was especially severe, cutting support to Kabul more than ten-fold in the decade to 1972, when it reached a nadir of US$2.35 million.[110] As a result, the Soviet Union strengthened its economic position in Afghanistan substantially: in 1973 its realised financial commitments were more than three times those of America.[111] With the benefit of hindsight, Leon Poullada commented bitterly that:

> It was in America's security interest... to support and encourage the democratic political development in Afghanistan – but again American diplomacy failed to rise to the occasion. A measure of this failure is the fact that *in every year of the democratic experiment, American economic aid declined.* No special effort was made to give strong visible support to the several prime ministers between 1963 and 1973.[112]

Afghan cabinets tried to expand domestic sources of revenue, but all their attempts were frustrated by the traditionalist parliament. The *Wakils* objected ferociously to any increases in land and livestock taxes, forcing the government to rely on indirect taxes and other inflationary means of fulfilling the budget.[113] One of the consequences of shrinking foreign aid and growing financial difficulties was that the state found it increasingly difficult to accommodate the swelling numbers of college-leavers:

> By the early 1970s unemployment among university graduates was becoming visible. Even for those successful in finding work, a career in government service was likely to add to the frustration of those without the right family connections... Salaries were low, providing ample incentive for corruption. Under 'New Democracy' rising inflation further reduced the real wages of government employees, and while their numbers increased dramatically, there was no corresponding investment in offices and other facilities, so working conditions also deteriorated markedly.[114]

Discontent amongst students and the lower echelons of the bureaucracy created excellent recruiting opportunities for nascent political groups espousing various ideologies, of which the communists were arguably the most active and successful.[115]

The Soviet Reaction

Meanwhile, the post-Khrushchev Soviet leadership had reasons to become concerned about the Afghan developments. Although its overall approach gave the appearance of tolerating the changes in Afghanistan, it could not afford to underestimate the risk of the changes re-orientating Afghanistan away from the Soviet Union, thereby undermining the USSR's sizable economic and military investment in Afghanistan since the mid 1950s, and broader Soviet interests in the region. One way to overcome the risk was to exploit the changes in the Soviet Union's favour. This came at a time when official modification in Soviet ideological behaviour towards the Third World was underway, prompted by realisation that thus far, military and economic aid on its own had failed as an instrument for diverting a Third World country like Afghanistan onto a non-capitalist or socialist path of development in alliance with the Soviet Union. From the mid 1960s, the Soviet leadership postulated that economic and military aid should be accompanied by an effort to help the development of an indigenous pro-Soviet communist party in the recipient country.

As the Afghan pro-democracy changes accelerated, they provided ample grounds for the Soviets to encourage the growth of such a party. The process of change opened the way for the Afghan intelligentsia to assume a greater role in politics. Small and mostly Kabul-based, but nonetheless expanding more than ever before, the intelligentsia was mainly composed of secularist, semi-secularist and religious intellectuals, professionals, bureaucrats, technocrats and military officers. While largely employed in the public sector, different segments of it immediately took advantage from 1964 of the new constitutional rights and freedoms to engage in informal group politics within and outside the legislative arenas. Within two years of the promulgation of the Constitution, diverse groups, ranging in their ideological-political disposition from liberal and social democrat to irredentist nationalist to Islamist, leftist and ultra-leftist, emerged on the political scene, either in opposition to the government or in response to one another. Many of them revolved around certain personalities; some operated on an ad hoc basis, without much organisational structure, and some modeled themselves on political parties.

Most of them published individual weekly or bi-weekly papers, serving as their unofficial organs, found a voice in the *Wolosi Jirgah* and also sought active support in higher and tertiary educational institutions, particularly Kabul University. Given the lack of a Political Parties Law, neither the King nor any Prime Minister apart from Maiwandwal, as mentioned earlier, made any serious attempt at forming a ruling party; but they all endeavoured in one form or another to manipulate the informal groups for the purpose of a parliamentary majority, political expediency and popular legitimacy.

A full discussion of all the diverse groups falls outside the scope of this study, but it is important for our purpose to focus briefly on the ones which

were either used as the main instruments of Soviet policy objectives or
emerged in opposition to Soviet communism. They included two leftist
groups, which, by 1966–1967, had become known as *Parcham* ('Banner')
and *Khalq* ('Masses'); one pragmatic/opportunistic network, which
informally operated as the 'Daoudist solidarity network'; and several
secularist and Islamist groupings.

Communists versus Islamists

Parcham was grounded in a pro-Soviet cell of Kabuli activists, which evolved
around Babrak Karmal. The latter came from a Dari-speaking mother, and
an urbanised, well-off Durrani Pashtun father, who rose to the rank of Army
General under Daoud, and whose family had become utterly dissociated
from their nomadic brethren by being landowners for some five generations.
Karmal was brought up and received all his education (including a degree in
Political Science and Law from Kabul University) in Kabul's Dari-speaking
urban environment, and moved generally in the fashionable intellectual circles
of the capital. He had become so urbanised that he could hardly relate to his
Pashtun background or speak the Pashtu language. As a leader of the
Students' Union at Kabul University during Prime Minister Shah Mahmud's
political reprisals, in 1952, Karmal, together with a fellow student and one
of the founders of the *Nida-ye Khalq* party (the Voice of the Masses), had
received a four-year sentence and 'gained first knowledge of the ideas of
scientific socialism in jail'.[116] However, while at the university, he had also
been brought to Daoud's attention through Ishaq Osman and Hasan Sharq
(who was subsequently appointed Deputy Prime Minister during Daoud's
presidency, and later assumed senior positions in the Soviet-installed *Parcham*
government in the 1980s). Daoud quietly encouraged Karmal in his
'reformist' activities as a means to advance his own power rivalry with his
uncle, Shah Mahmud. When Daoud became Prime Minister in 1953, the
conditions of Karmal's imprisonment were eased, leading to his release in
1956. Although restrained from doing anything openly against Daoud, in
the atmosphere of growing Afghan-Soviet friendship Karmal developed an
increasing commitment to Marxism-Leninism and ideological allegiance to
the Soviet Union, and began an underground process of organising a pro-
Soviet group. He was generally regarded as an element of the 'Establishment,
representing the modishly far left wing of the wealthiest and most powerful
Afghan families'.[117] He developed regular contacts with the Soviet Embassy,
and was a frequent and intimate participant in Soviet cultural functions. In
fact, the KGB 'curators' preferred to work with 'more liberal, pliant, and
less prone to leftist deviations; Babrak and his followers'.[118]

On the other hand, *Khalq* emerged from an essentially rural-based cell of leftist Pashtunist activists, revolving around Nur Mohammad Taraki. A self-educated romantic revolutionary, Taraki was born into a humble Ghilzai Pashtun family, whose tribe had permanently lost power, as explained in Chapter 1, to the rival Durranis' Mohammedzai clan since the mid nineteenth century. His leftist leanings largely stemmed from strong feelings about the impoverished and divided existence of rural Pashtuns and the ruling Mohammedzai family's inability or unwillingness to alleviate their conditions. In the late 1940s he had been absorbed into a pro-Daoud circle in Kandahar, and rose from obscurity through patronage by well-known Pashtunist entrepreneur, and originally an associate of Daoud, Abdul Majid Zabuli, himself of Taraki's tribe. Zabuli employed Taraki in 1949 in one of his export-import companies in Bombay before helping him secure a government position when Zabuli was Minister of National Economy. It was also during this period that Daoud's circle played an important role in the emergence of *Wikh-i Zalmayan* (as discussed in Chapter 4), which demanded accelerated political reforms from Shah Mahmud's government, but was exploited by Daoud to support his political ambitions.

In the early 1950s, Taraki moved to the Press Department, from where he was sent to Washington as a press attaché. But shortly after Daoud's rise to the premiership, and his crackdown on all forms of opposition, Taraki denounced the Nadiri dynasty's rule and returned home. Another influential Pashtun nationalist, Gholam Hasam Safi, interceded for him with Daoud, and Taraki was not arrested for anti-Mohammadzai propaganda. He continued to work as an interpreter and petty bureaucrat, including a stint with the American Embassy in Kabul, and also opened the Nur Translation Bureau, whihch he used as a cover for political activities. In the climate of Daoud's heightening Pashtunism and warm relations with the Soviet Union, Taraki's concern for Pashtuns increasingly led him to drift towards Marxism. Commencing in 1956, Taraki, together with Karmal and Shayan, started regular underground debating sessions for students, civil servants and army officers:

> The discussions at these meetings... Provided the first unmistakable evidence of Soviet-style Marxist rhetoric at work on the Afghan body politic. Nevertheless, the thrust of the discussions was not directed against Daoud's dictatorial government... Quite the reverse, the discussions supported Daoud's policies (as well, of course, as all things Soviet).[119]

He forged contacts with some Soviet-trained Pashtuns and the Soviet Embassy. By 1964, Taraki 'had become a contact man for the Soviet Embassy, using the tea shops where he liked to sit and talk as a place to introduce young staffers who were presumed to be members of... the KGB'.[120]

Following Daoud's resignation and the advent of the experiment with democracy, both Taraki and Karmal, prodded by the Soviet Embassy, stepped up their organisational activities to establish a political party. Taraki's position received an extra boost at this time from another, better-educated, fellow Ghilzai Pashtunist, Hafizullah Amin, who joined him in a common Pashtunist-Marxist cause. Amin was one of those who had benefited from Daoud's pro-Pashtunist policies, including expansion of education for Pashtuns. He had assumed secondary school teaching positions in the late 1950s, becoming a protégé of Daoud's Education Minister, Ali Ahmad Popal. He subsequently won a scholarship to study at Columbia University (1962–1965) for a Master's degree in education, where he conflated his Pashtunist and Marxist beliefs; and upon his return to Afghanistan, he came to Taraki's aid to construct a Marxist-Leninist Party. On 1 January 1965, Karmal and Taraki convened the first underground congress of the *Hizb-i Demokratik-i Khalq-i Afghanistan* (People's Democratic Party of Afghanistan, PDPA). Taraki was elected General Secretary of the PDPA Central Committee, and Karmal became his deputy. Embracing only a few hundred members, mostly teachers and students based in Kabul, the PDPA put forth a programme which was:

> an orthodox Communist one for the period, reflecting the analyses of the Third World conventionally associated with Khrushchev or Brezhnev... It called for an alliance of workers, peasants, progressive intellectuals, artisans, urban and rural smallholders and national bourgeois in one front, and for the unity of the working class of Afghanistan in the face of all tribal and ethnic differences.[121]

The PDPA was modelled very much on the late nineteenth century Russian Social Democratic Party, but decided to operate, given the existing circumstances, with a nationalist mask. Its aim was to work through the new 'bourgeois democratic' structure to cause the monarchy's eventual downfall. Yet the Afghan communists soon proved incapable of maintaining unity even within their meager ranks. The 27 delegates to the First Congress elected seven full members and four candidate members of the Central Committee; the next day one of those not elected quit the party in a huff.[122]

In late 1965, Taraki, Karmal and several of their supporters ran for election to the *Wolosi Jirgah*, with ample funds from unknown sources to finance their campaign. However, while Taraki failed, Karmal and a few of his supporters (most of all Anahita Ratebzad, who was reputedly Karmal's mistress – a matter of discredit for both of them in a traditional Muslim society) succeeded. This caused much disquiet among those party faithful who attributed Karmal's and his supporters' election to Karmal's links with the royal family, especially Daoud. Moreover, it soon became apparent that Karmal and Amin could not see eye to eye: Amin detested Karmal as an instrument of the 'ruling clan' and saw himself as better educated, a better Marxist-Leninist, and more of a Pashtun.

Soon personality and ideological differences, rooted mainly in the cleavage between Pashtu and Dari speakers, and the urban-rural dichotomy, resurfaced between the two sides. Despite frantic efforts by the Soviet Embassy, in 1967 the PDPA split into *Parcham* under Karmal and *Khalq*, led by Taraki and Amin. *Khalq*'s weekly, of the same name, was closed down by the government because of its attacks on religion and the monarchy, but *Parcham* was allowed to begin a weekly under its own name in March 1968. Except for a couple of hiccups, *Parcham*'s publication continued uninterrupted, although its content differed little from that of the banned *Khalq* – something again attributed to Daoud's patronage and protection. Although *Khalq* contested the election in 1969, and Amin this time secured a seat in the *Wolosi Jirgah*, *Khalq* portrayed itself as more revolutionary, along the lines of the Bolsheviks, and by implication presented the *Parchamis* as Afghan Mensheviks. In the *Wolosi Jirgah*, Amin quickly allied himself with a number of Pashtun deputies. *Parcham* and *Khalq* engaged in an intense war of words against one another inside and outside the legislative arena. On the recruitment front, the *Parchamis* concentrated mainly on the Dari-speaking intelligentsia, and sought to indoctrinate high school and university students. One of their prominent activists by the late 1960s was Najibullah, a medical student at Kabul University, who subsequently became head of the PDPA government's notorious secret police, KHAD (1980–86), then PDPA leader and President from May 1986 to April 1992. On the *Khalq* front, Amin increasingly focused on the Pashtun-speaking intelligentsia and on liaising between various political groups inside and outside the government, with a clear aim of gaining influence among Pashtun military officers, who traditionally dominated the armed forces.

The Soviets from the start had serious reservations about *Khalq*. They could find little comfort in either its rural-oriented ideological vulgarism or its Pashtunist nationalism, and did not regard it as trustworthy. By contrast, they perceived greater cohesion, loyalty and at the same time ideological flexibility and pragmatism in *Parcham*. They appreciated its leadership's intellectual strength, political sophistication and, above all, links with Daoud, an old friend of the Soviet Union. Still, since both *Parcham* and *Khalq* factions were claiming pro-Soviet loyalty, the Soviets found it for the time being politically expedient to support both separately, but without relinquishing pressure for their amalgamation.[123]

It is imperative not to overestimate the extent of Soviet involvement in Afghanistan's domestic politics in this period: the Kremlin had a good relationship with the King, and did not want to jeopardise it. When Taraki went to Moscow in 1965 to attend an international writers' conference, he was received only by a minor official in the International Department of the CPSU Central Committee, who in plain words explained to him, the top Afghan communist, that 'Afghanistan is not ready for a socialist revolution.'[124] Moreover, the PDPA 'unlike other "brotherly parties" never received invitations to send an official delegation to a CPSU congress in Moscow. Without doubt, this was done in order to maintain good ties with the regimes of Zahir Shah and Mohammad Daoud.'[125] It appears that the Kremlin viewed Afghan communists as a sort of 'fifth column', which could be activated at an appropriate moment and which, even in a state of disarray, would serve as a reminder to the authorities in Kabul not to drift towards the West. Zahir Shah understood the message very well.[126]

However, Afghanistan's democratic experiment, in conjunction with the growth of pro-Soviet groups in its wake, produced a number of unintended results. As successive liberal-minded governments pressed on with the democratic course, they found themselves on the horns of a dilemma. On the one hand, they had to cater to the needs of a monarchy that did not want to relinquish much of its power, the implication of this being a perennial crisis of self-confidence and loss of direction experienced by Cabinet members. On the other hand, parallel to the growing activities of the *Parchamis* and *Khalqis* and rising Soviet influence, various other ideological groups started to figure more prominently on the political scene. The main opposition to the rise of communism stemmed from non-pro-Soviet leftist and Islamist groups, and here the situation was quite different: 'While the government did not support the [pro-Soviet] Communists, at least not publicly, it began to [marginalise the non-pro-Soviet leftist groups] and brutally suppress the Muslim Youth movement, killing and imprisoning many of its leaders.'[127]

Opposition to Soviet Communism

Of these groups, the most active by the turn of the 1970s were organisations that had arisen in opposition either to the Soviet brand of communism, or communism in general. On the far left of the political spectrum was the *Setam-e Melli* ('National Oppression') movement, set up in 1966 by an original member of the PDPA's Central Committee, Taher Badakhshi.[128] Drawing mainly on support from Tajik peasants in northern Afghanistan, the Panjsher Valley in particular, as well as enjoying support from China, this group denounced the PDPA as agents of the Pashtun ruling class and professed the belief that 'armed struggle by the non-Pashtun peasantry against the Monarchy and its Soviet allies was necessary'.[129] Another Maoist faction coalesced in the beginning of 1968 around the weekly publication *Sho'la-ye Jawed* ('The Eternal Flame'), which gave this grouping its name. Rahim Mahmudi, the editor-in-chief and publisher of *Sho'la-ye Jawed*, was the nephew of Dr Abdur Rahman Mahmudi, a well-known nationalist and democrat, who was sentenced to imprisonment in 1952 and died shortly after being released in 1963. *Sho'la-ye Jawed* attacked both the Soviet Union and the US as revisionist and imperialist powers respectively; it advocated revolutionary forms of political struggle at the expense of parliamentarism, and severely criticised *Khalq* and *Parcham*. In the summer of 1968, *Sho'la-ye Jawed* organised mass demonstrations of students and workers in Kabul, which ended in violent clashes with the police. Subsequently, 14 leaders of this faction were arrested, and five of them, including Rahim Mahmudi's brother, Abdul Hadi Mahmudi, sentenced to 13 years behind bars.[130] In spite of harsh reprisals, *Sho'la-ye Jawed* remained the largest and most influential leftist group in Kabul in 1970.

Resistance to the creeping Soviet influence was also voiced by Islamist groups, which viewed Islam as a revolutionary ideology of political and social transformation, and demanded reformation of Afghanistan along Islamic lines as such. By 1965, a handful of theologians who had studied at Al-Azhar University in Cairo and had been imbued with the teachings of the *Ikhwan ul-Muslimin* ('Muslim Brotherhood'), had established informal groups to discuss Islam's role in the country and ways to save it from the threat of communism. These groups were initially confined to Kabul University, and led by Professor Ghulam Mohammad Niyazi, Dean of the Faculty of Theology. Amongst its founding members were Abdurrahim Niyazi, a number of future anti-Soviet Mujahideen leaders, such as Professor Burhanuddin Rabbani, and Abdurrasul Sayyaf, and several other students and instructors of that faculty. In 1968, they established the Islamists' organization called *Jamiat-i Islami Afghanistan* (the Islamic Society of Afghanistan), which in the wake of the Soviet invasion emerged as the main or at least one of the main Mujahideen resistance groups under the political leadership of Burhanuddin Rabbani. A year later, they joined forces with similar groups from the Faculty of Engineering, represented by Gulbuddin Hekmatyar (later Mujahideen leader of *Hizbi Islami* – Islamic Party),

Saifuddin Nasratyar, and Habib Rahman, who formed the *Nahzat-e Jawanan-e Musulman-e Afghanistan* ('Afghan Muslim Youth Movement'). The new organisation, with which the subsequent distinguished anti-Soviet and anti-Taliban Commander Ahmad Shah Massoud also reportedly interacted, held regular meetings at Burhanuddin Rabbani's house. According to one view, its activities were veiled in secrecy:

> Everything was conspiratorial: the structure of the organisation, its programme, leading figures, planning and implementation of various acts... The organisation had the so-called military section, which at the initial stage was busy recruiting Army junior officers into its ranks, and later on embarked on preparing for an armed uprising. The work of the military section was coordinated by G. Hekmatyar and S. Nasratyar; the same persons were involved in organising demonstrations and meetings.[131]

In the early 1970s, the Islamists controlled two thirds of the seats of the Student Union at Kabul University; they were well represented in the parliament and, to a lesser extent, in the armed forces. In Kakar's view:

> Because of the headway the Islamists had made, the leftist groups had gone on the defensive... The Islamic movement appeared to be on the way to becoming a party of the masses. Among other things, this threat prompted the communists to help Daoud to topple the monarchy in 1973.[132]

Daoud's Triumph

For much of his public life Daoud had endeavoured to combat what he perceived as religious or 'black' reaction, and in the early 1970s he continued to identify the Islamist movement as a major threat to modernising Afghanistan.[133] During his first premiership, he did not hesitate to move against religious figures who opposed his policies, particularly over the unveiling of women. In the assessment of the Muslim Youth, 'Godless' Daoud's aims were 'elimination of the Islamic order and liquidation of the followers of the humanist school (*maktab-e ensansaz*) in Islam'.[134] Daoud also distrusted Maiwandwal's PD and the newly emergent nationalist groups, such as the ultra-nationalist Pashtun *Jamiat-e Social-e Demokratik-e Afghanestan* ('Afghan Social Democratic Party', ASDP), whose formation was announced in the *Afghan Mellat* newspaper in April 1966. Headed by Engineer Ghulam Mohammad Farhad (also known as 'Papa' in Kabul), the ASDP, among other things, advocated Pashtunistan within a Greater Afghanistan, and called for the return of Afghan territories lost to Tsarist Russia in the nineteenth century.[135] Not being formally linked to any of the parties or ideological groups, Daoud had been watching the changing political situation closely, preserving and developing his own solidarity network within and outside the government.

Apart from senior public servants, such as Abdur Razaq Ziayee, Massoud Pohanyar and Mohammad Hasan Sharq, Daoud relied on the all-round support of influential figures in the uniformed services, such as General Ghulam Haidar Rasuli, a Mohammadzai; Qadir Nuristani, a high-ranking police officer; General Abdul Karim Mostaghni; and, apparently, General Ismael, chief of the intelligence service. Through such figures Daoud was kept fully informed of government decisions and policy initiatives. As explained before, his protégés in the *Wolosi Jirgah*, most notably Ishaq Osman, were constantly making pragmatic-opportunistic alliances with leftist factions, *Parcham* in particular, in order to undermine the government of the day. Temporarily united in disdain for the monarchical-democratic experiment, these two unlikely allies had different long-term objectives: accelerated modernisation of the country according to Daoud's vision, and establishment of a pro-Soviet regime in line with the *Parcham* programme. Successive government leaders were cognisant of *Parchami* and *Khalqi* obstructionism, as well as their links with the Soviet Union. They were also fully aware of the existence of the active Daoudist network, and the emerging ties between its members and the *Parchamis*.[136] For a number of reasons, however, they did little about these developments.[137]

First, none of them ever found it credible that the pro-Soviet groups would one day be in a position to bid for power, given their minute memberships, mutual hostilities and the unsuitability of their stated policies for Afghan conditions, especially in the climate of good relations between the Afghan and Soviet leaderships. Second, they were unable to take any action to counter communist infiltration of the armed forces,[138] as all things military were overseen personally by Zahir Shah and General Abdul Wali. Consequently, prime ministers had to rely on their judgment and vigilance, which proved inadequate: by mid 1973, there may have been as many as '800 hard-core Soviet trained communist officers in the army'.[139] Third, while identifying the Daoudist solidarity network as potentially most threatening, they continually found solace in the fact that Daoud's menace stemmed from the downturn in his relationship with the King, and therefore concluded it was a matter exclusively for the monarch to handle. In his turn, Zahir Shah, whenever Daoud's suspicious behaviour was reported to him (even by General Abdul Wali), dismissed such allegations on the basis of consanguinity: Daoud would have to remain loyal to him as his brother-in-law, as well as to the dynasty on the whole, in strengthening whose rule Daoud had played so illustrious a role. Zahir Shah even failed to take note of the fact that, from 1968, Daoud's discord with the King had reached a point where he would not allow his wife to visit her brother.

In summation, the persisting patrimonial character of the state in Afghanistan proved detrimental to an experiment with democracy. Constitutional law, freedom of speech and association, regular elections to the legislature, political parties and organisations, and other trappings of modern liberalism were superfluous under conditions where all real mechanisms of social control remained firmly in the hands of the Mohammadzai clan. The country may have acquired an imposing edifice of the 'institutional fiction of representation',[140] but for all practical purposes it remained close to the sultanistic ideal type of political system, that precluded the existence of moderate elements within both regime and opposition capable of negotiating a genuine democratic transition.[141] Moreover, the entire discourse and praxis of 'democratisation' was confined to the still numerically insignificant urban establishment, so there was no pressure from the bulk of the populace to follow this path, although neither did the haphazard conduct of liberal reforms elicit mass discontent. The deteriorating economic situation, which crippled the state's regulatory function, and the radicalisation of elitist opposition groups supported and ideologically guided by the Soviet secret service also played their part in undermining the reforms. However, the major threat to stability of the regime came from the internecine fight inside the governing elite, between the King's supporters and Daoud's, emanating from the endemic royal polygamic rivalries, and the degree to which this had made Afghanistan vulnerable to outside interferences for most of its modern history. Had it not been for rivalry within the royal family, and the Soviets' growing concern about their interests in Afghanistan and the region, the Afghan experiment with democracy might not have taken the hazardous course that it did. Also, as a consequence, Afghanistan might have not have been opened to Daoud's vindictive republicanism, which within a few years led the country down the path of ideological extremism and another phase of bloody conflict in the evolution of its politics and society.

7

Daoud's Republicanism

IN THE POST-SECOND World War period, Afghanistan, like many other countries throughout the Middle East, developed a peculiar form of étatism:

> The state became the central controlling force in society, not just by virtue of its monopoly on coercion but also by its vastly increased economic power – as owner of the basic industries, source of all major investments, only international borrower, and provider of all essential services.[1]

The non-coercive component of the mechanism of state domination was particularly significant in Afghanistan: even with a modern army and police force at its disposal, the central government preferred to secure the compliance of autonomous social units, particularly the Pashtun tribes, by channelling rentier income to them. As the major source of this income was foreign aid, not oil sales as in the Gulf States and Iran, the Afghan government encountered massive fiscal problems after the financial flow from abroad began to dry up, and had to default on debt repayments in 1970. The financial crisis had an important ramification for the most mobile and volatile section of the population – school leavers and university graduates, practically all of whom had to be employed in the government agencies: 'The number of state employees tripled in the late 1960s, even as the foreign aid financing the projects where they were supposed to work was declining.'[2] These underpaid youths with unclear career prospects swelled the ranks of the radical political organisations.

It is easy to explain the termination of the 'New Democracy' phase as a logical outcome of the 'prolonged economic distress, in which constitutional institutions are drained of their democratic content even in the absence of formal regime change'.[3] To understand why the regime change *did* occur, and what influenced the configuration and performance of its successor, is more difficult, and requires reference to the erstwhile themes of agnatic rivalry, foreign influences and ideological struggle in Afghanistan.

The credibility of monarchical rule was severely impaired by the drought that began in 1969 and lasted for three years. In 1971 and 1972, famine became a reality in Afghanistan, and may have claimed anywhere between 50,000 and 500,000 lives.[4] The government, headed by Dr Abdul Zahir (July 1971–November 1972), proved incapable of handling a crisis of such magnitude. Food prices went through the roof, foreign aid was squandered by corrupt officials and a reasonably efficient distribution of relief supplies did not begin until late 1972, by which time 20 per cent of the population had been driven to the very brink of survival.[5] Foreign Minister Musa Shafiq secured international help for the drought victims, liaised fairly successfully between the Cabinet and various parliamentary factions on constitutional issues, and worked hard to compel Zahir Shah to keep his promise to appoint him Prime Minister one day. The King did so on 5 December 1972, and this personnel move had far-reaching ramifications.

Shafiq's Premiership

Shafiq, educated both according to Islamic (Al-Azhar University) and western (Columbia University) canons, appeared to be the right man to put the democratisation process on a more stable course: a technocrat, a loyal, energetic trouble-shooter, and one of the original designers of the new constitutional political system in Afghanistan. Shafiq formed a cabinet comprising largely young, talented, liberal-minded ministers, untainted by the corruption that had tarnished many of their predecessors. He moved swiftly and shrewdly to placate liberal and Islamic oppositionists by drawing on both certain religious values and a commitment to consolidate 'Afghan democracy'. With more royal backing than the King had accorded any of his forerunners, Shafiq initiated a number of long overdue reforms, to make the constitutional process more effective and achieve greater political and social stability. He managed to break the executive-legislative impasse, and came very close to turning the Political Parties Bill into an operational law. Most importantly, he succeeded in rapidly reversing the negative economic trends: economic growth, based primarily on increased private industrial investments, resumed; exports grew, and so did tax revenues in Kabul and elsewhere.[6]

On the foreign policy front, Shafiq reaffirmed Afghanistan's stance of neutrality, non-alignment, and friendly relations with the Soviet Union. At the same time, he put special emphasis on developing regional cooperation in order to reduce the country's dependence on the Soviet Union. In the aftermath of the February 1971 Organization of Petroleum Exporting Countries (OPEC) Conference, Iran was clearly emerging as the strongest regional power, so Shafiq deemed it necessary to promote ties with Tehran. This could not be done without settling the long-standing dispute over distribution of the Helmand River's waters,[7] so he offered reasonable concessions to Iran[8] and signed a definitive settlement agreement with his Iranian counterpart, Amir Abbas Hoveyda, on 12 March 1973, opening the way for better relations and a concomitant promise of Iranian financial aid. Both left and right opposition inside Afghanistan was infuriated: Maiwandwal, for example, denounced the agreement as 'an undesirable deal to the detriment of the Afghan nation' and 'a plot against the people of Afghanistan'.[9] Shafiq planned to rectify outstanding problems with Pakistan in a similar vein. President Bhutto's two brief visits to Kabul in January and May 1972 had helped clear the logjam in bilateral relations, particularly in the economic sphere, and were largely the result of Shafiq's efforts while Foreign Minister. Shafiq believed that:

> Having a common history, cultural and racial ties, the people and Government of Afghanistan want the Pakhtoonistan issue, a remnant of colonial days and which is the only political difference between Afghanistan and Pakistan, to be solved through peaceful means so that the People of Pakhtoonistan may be given the right to self-determination.[10]

In the meantime, Shafiq pressed for the Chairman of the Presidium of the Supreme Soviet and Head of State of the USSR, Nikolai Podgorny, to visit Kabul, a break with past practice, whereby Afghan premiers visited Moscow first. Podgorny came in May 1973, but although the two sides exchanged assurances of friendship and understanding, the visit did not go as smoothly as Shafiq would have liked. Podgorny reiterated Brezhnev's proposal for an Asian Collective Security System, but Shafiq, reflecting Afghanistan's concern that the proposed system was essentially directed against China, politely refused to endorse it.[11] There was also a certain divergence on the Pashtunistan issue, with Moscow less inclined to reiterate its past support for Afghanistan.[12] These events unfolded against the background of three other hitches in Afghan-Soviet relations in the early 1970s. They concerned Afghanistan's unwillingness to allow the Soviets to establish a cultural centre in Kabul similar to that already operated by the USA; refusal to erect bridges across the Amu River; and opposition to Soviet plans to build a railroad from Kabul to the river terminal of Hairatan on the

Soviet border. Meanwhile, everything discussed at Cabinet meetings, including Shafiq's intention to balance the influence of the USSR and its proxies, could easily be leaked to the *Parchamis* and their Soviet friends. Namatullah Pazhwak and Mohammad Khan Jalalar, selected by Shafiq as Interior and Finance Ministers respectively, had close ties with *Parcham* and with Daoud,[13] who subsequently retained both in his Presidential Cabinet as Ministers of Education and Commerce.

It can be conjectured that, if successful, Shafiq's policies would have had three main implications for the Soviets and their supporters in Afghanistan. First, they would have entrenched the democratisation process, probably with significant Islamic qualifications. Second, they would have left little room for the communists and, for that matter, Daoudists, to manoeuvre against the government in an organised and institutionalised political space. Third, they would have checked the growth of Soviet influence in Afghanistan and the region on the whole. Moscow's greatest disadvantage at the time was the fact that its surrogate forces had thus far failed to gain much ideological credibility and popular support, losing in this sense even to *Sho'la-ye Jawed*, whose recruitment programme had yielded positive results among both the Kabul intelligentsia and the people in the northern provinces. *Parcham* and *Khalq* between them had only 1,500 hardcore members, virtually all of them in Kabul,[14] and could not submerge their enmity for the sake of long-term political expediency. To counter the possible menace from Shafiq's policies, the best the Soviets could count on was an alliance between Daoud and *Parcham* against the regime.

Daoud's Coup

This alliance was formalised in 1971, when officers representing the underground Marxist-influenced Army Revolutionary Organisation met with Daoud's confidant, Dr Mohammad Hasan Sharq, and reached agreement to start planning a coup.[15] It was widely rumoured that Zahir Shah's pathologically indecisive and purposeless leadership style, aimed at preserving royal privileges at whatever cost, would lead to regime change. The US Ambassador to Kabul, Robert G. Neumann, wrote in 1972 that the King was unlikely to cope with the 'crisis of survival'.[16] By the summer of 1973, at least three conspiracies were gaining momentum: Daoud's, ex-premier Maiwandwal's and General Abdul Wali's.[17] Daoud struck first. Daoud, leading many of his sympathisers and a group of *Parchami* servicemen in the armed forces, carried out an almost bloodless coup and toppled the monarchy on 17 July 1973, while the King was visiting Italy.[18] Musa Shafiq, Abdul Wali and many other government officials and military officers were imprisoned, the army offered no resistance and the bulk of the populace were apparently happy to see the 63-year-old Daoud return to power.[19] For many of them, the reality was simply that a different member of the royal family was assuming full political power.[20]

Afghanistan was proclaimed a republic, and a 17-strong Central Committee assumed executive power. The following day, 18 July 1973, the Central Committee elected Daoud President, Prime Minister, Minister of Foreign Affairs and Minister of Defence of the Republic of Afghanistan. Daoud declared a state of emergency, disbanded parliament, suspended the 1964 Constitution, banned all forms of opposition organisations, propaganda and agitation, and closed all private newspapers and magazines. In his first policy statement, he said that, under Zahir Shah, 'Democracy or the government of the people was changed into anarchy and the constitutional monarchy into a despotic regime.'[21] He made a solemn pledge to put the country on a path of genuine democracy 'which conforms to the true spirit of Islam'.[22] He also declared the continuity of foreign policy based on neutrality and non-alignment, praised Afghanistan's friendly relations with its great northern neighbour, the Soviet Union, singled out Pakistan as the only country with which Afghanistan had a major political dispute and declared his regime's full support for the people of Pashtunistan's right to 'self-determination'.[23]

Although initially the extent of *Parcham*'s involvement in the coup was concealed, it was considerable. When Daoud announced his first Cabinet, at least half of its 14 ministers were closet *Parchamis*.[24] One of the central figures of the coup, Major Abdul Qadir, a Soviet-trained *Parchami* sympathiser, was shortly thereafter promoted to Deputy Commander of the Air Force, while another of his pro-Soviet elements, Captain Zia Majid, a son of Colonel Majid, former chief of Afghan military intelligence, was made Commander of the Republican Guard.[25] Hundreds of *Parcham* supporters received gainful employment in the bureaucratic apparatus, and Daoud despatched 160 of their most energetic comrades-in-arms to the provinces, where they could promote 'enlightenment and progress' uninhibited.[26] The degree of Moscow's involvement in the events of July 1973 is more difficult to gauge. Scholars inside Afghanistan have tended to portray Zahir Shah's ouster as master-minded *and* implemented by the Kremlin,[27] but it has been widely suggested in the West that the Soviets had no role in the coup.[28] Indeed, there is very little hard documentary evidence of a direct Soviet role in the coup. However, there is abundant circumstantial evidence to support the view of a number of senior Afghan officials of the time that Moscow not only had prior knowledge of the coup, but also an indirect hand in it. Several factors account for this.

First, to anyone who was deeply involved in Afghanistan's politics at the time, it is beyond belief that Karmal and his senior colleagues would have done anything as substantial as participate in a coup without instructions and explicit permission from the Soviet Embassy. The reason why Karmal himself did not receive a position in Daoud's Cabinet is obvious. Daoud would not have agreed to it, but nor would the Kremlin have found it expedient to unmask Soviet involvement, particularly when they felt that they had to deal with a force as credible as Daoud to take advantage of the situation. Second, by the turn of the 1970s, despite growing political difficulties and uncertainties, the Kremlin had secured a comfortable position in the Afghan administration and armed forces. Its Afghan agents and sympathisers, as well as Soviet advisors, already occupied strategic positions, to the extent that no major Afghan decision or major military operation could be implemented without the prior knowledge and, in the Air Force, permission, of Soviet personnel. Third, the sheer weight Daoud gave to *Parchamis* in his first Cabinet signalled that the bargaining for ministerial posts was conducted with deference to the Soviets.

Whether or not it had helped instigate the coup, for the time being Moscow had reason to be happy with the turn of events, as Daoud and his *Parchami* collaborators moved to establish a system of government and elaborate a new foreign policy with which the Soviet Union could feel very comfortable. Daoud permitted members of the royal family, including General Abdul Wali, to join the King in Italy in return for the King's formal abdication a month after the coup,[29] and quickly established personal control over the government apparatus. He immediately put behind bars or liquidated a number of real and potential opponents in the administration and the army, and, at the instigation of the *Parchamis*, unleashed a brutal campaign against the Islamists and *Sho'la-ye Jawed*, exterminating or incarcerating many leading and rank-and-file members of these groups during the next two years.[30] However, his measures never acquired the form of a perpetual terror campaign, such as became a hallmark of the subsequent communist regime. 'Repressive measures applied only to active political opponents, and were usually undertaken with some measure of legality. There were no disappearances and at most a handful of unexplained deaths that might have been summary executions.'[31] In many instances, Daoud was forced to quell nascent coups and rebellions. In December 1973, a plot was uncovered in the army, instigated by the radical Muslim Youth Movement, but its main leaders managed to escape to Pakistan.[32] Other Islamist figures, such as Burhanuddin Rabbani and Gulbuddin Hekmatyar, joined them during 1974. They were welcomed by the Pakistanis who quickly spotted an opportunity to secure leverage against Daoud over his Pashtunistan stand: 'With arms, training and money in part supplied by the [Zulfiqar Ali] Bhutto government, and recruits from their following inside Afghanistan, groups of the Ikhwanis struck far and wide over the south-east and east of Afghanistan in the summer of 1975.'[33] One of the leading figures of the insurrection, who proved a very efficient field commander in the Panjsher Valley, was Ahmad Shah Massoud, a personality to be discussed later. In 1975, the anti-Daoud campaign received no popular support, and was rapidly quashed. Having lost some 600 men, Islamists retreated to Pakistan.[34] Between 1975 and 1977, they suffered a series of splits, which eventually led to the formation of *Hezb-e Islami*, headed by Hekmatyar, and Rabbani's *Jamiyat-e Islami*, forming the backbone of the future Mujahideen resistance to the Soviet occupation in the 1980s.[35]

Also included on Daoud's and *Parchami* hit lists was Maiwandwal. During the long years of his ambassadorship to the USA, he had been labelled a 'CIA agent' by the communists and had maintained a somewhat uneasy relationship with the Soviet Union;[36] but what made him dangerous in Daoud's eyes was his personal power ambitions. Having been arrested on 20 September 1973 and sentenced by a military tribunal to death on charges of high treason and conspiring against the state, Maiwandwal was found dead in his cell 12 days later.[37] The government claimed he had hanged himself, but it is now evident that he was killed by a *Parchami* who had custody of him.[38] Five more people were executed in connection with this case, and seven sentenced to life imprisonment.[39]

From the outset, Daoud adopted a belligerent position against Pakistan over Pashtunistan. Following his support of the issue in his inaugural speech, he characterised Pashtunistan as an incontrovertible reality. Kabul's financial and military aid to Pakistan's secessionist Pashtun and Baluchi movements increased, and relations with Pakistan deteriorated to the point of border skirmishes.[40] These developments alarmed the Shah of Iran, who, much in line with the 'Nixon Doctrine', regarded himself not only as the main regional bulwark against communism and communist subversion, but also, in then US Secretary of State Henry Kissinger's eulogistic words, 'a leader whom eight Presidents of both parties proclaimed – rightly – a friend of our country and a pillar of stability in a turbulent and vital region'.[41] This, together with Daoud's initial reservations concerning the Helmand River Treaty, prompted the Shah to declare that Iran would not tolerate any further disintegration of Pakistan after the creation of Bangladesh in 1971.[42] He promised Bhutto's government assistance in curbing secessionist activities in Baluchistan and the North-West Frontier Province (NWFP) by exerting pressure on Kabul, but, more importantly, by providing arms, in contravention of the existing US embargo.[43]

As Daoud reversed the course of democratisation, suppressed the forces which had posed a threat to Soviet interests and revived a foreign policy posture which had originally been a main factor in engendering Afghanistan's dependence on the USSR, he certainly pleased the *Parchamis* and their Soviet patrons. But this was not the whole story for Daoud. By pursuing these policies, he was buying time to consolidate his personal power. Whereas the *Parchamis* may have viewed the coup and the new regime's line as a prelude to a 'national democratic' revolution under their leadership, Daoud's long-ranging plans were dramatically different.

Daoud's Changes and Soviet Distrust

Clearly, from the beginning, Daoud's alliance with the *Parchamis* was not based on ideology. As noted earlier, Daoud's objective was to wreak vengeance on Zahir Shah and seize power in pursuit of his own vision for Afghanistan. Since he knew that pro-Soviet communists and Soviet advisors had gained a solid foothold in the armed forces, he was compelled to use their help to achieve his goal. But, above everything else, Daoud was a self-seeking, autocratic, nationalist reformer, ultimately not prepared to share power with anyone. In his radio broadcast to the people on the day of the coup, he referred to the ten years of Zahir Shah's constitutional experiment as 'a false democracy which from the beginning was founded on private and class interests, and on intrigues, plots, falsehood, and hypocrisy', eventually resulting in 'the complete decline and bankruptcy of the country's economic, administrative, social, and political state'.[44] A month later, on 23 August 1973, Daoud unveiled his modernisation programme, based on centralisation of power, increased state regulation of the economy and a whole cluster of social reforms, including equal rights for men, women and national minorities, expansion of education, better welfare service measures and an anti-corruption drive.[45] Its centrepiece was a comprehensive land reform, which he had been nurturing since the early 1950s. It was to be carried out over a period of 25 years, and:

> probably could have offered the optimal solution to the agrarian question. It took into account the existing realities, the peculiarities of the Islamic law, and envisaged gradual introduction of new forms of land tenure... Its success would have been linked to the authority of the President himself who was accustomed to achieving the goals he had set for himself. The reforms could have eventuated without much tumult.[46]

Daoud finally put an end to the legislative quagmire of the preceding period. He ruled by decree, enacting 36 laws between 1973 and 1977, including modern civil and penal codes which had been in the offing since the 1960s.[47] By the mid 1970s, he had succeeded in consolidating his power and re-establishing his credibility with the Soviets, and was no longer willing to tolerate the communists' influence, nor their irritating presence in the fabric of his regime. After appointing his brother, Mohammad Naim, as his special emissary in foreign policy, and shifting power decisively to his branch of the former royal family, he wanted only 'yes-men' around him, and certainly none who would seek to expand their own power bases and challenge him using extraneous support.[48] This also to some extent affected representatives of the Mohammadzai clan: Daoud, while continuing the traditional policy of promoting Pashtun supremacy, tried to broaden his base of support. He recruited amongst the Ghilzai at the expense of the Durrani – a development that eventually contributed to polarisation and fragmentation in the Pashtun-dominated armed forces and security agencies.[49]

Meanwhile, he needed far more aid than Moscow could provide to implement his grandiose schemes for a modernised Afghanistan. His Seven Year Development Plan (1976–1983) demanded expenditures to the tune of US$3,850 million, of which US$2,533 million would have to come as foreign aid; the Soviet Union had underwritten only US$570 million of that sum.[50] Yet in reasserting his approach to Afghanistan's foreign relations in the changing regional and international circumstances, he strove to avoid the mistakes which had cost him his premiership ten years earlier. It was clear to him that as long as he remained heavily dependent on the Soviet Union, he could neither become completely free of the influence of Moscow's proxies in Afghanistan, nor obtain sufficient support from non-Soviet sources, particularly the oil-rich states in the Persian Gulf and Middle East – the regions which now featured prominently in Daoud's foreign policy considerations, given the continuous decline in American aid to Afghanistan.[51]

Consequently, from 1975 on, he moved to break his partnership with the *Parchamis* and diversify Afghanistan's sources of external assistance, with a view to attracting the types of investment and advanced technology and know-how that the USSR could not offer. He did not aim to degrade Afghan-Soviet ties; rather, he aspired to put them on a more symmetrical basis with other relationships, so as to give himself greater independence in conducting both domestic politics and foreign relations as he deemed appropriate. To achieve this, he felt he could confidently count on his personal friendship with the Soviet leaders, on his assurance to them that he was committed to maintaining close relations, particularly in the military sphere, and on the changing regional and global imperatives, which now included the emergence of powerful second tier actors, most notably Iran.[52] Furthermore, he concluded that by now the Soviets must value him more than their ideological clients, who could never have acquired enough popular acceptance to enable them to safeguard Soviet interests in Afghanistan. Indeed, when, in December 1975, the Afghan-Soviet Treaty on Neutrality and Mutual Non-Aggression of 1931 was extended for another ten years, the joint communiqué expressed the two sides' 'deep satisfaction with the present state of friendly Soviet-Afghan relations and emphasised that in the wake of the establishment of the republican regime in Afghanistan these relations have ascended to a new stage'.[53] The Soviet media oozed honey about Daoud's regime:

> The young Afghan republic is on the threshold of an economic, social and cultural renaissance. It conducts the policy of positive neutrality and non-alignment to military blocs in the international arena, and thus deservedly enjoys respect of peace-loving nations.[54]

In the mid 1970s, even the KGB viewed Afghanistan as a friendly state which posed no threat to Soviet interests.[55] Daoud was able to initiate changes to diversify Afghanistan's foreign policy orientations without antagonising the Kremlin. He sought to realise his objectives through a four-dimensional approach. First, he intensified his contacts with the Soviet leaders, confirming his commitment to friendship and his ever-growing need for all-round Soviet aid.[56] The Afghan army began to receive increasing quantities of modern hardware: MiG-19 jet fighters, Su-7 ground support aircraft, surface-to-air missiles and T-62 main battle tanks.[57]

Second, under cover of these enhanced contacts, he speedily deployed his own loyalists, many of whom had served the monarchy and belonged in one way or another to the Mohammadzai clan, in important government positions. In a shake-up of the Cabinet, ostensibly in pursuit of greater efficiency, he either removed or sent abroad as ambassadors some of the communist members and their sympathisers, replacing them with his own protégés, so that by 1977 no leftists remained in the government[58] except Jalalar, who skilfully continued to hide his ideological leanings. The army, too, was purged in late 1975, but in less dramatic fashion; the bulk of pro-Soviet officers retained their positions.[59] US Ambassador Theodore Eliot wrote in 1975:

> Those leftist officials who have been fired have never had their ideological beliefs thrown up as a reason for dismissal, but only their corruption or inefficiency... We believe it most likely that Daoud, having used the left to gain power, is now methodically and cautiously trying to whittle it down... He is snipping away at some of the left's strength without leaving himself open to charges of discrimination against it.[60]

Daoud also activated his secret police for close surveillance of the communists. He even discreetly went as far as to give Iran's secret police, SAVAK, a generally free hand in assisting its Afghan colleagues to isolate Soviet agents.[61]

Third, after years of animosity towards Pakistan, he suddenly found it imperative to soften his stance on Pashtunistan and opted for rapprochement. His intentions were two-fold: to reduce his dependence on local communists and the Soviet Union as well as military expenditure, and expand economic and trade ties with Pakistan, and to open the door for substantial aid and investment from several oil-rich or technologically advanced Islamic states in the Persian Gulf and Middle East, with which Pakistan had developed friendly relations.[62] This led to direct talks between Daoud and Zulfiqar Ali Bhutto in Kabul in 1976. Although the problem of Pashtunistan remained unresolved, the two leaders agreed to pursue peaceful negotiations and improve existing relations: 'Contrary to expectations, phenomenal progress was made... Not only was a spirit of amity and goodwill generated during the visit, it also provided the opportunity to the leaders of both countries to make numerous gestures of friendship.'[63] Daoud was encouraged in this initiative by the Shah of Iran. Once Daoud had signalled his willingness to respect the March 1973 Afghan-Iranian Agreement and seek normalisation of relations with Pakistan, the Shah was more than pleased to help Daoud reduce Afghanistan's dependence on the Soviet Union. In 1975, the Shah promised Daoud financial aid, amounting to US$2 billion over ten years, for his developmental programmes and security purposes.[64]

Fourth, with Afghan-Pakistani tension subsiding, and the Shah pledging more assistance than Kabul could hope to procure from any other source, Daoud felt emboldened not only to become more forceful in dealing with the communists, but also to draw up an ambitious Seven-Year Development Plan (1976–1983) to achieve his dream of modernisation. Unlike the previous Five-Year Plans, in which Soviet aid had assumed the leading role, this Plan was to be financed largely by Iranian aid.[65] It envisaged a number of major projects, the most important of which were construction of the first Afghan railway network, linking Afghanistan with Iran in the west and Pakistan in the east; exploration and exploitation of oil deposits hitherto deemed uneconomic; establishment of several large industrial and agricultural schemes in the provinces of Herat and Kandahar; and expansion of the Hajigak iron ore mine, north-west of Kabul. While the railway, planned for completion by 1983, was primarily intended to give Afghanistan an overland route to Iranian ports, it would also be an important stimulus for the industrial and agricultural projects. In a daring step, rather than inviting Soviet partnership, Kabul approached Indians to do the feasibility study for the railway, and Japanese and French firms to participate in its construction, and asked the French company Total to help with the oil exploration.[66]

In the meantime, Daoud was sufficiently worried about the possibility of a *Parcham*-led attack against him to send his brother, Mohammad Naim, to Washington on 29 June 1976 to enlist the Ford Administration's support against the contingency. Naim met Secretary of State Henry Kissinger and other senior officials, informing them of Daoud's concern about what the communists could do to the incumbent government and requesting greater economic assistance to reduce Afghanistan's dependence on the USSR.[67] Although Kissinger expressed sympathy, he was either unwilling or unable to do more than urge him to turn to the Shah's government – now seen as the region's major bulwark against communism – and to supply some cooking oil.[68] Naim, accompanied by some senior State Department officials, met Iran's ambassador, the Shah's estranged son-in-law, Ardeshir Zahedi, in Washington, only to hear Zahedi merely reiterate his government's general promises of support. Meanwhile, in late 1977, State Department staff mooted the possibility of the USA downgrading its embassy in Kabul to the category of 'Mission', usually accredited to countries of least importance to the USA – indicating that America was not prepared to accord Afghanistan priority in any of its regional or international concerns. The task of upholding US policy there was in effect delegated to the Shah of Iran, who:

> during his 1977 visit to Washington... spent a good portion of his presentation to President Carter... expounding the shared American-Iranian interest in protecting Afghanistan's genuine neutrality. A strong Iran, backed by the United States, was clearly in a position to make a Soviet invasion of Afghanistan both more costly and internationally dangerous.[69]

Yet, despite his grand gestures, the Shah could not fulfil his promise of financial aid as quickly as Daoud wanted, because of a drop in Iran's oil income and domestic economic difficulties after 1975.[70] In early 1978, by which time Iran had disbursed only about $10 million in assistance, Daoud undertook an extensive trip to India, Saudi Arabia, Egypt and Libya in his quest for more aid.[71] He was warmly received and promised substantial assistance in Saudi Arabia and Egypt, but his visit proved poorly timed and ill conceived in terms of his relations with Moscow, which considered both states hostile.

Daoud's visit to Anwar al-Sadat's Egypt particularly alarmed the Soviets.[72] They could forgive Sadat neither for his abandonment of quasi-alliance with them in favour of close friendship with Washington and peace with Israel, nor for his de facto alliance with the Shah against what both described as 'Soviet subversive activities' in the Middle East.[73] In fact, Sadat's encouragement of Daoud to undermine the Afghan communists as he had undermined their Egyptian counterparts, and the lessons Daoud drew from this advice, were apparently leaked to the Soviets by a clandestine *Parchami* in Daoud's entourage. To Moscow, the bells warning of emerging 'Sadatism' in Daoud's policy must now have been ringing loudly. In April 1977, Brezhnev invited Daoud to come to Moscow for the second time since 1973. During the talks, Brezhnev rather arrogantly demanded that the President of Afghanistan dismiss all non-Soviet foreign specialists and advisors. Abdul Samad Ghaus who was present at the meeting has commented on this incident:

> Nothing like Brezhnev's words to Daoud had ever been heard before in any high-level Russo-Afghan meeting. It was obviously an intentional outburst by which Brezhnev had wanted to demonstrate the Soviet annoyance with the new trends in Daoud's domestic and external policies. He did it in a manner that he knew would be most displeasing to Daoud, by telling him to deal with an internal matter according to Russian wishes. But if he had wanted at the same time to chide and embarrass Daoud, his ploy had backfired pitifully, for he had received a formidable dressing down from the Afghan president in front of his peers and most of his close associates.[74]

The President's growing friendship with the Shah and Sadat could well confirm the Kremlin's worst fears about his motivation, especially if taken together with Daoud's structural changes in the Afghan government and continuous reprisals against *Parchamis* and *Khalqis*.[75] In January 1977, Daoud promulgated a new constitution. It prescribed a strong presidency and a one-party system; the National Revolutionary Party (*Hezb-e Enqelab-e Melli*), or NRP, was to be led by Daoud himself and he was elected as President for a six-year term by the *Loya Jirgah* that he had convened. Establishment of the NRP as the only legal party left no legal room for the communists; henceforth, their break with Daoud became final: *Parcham* rejected the new constitution and refused to join NRP,[76] and the *Khalq* was of course never part of Daoud's establishment.

Daoud immediately embarked on an extensive purge of *Parchamis* and *Khalqis*, prompting both factions to come out in public defiance of Daoud's rule; this led to further escalation of anti-PDPA purges in December 1977.[77] In David Chaffetz's words, the new spiral of persecution, 'more far-reaching and final in its intent than that of 1975, gave the *Khalq* and the *Parcham* the choice of liquidation or revolution'.[78]

When it became clear, probably through Jalalar, that Daoud planned to extend the purge of communists to the armed forces, Moscow could foresee only the likelihood of permanently losing whatever mechanisms of control it had thus far secured in Afghanistan. Two options were open to the Soviet leadership: either to accept a serious setback in Afghanistan and its consequences, particularly a dramatic shift in the regional balance of power, or to pre-empt it. There were several broader considerations that may have nudged Moscow towards the latter option. They related to the Brezhnev leadership's regional and global policy objectives.

Although pursuing détente in its relations with the West, especially the USA, the word 'détente' meant different things to the Kremlin and Washington. Whereas the USA construed it as mutual understanding and accommodation, based on the pre-1970s global status quo, Moscow interpreted it as a means of peaceful competition, especially with regard to Soviet relations with the First World, a quiet form of class struggle, which would secure the Soviet Union's position as a world power, if not the superior then at least the equal of the USA.[79]

In this context, acceptance of Daoud's exercises in Afghanistan could have meant a serious loss for the Soviet Union's growing influence in the Third World. By the mid 1970s, the Middle Eastern region had gained additional economic and strategic value, by virtue of OPEC's success in manipulating the international petroleum market and maximising producers' control over their oil resources and prices. The triumph of oil-rich states in West Asia created an environment that did not reduce but, on the contrary, encouraged more active involvement in the region by the Soviets' adversaries. It enabled many regional nations, led by Iran, to undertake ambitious pro-western programmes of social, economic and military modernisation; and this in turn provided expanding markets for the West, headed by the USA, to capture for both economic and strategic reasons. Given that the region was, as it still is today, riddled with seeds of ethnic, political and social instability and of intra-state conflicts, this confronted Moscow with considerable uncertainties over policy choices. The situation was further complicated by the seizure of power in July 1977 in Pakistan by an Islamic-oriented military regime under General Zia ul-Haq.[80] Under such circumstances, the Soviets could scarcely welcome Daoud's activities.

The PDPA Coup

As a result, in mid 1977, *Parcham* and *Khalq* found it imperative to reunite into their original People's Democratic Party of Afghanistan (PDPA) against their common enemy, Daoud.[81] From then on, they waged an active campaign against Daoud in the armed forces and the public arena and mobilised their resources, with the knowledge and help of Soviet advisors, to destabilise Daoud's regime. This led eventually to the PDPA's bloody but successful coup of 27 April 1978 and the subsequent elimination of Daoud and almost his entire family and network of senior colleagues. The events which triggered the communist takeover were the assassination of Mir Akbar Khaibar, one of the PDPA's leaders, on 17 April 1978; a massive demonstration on 19 April at his funeral; and the arrest by Daoud's police of seven PDPA Politburo members on 25 April.[82] Hafizullah Amin, the only PDPA ranking leader to escape arrest, and therefore able to activate PDPA supporters in the armed forces, claimed that the coup was entirely engineered by him and executed mainly by his supporters in the armed forces, albeit some two years ahead of plan.[83]

Many senior Afghan officials of the time widely believe that the Soviets had worked hard to change the course of Afghan politics in their favour and that they had a direct hand in the PDPA coup.[84] However, the Soviets' direct involvement in the coup remains a rather murky issue. Although some authors speculate that Moscow had prior knowledge of the coup, and may even have instigated it,[85] there is no documentary evidence to this effect. Georgii Kornienko, then First Deputy Minister of Foreign Affairs of the USSR, has reminisced that policy-makers in Moscow received news of the coup from Reuters, and added:

> There was also no advance intelligence from our special service agency. Even the names of the leaders who came to power – Taraki, Karmal, Amin and others meant nothing to Gromyko [Soviet Foreign Minister], or to other members of the Soviet leadership. They were only familiar to experts in the CPSU's Central Committee's International Department and to the KGB. At one time the PDPA leader, Taraki, in a conversation with me admitted that they had an opportunity to notify Soviet representatives in Kabul but abstained from doing so, fearing that Moscow would try to dissuade the PDPA leadership from a military takeover.[86]

Even more precarious are the assertions that Soviet personnel took part in combat engagements which claimed up to 2,000 lives in Kabul.[87] Lieutenant-General L.I. Gorelov, who headed the group of Soviet military advisors between 1975 and 1979, learned about the rebellion when 30 Soviet officers came under fire from Aslam Watanjar, who headed a Tank Brigade near Kabul, in the Ministry of Defence building.[88] No less an authority than Zbigniew Brzezinski, President Carter's national security advisor, commented that 'It was an internal coup, there was no evidence of Soviet involvement.'[89] While the removal of Daoud was to the Soviet Union's advantage, the installation of a PDPA or more specifically *Khalqi*-dominated government in Afghanistan was hardly the preferred choice of the CPSU International Department: 'In this sense, the observation may be justified that the coup had dumped an obviously Moscow-leaning government into their laps, ready or not.'[90] The best one can conclude is that the Soviet Embassy may have been behind the reunification of the *Parchamis* and *Khalqis* within the PDPA and aware of the projected PDPA plot, but its timing and leadership were not entirely with their grand design.

Daoud's Blunders

The dramatic demise of Daoud's rule was ultimately rooted in internal developments in Afghanistan. On the most general level, Daoud repeated Amanullah's mistake of pushing through changes without first building and maintaining a potent reform coalition. Although his policies might have been beneficial to the national bourgeoisie and, in the long run, the peasantry, these were not the actors a ruler should count on for survival in Afghanistan. Daoud alienated the Islamic establishment – one of the mainstays of the traditional society – and lost his hold over the burgeoning state bureaucracy and the army, the vital mechanisms of social control, to the leftists. His most glaring mistake was the abolition of the monarchy – one of the few symbols and forces that cut across Afghan society and contributed to the semblance of cohesion of the national elite. In William Maley's characterisation, 'The coup of April 1978 was fundamentally the product of the emergence of severe division within the national elite.'[91]

Daoud had a vision of a nationalist, modern, secular, neutral Afghanistan. His tragedy was that he failed to codify his programme in a way acceptable to the predominantly traditional and Islamic society: 'Essentially, his objectives amounted to no more than a loose set of self-serving principles and did not have the cultural legitimacy to make them acceptable to more than those who found their fortunes tied to Daoud's.'[92] As Daoud's attempts at mobilising mass public support failed, he gradually developed a siege mentality and started to demonstrate a pathological style of leadership.

This manifested itself in several ways. The first was related to his own autocratic and selfish nature. He neither believed in sharing power with anyone, let alone the communists, nor in allowing even legal opposition. For this very reason, he was initially happy to concur with his *Parchami* collaborators and move brutally against the *Sho'la-ye Jawed* and Islamists. Eventually people began to be seconded to important positions for no other reason than their loyalty to Daoud. Many of them proved poorly educated and incompetent. For example, he created a vice-presidential post, only to offer it to Sayyed Abdul-Ilah, an 'adopted son' and son of one of his former loyal ministers, of whom he had been very fond during his premiership. In his early thirties, Abdul-Ilah had little political and administrative experience and was largely ignorant of foreign policy issues.

Similarly, the man who came to handle foreign affairs as Deputy Foreign Minister, Waheed Abdullah, neither understood the sensitivity needed for the conduct of Afghanistan's foreign relations, nor achieved much beyond self-gratification. When the Preparatory Session for a non-aligned summit was to be held in New Delhi, shortly before Daoud was overthrown, Waheed Abdullah, in the presence of many diplomats, expressed opposition to membership in the non-aligned movement of Cuba, one of Moscow's key allies, whose capital, Havana, was eventually selected as the venue for the non-aligned summit. Furthermore, when Daoud finally found the burdens of office too much and relinquished the portfolio of Defence Minister, he appointed Lieutenant-General Ghulam Haidar Rasuli, a Mohammadzai, to that post. Rasuli proved so unaware of the situation that he 'innocently' even allowed a battalion commander of the 4th Armoured Brigade, Major Aslam Watanjar, a committed communist who, together with Abdul Qader, played a central role in toppling the Daoud regime, to penetrate his household and steal all military secrets from him. He also desperately lacked influence with the armed forces and in the end could not raise enough troops to resist the coup.[93] Daoud's mistrust of members of his own Cabinet went so far that in the last months of his rule no minister was allowed to authorise expenditure of more than 5,000 afghanis ($70).[94]

Second, Daoud underestimated the capability of the communists and overestimated the vitality of his personal relationship with the Kremlin. He most probably contrasted the communists' lack of popular support with what he saw as his own position as ruler; and concluded that neither would the communists have the capacity to bid for power, nor would the Soviets support them in such a venture. Thus he became a prisoner of his own beliefs and rhetoric, as is frequently the case with autocrats, and overlooked two things. One was that, although very limited in number, the *Parchamis* and *Khalqis* had, over the years, especially during the first two years of Daoud's own rule (when the *Parchamis* had gained a free hand in the government and the *Khalqis* were left unchecked to recruit inside the army), succeeded in placing members and sympathisers in important positions in the state agencies.[95] They had penetrated Daoud's secret police, which by and large proved inefficient in identifying even those communists who remained in Daoud's personal company to the last day of his rule. The other was that his attractiveness to the Soviets was impermanent. Why Daoud thought the Soviets would let him achieve what they had not wished his predecessors to accomplish remains profoundly puzzling. One can only conclude that Daoud never fully understood the wider regional concerns underpinning the Soviets economic-military aid and political support to Afghanistan. He failed to realise that the Soviets by then were not the same as those who had had dealings with Nasser in Egypt.

Third, and in a similar vein, Daoud's strategy to achieve more independence of action was badly conceived and implemented. He seemingly failed to foresee the implications of his decision to turn for aid at first to the Shah and, later, also to Sadat. The Soviets could interpret this only as a dangerous step to steer Afghanistan away from the USSR and ally it with the camp of 'reaction'.

In the final analysis, Daoud's dynastical antagonisms, poor judgment and faulty personnel policies go a long way towards explaining not only his own destruction, but also the tragedy which beset Afghanistan following his overthrow. Had Daoud been more prudent and perceptive, the incompetent PDPA would not have been in a position to bid successfully for power and thus open the way for the subsequent Soviet invasion of Afghanistan, and another bloody chapter in Afghan history.

8

Communist Rule, the Soviet Invasion and Resistance

THE LIQUIDATION OF DAOUD'S regime and its replacement by the pro-Soviet PDPA Marxist-Leninist government finally brought to an end the Mohammadzai rule and therefore the polygamic-based conflicts within the royal family that had bedevilled Afghan politics in one form or another for nearly two centuries. However, this did little to provide the Afghans with a breathing space. It provided unprecedented stimuli for ideological extremism and frictions to become a dominant force in Afghan politics, and enhanced the basis for major power intervention and rivalry in Afghanistan.

> [The new] regime was not in a position to exploit the traditional legitimacy that had helped sustain its predecessors, and in the context of its grossly overambitious programme of social transformation... it was obliged increasingly to resort to coercion to maintain its position.[1]

For the first time since the reign of Abdur Rahman Khan, violence emerged as the determining factor in state-society relations. The new masters of Kabul had to resort to the patronage of a single foreign power in order to subordinate the recalcitrant microsocieties. However, the 'fraternal ties' with a 'great and selfless northern neighbour' – the USSR[2] – turned out to be insufficient to guarantee success and ultimately led to innumerable victims, dramatic shifts in the make-up of Afghan society and the disintegration of Afghanistan as a governable sovereign state. The PDPA's internal dynamics (redolent of the Mohammadzai 'Royal Dualism'), the mainly ideologically unified Islamic resistance to communist rule, the peculiar nature of Soviet support and the active involvement of other extraneous actors contributed to this outcome.

The PDPA Policies

The PDPA's assumption of power, promptly recognised by Moscow, was opportunistic and premature, and it fell desperately short of Moscow's ideal of a victorious revolutionary takeover. The party lacked legitimacy, administrative capability and popular support. While a great majority of Afghans knew no more about Marxism-Leninism than the fact that it was a 'Godless' ideology and therefore repugnant to Islam, by April 1978, the PDPA's membership, mostly teachers, army officers and civil servants, was scarcely more than 11,000 to 12,000.[3] It was not well equipped to rule the predominantly Muslim, tribal and determinedly independent and nationalistic Afghans, especially given Afghanistan's permeable borders with the non-communist world.

After welcoming the new regime, Moscow rapidly committed itself to its survival, not out of ideological proximity between the CPSU and PDPA, but rather for purely pragmatic considerations. As the Soviet Ambassador to Kabul, Aleksandr Puzanov, summarised in a confidential missive dated 5 May 1978, the new government would likely be 'more sympathetic towards the Soviet Union, further consolidating and strengthening our position in Afghanistan'.[4]

Nonetheless, as could have been expected, the PDPA rapidly tore itself to pieces in factional fighting, with the *Khalqi* leaders – Taraki and Amin – gaining ascendancy in the new supreme organ of power, the Revolutionary Council of the Democratic Republic of Afghanistan. Although the new government formed at the Council's meeting on 30 April 1978 included several *Parchamis*, including Babrak Karmal as Vice President to Taraki, they were denied real authority.[5] By the summer of 1978, when Taraki had consolidated his position as the PDPA's General Secretary and President, and Amin had emerged as the regime's 'strongman', occupying the posts of Deputy Prime Minister and Foreign Minister, hundreds of *Parcham* members and sympathisers were arrested and purged or executed on charges of counter-revolutionary activities.[6] By the end of the year, the *Khalq*'s dominating position in all the country's governing bodies had become unquestionable. (See Table 8.1)

Furthermore, the ill-conceived *Khalqi* policies provoked nationwide civil and armed resistance to 'Godless communism'. Three decrees, issued by the Revolutionary Council between July and November 1978, proved particularly harmful to the new regime's ability to gain credibility. Decree No. 6 aimed at the 'liquidation of usury' in agricultural communities and establishment of production cooperatives. Decree No. 7 imposed age restrictions on marriage, curtailed polygamy, and abolished *mahr* (dowry).

Table 8.1 Composition of Supreme Organs of Power of the Democratic
          Republic of Afghanistan, end 1978

Decision-Making Body	Total Membership	*Khalq*	*Parcham*
Politburo of the PDPA			
Central Committee	7	7	–
PDPA Central Committee	36	30	6
Revolutionary Council	45	39	6
Government	17	14	3
Total	105	90	15

Source: A.A. Liakhovskii and V.M. Zabrodin, *Tainy afganskoi voiny*.

Government census-takers, led by inexperienced and dogmatic party
functionaries, poured into villages asking questions about women's status,
filling out forms with their names and ages, and otherwise infringing upon
family matters of the utmost intimacy: 'Country people ended up believing
that the communists were plotting to turn women into communal property!'[7]
Finally, Decree No. 8 dealt with large-scale land reform based on confiscation
and redistribution of parcels in excess of 30 *jaribs* (12.6 hectares), which
proved to be more symbolic than substantive in its importance. By mid 1979
some 250,000 hectares of land had been distributed amongst 296,000 of the
poorest families,[8] with each receiving land about the size of a large garden
rather than a small farm, therefore not enough to provide food or income.

This campaign hardly alleviated land starvation, but antagonised all classes
of the peasantry. The poorest elements were given allotments which could
not be sold, divided, bequeathed, mortgaged or otherwise alienated, and,
moreover, water supply arrangements were not changed; eventually they
began refusing to accept allotments and even returning them to their previous
owners.[9] The middle strata suffered from a lack of capital in the wake of the
moneylenders' expulsion and the state's failure to provide credits, seeds and
machinery. Large landowners, amongst whom were higher-ranking members
of the officer corps, state bureaucracy and religious establishment, received
no compensation for the lost land. In 1986, Dr Najibullah, who was soon to
be appointed *Parchami* General Secretary of the PDPA, castigated Taraki's
excessive radicalism:

> Such a vital issue as land and water we tried to resolve by issuing abstract
> documents, directing a stream of papers on peasants' heads. We started
> the agrarian reform from the wrong end, destroying the established
> production relations, disregarding national customs, traditions and mores.[10]

The dislocation caused by the ill-conceived reforms was exacerbated by the leadership style of Hafizullah Amin, who had rapidly become the most powerful actor within the *Khalqi* regime. In July 1978, while the *Parchamis* were virtually extirpated from the high echelons of power, and thousands of non-communists were gaoled in Pol-e Charkhi prison, he added the General Secretaryship of the PDPA Central Committee Secretariat to his other portfolios. Like Stalin half a century previously, Amin used control over the party apparatus to consolidate his own power base. During the Second World War, Stalin used Russian chauvinism as part of his state-legitimating ideology, and Amin followed suit, promoting the interests of the Pashtun ethnic group, with an emphasis on its Ghilzai elements, over all others.

In the words of Abdul Qarim Misaq, a Hazara and *Khalqi* Minister of Finance between May 1978 and December 1979:

> Amin was a communist. But he was a special sort of communist, like Stalin, he loved Stalin very much and tried to emulate him. He was also a Pashtun nationalist. He did everything to inflate his own personality cult; moreover, he desired fame not just inside Afghanistan but throughout the world. His ambitions truly knew no limits.[11]

It is no coincidence that the first instances of organised mass resistance to PDPA policies occurred in October 1978 in Nuristan in north-eastern Afghanistan, in reaction to an influx of Pashtun cadres and security forces.[12] Within months, people had started to rise up in other regions, Pashtun and non-Pashtun alike, led by the mullahs or local religious leaders. The apathy with which most of the populace treated the April coup quickly gave way to overt resistance to the *Khalqi* regime.

Soviet Involvement

It is doubtful whether PDPA rule could have been sustained for long without external support. The Soviet leadership did not hesitate to accord full assistance to the Taraki-Amin government, anti-*Parcham* purges notwithstanding, and encouraged its satellites to do the same. Within six months of the coup, 30 agreements, worth more than US$14 billion, had been concluded between the USSR and Afghanistan, complemented by 25 agreements with other COMECON states.[13] Immediately after the coup, Soviet civilian and military advisors flooded into Afghanistan. A high-ranking PDPA official at the time has recalled with bitter irony:

> So, a meeting of the Council of Ministers begins. We are taking seats around the table. Each minister has arrived with his own [Soviet] adviser.

The meeting goes on, the discussion ignites, and gradually the advisers are moving closer and closer to the table, consequently, our ministers are pushed away, and finally there are only advisers left at the table, arguing violently amongst themselves.[14]

The number of Soviet military advisors increased especially fast, to 700 by June and 2,000 by November 1979.[15] They were placed in every army unit from battalion upwards and took an active part in planning and implementing security and military operations. The PDPA regime's growing reliance on the USSR found reflection in a Treaty of Friendship and Cooperation, signed by Brezhnev and Taraki on 5 December 1978.

This document was conceived to complement the Afghan-Soviet Treaty of 1921. A clause in Article 4 paved the way for the Soviets to intervene, militarily if necessary, 'to guarantee security, independence and territorial unity' of Afghanistan on request and after consultations with its legitimate government.[16] Throughout 1979, the *Khalqi* regime experienced growing pressure from at least three directions. First, uncoordinated low-level armed resistance was on the rise in 24 out of the 28 provinces of Afghanistan.[17] Second, an organised Islamic opposition, which later became known under the generic name of Mujahideen, was busy recruiting guerrilla fighters from the 400,000 refugees in Pakistan and 60,000 displaced Afghans in Iran, as well as creating permanent operation bases inside the country (particularly in Nuristan, Hazarajat and Badakhshan).[18] Third, the PDPA leadership continued to be plagued by internecine struggles, with *Parchamis* trying to stage a comeback, while Taraki and Amin played a deadly game of political musical chairs. The Afghan army was in disarray and could conduct only limited defensive operations. In March 1979, the entire 17th Infantry Division stationed in Herat rebelled, and in the mayhem that followed dozens of Soviet citizens, advisors and members of their families, were slaughtered. The alarming developments in Afghanistan prompted lengthy debates in the Soviet Politburo during 17 to 19 March, which resulted in vastly increased shipments of military hardware, wheat and other strategic commodities to prop up the regime in Kabul.[19]

However, the *Khalqis* wanted more. Taraki, who visited Moscow on 20 March 1979, raised the question of despatching regular Soviet troops to Afghanistan. Brezhnev refused politely but firmly.[20] Still, between April and December 1979, the PDPA leaders, according to Soviet sources, approached Moscow for direct combat support approximately 20 times.[21] The Kremlin was invariably reluctant to respond positively: it appeared aware of the wider implications of deeper involvement in Afghanistan, wishing to avoid the possibility of getting bogged down in a Vietnam-type situation. This was made clear in a top-secret report circulated amongst Politburo members on 1 April 1979. Its authors – Foreign Minister A. Gromyko, KGB Chairman Iu. Andropov, Defence Minister D. Ustinov, Head of the CPSU CC International Department B. Ponomarev – claimed that:

> In view of the predominantly internal essence of the anti-government uprisings in Afghanistan, participation of Soviet troops in their suppression would, on the one hand, seriously damage the international prestige of the USSR and set the process of détente a long way back; and, on the other hand, disclose the weakness of Taraki's government and encourage counter-revolutionary forces inside and outside Afghanistan to step up anti-government activities.[22]

Yet, in December 1979, the same Soviet officials ostensibly supported the idea of invading Afghanistan. This change of heart was conditioned mainly by domestic developments in Afghanistan.

Hafizullah Amin continued his rise to power. He became Prime Minister in March 1979, and assumed control over Defence in July. As his powers grew, so apparently did his craving for personal dictatorship. Taraki, who had turned 62 (although he himself was not aware of his birthday until Amin staged a birthday party for him) and had problems with alcohol abuse, was turning into a mere figurehead. Amin was now in a position to implement his vision of the revolutionary process based on terror: 'We have 10,000 feudals. We shall destroy them, and the question will be resolved. The Afghans recognise only crude force.'[23] By September 1979, the notorious Pol-e Charkhi prison in Kabul was overflowing with 12,000 political prisoners, and firing squads had to work hard by night to rid Amin of his opponents and clear space for more victims.[24] The *Parchamis* (not including their leaders, who had been at first dispatched as ambassadors abroad and then shortly thereafter fired on embezzlement charges, forcing them to seek protection in Moscow), and Taraki's associates formed part of the gruesome grist for Amin's repressive machine. Six hundred *Parchamis* were arrested in Kabul in September–October 1979.[25] In early September, Amin decided to eliminate the remaining Taraki supporters from the Cabinet: Minister of Interior Aslam Watanjar, Minister of Tribal Frontiers Sher Jan Mazduryar, Minister of Communications Sayyed Mohammad Gulabzoy, and head of the security service (AGSA) Asadullah Sarwari. When these ministers tried to persuade Taraki to mount a counter-attack, he refused and reportedly told Gulabzoy: 'Son, I have protected Amin all my life, and I was beaten on the hands for that all the time. Look at my hands, they are swollen from beating...

Remember, my friend, for the sake of my salvation I will not kill a fly.'[26]

However, shortly after Amin's move against Cabinet supporters of Taraki, the latter, on his way back from a non-aligned summit in Havana, stopped in Moscow for a meeting with Brezhnev. He agreed with the Soviet leader that the time had come to broaden his power base by reincorporating the *Parchami* leaders into the PDPA leadership, bringing Karmal into the fold at the expense of Amin. But since Amin had one of his men in Taraki's entourage, word of the agreement had been leaked to him by the time Taraki returned to Kabul, allowing Amin to mount a counter-plot. Amin first arrested Mazduryar, whose three colleagues found asylum at the Soviet Embassy and were evacuated from the country; then three days later, on 14 September, with the support of the Chief of General Staff, Mohammad Yaqub,[27] he deposed Taraki, in a Cabinet shoot-out in the presence of the Soviet Ambassador, and assumed the presidency. A secret PDPA document circulated on 16 September 1979 gave the following reasons behind the coup:

> Comrade Taraki's cult of personality was the main obstacle in the way of accelerated advancement and intensified development. This cult of personality... overshadowed all ideological and organisational principles of our party. Comrade Taraki resorted to conspiracies and anti-party groupings against the Politbureau and all party organs, especially against Comrade Hafizullah Amin.[28]

Taraki was put under house arrest and then strangled on 8 October 1979.[29] While he was still alive, a grave was dug for him at Qul-e Abchakan cemetery, and a shroud prepared; Amin's story that Taraki had died of natural causes therefore convinced nobody.

This murder outraged Brezhnev, who had come to view Taraki as a close personal friend.[30] More significantly, Moscow was highly doubtful of Amin's methods of government and of his ability to keep a friendly regime afloat. Yet for a while the Kremlin stuck with *Khalq* and its new leader. The Politburo at a meeting on 31 October 1979 resolved to continue rendering Afghanistan all-round economic and military assistance and at the same time:

> to continue active work with Amin and with all the present leadership of PDPA and DRA [Democratic Republic of Afghanistan] so that Amin will have no ground to think that we do not trust him and do not want to do anything with him. To use contacts with Amin for exerting corresponding influence on him and at the same time finding out his true intentions.[31]

Amin's 'true intentions' became transparent soon enough: 'Like Daoud, Amin was more ambitious than he was loyal to Moscow. The armed forces were breaking up and insurgents were steadily taking over provincial areas. Counter-revolution was in the air.'[32] His leadership style was based on the quest for unlimited personal power and Pashtun chauvinism veiled in Marxist demagoguery. He quickly turned government, in the old Afghan tradition, into a family business, appointing his brother to oversee the four northern provinces, his nephew and son-in-law as security chief, and scores of other relatives and cronies to other influential and lucrative positions. He was determined to stay in power at all costs, resorting to genocide, if necessary. Amin's close associate, the *Khalqi* commandant of Pol-e Charkhi prison, Sayid Abdullah, was quoted as saying that 'Two million citizens loyal to the Revolution [that is, Amin] are enough.'[33]

The Soviet Invasion

In December 1979, the *Khalqi* regime's prospects seemed bleak. The government had virtually lost control over the countryside to the Mujahideen and their supporters. Nearly half the army had deserted; many servicemen had joined the resistance with their weapons and ammunition.[34] The 40,000 Mujahideen operating in Afghanistan from bases in Pakistan almost equalled the combat-ready troops at Kabul's disposal.[35] Soviet sources claim that Amin kept on asking for Soviet troops to prop up his foundering authority.[36] While prompting Amin to make overtures to some Mujahideen leaders, especially Gulbuddin Hekmatyar, and their American and Pakistani backers,[37] this confronted the Soviet leadership essentially with two policy options: either to send troops into Afghanistan to salvage the communist regime, and therefore the mechanisms of Soviet control and foundations of influence in the country; or to let an Islamic regime take over Afghanistan. It opted for the former.

On 27 December 1979, Amin invited members of the PDPA Politburo to a dinner, during which he triumphantly declared:

> Soviet divisions are on their way here. I've always told you that the great neighbour would not leave us alone. Everything is going fine. I am constantly speaking with Comrade Gromyko over the phone, and we are discussing one question: what is the best way to formulate the news about Soviet military help to us for the world.[38]

Indeed, the Soviet 40th Army, 75,000 men with aviation, tanks and artillery, had begun its two-pronged march into Afghanistan. However, as the *Khalqi* leadership belatedly realised, the Soviet troops did not come to salvage it: 'Their objective was simple enough – to replace the regime of Hafizullah Amin with one headed by Babrak Karmal – a regime designed to secure broader support from the people and the party.'[39] Shortly before the intervention, Amin was advised by Soviet security officers to change his residence from the centrally located Arg palace to a refurbished compound of Dar ul-Amman on the edge of Kabul's suburbs for 'safety reasons'. In reality, this relocation enabled them to control the President's moves, and made preparations for his physical elimination easier.

There is a point of dispute among scholars as to whether the Soviet action amounted to an invasion or intervention. According to some, the Soviet forces did not 'invade' Afghanistan, but 'intervened' at the invitation of the then head of both state and government, Hafizullah Amin. Yossef Bodansky has argued that initially the direct involvement of Soviet troops in Afghanistan was an escalation of Moscow's previous policies rather than an invasion with the aim of achieving direct and complete control over the country:

> At the time, the Soviets considered the invasion to be merely a further development of a predetermined policy. They expected the Afghan Army to go over to the offensive, while the insurgents would be reluctant to take on such odds. Soviet troops were supposed only to provide the initial stiffener and were therefore organised for a brief stay of a few months among a friendly and safe population which would welcome the new leadership they brought in.[40]

However, since the PDPA's regime lacked any kind of legitimacy from the start and since among the Soviets' first acts after their arrival was to kill Amin and install a government of their own choice under Babrak Karmal, the world widely and appropriately recognised the Soviet action as an 'invasion'. It is in relation to this fact and the Soviets' post-entry behaviour that the Soviet action was nothing less than an invasion.

Whereas, at the time of the April 1978 coup, Moscow was committed to providing diplomatic support and economic and technical assistance to the new regime, after signing the December 1978 Treaty it had to resort to massive deliveries of military hardware to keep the *Khalqi* government running and, throughout 1979, the Soviets had been growing increasingly frustrated with faction fighting in the PDPA, and Amin's recalcitrance and extremism. When, despite his absolute dependence on the Kremlin's support, Amin proved unreliable, it was only a matter of time before he would be replaced. The newly appointed Soviet Ambassador, Fikrat Tabeev, thus assessed the situation in December 1979:

> There was a real danger of a counter-revolutionary coup under the banner of Islamic fundamentalists. They had accumulated great strength by then. On the contrary, Kabul had been weakened. The army after Amin's purges

and reprisals was decapitated. The clergy had been alienated. The peasants were against [the regime]. So were the tribes, who had suffered from Amin. There were just a handful of sycophants left around Amin who, like parrots, repeated after him various idiocies about 'building socialism' and 'the dictatorship of the proletariat'. The so-called 'Kunar grouping' of the insurgents created in the east was capable of capturing Kabul within 24 hours.[41]

The selection of Babrak Karmal and the *Parchamis* as the backbone of the new government was natural for Moscow. As discussed in Chapter 6, they traditionally had close ties with the KGB, and it was under Iurii Andropov's pressure that the Politburo decided to switch support to the malleable, moderate and relatively liberal *Parchamis* in autumn 1979.[42] Four former members of the PDPA Central Committee[43] were put under protection (and supervision) of the KGB 'Alfa' group, which smuggled them into Afghanistan on 14 December 1979, and orchestrated their instalment in Kabul a fortnight later.[44] Hafizullah Amin was killed by Soviet special forces on the evening of 27 December 1979.[45]

In addition to internal Afghan developments, a number of other factors entered the Kremlin's calculation in support of invasion. They ranged from an Islamic resurgence in the region, with the advent of Ayatollah Khomeini's Islamic radicalism in Iran and of Zia ul-Haq's reassertive Islamist policies in Pakistan, and the growing ties between Islamabad and Beijing, which had rejected the PDPA regime from the outset, to the US naval build-up in the Persian Gulf with the 'Iranian hostage crisis', the flourishing Sino-US rapprochement, Washington's decision in 1979 to increase its military spending and NATO's decision to deploy Pershing II missiles in Western Europe.[46] If not to the Soviet military, at least in the minds of certain senior Politburo members who were more swayed by their conservative leanings and personal impulses, all these factors raised Brezhnev's threat perception.

Washington, of course, was well informed of these developments. President Carter had been warned by his national security advisor, Zbigniew Brzezinski, as early as March 1979 about the Soviets' 'creeping intervention in Afghanistan', and the US administration soon after began generating plans for covert support to the Afghan insurgents. However, the White House continued to pay little more than lip service to Afghanistan's problems. This was partly because the whole Afghan question had previously been delegated under the 'Nixon Doctrine' to the Shah of Iran, who had by now been overthrown and replaced by Khomeini's anit-American Islamic regime; and partly because of a conflict between Brzezinski and Secretary of State Cyrus Vance. In contrast to Brzezinski's espousal of a 'Soviet Vietnam', the State Department constantly urged President Carter to avoid a quarrel with the

Soviet Union, for fear that Congress might not ratify the second Strategic Arms Limitation Treaty (SALT II).[47] The killing of the American ambassador to Afghanistan, Adolph Dubs, in a shoot-out between the Afghan anti-terrorist squad and his kidnappers in Kabul on 14 February 1979, had already clouded Vance's attitude towards Afghanistan, resulting in further downgrading of bilateral relations.[48]

The US willingness to remain once again insensitive and indifferent over Afghanistan proved fatal. When finally the Brezhnev leadership decided on invasion, it appeared to expect no major international impediment to its action. In sharp contradistinction to the concurrent crisis in Poland, the Carter administration never issued a *public* warning to Moscow about the possible repercussions of direct Soviet intervention in Afghanistan. One can only speculate on Brezhnev's reaction, had he received a list of American punitive sanctions before the invasion: 'Who knows, perhaps it would even have made him look for other ways of solving his problems in Afghanistan'.[49] However, Brzezinski has indicated that he wanted to lure Moscow into the Afghanistan adventure as part of a Cold War strategy to humiliate the Soviets and return to them what they had given the Americans in the Vietnam war.[50]

In retrospect and in the context of subsequent Soviet actions, two facets of the invasion need to be reiterated. First, it followed a long and complex period of growing Soviet involvement in Afghanistan. In shaping this background, unforeseeable political developments in Afghanistan, and the frequently naïve and short-sighted actions of successive Afghan leaders, played as much a part as did Soviet perceptions and actions. However, changing regional and international circumstances, which reflected a continuous marked US indifference over Afghanistan, finally compounded by the emergence of Khomeini's Islamic regime in Iran and Zia ul-Haq's Islamic rule in Pakistan, provided specific challenges and opportunities for the Soviet Union. All this created a crisis in and over Afghanistan that led the Kremlin leaders to choose invasion as the best option in terms of their perceived interests.

Second, the underlying *urgent* objective of the invasion was to be *pre-emptive assertion*, not necessarily *outright expansion*. It was to pre-empt the imminent collapse of PDPA rule under Amin and its replacement with a (probably hostile) Islamic regime; and to secure the Soviet hold on its long-standing interests, investments and political initiatives in Afghanistan. It was also to maintain the credibility and status of the Soviet Union as a superpower in the face of what the aged, conservative Kremlin leaders may have regarded, rightly or wrongly, as both adverse and favourable developments in regional and global politics.

The US-Led Counter-Interventionist Strategy

The invasion, however, failed to achieve its central objective of consolidating the PDPA rule and making the party an effective ruling body. It caused, both directly and indirectly, horrendous losses and devastation for the Afghan people, involving, until mid 1988, 1.24 million killed and about five million (or nearly one third of the Afghan population) becoming refugees, with approximately three million in Pakistan and two million in Iran.[51] Yet it could not stamp out bloody factionalism within the PDPA.[52] Nor could it contain the outrage of the Afghan people, who became more determined than ever to support the Mujahideen, preventing the foreign interlopers and their surrogates from securing any more than the Kabul regime originally held when the invasion occurred.[53] Nor could Moscow hope to satisfy the world community by asserting, as when Soviet forces occupied Bukhara and Khiva more than five decades earlier, that a 'limited contingent' of Soviet forces had been dispatched 'at the request of the Afghan government' and would be withdrawn as soon as 'imperialist-backed' threats to Afghanistan's independence ceased.[54]

The invasion attracted massive international condemnation, complicating the Soviet Union's regional and international relations, and serving to blot Soviet prestige. Regional countries, particularly China and the Muslim states, headed by Pakistan, found it reprehensible, professing to be deeply concerned about the threat of Soviet expansionism;[55] and the West treated it as unacceptable and a serious breach of international order. Despite Brzezinski's quiet delight over the possibility of having an opportunity to humiliate the Soviets in Afghanistan, President Carter personally felt cheated and degraded by the Soviet action.[56] The US government now found it necessary and opportune to formulate an effective counter-interventionist strategy. At first it focused on a moderate response, involving mainly:

> the imposition of economic sanctions, the Olympic games boycott, the acrimony of US condemnations of the Soviet action, as well as increases in defence spending and attempts to create co-operative links with the regions affected, to improve America's ability to protect its interests more effectively.[57]

However, the USA soon escalated its response. Despite its reservations about Zia ul-Haq's dictatorship, Washington began a programme of massive economic and military aid to Pakistan as a frontline state and conduit for similar assistance and logistic support to the Afghan Islamic resistance forces, the Mujahideen.[58] As worldwide condemnation of the Soviet move gathered pace and the Muslim world, especially Saudi Arabia, Egypt and Iran, as well as China, denounced the Soviet action, the USA could press on with its counter-interventionist strategy with almost global immunity. The CIA was empowered to coordinate international delivery of arms to the main Sunni Mujahideen groups, which represented the majority of the Afghan people and had established their political headquarters in Pakistan. It immediately developed close links with Pakistan's military intelligence (ISI), which General Zia ul-Haq entrusted with Pakistan's Afghanistan and Kashmir policies from the beginning of the 1980s. Because the Afghan cause gained bipartisan support in the US Congress, President Ronald Reagan, who assumed the presidency in January 1981 with a strongly anti-Soviet agenda, was in a position to increase America's aid to both Pakistan and the Mujahideen dramatically. Although the anti-American Iranian Islamic regime, which had overthrown the pro-western government of Mohammad Reza Shah Pahlavi in the revolution of 1978–1979, could not cooperate with the US, Tehran also delivered assistance, mostly to the minority Shi'ite Mujahideen groups. Moreover, as the Soviet casualties mounted – as of March 1989 they numbered 13,833 dead and 49,985 wounded[59] – and as the war dragged on with no end in sight and the Soviet conscripts received poor treatment, the war also became increasingly unpopular with the Soviet public. Each day of military presence in Afghanistan cost the Soviet budget US$15 million – a luxury the country's stagnating economy could ill afford.[60] Although opposition from the Soviet public to the war was not comparable to the outcry in the USA against the Vietnam War, it was sufficient to cause serious concern to the authorities.

As a result, whatever political and military measures the Soviets undertook inside Afghanistan, and whatever international propaganda they waged in support of their Afghan campaign, they were ultimately unable to conceal the extent of their failure and the fact that they had entangled themselves in a very costly and unwinnable war. By July 1987, even President Najibullah – whom the Soviets had installed in place of Babrak Karmal 14 months earlier, due to Karmal's failure to fulfil Soviet expectations and his own achievements as head of the KGB-run Afghan secret police, KHAD – had admitted this. Adding to a previous statement that the Mujahideen controlled at least two thirds of the country, he proclaimed that 'if we continue our present policy, it will take another 20–30 years to normalise the situation. Instead of resolving all problems through military means, the urgent task should be the achievement of national reconciliation.'[61] The factors contributing to the regime's weakness included the continuation of bloody factionalism within the PDPA under Najibullah,[62] the limited fighting capacity of the Afghan armed forces,[63] and the Soviets' failure to win international legitimacy for their intervention. The situation was critical for Najibullah's survival, despite the divisions among the Mujahideen, and their inability to match Soviet organisational sophistication, equipment and firepower.[64]

The Soviets still appeared willing, at least until 1985, to press on with military pacification as the best means available to them. But two developments dramatically changed the situation. The first was a decisive augmentation of the Mujahideen's military capacity in mid 1986, when supplies of American Stinger and British Blowpipe missiles substantially strengthened their ability to counter Soviet airpower. As a result, they were able sharply to raise the cost of the war for the Soviets, shooting down almost one aircraft or helicopter daily and exerting greatly increased pressure on the main cities, most importantly Kabul.[65] The second emanated from the aged post-Brezhnev leadership's replacement in March 1985 by Mikhail Gorbachev. The Afghan crisis evidently fell more and more out of place in his scheme of priorities. Given his policies of *glasnost* ('openness'), *perestroika* ('reconstruction') and *demokratizatsiia* ('democratisation') to revitalise Soviet society, promote the USSR's international image as a constructive world power and, by the same token, make a break with the Brezhnev era, he simply could not let this crisis imperil his reformist efforts in other areas.[66]

The 'Geneva Accords' and Soviet Withdrawal

After Gorbachev's description of the crisis as a 'bleeding wound' on 25 February 1986,[67] the Gorbachev leadership decided in principle at the November Politburo meeting to cut Soviet losses and find a way out of the Afghan problem. Gorbachev launched a vigorous campaign to achieve this objective, premised on accomplishing three things. The first was to remove the Soviet forces in a way that could be presented as an 'honourable' withdrawal, in order to avoid any conservative backlash. This meant, however, that he should procure whatever was needed to replace direct Soviet combat involvement to ensure the PDPA regime's survival – most significantly abandonment of the resistance by its regional and western supporters. The second was to achieve the first objective in conjunction with, not in isolation from, his international diplomacy. He felt that he needed American cooperation, and through it Pakistan's concurrence, for the type of face-saving he sought. The third objective was to shift the blame for the Afghan fiasco onto the Brezhnev leadership, with a view eventually to declaring it a 'mistake'.[68] Withdrawal would have to be achieved within the broader framework of changes in the Soviet domestic environment.[69]

Gorbachev initiated a series of diplomatic offensives to accelerate the process of UN-sponsored indirect Geneva 'peace talks', which had been staged fitfully since mid 1982 between the PDPA regime and the Pakistan government, endorsed by both Moscow and Washington.[70] His efforts, coordinated with Moscow's initiatives at a global level, finally paid off on 14 April 1988, when the PDPA regime and Pakistan signed the Afghan Geneva Accords, with the USSR and USA as co-guarantors.[71] The Accords involved four elements: a non-interference agreement between Pakistan and Afghanistan – something the PDPA and Soviets had wanted from the beginning; Soviet commitment to withdraw its troops within ten months, by 15 February 1989; the voluntary and safe repatriation of the Afghan refugees in Pakistan, but not necessarily those in Iran; and guarantees of the Accords by the USA and USSR.[72]

The Accords, to the negotiation of which the Mujahideen had never been a party, and which they rejected as a 'fraud' and totally unacceptable,[73] were signed in conformity more with what the Soviet Union wanted than with what was needed to produce a viable settlement of the Afghanistan problem. Under the Accords, in return for a mere withdrawal of their uniformed troops, the Soviets were permitted to maintain as much direct non-combat support for the PDPA regime as they deemed necessary. Similarly, they were not required to abrogate their past treaties with Afghanistan, most importantly the 1978 Treaty, nor to sever the organic links they had forged with the PDPA.

In short, the Accords provided little comfort for the opposition. They went much too far towards meeting Soviet needs. It was apparently hoped that the resistance would settle for a subordinate role with the PDPA regime as part of a Soviet-PDPA orchestrated policy of 'national reconciliation'.[74] Failing this obviously unacceptable 'option', they were expected to take comfort from a unilateral American declaration that Washington would continue its arms supply to the Mujahideen for as long as Moscow continued to do the same for the regime. As such, the Accords did not provide for a ceasefire, let alone peace. They were designed simply to enable the Soviet Union to end its humiliating military involvement by an ostensibly 'honourable' withdrawal. Moscow intended them to *Afghanise* the war, retaining sufficient leverage to maintain Soviet interests.

In Afghanising the war, the Soviets adopted a two-fold strategy. One dimension was to do everything possible to unify the PDPA under Najibullah. Another was to engage in an accelerated scheme to strengthen the PDPA's military capability. The Soviet Union helped not only in setting up an elite Presidential Guard under Najibullah's direct command, and tightening the efficiency of the regime's brutal secret police and the special militia of Sarandoy,[75] but also in supplying the regime with three to four times more weapons than its standing army required.[76] Some of the arms supplied were among the most sophisticated in the Soviet inventory, including MiG-27 aircraft and a variety of SS-1 (SCUD) missiles.[77] This was backed by unprecedented efforts to fortify Kabul by laying a ring of minefields around it.[78] Thus, the Soviets laid the groundwork for the war to continue after their withdrawal, possibly even at greater intensity, preventing an early return of the Afghan refugees – a goal which ironically had served as Pakistan's main motive for signing the Accords.

The major question is: why did Islamabad conclude the Accords and Washington undertake to serve as their co-guarantor? Pakistan did so very reluctantly. It initially wanted a Mujahideen-led government in place before the Soviets commenced withdrawal. This was not, however, something which could be accommodated by Moscow in any form. Although publicly supporting the Mujahideen's internationally backed demands for unconditional and total withdrawal of Soviet troops and the right of the Afghan people to free self-determination, Washington in the final analysis changed its position to accommodate what the Soviets rather than Pakistan and the Afghan people wanted.[79]

It did so for two main reasons. First, bureaucratic elements centred largely in the State Department, which finally succeeded in shaping the US response to Gorbachev's initiatives, had all along been interested in the Afghan problem in terms of its perceptions of the US global position rather than any great concern for the future of the Afghan people. Second, the US administration fundamentally came around to the view that it was important to secure first of all the withdrawal of Soviet troops as the precondition for any settlement of the Afghan problem, and in the process also to try to moderate the Islamic tone of the Afghan resistance so that a Mujahideen-led government, should it eventuate after the Soviet pull-out, would not be as extreme as that of the anti-American Ayatollah Khomeini in Iran. In this respect it came to share a common position with Moscow and New Delhi, although through a thoroughly misguided analysis of the nature of social forces in Afghanistan, which would inevitably make any Islamic government there very different from that in Iran. Consequently, it appears that because of this and broader American objectives for improved relations with a changing Soviet Union under Gorbachev, Washington found it acceptable to pressure Pakistan to sign the Accords.[80]

Of course, the 'Afghanisation of the war' option was pursued in conjunction with an attempt to achieve a favourable coalition settlement, before completion of the Soviet withdrawal, between the PDPA and, if not all, at least some of the opposition forces. The main aim of such a settlement was to broaden the power base of the PDPA, so as to enable it, and consequently the Soviets, to continue to play a central role in post-withdrawal Afghan politics, although within a pluralist power structure. To this end, as the Soviet pullout gained momentum, Moscow launched a vigorous diplomatic campaign to bring as much pressure as possible to bear on the Mujahideen and their international supporters, most notably Pakistan, to accept a ceasefire and abide by the 'non-interference' provision of the Geneva Accords. As part of this, before the end of 1988, Moscow even made a dramatic turnabout, by opening direct talks with the Afghan opposition forces.

The Soviet Deputy Foreign Minister and newly appointed Ambassador to Kabul, Yulii Vorontsov, held two meetings – one in early December 1988 in Taif, Saudi Arabia, and another a month later in Islamabad – with a delegation of Pakistan-based leaders of the seven main Mujahideen groups,[81] which had provided most of the resistance and had a determining role to play in any settlement. Meanwhile, as a further measure to bring pressure on these groups and their regional supporters, Vorontsov also held separate talks in Rome with Zahir Shah, and in Tehran with the leadership of eight Iran-based Mujahideen groups. Vorontsov also met with Saudi, Pakistani and Iranian leaders.

However, as could have been expected, the Soviet efforts soon reached a dead end. Vorontsov's unbending support for the PDPA's claim to play a pivotal role in a settlement, and his insistence that the Soviet Union would continue to support the PDPA even after its troop withdrawal, finally prompted both the Sunni and Shi'ite Mujahideen leaders to perceive the discussions as nothing but a divisive ploy to enable the Soviet Union to achieve politically what it had thus far failed to accomplish militarily. While all along opposed to any deal with the PDPA as anathema to their struggle, both the Sunni and Shi'ite Mujahideen leaders, in an unprecedented display of unity at the Islamabad round of talks, rejected any further discussion with the Soviets until all their troops had withdrawn from Afghanistan and the PDPA regime had been overthrown.[82] The situation did not change in August 1991 during tripartite talks in Islamabad between representatives of Pakistan, the USSR and the Mujahideen.[83] Soviet diplomacy equally cut little ice with Zahir Shah, any other credible figures from past Afghan regimes, or the Mujahideen's regional supporters.

Moscow's efforts, nonetheless, exacerbated two pre-existing schisms within the Afghan resistance. They not only intensified divisions in the resistance along leadership and traditional ethno-tribal and linguistic lines, but also aggravated the sectarian Sunni-Shi'ite split, which could easily be manipulated by elements from inside and outside Afghanistan for self-serving purposes. Furthermore, they brought to the fore the rival and conflicting

interests of the Mujahideen's regional supporters. Whereas Pakistan and
Saudi Arabia augmented their support for their favourite Mujahideen leaders
from amongst the seven Pakistan-based Sunni resistance groups, Iran sought
to single out the Shi'ite Mujahideen group of *Wahdat* ('Unity'), as its
preferred platform for exerting greater influence than the total demographic
strength of the Shi'ites would warrant in the politics of post-Soviet
Afghanistan.[84] In January 1989, the Iranian-based Alliance of Eight demanded
one quarter (120 out of 480) of all seats at the Mujahideen *Shura* convened
to form the post-Najibullah government.[85] When its demands were rejected,
the Shi'ites boycotted the *Shura*.

US Policy

To complicate the situation further, the USA had its own regional and
international interests.[86] Since Washington's counter-interventionist policy
had all along been guided more by how it could benefit the USA against the
Soviet Union rather than by what might be conducive to bringing peace and
stability to Afghanistan, in the process, Washington neglected to give
sufficient thought to what could become of Afghanistan after the Soviet
withdrawal. This was evident in both its policy priorities and distribution of
weapons to the Mujahideen. It channelled arms through Pakistan, more
specifically through Pakistan's military intelligence (ISI), to those Afghans
who received ISI endorsement.[87] No mechanism was put in place to check
the credentials and future usefulness of such individuals. The question of
how to distribute the arms was left entirely to the ISI, allowing it to favour
whomever it wanted.

It was in this context that one of the most destructive forces in the Afghan
resistance was nurtured: the extremist *Hezb-e Islami* (Islamic Party) of
Gulbuddin Hekmatyar. As a self-styled radical Islamist, Hekmatyar had been
from the start an obedient client of the ISI, which bolstered his *Hezb-e Islami*
for no other purpose than to enable Pakistan to control the Afghan resistance
and to be in a strong position to place its own clients in power in Kabul after
a Soviet withdrawal. As a result, Hekmatyar emerged not only as the most
single-minded and power-hungry strongman, but also the best armed and
wealthiest, among the Mujahideen leaders.[88] Because of his lack of popular
support, this made him a destabilising factor in the resistance during the
Soviet occupation and the most destructive force after the collapse of
communist rule. Despite repeated warnings by serious analysts of Afghan
politics, and by the British government from 1986 on, Washington
continuously turned a blind eye to the ISI's transfer of a lion's share of its
arms to Hekmatyar.[89]

The Soviet Union withdrew its troops on time by 15 February 1989, ending the longest period of sustained foreign occupation in modern Afghan history. While Moscow tried to present its defeat as a withdrawal with honour, Washington was quick to claim credit for the biggest humiliation the Soviets had suffered in the post-Second World War era. Upon achievement of this goal, Washington's interest in Afghanistan also began to wane rapidly. Its annual military aid to the Mujahideen dwindled from some US$600 million at the height of the Afghan war to less than US$280 million immediately after the Soviet withdrawal, to nothing in 1992.[90] Little attempt was made to focus US energy and aid either on creating the conditions and mechanisms for ensuring a relatively bloodless transfer of power to the Mujahideen, or on catering for the Afghans' humanitarian needs during a transitional phase. The USA appeared to be in a hurry to find the quickest way out of the Afghan problem.

The Collapse of Najibullah's Government

Najibullah's government survived the Soviet withdrawal for another three years, albeit on the basis of a Soviet-provided life support system. The arsenals left by the Soviets were undoubtedly crucial for the PDPA regime's continuation in the wake of the 40th Army's withdrawal. No less important were Najibullah's political skills – skills that would have earned the commendation of Niccolò Machiavelli, who wrote half a millennium earlier that a prudent ruler must 'know how to act like a beast, he should learn from the fox and the lion'.[91] Najibullah practised what Joel Migdal has called the 'politics of survival': a style of leadership aimed at preserving personal power at all costs, including 'illegal methods or quick changes of the law to remove key state figures, pre-empting the emergence of competing power centres, and weakening and destroying groups in agencies already powerful enough to threaten the rulers' prerogatives'.[92] While he managed to cling to the presidential post for another three years, he did so at the expense of institutionalised state social control. Particularly after the abortive coup by his Minister of Defence, General Shah Nawaz Tanai, who defected to Hekmatyar in March 1990,[93] Najibullah was prepared to compromise with literally any strongman inside or outside the country. Between 1989 and 1991, 354 field commanders with some 140,000 men 'joined the policy of national reconciliation', which in real life meant that the central authority had given them complete freedom in running affairs in their localities in exchange for a vague promise not to fight against the regime in Kabul.[94]

Najibullah quickly shook off all ideological trappings of Marxism-Leninism. Beginning in 1989, communist rhetoric in the government and state-controlled media declined sharply. Terror abated somewhat, and limited freedom of speech and association was allowed.[95] On 27 June 1990, the Second PDPA Congress changed the party's name to *Hezb-e Watan* (Homeland Party), renounced its 'leading and guiding' role in Afghan society, proclaimed its adherence to the principles of Islam, and adopted a new programme envisaging 'expansion of democracy, strengthening of the political system based on a multiplicity of parties, and creation of coalition government in the centre and periphery'.[96]

In early 1992, with the Soviet Union consigned to history and no further aid flowing from Russia to support his regime, Najibullah referred to the Soviet troops as 'enemy forces in Afghanistan'.[97] He dispatched his Foreign Minister, Abdul Wakil, and Minister of State Security, Faruq Yaqubi, to Geneva in a last-ditch attempt to persuade Zahir Shah to return to Afghanistan and become Head of State again.[98] It was too late: by that time the central authority as locus of power had ceased to exist. The recycled PDPA and army were disintegrating; provincial governors, various warlords and field commanders were busy carving up autonomous principalities, striking alliances of convenience with a healthy disregard for ideological differences.[99] The political process degenerated into direct bargaining by primary groups, resulting in the simplified exercise of authority based on military might.

The most disturbing legacy of Najibullah's last years in office was exacerbated ethnic tension. Kabul eagerly employed ethnic formations from the north in pacifying Pashtun territories. The 53rd Infantry Division of General Abdul Rashid Dostum, made up mostly of Uzbeks from Jawzjan, particularly excelled itself in combat near Khost and Kandahar; its members were called 'national heroes' by Najibullah.[100] In the meantime, Dostum never concealed the fact that he had his own agenda in Afghan Turkestan. As early as July 1990, he said in Moscow: 'Uzbeks and Turkmens in the north of Afghanistan will not allow the situation where Pashtuns would be in charge of everything, as in the days of old.'[101] Najibullah's efforts to reassert Pashtun control over the north finally backfired: when in January 1992 he attempted to replace General Abdul Mumin, the Tajik commander of the 70th Infantry Division, with a Pashtun officer, Dostum came to Mumin's support and eventually entered an alliance with mostly non-Pashtun forces north of the Hindu Kush, including the Mujahideen of Ahmad Shah Massoud, the Ismaili formations of Sayyed Mansur Naderi and the Shi'a *Hezb-e Wahdat*.

In this unlikely coalition of northern forces, Massoud stood out as the strongest and the most disciplined and visionary, enjoying the secret support of many ranking *Parchamis* in Kabul and throughout the country. In contrast, while Massoud and many of his fellow Mujahideen commanders had fought for their religion and country, some observers identified Dostum as a devout communist.[102] In fact, Dostum was nothing more than a warlord, and a quintessential representative of the new breed of strongmen who came to the fore through the collapse of the centralised state in arms-saturated Afghanistan, and to whom no political ideology conceptualised in modern western terms could credibly be ascribed. He made his way to the top by first allying himself with Najibullah's government and subsequently when this government's fate seemed sealed, he joined the Mujahideen as the 'strong man' of the Uzbek minority, over whom he had gained influence. He was as self-centred as Hekmatyar, except that Dostum built a power base through what he could gain from a manipulation of both communism and Islam. Nonetheless, Dostum's defection to the opposition and his seizure of Mazar-e Sharif on 19 March 1992 fatally undermined Najibullah's grip on power. The shift that this produced in the configuration of forces caused many high-ranking Pashtun government officials, regardless of their factional affiliation, to flee en masse to the Mujahideen.[103] As Barnett Rubin has noted: 'Many Pashtuns in both the resistance and government feared an attempt by the northerners to capture power at their expense. Hekmatyar continued to play on Pashtun ethnic fears. In Kabul there had been talk for some time of a "Pashtun solution".'[104]

At this stage, Massoud, Dostum Ali Mazari and Ismail Khan (another powerful Mujahideen commander affiliated with *Jamiat*), controlled most of northern, western and central Afghanistan. Massoud controlled Takhar, Badakhshan, Kapisa, Parwan and several districts in Kunduz. Dostum reigned strong in the provinces of Jawzjan, Baghlan, Balkh, Faryab, Samangan and parts of Kunduz. *Hezb-e Wahdat* held Bamyan, most of Uruzgan and parts of Ghor and Ghazni. Ismail Khan was in charge in Herat, Badghis and Farah. The Pashtun provinces in the south-east, south and south-west were carved up amongst innumerable field commanders affiliated with the seven major Pakistan-based Sunni resistance organisations. Under the circumstances, Najibullah's government could not continue for much longer. As Najibullah offered to resign, the UN Secretary General's Special Representative for Afghanistan, Benon Sevan, made a last-minute frantic effort to help him find a way out of what was emerging as a chaotic situation, with no transfer of power mechanism or Mujahideen coalition takeover in place. Najibullah, with the help of Sevan, sought to escape to the Kabul airport for exile in India. But his plans came unstuck when he was blocked by night guards from his own forces, and by Dostum's troops, who had been allowed to stay overnight at Kabul airport on the understanding that they were going to help the government. As a result, he returned to the UN Mission in Kabul, where he was provided asylum until the Taliban takeover of Kabul and the militia's brutal killing of him and hanging of his body from a pole – an early sign of what was to transpire under the Taliban rule.[105] Meanwhile, Najibullah's Foreign Minister, Abdul Wakil, had entered negotiations with Massoud, essentially calling on him to take over Kabul, in the face of an imminent *Hezb-e Islami* attack on the city. Massoud's forces secured much of Kabul by 25 April 1992, inaugurating the establishment of the Islamic State of Afghanistan.

The most lucid illustration of the modalities of Marxist rule in Afghanistan is the model of four vicious circles created by the PDPA policies:

> To offset the lack of state capacity, the regime intervened in society, thereby sharpening social resistance to the state; to redress the excesses of the initial radical phase, it made compromises with the society, which alienated some support while failing to attract significant compensatory sections of the opposition; to redress further the isolation of the regime it then tried to find compromises with other forces inside society, but this served to ally it with elements that were unreliable and ultimately rebellious; to offset its internal weakness it fell back on external support – thereby sharpening national resistance to the alien military presence.[106]

In the process, resistance leadership structures in microsocieties, particularly in the countryside, experienced a dramatic change. Traditional bearers of authority (clan or village elders, khans, mullahs and Sufi figures) who implemented functions of political exchange according to the well-established canons of group solidarity were augmented (often supplanted) by the new type of strongmen. These were Mujahideen commanders who were linked to institutions beyond the traditional localised continuum: various Islamic parties and groups, foreign countries, and international organisations. When Najibullah's regime finally disintegrated, reconstructing political space with these new actors proved an extremely hazardous task.

9

Mujahideen Islamic Rule, Taliban Extremism and US Intervention

IN MID APRIL 1992, the disintegration of the Soviet-installed Najibullah government in Kabul and the takeover of the capital by the Mujahideen, led by Commander Ahmad Shah Massoud, opened an initially euphoric but ultimately another painful phase in the historical evolution of Afghanistan. The removal of the Najibullah regime essentially vindicated the Afghans' popular Islamic resistance and the US-led support for it against the attempted imposition of 'Godless' Soviet-style socialism. The Mujahideen declared Afghanistan an Islamic state for the first time in its history, and their takeover was welcomed by many Afghans in the expectation that their war-ravaged country would return to peace and order. However, their expectations were soon to be confounded. The Mujahideen victory quickly turned sour: Soviet occupation gave way to Pakistan's 'creeping invasion' and the Mujahideen's claimed Islamic rule was rapidly upstaged by the Taliban's extremist medievalism in the name of Islam, with further tragic losses for the Afghans.

This chapter focuses on the swing of the political pendulum from the moderate Islamism of those Mujahideen who took over the reins of power in Kabul to the Taliban's Islamic extremism. What went wrong with the Islamist government of President Burhanuddin Rabbani and its strong military commander, Ahmad Shah Massoud, which sought to govern Afghanistan from June 1992 until it was forced by the Taliban militia to retreat north in September 1996? How did the Taliban transform Afghanistan into a hub of extremism and international terrorism? Among the main problems in the body politic of Afghanistan during the period under discussion, the following were of crucial importance: a deficit of political legitimacy, which dogged the Rabbani-Massoud government from its inception; the failure of elite settlements to secure the position of this government; party rule and intra-party conflict, which had few if any historical precedents in Afghanistan and which the Rabbani-Massoud leadership could not master effectively; and foreign intervention, especially by Pakistan which from the start distrusted the Rabbani-Massoud government and was determined to replace it with one which would be under the control of one of its protégés.

Political Legitimacy

As the collapse of the Najibullah government approached, the Mujahideen remained as fragmented along ethno-linguistic, tribal, sectarian and personality lines as ever. The Pakistan-based leaders of the seven main Sunni Islamic Mujahideen groups had failed to agree on a common political platform, and there was little cohesion among the leaders of the minority Shi'ite Islamic groups, who were based in Iran. Nor were there any effective links between the Shi'ite and Sunni groups. Not one of the groups or their respective leaders had managed to develop a national profile or a nationwide following. Most groups functioned as fighting militias within specific localities from which their leaders originated, and enjoyed support substantially along lines of ethnic or tribal identification. Six of the seven Sunni Mujahideen organisations were dominated by Pashtuns.

> While this multiplicity of organisations during the war against the Soviets enabled the Pashtuns to receive more than their fair share of foreign military and financial aid, it also promoted rivalry, suspicion, and frequently violent clashes between them. This intra-Pashtun conflict prevented the leaders of Pashtun-dominated organisations to... take a united political stand during the chaotic downfall of the communist regime.[1]

Quite often the groups' leaders exercised only nominal influence over their commanders and other autonomous resistance figures in the field.[2]

These problems were exacerbated by the fact that most leaders had been either cultivated or adopted in one form or another by rival international patrons of the resistance. The bulk of money and weapons were channelled to the Mujahideen through Pakistan. The ISI's Afghan Bureau, which numbered 360 officers in 1984, carried out the day-to-day management of these operations and supervised training of Afghan fighters.[3] As has been mentioned, Gulbuddin Hekmatyar, who led the extremist *Hezb-e Islami Afghanistan*, was particularly nurtured by the ISI with the view that he should head the post-communist government in Kabul in order to further Islamabad's wider regional interests,[4] and, naturally, was the major recipient of foreign largesse.[5] Abdul Rasoul Sayyaf, the leader of another smaller Pashtun-dominated group, the *Ittehad-e Islami*, was strongly backed by Saudi Arabia, whose agenda was to disseminate its primarily anti-Iranian Wahhabi Islam, given Saudi Arabia's traditional claim of leadership of Sunni Islam against Iran's promotion of Shi'a Islam. Sayyaf, who initially had little or no influence inside Afghanistan, 'arranged for funds from Saudi Arabia to be paid into his own account, and literally bought groups of resistance fighters coming to Peshawar for arms by giving them what they wanted in return for their nominal support'.[6]

Iran's strategy in Afghanistan after 1982 focused very much on strengthening the leader of a relatively small organisation, *Sazman-e Nasr* (Organisation of Victory), led by Abdul Ali Mazari, to head an alliance of Shi'ite resistance groups based in Iran. In 1990, Mazari became the leader of *Hezb-e Wahdat*, which established itself as a major player in Afghan politics. Combat units affiliated with this party were often directly linked to particular religious leaders in Iran and were supervised by Iranian intelligence officers who knew (or cared) little about grassroots politics in Afghanistan. As a result, Hazara strongmen in the period between 1992 and 1996 became involved in countless clashes with other Mujahideen, to the detriment of the post-communist settlement in that country. Mazari's assassination by the Taliban in March 1995 was widely interpreted as a 'horrendous blow for Iran, because nobody is in doubt that this Shi'ite leader was "Tehran's man" in Kabul'.[7]

The two strongest groups – *Jamiat-e Islami*, led by Rabbani and his chief commander, Massoud, and Hekmatyar's *Hezb-e Islami* – were locked in a bloody power struggle. This was partly due to Hekmatyar's excessive power ambitions and rivalries with *Jamiat* leaders (especially Massoud), and partly to traditional ethno-linguistic as well as ideological differences. The *Jamiat* was dominated by ethnic Tajiks concentrated in Kabul, and north-eastern and western Afghanistan. It expounded a largely moderate, progressive Islamist ideology, conducive to modernity minus what were regarded as un-Islamic western cultural values and influences. The *Jamiat* could not boast a substantial representation of other important non-Pashtun minorities, such as the Uzbeks, Turkmens and Hazaras, but compared to practically mono-ethnic Pashtun organisations it had a greater 'tribal and regional cross-section'.[8] Its leaders were in general conscious of the fact that ultimately only a rainbow coalition of various ethnic groups could deliver Afghanistan a stable order.

The *Hezb* consisted overwhelmingly of ethnic Ghilzai Pashtuns concentrated mainly in south and south-eastern Afghanistan, but with sizeable pockets scattered through the north. It revolved around Hekmatyar, who was an ambitious, opportunist firebrand Islamist, whose entire goal was one day to become the unchallenged ruler of Afghanistan. Hekmatyar had been adopted politically by Pakistan's military ruler, General Zia ul-Haq, and backed by the ISI as the main instrument to control the Afghan resistance in pursuit of Pakistan's regional interests. The *Hezb*, which boasted the most tightly knit organisational structure among all the Mujahideen groups and was radical (at times bordering extremist) in its ideological disposition, mostly attracted detribalised urban Pashtuns and segments of the Ghilzais resettled in the north. Hekmatyar was born into a family of such settlers who represented the marginal Kharruti tribe of the Hotak group of the Ghilzais; hence his influence amongst major Pashtun tribes, especially the Durrani, was negligible. The *Hezb* was even less rooted in Afghan society than the Pashtun groups of Yunus Khales (*Hezb-e Islami*), Sebghatullah Mojaddedi (*Jabha-ye Nejat-e Melli*) and Sayyid Ahmad Gailani (*Mahaz-e Melli-ye Islami*), which were built largely around traditional patronage networks. Of the last three groups, Khales' *Hezb-e Islami* adhered to a traditionalist form of Islam, whereas the Mojaddedi and Gailani organisations espoused moderate Islamism, with a special disposition towards the exiled King Zahir Shah and the West.

In 1983, when Soviet occupation was at its zenith, Rabbani wrote the following prophetic words:

> We must avert the fratricidal war between us after the Russians withdraw from Afghanistan. We should prepare a government, a program of its activities. We must act in a way so that our friends in Islamic world would not fear the commencement of a civil war between the Mujahideen in Afghanistan, the more so as such a war would give the Russians an excuse for a new interference under the pretext of maintaining security of their southern frontier.[9]

All the same, the infighting among various Mujahideen groups and commanders never ceased. Olivier Roy has made a poignant observation that those conflicts were always treated as 'misunderstandings', or attributed to corrupt individuals and foreign plots: the Afghan leaders in Peshawar simply failed to produce a political explanation of divisions and segmentations and work towards rectifying them.[10]

After the Soviet withdrawal, the 'misunderstandings' intensified, resulting, for instance, in ferocious battles between the *Jamiat* and the *Hezb* in Logar and Parwan in June 1990, which caused hundreds of casualties on both sides.[11] Not surprisingly, the resistance was not in a position to invoke any legal or for that matter conventional processes of political change to create a broad-based and representative Islamic government to replace the regime of Najibullah. In this setting, no outside mediation could produce any desirable result either. The UN efforts to put together a transitional team, composed of 'neutral' Afghans, proved futile, although the inability of the Secretary-General's representative Benon Sevan to develop an appropriate understanding of the nature of the Afghan conflict also played its part in this respect.[12] This was all beneficial to the survival of Najibullah's regime in the short run, but the regime still could not hope to endure for long, given its continued deep internal problems and the loss of its lifeline with the disintegration of the Soviet Union. The collapse of Najibullah's regime provoked a scramble among the Mujahideen leaders for power.

Ahmad Shah Massoud was the Mujahideen leader who was best positioned to take over Kabul. He had already distinguished himself as a visionary and innovative Islamist and nationalist as well as a shrewd political and military strategist, with commanding skills in guerrilla warfare. Born in the summer of 1952 in the Panjsher Valley (60 miles north of Kabul), he was the son of a former army general. He had risen from the ranks of young Islamists of the early 1970s. While in his early twenties, he organised his first Islamist uprising in Panjsher in 1975 against President Mohammad Daoud's anti-Islamist policies. Although he failed in that stand, he soon found himself in a bigger struggle against the Soviet-backed communist regime in Afghanistan from April 1978. He was the only Mujahideen leader who did not leave Afghanistan during the almost decade-long Soviet occupation. He turned the Panjsher Valley into a robust fortress. The Soviets made several massive military attempts to eliminate or capture him, but he survived all of them and went on to grow in stature and influence. He became known as the 'Lion of the Panjsher'. He rapidly proved to be one of the world's most remarkable liberation strategists and fighters – a position that he augmented subsequently by leading the anti-Taliban and anti-al-Qaeda forces until his assassination on 9 September 2001.

It was Massoud's relatively better-organised and disciplined forces that succeeded, in alliance with those of the Uzbek warlord, Abdul Rashid Dostum, in seizing power in Kabul as Najibullah's government fell apart. Massoud was the second Tajik leader after Habibullah Kalakani (discussed in Chapter 3) in the history of modern Afghanistan to achieve a dominant position in Kabul. Nonetheless, the control of the capital by Massoud's forces was by no means complete, as they were not able to prevent other Mujahideen groups from occupying the suburbs of Kabul. The city was divided amongst different factions into 12 sectors. *Hezb-e Wahdat* was especially successful, occupying 30 per cent of the capital. The bulk of Hekmatyar's forces, however, remained to the south of Kabul in readiness to launch an attack on their former allies.

Elite Settlement

As he stood poised to enter Kabul, Massoud was acutely aware of two overarching imperatives. One was that Afghanistan's contemporary history had shown that no single ethnic group could effectively rule the country on its own and that the best way to proceed was to secure a broad-based transitional coalition as the first step towards creating a legitimate national government. The other was that in order to achieve this objective, the Mujahideen leaders had to reach a power-sharing agreement among themselves. He thus called on the Pakistan-based Mujahideen leaders to work out such a deal. The only hope for stability lay in an elite settlement,[13] whereby various leaders, not only acting on behalf of their respective Mujahideen groups but also in effect claiming representation on behalf of different ethno-linguistic categories, would construct a power structure whose durability and effectiveness would rest solely on the goodwill of the individual signatories to respect each other's end of the bargain, as well as on their capacities to control their subordinate forces.

The result was the Peshawar Agreement of 24 April 1992, forged between the Pakistan-based Mujahideen leaders, but with the heavy involvement of the Pakistani government of Prime Minister Nawaz Sharif.[14] The latter had succeeded Benazir Bhutto following her election in the wake of General Zia ul-Haq's death in a mysterious air crash in August 1988. The Agreement was designed essentially to provide a framework for an interim government, to be implemented in two stages. The first was to dispatch to Kabul the leader of a small Pashtun Mujahideen group, Sebghatullah Mojaddedi, as a compromise choice, to head a two-month transitional government. The second was to enable a longer-term interim coalition government, headed by Rabbani – whose control of Kabul through Massoud provided him with extra political clout – to take over from the transitional government for a period of four months. This was to be followed by the holding of a 'Council of Experts on Solving and Binding' (*Shura-ye ahl al-hall wa l-aqd*)[15] to constitute an interim government for 18 months as a prelude to a general election for creating a popular government. Amid some controversy over the representativeness of its membership, a *Shura* was convoked in late 1992 which endorsed the continuation of the Rabbani administration for 18 months – an administration in which several Pashtun Mujahideen leaders, most. importantly Sayyaf, remained loyal participants.

However, the settlement's Achilles heel was that it only needed the disaffection of one key party to destroy the whole design. And this was precisely what happened. Hekmatyar's thirst for power and his ISI patrons' displeasure with not having him at the helm in post-communist Afghanistan rapidly led them to work against the Peshawar Agreement, under which the post of Prime Minister had been allocated for the *Hezb*, but which Hekmatyar had not signed. The *Hezb* leader fancied himself to be the sole ruler of Afghanistan: 'In our country coalition government is impossible because, this way or another, it is going to be weak and incapable of stabilising the situation in Afghanistan.'[16] In opposition to Massoud, Hekmatyar argued that under the Agreement the position of Prime Minister should not be subordinated to that of the President; and that the position of Defence Minister, to which Massoud had been appointed by Mojaddedi, should function at the behest of the Prime Minister. Although Mojadeddi's efforts to prolong his transitional presidency from two months to two years had created considerable difficulties between him and Massoud, who viewed the unswerving implementation of the Peshawar Agreement as the best course of action, ultimately it was Hekmatyar's and his Pakistani backers' obstructionism that rendered the Agreement totally ineffective.

Initially, under pressure, Hekmatyar nominated one of his aides, Abdul Saboor Farid, to assume the premiership, but he himself refused to enter Kabul and used every excuse possible to undermine the Rabbani government. While *Wahdat* demanded representation in the Cabinet disproportionate to that warranted by the size of the Shi'ite segment of the Afghan population, Hekmatyar requested that the troops of Dostum (who had allied with the government) leave Kabul. When Rabbani acceded to this ultimatum, Dostum refused to comply and, in his turn, requested the immediate inclusion of his group's representatives into the government. In the meantime, Mujahideen of Mazari and Sayyaf were busy battling each other and residents of Kabul in street fighting. Ceasefires, truces, and power-sharing agreements were produced in ever-growing quantities, and Massoud made a frantic effort to reach a face-to-face agreement with Hekmatyar, offering to step down as Defence Minister, as he subsequently did, in order to placate Hekmatyar. The *Hezb* leader was again named Prime Minister pursuant to an agreement signed in Islamabad in March 1993,[17] and reaffirmed in Mecca at the invitation of Saudi authorities, but still stayed outside Kabul, imposing a blockade of the city.

In early August 1992, Hekmatyar had launched a barrage of rockets against Kabul, killing 1,800 civilians and destroying a great deal of southern parts of the capital over a period of three weeks. Concurrently, Dostum, who had all along acted as nothing more than an opportunist Uzbek warlord, promised to create a 'democratic secular republic' in northern Afghanistan if 'rabid mullahs in Kabul' did not change their line.[18] This threat of secession appeared to be real: a number of northern provinces under his tutelage had substantial armed forces, an autarkic economy and good relations with Uzbekistan and Russia. High-ranking officials from Tashkent frequented Mazar-e Sharif without notifying Kabul, and there were rumours that Dostum's son could one day marry the daughter of President Islam Karimov of Uzbekistan.[19] Karimov was keen to see Dostum controlling the region from Uzbekistan's border to the Hindu Kush as part of his rivalry with Tajikistan and Russia for influence in Central Asia. Yet Dostum also maintained representation, though unofficial, in Moscow, and the trade turnover between companies in northern Afghanistan and Russia reached an impressive US$800 million in 1993.[20] Dostum was also backed by Turkey, which was keen to see Karimov succeed in his quest for supremacy in Central Asia, as part of Turkey's efforts to prevent its long-standing rival, Russia, from making a comeback to the region.

As Rabbani and Massoud were trying to broaden the base of the government, Hekmatyar, Mazari and Dostum, in loose association with Mojaddedi, secretly formed a new anti-government alliance, the so-called *Shura-i Hamahangi* ('Council of Coordination'). On 1 January 1994, they launched a blistering attack on Kabul. This was done at the instigation of and pursuant to a secret agreement between Hekmatyar's and Mazari's patrons: the Pakistani and Iranian intelligence services. A western analyst employed a Shakespearean allegory explaining this move: 'It sounds outrageous, the president is pained, but no one is very surprised. Self-interest is an acceptable morality, as it was in medieval England, even though tanks and aircraft have replaced horses as instruments of warfare.'[21] Dostum's spokesperson provided a different version in his statement: 'We launched an attack because we want to change the political system and make it accessible for all national minorities... As to Rabbani, he rules the country only in the Tajiks' interests.'[22] By the end of 1994, the indiscriminate bombardment of Kabul by Hekmatyar and his new comrades-in-arms had managed to destroy half of the city and killed some 25,000 of its citizens, with all sides committing massive human rights violations in one form or another.[23] Numerous peace efforts, pursued by various Mujahideen leaders, the Organisation of the Islamic Conference (OIC) and the United Nations, produced no result.[24]

In all his operations, Hekmatyar had three objectives. The first was to make sure that Rabbani and Massoud were not allowed to consolidate power, build a credible administration, or expand their territorial control,[25] so that the country would remain divided into small fiefdoms, run by various

Mujahideen leaders and local warlords or a council of such elements, with only some of them allied to Kabul. The second was to ensure that the Rabbani government acquired no capacity to dispense patronage, and to dissuade the Kabul population from giving more than limited support to the government. The third was to make Kabul an unsafe city for representatives of the international community and to prevent the Rabbani government from attracting the international support needed to begin the post-war reconstruction of Afghanistan and generate a level of economic activity which would enhance its credibility and popularity. His tactics proved highly successful in all these respects.

Jamiat's Weaknesses

The factional conflict also exposed and exacerbated some of *Jamiat*'s inherent problems as the central component of the Rabbani government. As discussed in Chapter 6, the *Jamiat*, from which the *Hezb-e Islami* of Hekmatyar splintered when the latter went his own way in the wake of the Soviet invasion, had its origins in the Islamic movement for reform of Afghanistan, which was founded in the Faculty of Theology, Kabul University, in the late 1960s. Its structure and functions were very much defined under the leadership of Rabbani, shortly after he went into exile in Pakistan in 1974. It was essentially reborn as an Islamic resistance coalition. While containing some Pashtun elements, especially from the north, it was dominated by Badakhshis and Panjsheris, who were kindred, led by Rabbani and Massoud respectively.[26] *Jamiat* rapidly evolved as a political-military organisation, but with rather loose links between its political and military wings. Whereas Rabbani assumed the overall leadership and developed the party structure of *Jamiat*, with various committees to discharge different political, economic, military and socio-cultural functions, Massoud built up a cluster of fighting groups, which were drawn mostly from the six northern and north-eastern provinces and at the core of which lay his own ethnic Panjsheri devotees, to provide the armed resistance of the coalition inside Afghanistan. To place this cluster within a coherent military-political structure, Massoud set up the Supervisory Council of the North (*Shura-ye Nazar-e Shamoli*) during 1985–1986, which grew into an almost self-contained entity, with less than organic ideological, political and military links with the *Jamiat*. The territory around the city of Taloqan embodying Takhar and Panjsher was often referred to as 'Massoud territory' in the foreign press, for Massoud acted not only as the supreme military commander there, but also as the chief executive. His administration included several functional committees, dealing with maintaining law and order, economic development and provision of services to the people. In the early 1990s, there were 400 schools in Takhar, including some for girls – 'a radical development for the mediaeval society in this rural area'.[27]

Thus, from the outset, the *Jamiat* developed an oddly bifurcated structure: a political wing, with only limited input in military operations, under Rabbani; and a military-political wing operating inside Afghanistan under the full and charismatic leadership of Massoud. During the years of resistance this dichotomy did not cause much inter-party friction, and the two wings worked together quite harmoniously, but the situation changed when Massoud's forces took over Kabul. The former division of military and political responsibilities complicated the daunting task of transforming resistance forces into a governing body, a situation aggravated by four specific factors.

First, it was now Massoud and his Supervisory Council who stood supreme, as the security of Kabul and other *Jamiat*-dominated areas rested in their hands. Without them, the organisation's political wing could not have played a central role in establishing a government. The upshot of this was a desire by elements in the Supervisory Council to have a determining share in the power structure and substantial input in shaping the Rabbani government's policies.[28] Yet those senior *Jamiat* functionaries who had returned with Rabbani from exile wanted their expertise to be recognised and to fill most of the important governmental and bureaucratic posts.

Second, ethnicisation took hold within each of the *Jamiat*'s wings. Although the Supervisory Council and the political wing of *Jamiat* contained representation from a wide range of non-Pashtuns, in the growing atmosphere of distrust which had beset the Afghan nation in general, and the *Jamiat* in particular, ethnic loyalty to both Massoud and Rabbani rapidly came to take precedence over the need to develop a multi-ethnic administration and military force. Whereas Massoud became more and more reliant on his core Panjsheri supporters, Rabbani surrounded himself largely with staff and armed personnel who had come from his native Badakhshan province. This gave rise to divisions even within the Supervisory Council and the *Jamiat* party, as well as between them; and to plotting by factions against each other in ways which served the interests only of those who resented any form of Tajik rule. *Jamiat* members and supporters could be divided into three broad categories: the core, who were ethnically loyal to either Massoud or Rabbani; the middle circles, whose loyalty was questionable but who, for reasons of political expediency, were allowed to penetrate the administration at some strategic points; and those ostensibly supportive of the Rabbani administration, but mindful of maintaining the possibility of supporting Hekmatyar or whoever else could triumph in the power struggle between the Rabbani-Massoud camp and the *Hezb*. This was hardly a recipe for stability.

Third, when Rabbani assumed the presidency, he formally resigned as the head of the *Jamiat*, in order to depoliticise the office of presidency and free himself from party restrictions and accusations of political bias. In reality, Rabbani still remained very closely attached to the *Jamiat*, and more specifically to his Badakhshi clique, for loyalty and support. As his power base remained confined to the *Jamiat*, he simply could not depoliticise his position. Thus his resignation as the head of *Jamiat* had two unforeseen consequences. On the one hand, since during the years of resistance he had grown to personify his party, it caused a great deal of confusion among those of his supporters who had little understanding of party politics and were traditionally accustomed to the personalisation of politics. On the other, it did nothing to reduce his vulnerability to accusations of political bias and ethnic cronyism – a fact which came rapidly to permeate Rabbani's administration at all levels.

Fourth, the relationship between the *Jamiat*-led government and Governor Ismail Khan in Herat could not be effective. On the one hand, the governor's alliance with the government was a source of comfort to Rabbani and Massoud. On the other, his growing stature and strength as the *Amir* (ruler – as he was addressed) of all western Afghanistan ultimately became disconcerting for some of the Kabul authorities. This, together with the fact that Ismail Khan rapidly succeeded in transforming Herat into a peaceful haven with a thriving social and economic life, prompted some in the Rabbani-Massoud camp to view the governor's power with a degree of disdain and jealousy. *Jamiat*'s clumsy attempts to gain a strong foothold in the running of Ismail Khan's administration[29] led to bad feelings between the two sides, thus undermining the close cooperation which was required to enable them to develop a national government. This, together with Ismail Khan's own problems of internal dissension, mismanagement, and administrative malpractice, made his local government vulnerable. It was against this backdrop that the Taliban was able to overrun Herat without much fight in September 1995. The defeat of Ismail Khan, resulting in his flight and that of his core supporters to Iran and the fall to the Taliban of the large Shindand air base with many of its jet fighters, as well as a huge amount of other military equipment, proved very damaging to Rabbani and Massoud. It had serious psychological and material impact on their forces, making their grip on Kabul increasingly tenuous.

Pakistan's 'Creeping Invasion'

However, despite all the alliances he made and the carnage and destruction he engendered, Hekmatyar was unable to wrest power from Rabbani and

Massoud. This led Islamabad to make two inescapable conclusions. One was that Hekmatyar had become a serious liability for Pakistan.[30] Another was that now Pakistan lacked a viable Afghanistan policy to enable it to secure a receptive government in Kabul to settle once and for all the long-standing Afghan–Pakistan border dispute in line with Pakistan's interests. In other words, after the Soviet withdrawal, Islamabad essentially would have liked to see an enmeshing of the identity of Pakistan's and Afghanistan's Pashtuns and a transformation of Afghanistan into a Pakistan-influenced Pashtun-ruled enclave to assist it with wider objectives.[31] In addition, there was now also another consideration that appeared to influence Islamabad's policy thinking: it related to the disintegration of the Soviet Union and the sudden opening up of the potentially resource-rich Muslim Central Asian republics, where Pakistan wanted to have influence, preferably through Afghanistan as the most direct route. In July 1992, General Mirza Aslam Beg wrote:

> The emergence of the newly independent states of Soviet Muslim periphery requires a complete re-evaluation of the frontiers of Central Asia… the weakening of Russian influence has created a potential vacuum for other regional powers to extend their political, economic and cultural influences.[32]

So Pakistan was keen to gear up for a breakthrough in Central Asia.

However, the *Jamiat*'s domination of post-communist power in Kabul had proved very unsettling for these plans. Islamabad could not possibly expect the new Islamic government leaders, especially Massoud (who had always maintained his independence from Pakistan), to subordinate their own nationalist objectives in order to help Pakistan realise its regional ambitions. Although originally, at the political level, Islamabad had little choice but to recognise this reality, the ISI was given a free hand to do whatever it could to shift the balance of power in favour of Hekmatyar. Hence the ISI's continued support for Hekmatyar's military actions against the Rabbani government.[33] Had it not been for the ISI's logistic support and supply of a large number of rockets, Hekmatyar's forces would not have been able to target and destroy half of Kabul.

Yet Hekmatyar's failure to achieve what was expected of him prompted the ISI leaders to come up with a new surrogate force. That force was the Taliban, or the ultra-orthodox Sunni Islamic militia of young Pashtun students from *madrasas* or religious schools in Pakistan, who had come from both sides of the Afghan-Pakistani border. A chain of *madrasas* had been created by Pakistan, with US consent and Saudi funding, in the mid 1980s 'as a religious-political belt along the Afghan-Pakistani border in order to support the combat spirit of Mujahideen'.[34] These *madrasas'* curriculum focused on the teaching of a strictly puritanical Islam, based on the orthodox and in many ways medievalist teachings and interpretations of the Saudi Wahabi brand of Islam and Deobandi school of Islam, which had grown in northern India since the nineteenth century with the influence of Wahabism.[35] The *madrasa* students were trained to be totally dedicated not only to a particular, in one sense traditionalist and, in another sense, radical Islamism, bult also with devotion to the concept of Islamic *jihad* in the combative meaning of the term. This included a readiness to participate in a *jihad* and make self-sacrifice whenever necessary to liberate Muslim lands from, and defend them against, control by infidels and their Muslim surrogates, and to unite Muslims within a single *umma* (community) under an Islamic government.

The 'godfather' of the Taliban was essentially Pakistan's then Minister of the Interior, Naseerullah Babar. In late 1994, he recruited, trained and armed a number of *madrasa* students to join a few former Pashtun Mujahideen fighters from southern Afghanistan to provide protection for a Pakistani convoy en route to Central Asia through Afghanistan.[36] The initial success of the group, which assumed the name 'Taliban' (Islamic students) immediately received approbation of Pakistan's military/ISI leadership as well as Mawlana Fazlur Rahman, the leader of the *Jamiat-e Ulema Islam* party, who was a coalition partner of Benazir Bhutto and also headed the foreign affairs committee of the Pakistani parliament. The ISI urgently took over the project to develop the Taliban into a credible ideological and fighting force. It lavished the militia with training, arms, fighters, logistic support and money. It appeared to uphold the militia's ideological extremism and draconian measures of rule imposition as critical to its success in claiming higher moral grounds and winning among the conflict weary and exhausted Afghan people against the divided, battling Mujahideen forces, including those constituting Rabbani's moderate Islamic government.

In November 1994, the Taliban took over Kandahar in a surprise attack and continued to press towards Kabul. By February 1995, their ranks had swollen from 800 to 25,000, mostly due to the influx of Pashtuns from the frontier tribes who had done service in the border troops of Pakistan's Ministry of the Interior.[37] Their leader was an unknown figure by the name of Mullah Mohammad Omar, a former Mujahideen fighter of the *Hezb-e Islami* of Yunus Khales, who had lost one eye when fighting against Soviet forces. Although he was later exalted to the position of *Amir al-Mo'mineen* (Commander of the Faithful), Omar was essentially a poorly educated, impoverished Ghilzai Pashtun who had come from Sangisar in southern

Afghanistan. Initially, the Taliban leaders announced that their desire was to bring peace to Afghanistan by disposing of all Mujahideen factions.[38] But as the militia's territorial control expanded, its political-ideological agenda made it explicit that their ultimate goal was to transform Afghanistan into a 'pure Islamic Emirate' as a prelude to achieving wider regional objectives.

As such, the Taliban quickly overwhelmed Hekmatyar's forces and proved a formidable foe to the Rabbani and Massoud forces. They fought and bought their way to the southern gates of Kabul within a few months of their emergence. After March 1995, they periodically bombarded the capital city using old artillery and missile sites of Hekmatyar. By September 1995, they had managed to capture Herat and gain control over 27 out of the country's 32 provinces including the entire length of the 880-kilometre road linking the Pakistani town of Chaman with the northern Afghan town of Turghundi on the border with Turkmenistan. Wherever they conquered, they immediately imposed what amounted to a highly brutal, medievalist rule, which produced 'security', for which the people were yearning, but discriminated savagely against not only those who actively opposed them, but also women and Shi'a minorities and any form of cultural and social practices which happened to be at variance with their idiosyncratic preaching and understanding of Islam. They also allowed poppy cultivation, heroin production and drug trafficking in the areas under their control as the best revenue raising means to help finance their territorial conquests and political and ideological impositions.[39]

Massoud defined the goals of the Taliban and their foreign patrons as follows:

> As always, it is the question of money. Western companies are interested in resources-rich territories of northern Afghanistan. They also want to penetrate the adjacent countries of Central Asia: Tajikistan, Turkmenistan, Uzbekistan. Gold and aluminium. But most importantly – oil and gas. All these, according to the plans of the true instigators of war, must go by the shortest route – through Afghanistan – to the Pakistani seaport of Karachi. This is the essence of the war, not the struggle for the 'true faith'. The Holy Quran and jihad are, unfortunately, only cover in this rather dirty affair.[40]

In the face of this and the world's unwillingness to refocus its attention on Afghanistan – this time to prevent what was widely believed to be Pakistan's 'creeping invasion' of Afghanistan – from early 1996, Rabbani forged a renewed alliance with *Hezb-e Wahdat* (now under Karim Khalili, who replaced Mazari as the group leader in March 1995 following the Taliban's killing of Mazari) and reinvited Hekmatyar to join them in an anti-Taliban coalition to fend off the Taliban onslaught. Given his isolation and abandonment by Pakistan, Hekmatyar joined the coalition as Prime Minister in March 1996, establishing finally a coalition government in May 1996, which would have been authoritative and representative four years previously, but now proved helpless in the face of the Taliban threat. Rabbani and Massoud made a last frantic effort to broaden the government's power base. The reconciliation with Hekmatyar was perhaps the worst strategic mistake that the Rabbani leadership committed, a severe miscalculation which badly backfired, subjecting the *Jamiat* to destructive internal and external pressures. Hekmatyar's inclusion achieved the reverse of what was intended: it resulted in the government's power base contracting rather than expanding. There were many in the Rabbani and Massoud camp fiercely opposed to Hekmatyar, holding him responsible for the predicament in which the government was placed. They could not bring themselves to serve a Prime Minister who had done everything possible to destroy them. This led to a profound collapse of morale within the government and its military defenders, and the end result was disastrous.

A great deal of controversy surrounds the role of countries other than Pakistan in the orchestration of the Taliban. Pakistan's then Prime Minister, Benazir Bhutto, has disclosed that Pakistan was not alone in setting up the Taliban. She has claimed: 'Weapons were supplied to the Taliban by the USA and Britain with money from Saudi Arabia... Pakistan's territory was used to train solely the Afghan refugees – Pashtuns, who made up the backbone of the Taliban movement.'[41] While Bhutto's claims must be treated with due caution, there is no doubt that once Babar conceived and launched the genesis of the Taliban, Saudi Arabia and the United Arab Emirates (UAE) were happy to provide finances to ensure its rapid expansion and success, and the USA appeared willing to wear it without any qualm. The Taliban suited the interests of not only Pakistan, but also these countries in different ways. Given the Sunni, but anti-Shi'a and anti-Iranian, character of the Taliban, the Saudi, UAE and US objectives were very much shaped by a common desire to contain the Islamic Republic of Iran and prevent it from gaining influence in Afghanistan and in the newly emerged mineral and market-rich region of Central Asia. The Saudi and UAE funding came from both the government and wealthy private citizens, whose past support, together with that of the USA, had also been critical to hundreds of Arab volunteers who had come to fight alongside the Mujahideen in a *jihad* against the Soviets and their surrogates in Afghanistan in the 1980s.[42]

Rabbani's and Massoud's uneasiness and eventual public expression of concern about Pakistan's behaviour precipitated a sense of mutual distrust and recrimination. As the Taliban made rapid territorial gains, Rabbani and Massoud became increasingly vocal in their condemnation of Pakistan's interference in Afghanistan's internal affairs, notably at the UN General Assembly and Security Council meetings from mid 1995. This coincided with anti-Pakistan demonstrations in Kabul, which led to the sacking of the Pakistani Embassy in September 1995 and the death of one of its employees.[43] Islamabad not only closed down its embassy, and demanded an official apology and compensation, but also dropped any pretence which it had so far exhibited of supporting Rabbani's government.

In early 1995, Prime Minister Benazir Bhutto, under pressure from the ISI and the military, whose leadership have always been interchangeable, publicly attacked Rabbani's policies and declared his government 'illegitimate'. She argued that Rabbani was supposed to have stepped down from the presidency by mid 1994, and that his failure to do so was the main cause of the ongoing fighting in the country.[44] Yet she ignored two key facts. First, the Peshawar Agreement, the basis for her claim, had been massively violated when Pakistan's client, Hekmatyar, mounted his coup attempt in January 1994; and to suggest that Rabbani remained bound by it when no other party treated it as meaningful was ludicrous. Second, UN mediation had not succeeded in putting in place any viable transitional mechanism which could allow Rabbani to step down, without jeopardising still further the security of thousands of people in areas under government control. Ms Bhutto also ignored the fact that no Afghan government had ever come to power on a popular base of legitimacy, and that the question of what has historically constituted a legitimate government in Afghanistan was a highly academic one.

From then on, it was clear that Pakistan would do everything possible to wreck Rabbani's government and its claim to any form of legitimacy in favour of a decisive Taliban win. It paid little more than lip service to UN mediation efforts and circumvented every gesture made by the Rabbani government in the hope of building a better working relationship. Although publicly maintaining a policy of denial of any support for the Taliban, her government expanded its logistic and military assistance to the militia, as was subsequently confirmed by hundreds of Pakistani officers, troopers and volunteers who were captured by anti-Taliban forces.[45] On 10 September 1996, the Taliban captured Jalalabad and followed this with a relentless thrust towards Kabul. As the militia launched its final assault on Kabul, it was Hekmatyar's commanders who surrendered one after another en route from Jalalabad to Kabul, and Massoud's forces could not hold the dam once it had burst. By September 1996, Kabul had become indefensible; Massoud found himself with little choice but to retreat to his native Panjsher Valley and to shift the government, including its leaders, especially Rabbani, Sayyaf and Hekmatyar, to the north in order to be able to fight the Taliban from a more secure base.

The fall of Kabul to the Taliban was achieved with Pakistan's generous logistic and combat assistance, even including night-vision binoculars – a contraption which had not been provided to the Mujahideen to fight against the Soviets. It also opened a bloody new phase in the evolution of Afghan and regional politics. Pakistan 'won', but only to face bigger problems in Afghanistan and in the region[46] – a development too familiar to students of Afghan politics and history, who had witnessed similar Pyrrhic 'victories' for the British in Afghanistan in the nineteenth century and the Soviets in the 1980s. In a subsequent Taliban assault on Mazar-e Sharif in August 1998, as many as 1,500 Pakistani military personnel took part in the attack, which led Afghanistan's ambassador in Moscow, Abdul Wahhab Asefi, to accuse Pakistan of the intention to occupy that country 'emulating the shameful Soviet experience'.[47]

The US Attitude

Islamabad immediately condoned the Taliban's capture of Kabul and, in May 1997, officially recognised the Taliban as the legitimate government of Afghanistan and urged the rest of the world to do the same. Although its call for recognition fell on deaf ears in general, Riyadh and Abu Dhabi followed suit. Islamabad launched a massive diplomatic and public relations campaign to promote the Taliban as the strongest and most popular force in Afghanistan. It exalted the militia as the only force capable of bringing stability to Afghanistan and successfully secured increased Saudi Arabian and UAE financial aid to the militia, urging the USA to view the Taliban in the best light possible as an aide to US interests in the region. A former advisor on Afghanistan to the Bush administration and later President George W. Bush's envoy and ambassador to Afghanistan, Zalmay Khalilzad, even went so far as to urge the Clinton administration to engage with the Taliban.[48] Pakistani leaders argued forcefully that a stable Afghanistan under the Taliban could open up a valuable transit route to the Central Asian Muslim republics, and that at least two international consortia, one led by UNOCAL of the USA and Delta Oil of Saudi Arabia and another comprising Bridas of Argentina, could compete for contracts to construct pipelines at the cost of $2 billion through Afghanistan for the import of gas from Turkmenistan to Pakistan and beyond.[49] The financial windfall for both the Taliban and Pakistan was considered to be critical for sustaining their operations in Afghanistan. Despite its public denial of any association with the Taliban, in reality Washington maintained a conspicuous silence over their human rights violations and medievalist theocratic approach to governance and voiced only muted criticism as they destroyed Afghanistan's distributive and administrative institutions, turning the country into a hub for poppy cultivation, drug trafficking, narco-economic activities. This indulgence continued for almost two years.

Washington also expressed no qualms over the large number of Arab and non-Arab volunteers who moved into Afghanistan via Pakistan in support of the Taliban, especially in the wake of its capture of Kabul. One of those volunteers, who arrived now for a second visit to Afghanistan but this time with more dramatic consequences, was of course the Saudi multi-millionaire dissident, Osama bin Laden. He had originally visited Afghanistan via Pakistan in the early 1980s to fulfil what he regarded as a religious duty by participating in the Afghan *jihad* against Godless communists. He had done so with indirect, if not direct, support of the CIA, which in alliance with the ISI had actively sought international Islamic support for the Mujahideen, and in some cases monitored and guided the movements and operations of all volunteers.[50] After coming into close contact with a number of Pakistani radical Islamists, it was in Peshawar that bin Laden set up the original cell of his al-Qaeda network, essentially to help the Arab volunteers. However, following the defeat of the Soviets in Afghanistan, bin Laden returned to Saudi Arabia, where he soon made a public stand against the Saudi regime for being 'corrupt' and against the USA for maintaining such a regime and enabling Israel to maintain its occupation of Jerusalem (Islam's third holiest city after Medina and Mecca) and its brutal suppression of Palestinian resistance. When the Saudi authorities stripped him of his citizenship, he first moved to Sudan but, by 1996, he had returned to the country that he knew best: Afghanistan. Yet this time he returned to an Afghanistan where a new ISI-run militia – that is, the Taliban, which was ideologically very amenable to bin Laden's brand of Islam – had seized power in Kabul. The ISI wanted to use his wealth and Arab connections in support of the militia's adventures and also therefore in support of Pakistan's expanded regional policy goals.[51]

Bin Laden forged an organic alliance with Mullah Mohammad Omar, based on the Saudi dissident providing the Taliban with money and Arab fighters and the Taliban giving the Saudi dissident and his supporters sanctuary and all the logistic support that they needed to set up terrorist training camps and expand al-Qaeda into a trans-national network. Nor did Washington seem to be particularly disturbed by bin Laden's al-Qaeda merging with the militant Egyptian Islamic Jihad of Ayman al-Zawahiri, who joined bin Laden in Afghanistan in early 1997. On the contrary, the Clinton administration allowed senior officers from both the State Department and the CIA, including Assistant Secretary of State for South Asia Robin Raphel, to meet Taliban leaders on a regular basis inside and outside Afghanistan.[52] Washington proved astonishingly calm in the face of the Taliban-al-Qaeda alliance – something which could not have materialised without the active support of the ISI, which acted as the mastermind of the Taliban's policy behaviour and actions. The USA voiced no strong criticism of the Taliban's theocratic medievalism and cultural vulgarism until November 1997. Only then, while coming under public pressure over the Taliban's treatment of Afghan women and girls, who were banned from working and going to school, did Secretary of State Madeleine Albright describe the Taliban's policies towards women as 'despicable' and make it clear that the Taliban rule of Afghanistan was not assured given the presence of other forces in the country.[53]

This proved to be a precursor to stronger American criticisms, especially following the al-Qaeda bombing of American embassies in Kenya and Tanzania at the cost of hundreds of lives in August 1998. Even so, Washington still remained somewhat passive and confused in the face of the challenge posed by the Taliban-al-Qaeda-ISI alliance. It retaliated over the embassy bombings by rocketing a drug factory in Sudan, which it wrongly identified as linked to bin Laden and producing chemical weapons, and bin Laden's camps in eastern Afghanistan. It also made a couple of abortive attempts to capture bin Laden, but made no attempts to pressure Pakistan to the extent necessary to reform its domestic structures or change its Afghanistan policy, the source of many of the problems in the war-torn country. In the face of the late 1999 coup in Pakistan, led by General Pervez Musharraf, which overthrew the elected government of Prime Minister Nawaz Sharif and placed Pakistan once again under military dictatorship, with a subsequent declaration that Pakistan's support of the Taliban was a 'national security imperative', the USA simply sought policy coordination with India and Russia in a common anti-terrorist cause. It supported increased UN pressure on the Taliban. However, this was something that the Taliban and al-Qaeda could easily defy as long as they had the support of Pakistan.[54]

At the same time, the USA did nothing to provide financial and miliary support for the badly pressured and poorly equipped and trained forces of Commander Massoud, who had been squeezed into north-eastern Afghanistan by late 1998. It repeatedly ignored Massoud's warnings about Afghanistan being turned into a centre for not only medievalist theocracy, but also international terrorism, involving thousands of al-Qaeda Arab,

Pakistani, Kashmiri and Chechen operatives – all in the name of an Islam that Afghans had never experienced in their history. Washington's response continued to be 'no help to any faction' in Afghanistan.

This gave rise to a serious shift in the strategic picture in the region, alarming not only Rabbani and Massoud, but also Iran, the Central Asian republics, Russia and India. While Tehran viewed the whole development as an attempt to enforce the American policy of containment of Iran,[55] the secularist Central Asian leaderships felt threatened by the possible spread of the Taliban's Islamic extremism. Moscow came to perceive the changing situation as threatening to its vital strategic interests in its former Central Asian republics,[56] and New Delhi found the changes upsetting the regional balance in favour of Pakistan.[57]

The unwavering Pakistani support of the Taliban and quiet complicity in the Taliban-al-Qaeda alliance invited greater involvement on the part of those other regional actors which found both the politics of the Taliban and their patron repugnant to their individual national and regional interests. Iran for a long time remained indecisive as to whether to increase its aid solely to *Wahdat* or also to provide some help to the Rabbani government. It was only after the August 1998 crisis in Mazar-e Sharif, where the Taliban captured and killed several Iranian diplomats and truck drivers, that Rabbani secured pledges of some assistance from Tehran.[58] Uzbekistan dramatically increased its military and logistic support to Dostum under the euphemism of 'humanitarian and technical aid'.[59] Tajikistan could provide little help since it remained embroiled in the complications of its own civil war, although it served as an important transit point for a trickle of Russian assistance to Massoud. The best the country could do was to provide Massoud with a vital strategic outlet to the outside world and let its airfield in Kulob be used for transit of goods to Massoud's forces, including some 15,000 tonnes of fuel in 1997.[60] Beyond this, in August 1998, President Rakhmonov of Tajikistan announced that he would invoke the clauses of the CIS Collective Security Agreement and ask Russia to beef up its military presence on the border with Afghanistan.[61]

Concerned about the implications of the Taliban ascendancy for its interests in Central Asia, Russia certainly began supplying some arms to the anti-Taliban forces, particularly after the Chief of Russian General Staff, Anatolii Kvashnin, met with Rabbani's emissaries in Tajikistan on 19 August 1998.[62] India joined efforts with Iran and Russia in turning up the diplomatic heat on Pakistan and in dissuading the international community from according recognition to the Taliban, particularly in the wake of the news about acts of genocide and 'ethnic cleansing' committed by the militia, especially against the Shi'a after its capture in late 1998 of Mazar-e Sharif and the central province of Bamiyan.[63] Following the bombing of American embassies in Africa, even Saudi Arabia found itself with little choice but to freeze its diplomatic ties with Kabul. Although the UAE maintained its ties, it felt more and more isolated by the day, and therefore ready to break off ties whenever warranted by Washington.

The shift of the Rabbani government from the capital to the north of Afghanistan simply inaugurated a new phase in Massoud's and his followers' struggle for the soul of Afghanistan. While the Rabbani government still retained Afghanistan's UN General Assembly seat and most of the country's diplomatic missions, Massoud relentlessly toiled to maintain a level of resistance whereby the Taliban and their Pakistani and Arab backers would be prompted to settle for a negotiated settlement of the Afghanistan problem. After the Taliban overran most of the north by late 1998, defeating Dostum, who had joined Rabbani-Massoud's anti-Taliban alliance in late 1996, and capturing Ismail Khan (who two years later escaped their captivity), Massoud made strenuous efforts to widen the resistance by strengthening what he had forged under the name of *Jabhi-e Mutahid-e Islami bara-e Nejati Afghanistan* (the United Islamic Front for the Salvation of Afghanistan) or what the Pakistanis disparagingly dubbed 'the Northern Alliance'. He once again brought Dostum, Ismail Khan and the former Mujahideen governor of eastern Afghanistan, Haji Abdul Qadeer, into the fold to generate new fronts against the Taliban and their outside backers. In early 2001, he made a celebrated visit to the European Union at the invitation of the European Parliament, to drum up international support, and a secret visit to New Delhi to secure some Indian military assistance. As the international situation was tipping against the Taliban and Pakistan, and as Massoud was preparing to launch his late summer offensives, the Taliban and their foreign backers had already plotted Massoud's murder. Two al-Qaeda agents posing as journalists assassinated Massoud on 9 September 2001, in what appeared to be a prelude to the apocalyptic actions against the USA which materialised two days later and in which 2,752 people, mostly Americans, were killed.

Had it not been for those acts of terrorism, the Afghans would have continued to languish under the Taliban rule. In a curious twist of fate, bin Laden and al-Qaeda finally alerted the USA and the international community to the Afghans' plight. The US decision to lead an international military campaign to destroy al-Qaeda and its harbourers, the Taliban, left the Musharraf military regime, which until 11 September had vehemently defended Pakistan's Afghanistan policy, with no choice but to side with the USA against its clients or invite American wrath. Musharraf's immediate and unconditional support of the USA provided Afghanistan with an opportunity to engage in a process of self-determination, without interference by its neighbours, for the first time in 23 years of conflict. By late 2001, the Taliban's rule had been dismantled, al-Qaeda was on the run and, with the help of the USA and the international community as a whole, Massoud's forces had at last succeeded in playing a central role in the US-covered ground war and in leading various Afghan factions to create an internationally supported government, led by a former Mujahideen fighter, Hamid Karzai. This opened a new chapter in the turbulent and tragic evolution of Afghan politics and society, whose future remains as unpredictable ever.

Conclusion

AFGHANISTAN'S POLITICS AND SOCIETY in modern history have been shaped by interaction between variables with which few other countries have had to cope. The variables *royal polygamy*, *major power rivalry* and *ideological extremism*, which underlined the themes of this book, have not all been of equal weight with equal impact in the process. However, their confluence, in conjunction with certain peculiar geo-strategic aspects of Afghanistan as a traditional, ethno-tribal and a crossroad, landlocked Muslim country, has played a determining role in the evolution of the Afghan state and politics and in influencing the material life and psyche of its citizens as well as the country's relevance to the outside world. Most historians and analysts of Afghanistan have too often, for one reason or another, not found it analytically appropriate to focus on these variables in a *cognate form* to the extent necessary. Yet without this, one would be seriously disadvantaged in providing a clear and realistic explanation of some of the complex and less accessible dimensions of the historical development of Afghanistan – which has been so hazardous and, in many ways, different from the countries in its neighbourhood and further afield.

The three variables have undoubtedly been the subject of much scholarly research and writing. But this has been conducted with a focus on them *individually*, rather than in an integrative manner that emphasises the primacy of intersection between royal polygamic-based power struggles and major power rivalries and interventions as contributing centrally to the kind of conditions which have kept the Afghan state weak and vulnerable to ideological extremism as a significant outcome. It is in this sense that the variables have also been largely responsible for Afghanistan's historical journey taking a very turbulent and violent path, punctuated by only one long period of relative peace and stability, that is 1930–1978, in the more than 250 years since the country's coalescence as an identifiable political entity and its acceptance as such in the international system.

Modern Afghanistan made a promising start under its founder, Ahmed Shah Abdali. Within a quarter of century of Ahmed Shah's patrimonial, centralised and charismatic rule, not only had Afghanistan crystallised as a political and territorial entity, but it had also developed a number of political and institutional practices which laid the foundations for the growth of a central authority with some distributive and administrative attributes. Although the Durrani tribal units held the reins of power and subordinated other, mostly non-Pashtun, microsocieties, elements from the latter were selectively and expediently coopted into the governing structures to make the Afghan state – in the narrow sense of the term – work and become resilient in ensuring its longevity. Yet what substantially thwarted the progress of this state beyond what had crystallised under Ahmed Shah was not that the microsocieties successfully revolted against the centre and one another, resulting in an internal breakdown, but rather that Afghanistan witnessed a fragmentation of power, largely due to dynamic interaction between royal polygamic-based power struggles and outside powers' rivalries over Afghanistan. While the practice of polygamy had its roots in Islam, its use by Afghan rulers was fundamental to producing rival contenders for the throne and therefore inter-dynastic power intrigues and rivalries, which in the absence of institutionalisation of politics and clear-cut leadership succession procedures invariably led to bloody fighting between various full and half-brothers, and competing branches of successive ruling families. Such polygamy-based power rivalries have by no means been exclusive to Afghanistan. It has been a feature of rule in many Muslim countries ever since the early centuries of Islam. It became pronounced during the Abbasid Empire (750–1250), and continued to grow under the Ottomans and has lingered on in many patrimonial Arab states in various forms to the present day. In modern times, Saudi Arabia, Jordan, Morocco and some of the smaller Arab states in the Persian Gulf have suffered from it. Even so, no country has borne the brunt of it so much as has Afghanistan.

Indeed, the Afghan polygamic-based power fragmentation would not have attracted much outside attention had it not been accompanied by certain geo-strategic imperatives. Despite being a collection of poor, traditional, ethno-tribal Muslim microsocieties, Afghanistan's location as a landlocked crossroad territory had always made it the subject of focus by rival major powers. This is what provided the nexus between royal polygamic-based power struggles in Afghanistan and their relevance to rival outside powers right up to the 1970s. The internal situation of the inter-dynastic conflict interacted dynamically with the need of the rival powers to recycle one another from gaining advantage in the crossroad territory to render Afghanistan weak from within and under constant pressure from outside. As the domestic power conflicts continued through the nineteenth century, so did the Anglo-Russian interferences in Afghanistan in pursuit of conflicting regional and wider interests. Afghanistan's inability to build enduring domestic structures and institutions played into the hands of the rival powers, and major power competition entrenched the country's status as a weak state, where the microsocieties, either in alliance with one or the other major power or as enclaves without loyalty to any central government, stood strong.

However, despite the resulting fragmentation, Afghanistan always survived as a political-territorial state, as neither of the rival powers found it beneficial to conquer Afghanistan. But it was a state without much internal cohesion and distributive-administrative power. This is how Afghanistan existed, until the formula somewhat shifted with the rule of Amir Abdur Rahman Khan and his son, Habibullah Khan, when the British achieved ascendency in Afghanistan, and the Russians found themselves incapable of doing anything substantial about it, except to nibble their way into Central Asia almost to the borders of present Afghanistan with the Central Asian republics. Had it not been for British backing and a weakened Russia, it is doubtful whether Abdur Rahman Khan and his son would have been able to undertake the brutal processes of domestic power centralisation and a measure of top-controlled liberalisation which featured in the rule of the father and son respectively. The Anglo-Russian rivalry, on the one hand, interacted with domestic power struggles to contribute substantially to preventing Afghanistan from achieving sufficient national cohesion, and political and social development to become a viable state, and, on the other hand, was instrumental in preserving Afghanistan as a state in the minimal sense of the term.

The advent of independence and radical modernisation under King Amanullah certainly ushered in a new era in the process of construction of the Afghan state. Not only were the polygamic-based power rivalries contained and a serious attempt made at political institutionalisation and accelerated modernisation – thanks to the enlightened monarch's monogamous and reformist efforts – but also the British influence was countered by a policy of forging closer ties with the new Soviet regime. However, in the end, Amanullah had to pay a high price for radical modernisation and challenging the British, as his decade-long rule came to an end amid domestic backlashes and, if not active British intervention, at least assertive British indifference.

Perhaps the only period when Afghanistan secured a breathing space from the effects of Great Power rivalry was during the first two decades of the Musahiban rule. Nadir Shah and his two brothers consolidated Afghan independence with minimum outside interference in Afghanistan's internal affairs, largely because of favourable regional circumstances. Nevertheless, this came at a price. Amanullah's radical modernisation was replaced with a process of 'gradual development', his anti-British tilt towards the Soviet Union was modified in favour of a pro-British neutrality and his standing on monogamy was reduced with the inherent polygamic rivalries within the Musahiban household. Although the development of the latter was contained on the surface, the growth of polygamic-based 'royal dualism' underpinned the rule of the Nadiri dynasty. With Mohammad Daoud's assumption of the premiership in 1953, 'royal dualism' took a sharp turn towards bitter rivalry, and Afghanistan became vulnerable to Soviet influence in the context of the US failure to help Daoud with his modernisation drive and disputes with Pakistan, and of the Soviet Union's willingness to contest the US policy of containment of the USSR at its weakest points. As a result, Afghanistan drifted towards the Soviet Union a lot more than had happened under Amanullah or than Daoud could have anticipated.

Yet the nature of the Musahiban's 'royal dualism' was very different from previous phases of polygamic-based power rivalries. This one did not result in open-armed conflicts, as had been the case in the nineteenth century; it was played out at a more sophisticated and policy-orientated levels – perhaps a sign of the maturity of the players, as well as changing times and circumstances. Daoud's modernisation, Pashtunistan policy and friendship with the Soviet Union and Zahir Shah's experiment with democracy, involving rationalisation of Afghanistan's foreign relations, with an effort to reduce the country's dependence on the Soviet Union, were part of the players' strategy against one another. It was also inadvertently in this context that ideological extremism, at first in the form of Marxism-Leninism, was nurtured in Afghan politics. If it had not been for Daoud's friendship with the Soviet Union and his protection and use of elements of pro-Soviet Afghan communists in the 1960s and early 1970s, in pursuit of an agenda against the Zahir Shah camp within the royal family, and finally his deployment of some of these elements to overthrow Zahir Shah's monarchy in the coup of 1973, communism would have stood little chance of gaining any ground in Afghan politics. For Daoud, close ties with the USSR and its Afghan protégés were an instrument in pursuit of a political, not ideological, goal. And this became clearer than ever before when he at last triumphed over his rivals in the royal family and declared Afghanistan a republic under his presidency. Despite his initial reliance on the *Parchami* faction of the PDPA, he soon turned against them, and sought a reduction in his dependence on the Soviet Union by courting closer ties with the USA and its friends in the region. In this, he was prepared to sacrifice even his Pashtunistan policy.

However, this was enough to provoke the PDPA in 1978, with if not direct at least indirect Soviet support, to topple Daoud's regime, liquidate him and his entire family, terminate the long rule of the Mohammadzai clan and all its inherent polygamic-based power rivalries and declare Afghanistan a 'Democratic Republic' with fraternal ties with the Soviet Union. The ideology-free nationalist rule of the Nadiri dynasty at last gave way to usurpation of state power by pro-Soviet Marxist-Leninists – a development unprecedented in Afghan history. It was clear from the outset that the PDPA could not impose its rule without extensive Soviet support. As the PDPA tore itself apart and the Muslim Afghan population rejected its 'Godless' communist rule, the Soviets naïvely resorted to invading Afghanistan in late December 1979, without adequate attention to what had happened to previous invaders of Afghanistan in history. With the Muslim world and most of the other members of the international community rallying behind the Afghan cause, the USA had plenty of justification now to adopt a counter-interventionist strategy in support of the Afghan Islamic resistance to break the back of the Soviet power and eventually win the Cold War. Yet given the US failure to manage post-communist Afghanistan prudently and effectively, a variety of Islamist groups with various ideological dispositions emerged to fill the power vacuum created by the communists and their discredited ideology. Afghanistan drifted from one ideological extreme to the next, especially with the rise of the Pakistan-orchestrated medievalist Taliban militia, who instituted a reign of terror and turned Afghanistan into a source of international terrorism – all in the name of an Islam which had historically been alien to Afghans. A great majority of the Afghans had been and still are followers of the *Hanafi* school of Islam, which is the most moderate and flexible of the four schools to which most of the Muslims around the world belong.

Meanwhile, it was this extremism that finally also helped the Afghan people to be given a way out of the latest vicious phase of violence and destruction which had seized them following the communists' overthrow of Daoud. But of course this came at another price: al-Qaeda's apocalyptic attacks on New York and Washington on 11 September 2001, which not only killed 2,752 people (mostly Americans) and caused massive property destruction, but also challenged America's status as the only superpower following the disintegration of the Soviet Union at the end of 1991. The USA had to act in pursuit of self-reassertion and did so with widespread international support. This marked the beginning of the phase of a third world-power involvement (after the British and the Soviets) in Afghanistan. Following pressure to entice the Pakistani military government of General Pervez Musharraf to join the USA and its allies in the war against Pakistan's clients in Afghanistan, the American-led intervention had, by December 2001, resulted in the dismantling of the rule of the Taliban, and their al-Qaeda and Pakistani allies, and the formation of an internationally-backed Interim Administration, led by Hamid Karzai, in Afghanistan.

Karzai was a moderate, progressive Kandahari Pashtun, who had joined the Mujahideen against the Soviet occupation and had briefly served as Deputy Foreign Minister in the Rabbani government. He was even nominated by the Taliban to represent them at the UN, but soon thereafter had denounced Taliban rule and left to live in the USA, where his family had been running businesses for many years. He returned to southern Afghanistan following 11 September 2001 to fight the Taliban with full American political and military backing. The USA and its allies, especially Britain, pledged not to leave Afghanistan in the lurch again. They promised to do everything possible to help the Afghans to reconstruct their county, and achieve peace and stability, with a lasting 'democratic' order, as soon as possible, so that the country would never again become a source of international terrorism.

The Karzai government initially came into existence as an interim administration for six months, starting from 22 December 2001. It originated from the Bonn agreement, signed two weeks earlier between the United Islamic Front for the Salvation of Afghanistan, led by the forces associated with the late Ahmad Shah Massoud; the Zahir Shah group; and two smaller Pashtun groups. Under the Bonn agreement, in whose formulation the UN and the USA, as well as Germany, played a critical role, Karzai was appointed as compromise choice to head the Interim Administration, with one of its central tasks being to convene an Emergency *Loya Jirgah* to appoint an 18-month-long Transitional Administration to pave the way for holding a general election for the creation of a popularly-mandated regular government. In the meantime, whereas the USA established bases in Afghanistan to stamp out the remnants of the Taliban and al-Qaeda and help America's anti-terror operations beyond Afghanistan, again as provisioned in the Bonn agreement, an International Security Assistance Force (ISAF) was deployed in Kabul to protect the Karzai government and maintain security in the capital.

The Emergency *Loya Jirgah* was held in Kabul from 11 to 19 June 2002, and despite some irregularities in its composition as a largely elected and partly appointed body, and American intervention to keep the lid on factional discontent, especially on the part of supporters of Zahir Shah who had himself returned to Kabul in May 2002 after 29 years in exile, the *Loya Jirgah* proved a success under the circumstances. Probably it was the most democratic *Loya Jirgah* ever held in Afghanistan. It 'consisted of over 1,600 delegates, the majority of whom represented various ethnic groups within Afghanistan. Some were appointed by various warlords and power brokers; others came from abroad representing Afghans living around the world'. After lively and at times heated debate, an overwhelming majority, 1,295 of the delegates, 'voted for Karzai as the head of state'.[1] The two other candidates – one woman, Massouda Jalal and another man, Mahfouz Nadaeei – accepted their defeat without disputing the results. Concurrently, the UN – and for that matter the international community – commenced massive aid operations to sustain the Karzai government, to rebuild Afghanistan and facilitate the return of some three to four million refugees from Pakistan, Iran and other parts of the world.

The US intervention, however, is very different from those by other powers, namely the Soviet Union and Imperial Britain, before it: all the major powers, especially Russia and China, have either actively supported or consented to this intervention. It is also part of a wider US-led global campaign against 'international terrorism', in relation to which the USA has managed, among other things, to secure a firm strategic foothold in Central Asia, where the Russians had historically claimed supremacy. This means that America and its allies are most likely to remain focused on Afghanistan for some time to come, and thus maintain American pre-eminence in the area on a long-term basis. But Afghanistan's problems are by no means over. On the contrary, the challenges facing the Afghans in building a viable polity, with an assertion of full state sovereignty, are enormous.

Certainly, the age of the traditional factors of royal polygamic-based power struggles and major power rivalries, fuelling long periods of instability and conflict and opening space for ideological extremism, is now in the past. The Afghans have reasons to look back at such factors with disdain and trepidation. Yet this is not to claim that the future is not already impregnated with serious risks, problems and endless uncertainties. It is indeed early days to be judgmental about the new phase in Afghanistan's historical journey. However, it may be safe to surmise that Afghanistan is now in the grip of a situation where power still remains seriously fragmented and the American pre-eminence has once again proved that rarely in modern Afghan history has a government come to power and remained in power without a foreign force backing it. The Karzai government has little writ outside Kabul and its authority is limited by various power-holders, ranging from local charismatic and religious leaders to armed commanders and straight-out warlords in different parts of the country. These power-holders have roots in and control over various parts or the whole of microsocieties, whose boundaries and modus operandi may have changed as a result of years of warfare but whose internal dynamisms to enable them to reassert themselves in the context of traditional social divisions and vulnerability to manipulation by both domestic opportunists and outside forces remain very much in place.

Despite its best efforts, the Karzai government has so far remained deeply preoccupied with, and for that matter marred by, the question of how to govern in order to cater to ethnic, factional and family politics. The challenge ahead is to establish an appropriate legal-rational framework and *culturally relevant* processes and institutions to ensure the development of a governmental system and polity, whose operations would be underpinned by principles of public participation, transparency, accountability, administrative-bureaucratic efficiency, social equity, observation of basic human rights, and promotion of merit rather than family connection and ethnic affiliation as the basis for governmental appointments.

Meanwhile, human security in military and economic terms still eludes Afghanistan to a considerable extent. Although, since the defeat of the Taliban, Kabul has become largely safe and stable, as much cannot be said for the rest of the country. On the one hand, the military security of various parts of Afghanistan rests with local power-holders, some of whom have managed to build personalised armies. To expand its authority and create national unity, the Karzai government urgently needs to subordinate such individuals to the authority of the central government. Yet this cannot be done without first of all establishing the necessary processes and institutions, and above all building a professional national army and security force. The Karzai government appears to be overwhelmed by politics of ethnicity and factionalism. Furthermore, even if the USA and its allies provide what it takes to construct new national armed and security forces, as they have indeed promised, the objective will take years to achieve. On the other hand, remnants of the Taliban and al-Qaeda, supported by Gulbuddin Hekmatyar, who has declared *jihad* against the Karzai government and foreign forces, still strut the long, treacherous Afghan-Pakistan border, over which neither the Pakistani government nor the Americans have established control. More disturbing, many in the Pakistani military and ISI as well as Pakistan's Islamist parties (which in the October 2002 general election gained control over local legislative assemblies in the North-West Frontier Province and Baluchestan, as well as one third of seats in the National Assembly) continue to back the

Taliban and their al-Qaeda allies. There are ongoing reports of cross-border infiltrations into Afghanistan.

As long as the Afghan-Pakistan border remains uncontrolled, Pakistan's repeated declaration of support for the new order in Afghanistan will prove to be ineffective. At the same time, no one can control the border if the old Afghan-Pakistan dispute over it is not settled. The Durand Line demarcation of 1893 was thought to be valid for 100 years, notwithstanding Afghanistan's rejection of it. If so, the agreement has lapsed by a decade, and negotiations must start immediately for a new agreement. But with the Karzai government very weak and its main international backer, the USA, more interested in keeping nuclear-powered Pakistan on board in its war on terror, there seems little chance of such negotiations eventuating soon – an issue which presents another major challenge to the struggling Afghan government. It may well be that an issue of this type could appropriately be remitted to the International Court of Justice for a binding determination.

On the national reconstruction front, the task seems even more daunting. It is a common view within and outside Afghanistan that the country's future peace and stability rests very much on how rapidly its economic and social life is rebuilt as a precondition to prompting the Afghans to change their culture of the gun to that of peace. To this end, the international community in January 2002 pledged $4.5 billion aid over the next five years and mostly fulfilled its commitment of $1.8 billion for 2002. But the problem has been that it is widely believed that Afghanistan's rapid reconstruction to the level to bring about long-term stability and security as inter-related factors would require $15–20 billion, and of the amount provided for 2002, much of it had to be spent on urgent humanitarian assistance and on UN and NGO operations. There has also been the argument that Afghanistan could not absorb any more than has been promised, given its very limited infrastructural and human resource capacity. This is not to claim that the Karzai government has not been able to commence the difficult task of national reconstruction; it has, especially with its centrepiece in 2002 being the start of the reconstruction of the Kabul-Kandahar-Herat highway. The point is that national reconstruction has had a very slow start, with its future looking somewhat murky in view of shortcomings in many other areas, not to mention the old Afghan practices of nepotism, kickbacks and bribery which have already made their growth felt across the board.

In addition, given the fact that US involvement in Afghanistan has been more motivated by America's war on terror than what might be best for the Afghan people in the long run, one cannot but be sceptical of the USA's commitment to rebuilding the war-torn country, and empowering the Afghans to run and protect their country independent of any foreign military involvement. There is every chance that Washington will let its Afghan policy be guided more by fluctuations in its war against international terrorism and America's globalist interests. The USA has been insensitive towards and neglectful of Afghanistan's needs and aspirations before, as discussed in this book. It may go down the same path once more.

For most of its modern history, Afghanistan has lived dangerously between the jaws of major or regional powers in one form or another. This time, it is landed between being once again very weak and vulnerable nationally and the USA's geo-strategic pre-eminence which recognises no limitations when it comes to America's interests as the greatest and most powerful actor ever to have existed on earth. The biggest challenge of all confronting the Afghans is how to steer their way out of this situation and ensure the development of Afghanistan as an independent and viable state for the new millennium.

Notes

Introduction

1. Mountstuart Elphinstone, *An Account of the Kingdom of Caubul*, Vol. I, Karachi: Oxford University Press, 1972, p.198.

2. Fazal-ur-Rehman, 'Power Struggle in Afghanistan', *Strategic Studies*, 16(4), 1994, pp.27–8.

3. Henry VII of England, Louis XI of France and Vasilii III of Russia are but a few examples of 'ambitious and highly successful rulers' who used kin-related institutions and practices in centralisation efforts. Robert O. Crummey, *The Formation of Muscovy, 1304–1613*, London and New York: Longman, 1987, p.84.

4. Martha Mundy, *Domestic Government: Kinship, Community and Polity in North Yemen*, London and New York: I.B.Tauris, 1995, p.107.

5. For a concise review of multiple marriage practices in the Middle East, see Dawoud Sudqi el Alami and Doreen Hinchcliffe, *Islamic Marriage and Divorce Laws of the Arab World*, London: Kluwer Law International, 1996, pp.5–32.

6. For example, Amir Dost Mohammad had 27 sons, at least 12 of whom survived him and were locked in a fierce fight for the throne in Kabul after his death. The same was true of Timur Shah, the son of the founder of modern Afghanistan, Ahmad Shah Abdali, whose rival sons plunged Afghanistan into a long period of inter-dynastic fighting. In the recent past, the polygamic-based rivalry between two branches of the Nadir Shah family (1930–1978) proved to be disastrous for Afghanistan, as discussed in Chapters 4, 6 and 7.

7. A.A. Kohzad, 'Men and Events in Afghanistan through 18th and 19th Century', *Afghanistan*, 11(4), October–December 1956, pp.60–1.

8. Igor M. Reisner, *Afganistan*, Moscow: Gosizdat, 1929, p.85.

9. Shmuel Eisenstadt has called such regimes 'neo-patrimonial', particularly stressing the distributive and guardianship roles of the state in them. Shmuel N. Eisenstadt, *Traditional Patrimonialism and Modern Neo-Patrimonialism*, Beverly Hills: Sage, 1973, p.59.

10. M. Siddieq Noorzoy, 'Soviet Economic Interests in Afghanistan', *Problems of Communism*, 36(3), May–June 1987, pp.43–53.

11.   Victor L. Mote, 'Afghanistan and the Transport Infrastructures of Turkestan', in Milan Hauner and Robert L. Canfield (eds), *Afghanistan and the Soviet Union: Collision and Transformation*, Boulder: Westview Press, 1989, pp.120–59.

12.   Miron Rezun, *Intrigue and War in Southwest Asia: The Struggle for Supremacy from Central Asia to Iraq*, New York: Praeger, 1992, p.42.

13.   Malcolm E. Yapp, 'A Little Game: Afghanistan Since 1918', *South Asian Review*, 8(4), 1975, p.406.

14.   Richard S. Newell, 'Afghanistan: The Dangers of Cold War Generosity', *The Middle East Journal*, 23(2), Spring 1969, p.170.

15.   See Thomas T. Hammond, *Red Flag Over Afghanistan: The Communist Coup, the Soviet Invasion, and the Consequences*, Boulder: Westview Press, 1984; Henry S. Bradsher, *Afghanistan and the Soviet Union*, Durham: Duke University Press, 1983; Anthony Arnold, *Afghanistan: The Soviet Invasion in Perspective*, Stanford: Hoover Institution Press, 1981; William Maley, *The Afghanistan Wars*, London: Palgrave Macmillan, 2002.

16.   Dennis Smith, *The Rise of Historical Sociology*, Philadelphia: Temple University Press, 1991, p.183.

17.   Michael Edwardes, *Playing the Great Game: A Victorian Cold War*, London: Hamilton, 1975, p.viii.

18.   A monograph by Jonathan L. Lee, *The 'Ancient Supremacy': Bukhara, Afghanistan and the Battle for Balkh, 1731–1901*, Leiden, New York, Köln: E.J. Brill, 1996, provides a convincing account of how cis-Oxanian Turkestan became 'Afghan' due to the incompetence of British officials. There is an excellent study of Germany's unrealistic plans concerning penetrating Afghanistan between the First and Second World Wars: Francis R. Nicosia, '"Drang Nach Osten" Continued: Germany and Afghanistan during the Weimar Republic', *Journal of Contemporary History*, 32(2), April 1997, pp.235–58.

19.   The KGB, military and diplomatic personnel on the ground, as well as respective services' analysts in Moscow all advised different courses of action. See G.M. Kornienko, 'Kak prinimalis' resheniia o vvode sovetskikh voisk v Afganistan i ikh vyvode', *Novaia i noveishaia istoriia*, No. 3, May–June 1993, pp.107–118; 'Dokumenty sovetskogo rukovodstva o polozhenii v Afganistane. 1979–1980', *Novaia i noveishaia istoriia*, No. 3, May–June 1996, pp.91–9.

20.   Ijaz Khan, 'Afghanistan: A Geopolitical Study', *Central Asian Survey*, 17(2), 1998, pp.489–502.

21.   Tara Kartha, 'The Diffusion of Light Weapons in Pakistan', *Small Wars and Insurgencies*, 8(1), Spring 1997, pp.71–87.

22.   Maley, 'Afghanistan Observed', *Australian Journal of International Affairs*, 51(2), 1997, p.267.

23.   *Itogi*, No. 7 (92), 1998, p.32.

24.   Ernest Gellner, *Postmodernism, Reason and Religion*, London and New York: Routledge, 1993, p.64.

25.   In Dale Eickelman's categorisation, the former can be referred to as 'formal ideologies' and the latter as 'practical ideologies'. Dale F. Eickelman, *The Middle East: An Anthropological Approach*, Englewood Cliffs: Prentice Hall, 1989, p.148. Both types are concerned with the legitimation of collective action, albeit on different levels: macro and microsocietal.

26.   M. Nazif Shahrani, 'The Future of the State and the Structure of Community

Governance in Afghanistan', in Maley (ed.), *Fundamentalism Reborn? Afghanistan and the Taliban*, London: Hurst & Co., 1998, p.233.

27. Barnett Rubin has observed that the particular growth of various 'nationalist', 'communist' and 'Islamic' opposition groups occurred after 1973, when 'for a variety of reasons... the superpowers and regional powers began to aid anti-system actors'. Barnett R. Rubin, 'Women and Pipelines: Afghanistan's Proxy Wars', *International Affairs*, 73(2), 1997, p.285.

28. For example, the ultra-left *Setam-e Melli* party established in 1968 enjoyed a degree of support in Badakhshan not because local peasants were taken by Mao Tse Tung's ideas, but mostly because its leader, Tahir Badakhshi, originated from Faizabad and could claim parochial loyalty in his home region.

29. Joseph C. Furnas, *The Americans: A Social History of the United States, 1587–1914*, New York: Putnam, 1969, p.9.

30. Trevelyan was in a position to utilise the experience of at least two centuries of classic historical sociology, originating with David Hume's *History of England* (1754). In the same fashion, Fernand Braudel and other *Annalistes* could draw on the heritage of Herder and French encyclopaedists to afford the luxury of looking 'beyond the diplomatic files, to real life'. Fernand Braudel, *The Mediterranean and the Mediterranean World in the Age of Philip II*, Vol. I, trans. Siân Reynolds, London: Collins, 1972, p.19. As far as Afghanistan is concerned, the critical mass of empirical knowledge and interpretative works necessary for a similar effort has not yet been achieved.

31. Polity is understood to be an entirety of contenders for power within a given population who have the routine means of making claims on the government that are accepted by other contenders and the agents of the government. The life of the polity is characterised by the attempts of non-members to influence the government, including attempts to gain membership. See Charles Tilly, 'Town and Country in Revolution', in John Wilson Lewis (ed.), *Peasant Rebellion and Communist Revolution in Asia*, Stanford: Stanford University Press, 1974, pp.278–80; James B. Rule, *Theories of Civil Violence*, Berkeley: University of California Press, 1988, pp.176–92.

32. Anthony Giddens, *Central Problems in Social Theory: Action, Structure and Contradiction in Social Analysis*, London: Macmillan, 1979, p.230.

33. Vadim M. Masson and Vadim A. Romodin, *Istoriia Afganistana*, Vols I and II, Moscow: Nauka, 1964–1965.

34. Vartan Gregorian, *The Emergence of Modern Afghanistan: Politics of Reform and Modernization, 1880–1946*, Stanford: Stanford University Press, 1969.

35. Louis Duprée, *Afghanistan*, Princeton: Princeton University Press, 1980.

36. For instance, a thoughtful, relevant and otherwise impeccable discourse on gender issues, once elevated to the status of an *ultimo ratio* of the PDPA policies, culminates in the conclusion that the demise of the Marxist regime in Afghanistan had been caused by the politicisation of gender in that country. Valentine M. Moghadam, 'Patriarchy and the Politics of Gender in Modernizing Societies: Iran, Pakistan and Afghanistan', *South Asia Bulletin*, 13(1–2), 1993, pp.129–31.

37. John M. Roberts, *History of the World*, London: Hutchinson, 1976, p.11.

38. Syed Abdul Quddus' effort can serve as an example here. This author has covered an amazing array of subjects in a meagre 200 pages, ranging from Hellenistic culture to poultry farming to the peace-loving nature of the Pakistani nation, in

what was promised to be, for many years, 'the source-book for all reference material not only on the history of the development of Pakistan's external relations with Afghanistan but also on the outside interests in this strategic area'. It all eventually degenerates into repetitive invectives against Indian opportunism and calls for Muslim solidarity. Syed Abdul Quddus, *Afghanistan and Pakistan: A Geopolitical Study*, Lahore: Ferozsons Ltd., 1982.

39.   Leon B. Poullada, *Reform and Rebellion in Afghanistan, 1919–1929: King Amanullah's Failure to Modernize a Tribal Society*, Ithaca, NY: Cornell University Press, 1973.

40.   Duprée, *Afghanistan*, p.xxi.

41.   Nancy Shields Kollmann, *Kinship and Politics: The Making of the Muscovite Political System, 1345–1547*, Stanford: Stanford University Press, 1987, p.180.

42.   Mir Gholam Mohammad Ghobar, *Afghanestan dar masir-e ta'rikh*, Kabul: Markaz-e nashr-e inqelab, 1988; Fayz Muhammad, *Memoir of the Coup*, trans. from Russian by R.D. McChesney, unpublished manuscript, April 1996; Robert D. McChesney, *Kabul under Seige: Fayz Muhammad's Account of the 1929 Uprising*, Princeton: Markus Wiener Publishers, 1999; Khalilullah Khalili, *'Ayyori az Khorasan, Amir Habibullah Khadem-e din-e rasulullah*, Peshawar: no publisher, 1984; Burkhan-ud-Din-khan-i-Kushkeki, *Kattagan i Badakhshan*, Tashkent: Gosudarstvennoe izdatelstvo, 1926; Ahmad Makhdumi Donish, *Risola yo mukhtasare az ta'rikhi saltanati khonadoni manghitiya*, Dushanbe: Sarwat, 1992; Fitrat, *Dawrai hukmronii Amir Olimkhon*, Dushanbe: Palatai davlatii kitobho, 1991. An excellent review of Afghan official historiography in the second half of the nineteenth and the early twentieth centuries can be found in: Romodin, *Afganistan vo vtoroi polovine XIX – nachale XXv. Ofitsialnaia istoriia i istoriografiia*, Moscow: Nauka, 1990.

43.   Rubin, *The Fragmentation of Afghanistan: State Formation and Collapse in the International System*, New Haven: Yale University Press, 1995.

44.   Asta Olesen, *Islam and Politics in Afghanistan*, Richmond: Curzon Press, 1995.

45.   Olivier Roy, *Islam and Resistance in Afghanistan*, Cambridge: Cambridge University Press, 1986; O. Roy, *Afghanistan: From Holy War to Civil War*, Princeton: The Darwin Press, 1995.

46.   Nancy Tapper, *Bartered Brides: Politics, Gender and Marriage in an Afghan Tribal Society*, Cambridge: Cambridge University Press, 1991.

47.   Akbar S. Ahmed, *Pukhtun Economy and Society*, London: Routledge & Kegan Paul, 1980.

48.   V.G. Korgun, *Intelligentsiia v politicheskoi zhizni Afganistana*, Moscow: Nauka, 1983.

49.   Abdul Samad Ghaus, *The Fall of Afghanistan: An Insider's Account*, Washington: Pergamon-Brassey's International Defense Publishers, 1988.

50.   Ahmed Rashid, *Taliban: Militant Islam, Oil and Fundamentalism in Central Asia*, London: I.B.Tauris, 2000; Maley (ed.), *Fundamentalism Reborn?*

51.   Harold Bloom, *The Western Canon: The Books and School of the Ages*, New York: Harcourt Brace, 1994, p.521.

Chapter 1: From Tribal Confederacy to National Coalescence

1.   Ronald Cohen, 'State Origins: A Reappraisal', in Henri J.M. Claessen and Peter Skalnik (eds), *The Early State*, The Hague: Mouton Publishers, 1978, p.55.

2. Hudud al-'Alam, *'The Regions of the World': A Persian Geography 372AH–982AD*, Oxford: Oxford University Press, 1937, p.91.

3. See Duprée, *Afghanistan*, p.xvii.

4. An *ethnie* is a given population, a social group 'whose members share a sense of common origins, claim a common and distinctive history and destiny, possess one or more distinctive characteristics, and feel a sense of collective uniqueness and solidarity'. Anthony D. Smith, *The Ethnic Revival*, Cambridge: Cambridge University Press, 1981, p.66. Thus, the preponderance of 'primordial' cultural traits distinguishes this phenomenon from a modern nation with its overlay culture based on various formal institutions, such as state, territorial sovereignty, predominant ideology, and so on.

5. As Mountstuart Elphinstone observed in 1814, 'the name of Afghaun... is, probably, modern. It is known to the Afghauns themselves only through the medium of the Persian language. Their own name for their nation is Pooshtoon'. Elphinstone, *An Account of the Kingdom of Caubul*, Vol. I, p.200.

6. Both Pashtuns and Tajiks are Indo-Iranian peoples. However, Pushtu (Pashto, Pakhto) belongs to the Eastern Iranian group of the Indo-Iranian branch of the Indo-European language family, whereas Dari, the tongue of Afghan Tajiks, is a Western Iranic language, very similar to Persian. According to Elphinstone, in the nineteenth century the name of Tajik was applied indiscriminately 'to those inhabitants of countries where Toorkee and Pushtoo are spoken, whose vernacular language is Persian'. Elphinstone, *An Account of the Kingdom of Caubul*, Vol. II, p.404. Contemporary Tajik scholars believe that: 'until the 17–18th centuries, southern and eastern provinces of today's Afghanistan were populated predominantly by Tajiks who throughout the Middle Ages suffered from regular marauding raids of Pashtun brigands – hence the nickname "Afghan", derived from Persian "feghan" – a cry of despair that people uttered while being assaulted and robbed by that tribe.' Saidi Sa'di, *Mukhtasari ta'rikhi siyosii Tojikoni Afghoniston*, Dushanbe: Oli Somon, 1995, p.26.

7. Hasan Kawun Kakar, *Government and Society in Afghanistan: The Reign of Amir 'Abd al-Rahman Khan*, Austin and London: University of Texas Press, 1979, p.xvii.

8. L.N. Kiseleva, *Iazyk Dari Afganistana*, Moscow: Nauka, 1985, p.12.

9. Masson and Romodin, *Istoriia Afganistana*, Vol. I, p.11.

10. Olesen, *Islam and Politics in Afghanistan*, p.29.

11. In the eighteenth century, there existed in excess of 380 Pashtun tribes belonging to four major tribal groups – Sarbani, Mati, Gurgushti and Karrani. Ni'mat Allah, *History of the Afghans*, London: S. Gupta, 1965, pp.40, 122. The Uzbeks and the Turkmens were each divided into nine tribal clusters. Kh. Khashimbekov, *Uzbeki severnogo Afganistana*, Moscow: IVRAN, 1994, p.15; A.K. Babaeva, 'Turkmeny severo-zapadnogo Afganistana: k voprosu o rasselenii turkmenskikh plemen', in *Afganistan: ekonomika, politika, istoriia*, Moscow: Nauka, 1984, p.119. The Tajiks, although devoid of tribal divisions, did not have a strong sense of ethnic community and identified primarily with historical and geographic regions, such as Kuhdaman, Kuhistan, Badakhshan, Panjsher and so on. The same situation prevailed amongst other Farsi-speaking ethnic communities, such as the Khorasanis, who, alongside the Tajiks, were known under the generic name of *farsiwans*.

12. The first Russian diplomatic mission sent by Tsar Ivan III arrived in Herat in 1464. M.R. Arunova, 'Iz istorii pervykh russkikh posolstv na territorii Afganistana',

in *Afganistan: ekonomika, politika, istoriia*, Moscow: Nauka, 1984, p.97. Russia's systematic colonial expansion into Central Asia commenced at the beginning of the eighteenth century under Peter I, but acquired paramount significance in Tsarist foreign policy only in the wake of the disastrous Crimean War of 1853–1856.

13. In dealing with Pashtun tribal structure, the following classification will be employed, in descending order of complexity: Tribal Groups; Tribal Confederations; Tribes; Clans. The Sadozais, for example, formed the dominant clan (*khan-khel*) of the Popolzai tribe of the Abdali tribal confederation of the Sarbani tribal group. For an alternative categorisation, see Rubin, *The Fragmentation of Afghanistan*, p.28.

14. During the *Jirga*, several Abdali *khans*, particularly from the strongest Barakzai tribe, laid claims to leadership. After eight rounds of negotiations, the candidature of Ahmad Shah Sadozai was approved, for his clan appeared to be the weakest amongst the contenders. The support of an eminent Sufi leader, Sabir Shah Kabuli, must have also been instrumental in Ahmad Shah's selection. *The Life of Abdur Rahman, Amir of Afghanistan*, Vol. II, London: John Murray, 1900, pp.215–17.

15. As Igor Reisner has argued, the Abdalis were perhaps better geared to tackling the onerous task of state-building in Afghanistan than other tribal confederations: 'In contrast to the Yusufzais and Bannuchis, as well as the Ghilzais, the Durranis were a relatively peaceful people, which could be explained by a relatively greater authority of the khans, and also by the fact that the chief of the tribe and the chiefs of the units, together with the jirga, not only had the right to mediate between the conflicting parties, but could also settle the matter without their consent, their decision being final and obligatory. Blood feuds were not widespread among the Durranis. The Sadozai chiefs of that tribe repeatedly called on the Durranis never to raise a sword against one another.' Reisner, 'Specific Features of the Development of Feudalism among the Afghans', in *Afghanistan: Past and Present*, Moscow: USSR Academy of Sciences, 1982, pp.52–3.

16. For an excellent essay on the peculiarities of authority, legitimation and transmission in Pashtun polities, see Jon W. Anderson, 'Khan and Khel: Dialectics of Pakhtun Tribalism', in Richard Tapper (ed.), *The Conflict of Tribe and State in Iran and Afghanistan*, London and Canberra: Croom Helm, 1983, pp.119–49.

17. The Durrani ascendancy was based on a solid amalgam of Islamic ideology and tribal codes of behaviour: 'To be a Durrani means more than just being a Sunni and indicates the ability to trace unbroken descent to a recognised Durrani ancestor and through him via the accepted genealogies to the ancestor of all Pashtuns, Qais Abd al-Rashid, who is said to have been among the first voluntary converts to Islam. Thus descent gives Durrani, and in theory other Pashtuns, a claim to religious superiority over all groups other than Sayyids. Moreover, in the Durrani view, all Pashtun custom is hallowed because it conforms strictly with religious prescriptions; they rarely make a distinction between custom and religious law and frequently are unable to do so. Things Pashtun and things Muslim are identical. As a buttress for their notions of their religious superiority, Durrani form a separate religious community and have slight interest in the teachings of religious leaders of other ethnic groups.' N. Tapper and R. Tapper, 'Marriage Preferences and Ethnic Relations among Durrani Pashtuns of Afghan Turkestan', *Folk*, 24, 1982, p.162.

18. In Arnold Fletcher's florid characterisation, 'the story of Ahmed Shah is one in which a father's reputation has suffered from the sins of his children. One of the most imposing figures in Asian history, a brilliant military commander, and the founder of a nation, he nevertheless remains almost unknown to the outside world. Endowed with all the qualities that make for successful leadership, Ahmed had few of the defects that sully the records of so many Asian rulers... Toward his own people he was benevolent, free from pride of station, and approachable by the poorest... That Afghanistan still exists as a kingdom after two centuries of vicissitudes is due not a little to a monarch who is known not as The Great but by the warmer tribute of Baba, "Father".' Arnold Fletcher, *Afghanistan: Highway of Conquest*, Ithaca, NY: Cornell University Press, 1965, p.57.

19. Masson and Romodin, *Istoriia Afganistana*, Vol. II, pp.92–4.

20. Elphinstone, *An Account of the Kingdom of Caubul*, Vol. II, p.301. The concept of an elite force recruited from non-indigenous elements who enjoyed better conditions of service than other corps and were particularly loyal to the ruler was, of course, an age-old tradition; suffice it to mention the scholarians of Constantine I, the Turkic cavalry of the Samanids, or the Janissaries in the Ottoman Empire.

21. In 1757, Ahmad Shah assumed the title of *Ghazi*, that is, Champion of the Faith, and his subsequent campaigns in India were justified by the need to 'defend Islam from the assaults of the Hindu infidels, who were in great force and threatened to over-power the followers of the Prophet'. George P. Tate, *The Kingdom of Afghanistan: A Historical Sketch*, Karachi: Indus Publications, 1973, p.78.

22. This paternalistic political praxis is called *mardomdari*, or 'taking care of people', in Afghanistan.

23. According to some scholars, Ahmad Shah was successful because of his exceptional skills, incredible luck and favourable geopolitical situation. There were no objective prerequisites for the emergence of the sense of nationhood in Afghanistan as yet. Ahmad Shah 'was considered to be a chief of chiefs and he earned high personal loyalty and respect for himself, but there is little in the structure or character of his rule or in subsequent developments to indicate that this *ramassement* of tribal power, held together by the charisma and magnetism of a bold leader, ever grew into a mature sense of nationhood in which the loyalty of the tribesmen was transferred from their own kinship groups to a central authority, much less to any concept of a state or even an ethnic "nation".' L.B. Poullada, *Reform and Rebellion in Afghanistan*, p.3.

24. As Olaf Caroe has put it, Ahmad Shah is still 'the very ideal of the Afghan genius, hardy and enterprising... He founded an Afghan monarchy which endured, and still finds its royal house from Ahmad's tribe, the Durranis... The fame of his house, the Saddozai sect of the Popalzai Durranis, still evokes an Afghan sense of loyalty which to some extent even crosses international frontiers.' Olaf Caroe, *The Pathans: 550 BC–AD 1957*, Karachi: Oxford University Press, 1980, p.259.

25. Caroe, *The Pathans*, p.12.

26. John Gray wrote in 1895: 'the Ghilzai is a very numerous and powerful tribe... They are a race of fighting men, but have not given a ruler to Afghanistan. One reason for their submission to the government of the Duranis [sic] at Kabul, is the fact that a large portion of the tribe is nomadic in its habits, moving from highlands to lowlands with the seasons.' John Alfred Gray, *At the Court of the Amir: A Narrative*, London: Darf Publishers Ltd, 1987, p.203. Generally, the

Ghilzais were at a lower stage of social development than the Abdalis: 'There was no powerful tribal nobility among the Ghilzais. Although they had their own khan-khel (he belonged to the Hoteki unit) which was a hereditary supplier of chiefs of the entire tribe, this khan family did not enjoy any special privileges (in contrast to the Sadozais in the Durrani tribe). The Ghilzai khans did not have any established coercive power over their fellow-tribesmen.' Reisner, 'Specific Features of the Development of Feudalism', p.56.

27. Lee, *The 'Ancient Supremacy'*, pp.92–9.

28. Qur'an: 4:3; Nawal el Saadawi, *The Hidden Face of Eve: Women in the Arab World*, Boston: Beacon Press, 1982, p.196.

29. Patriarchy is interpreted here in the broadest sense, as a 'kinship-ordered social structure with strictly defined sex roles in which women are subordinated to men'. Moghadam, 'Patriarchy and the Politics of Gender in Modernizing Societies', p.122.

30. In the late tenth century a petty Muslim ruler of the locality of Banihar, presumably near today's Jalalabad, had no fewer than 30 wives and concubines. Hudud al-'Alam, *'The Regions of the World'*, p.91. As late as the 1960s, in a rural community in Central Hindukush some 15 per cent of married men had more than one wife; 'these polygynists are the well-to-do, in the upper half of society'. J.P. Singh Uberoi, 'Social Organisation of the Tajiks of Andarab Valley, Afghanistan', Ph.D. Thesis, Australian National University, Canberra, 1964, p.27.

31. In Nancy Tapper's opinion: 'marriage is an integral part of on-going political relations at all levels of social organisation from the household to the ethnic group… marriage and political activity are inextricably linked in Durrani thought.' N. Tapper, *Bartered Brides*, p.65. Two important observations should be made here: (1) since, for Durranis, wife-takers were always equal or superior to wife-givers, excessive procurement of wives by the Durrani khans from other tribes and ethnic groups, especially at the early stages of state-building, was an important mechanism of asserting their exalted social status; (2) through strict enforcement of the ban on hypogamy, the Durrani aristocracy maintained its exclusivity and cohesion vis-à-vis external forces.

32. Caroe has made a strong argument that whenever a Durrani monarch arranged a tribal marriage for himself, tribal affection was focused on the *son* of that marriage, not the monarch, and during the succession struggle tribes would naturally support their respective offspring. Caroe, *The Pathans*, p.260.

33. Amir Abdur Rahman Khan (1880–1901) summarised the succession routine in Afghanistan thus: 'It is quite clear by our religion, as well as by our customs, that the eldest son succeeds to the throne, provided he is fitted for the post, and is also approved and selected by the nation. There have, however, been instances where younger sons have been nominated by fathers who were so weak as to allow themselves to be influenced by the mothers of such sons. The result has invariably been to plunge the country into civil wars, struggles and failure.' *The Life of Abdur Rahman*, Vol. II, p.9. (The authorship of the second volume of Abdur Rahman's book is often ascribed to his former secretary, Sultan Mohammad Khan. Nonetheless, the quoted opinion may be regarded as broadly shared by Afghanistan's ruling elite at the time. See Romodin, 'Taina sensatsionnoi publikatsii Sultan Muhammad-khana', in *Strany i narody Vostoka*, Vyp. XVIII, Moscow: Nauka, 1976, pp.116–24.) The order of seniority and precedence among members of the Afghan ruling elite was complicated even further by the fact that 'in the

condition of several, well-spaced marriages on the deceased father's part, as is common among polygamists, the succeeding generation is very likely to include full brothers and father's sons of widely differing ages'. Uberoi, 'Social Organisation of the Tajiks of Andarab Valley', p.126.

34. The turbulent reign of Dost Mohammad was illustrative in this respect. His mother was from the Jawan Sher group of the Qizilbash of Kabul who, among other things, had facilitated the Qizilbash migration to Peshawar. Qizilbash fighters remained a loyal force behind Dost Mohammad during his struggle against his half-brothers.

35. He was survived by 23 sons. William K. Fraser-Tytler, *Afghanistan: A Study of Political Developments in Central and Southern Asia*, London: Oxford University Press, 1967, p.67.

36. In the eyes of the Durrani aristocracy, the eldest son of Timur Shah, Humayun, was much more suitable for succession since his mother was a pure Sadozai. Caroe, *The Pathans*, p.261; Tate, *The Kingdom of Afghanistan*, p.94.

37. Karl Marx thus characterised the political situation at that time: 'Napoleon was plotting in the East as well; Calcutta's "office-boys" trembled at the combination: *France, Persia, and Afghanistan*.' Karl Marx, *Notes on Indian History (664–1858)*, Moscow: Foreign Languages Publishing House, 1956, p.126.

38. The first agreement between an Afghan monarch and a European power – an anti-Napoleon treaty – was signed in 1809 by Shah Shuja and Britain's Mountstuart Elphinstone and has been assessed by contemporary historians as 'a useless measure against an imaginary Franco-Persian combination'. James A. Norris, *The First Afghan War, 1838–1842*, Cambridge: Cambridge University Press, 1967, p.14.

39. N.A. Khalfin, *Rossiia i khanstva Srednei Azii*, Moscow: Nauka, 1974, p.366.

40. Compare William Moorcroft's despatches on the mythical 'monstrous plan of aggrandisement' – Russia's penetration of India via Kashgar, circa 1825, and the absurd conviction of A.I. Bariatinskii, the Caucasus Governor, that the British were planning to launch a two-pronged attack on Russia, from the Persian Gulf in the South and Afghanistan in the East, circa 1857. Peter Hopkirk, *The Great Game: The Struggle for Empire in Central Asia*, New York: Kodansha International, 1992, p.95; N.A. Khalfin, *Prisoedinenie Srednei Azii k Rossii*, Moscow: Nauka, 1965, p.97.

41. Russia's Foreign Minister, Prince Gorchakov, wrote in 1864: 'The situation of Russia in Central Asia is identical with the situation of all enlightened states that come in touch with semi-barbaric itinerant peoples devoid of stable social organisation. In such cases the interests of the safety of borders and trade links always demand that a more enlightened state have a considerable power over its neighbours.' O. Bokiev, *Zavoevanie i prisoedinenie Severnogo Tadzhikistana, Pamira i Gornogo Badakhshana k Rossii*, Dushanbe: Irfon, 1994, p.14.

42. The first comprehensive policy document outlining Russia's interests in Central Asia appeared in 1859. It proclaimed that the Tsarist Empire 'presently does not envisage any actions of conquest for this part of Asia', stressing, at the same time, the importance of establishing ties with the Emirate of Bukhara in order to 'avert British interference into Central Asian affairs', and measures aimed at securing Central Asian markets and 'pushing the British aside, preferably completely, from trade there.' Khalfin, *Prisoedinenie Srednei Azii k Rossii*, pp.110–11.

43. Actually, it was Captain Arthur Conolly of the 6th Bengal Native Light Cavalry who originally coined the phrase, circa 1831. Hopkirk, *The Great Game*, p.123. Kipling's use of this expression dates from 1901.

44. First evidenced in 1838, 'the British push toward Afghanistan and occupation of
     advanced positions there came to be called *forward policy*. This policy was at times
     discontinued in favour of a more restrained *masterly inactivity*, but it was clear
     that the latter attitude merely meant the forswearance of *military* intervention
     and occupation and not the total cessation of *political* interference. Then, for the
     sake of the defense of India, a time came when the British were ready to test the
     merits of a third formula: the establishment of Afghanistan as a buffer state between
     the Russian empire and India'. Ghaus, *The Fall of Afghanistan*, p.2.

45. George N. Curzon, *Persia and the Persian Question*, Vol. I, reprint, London: Frank
     Cass, 1996, pp.3–4. Curzon was echoed by such a penny-counting administrator as
     Lord Lytton, Viceroy of British India, who opined in 1876 that 'Potentates such as
     the Khan of Khelat or the Ameer of Kabul are mere dominoes, or counters which
     can be of no importance to us were it not for the costly stakes we put upon them in
     the great game for Empire we are playing with Russia.' Quoted in Anthony Verrier,
     Francis Younghusband and the Great Game, London: Jonathan Cape, 1991, p.49.

46. Negotiations concerning the power struggle in Central Asia and the avoidance of
     a head-on collision between Britain and Russia commenced in 1869, on the former's
     initiative, and ended in 1873. As a result, despite lip service to the 'neutral' status
     of Afghanistan's northern border, 'each power in practice recognised the sphere
     of influence of the other, beginning on the far bank of the Amu-Darya. Britain
     thus obtained Russia's promise not to cross Afghanistan's frontier, while Russia
     secured recognition of her influence over Bukhara and, by inference, Kokand
     from the only other imperialist power with interests in Central Asia'. Seymour
     Becker, *Russia's Protectorates in Central Asia: Bukhara and Khiva, 1865–1924*,
     Cambridge, MA: Harvard University Press, 1968, p.63. The compromise between
     the two colonial powers was beneficial to the Afghan Amir and disadvantaged
     independent non-Pashtun rulers of the region: 'It has been decided that, without
     reference to nationality, everything south of the Oxus belongs to Cabul.' Sir Henry
     Rawlinson, *England and Russia in the East*, reprint, New York: Praeger Publishers,
     1970, p.277. Thus, autonomous Uzbek principalities of Balkh, Khulm and Qunduz
     that hitherto had been in the sphere of influence of Bukhara were gradually
     absorbed by the Afghan state. Another consequence of the settlement was the
     inclusion of Badakhshan and Wakhan, the territories populated by Mountain Tajiks
     that did not belong to Afghanistan, into the realm of Amir Sher Ali Khan. Bokiev,
     Zavoevanie i prisoedinenie Severnogo Tadzhikistana, p.171.

47. The most striking example of proxy fighting was the unsuccessful siege of Herat
     in October 1837 by the Persians. There were several Russian military advisors in
     the Persian army of Mohammad Shah Qajar under the command of Captain I.
     Blaramberg, whereas British Lieutenant Eldred Pottinger played a crucial role in
     organising the defence of the city on behalf of its Sadozai ruler Kamran Khan.
     Masson and Romodin, *Istoriia Afganistana*, Vol. II, p.182.

48. In 1838, on the eve of the first Anglo-Afghan War, the power of the incumbent
     Afghan monarch, Dost Mohammad, did not spread beyond the principality of
     Kabul, marked by Parwan in the North, Moqur in the southeast, Bamian in the
     northwest and Khyber Pass in the east. M.A. Babakhojaev, *Bor'ba Afganistana za
     nezavisimost': 1838–1842*, Moscow: Nauka, 1960, p.6.

49. During the 1850s alone, the British concluded more than 20 treaties with
     independent Pashtun tribes, securing their loyalty and pitting them against each

other and Durrani rulers. L. Temirkhanov, *Vostochnye pushtuny v novoe vremia*, Moscow: Nauka, 1984, p.47.

50.   See Fraser-Tytler, *Afghanistan*, pp.188–91. In the words of Abdul Samad Ghaus: 'for his acceptance of the Durand Line, Amir Abdul Rahman Khan to this day stands accused by the people of Afghanistan, especially the intelligentsia, of betraying the Afghan nation and its vital interests.' Ghaus, *The Fall of Afghanistan*, p.16.

51.   Curzon wrote in 1889 that the Russian ultimate object 'is not Calcutta, but Constantinople; not the Ganges, but the Golden Horn. He believes that the keys of the Bosphorus are more likely to be won on the banks of the Helmund than on the heights of Plevna. To keep England quiet in Europe by keeping her employed in Asia, that, briefly put, is the sum and substance of Russian policy'. George N. Curzon, *Russia in Central Asia in 1889 and the Anglo-Russian Question*, reprint, London: Frank Cass, 1967, p.321. It is important to note, however, that Russia's expansion in Central Asia unfolded, to a substantial degree, due to the personal efforts of its generals, whose deeds civil authorities in St. Petersburg were prone to abet. Officials in British India had good reasons to worry after reading 'revelations' on the lines of a Colonel Sobolev's vision that 'there can be hardly a doubt that the whole of northern Afghanistan, from the Amu Daria to the Hindoo Koosh, will, by force of circumstances, become included within the sphere of the immediate influence of Russia'. Charles Marvin, *The Russian Advance Towards India*, London: Sampson Low, Marston, Searle & Rivington, 1882, pp.67–8.

52.   The major events that marked Russia's expansion to Central Asia during this period were as follows: between 1824 and 1854, the Kazakh steppes were subjugated; in 1865 Tashkent fell to Russian troops; in 1867 the General-Governorship of Turkestan was established; in 1868, Bukhara became a Russian protectorate and Khiva followed suit in 1873; in 1876, the Khanate of Kokand was annexed. One has to agree with Helene Carrere d'Encausse's verdict: 'despite initial anxieties as to the supposed strength of existing Muslim states and English opposition, the conquest of Central Asia had been, in the final analysis, rapid, and, on the whole, not very bloody, at least for Russia.' Helene Carrere d'Encausse, 'Systematic Conquest, 1865 to 1884', in Edward Allworth (ed.), *Central Asia: A Century of Russian Rule*, New York and London: Columbia University Press, 1967, p.149.

53.   Suhash Chakravarty, *From Khyber to Oxus: A Study in Imperial Expansion*, Delhi: Orient Longman, 1976, p.20.

54.   Duprée, *Afghanistan*, p.407.

55.   Afghan troops invaded Shughnan and Roshan, independent territories beyond the Afghan frontier as defined in the 1873 agreement, claiming that they were historically part of Afghan Badakhshan. 'Afghanistan's occupation of Shughnan and Roshan in 1883 and the ensuing Russian protest… brought into the open the problem of Afghanistan's northeastern boundary, which had never really been settled.' Becker, *Russia's Protectorates in Central Asia*, p.104. The oasis of Panjdeh, inhabited by the Turkmens, was located in disputed territory, but the Afghan Amir had a legitimate claim on its ownership, 'an ownership based on the payment of occasional tribute to the Afghan Governor of Herat, who seems otherwise to have little jurisdiction over an outlying oasis and an alien people'. Fraser-Tytler, *Afghanistan*, p.163.

56.   A detailed account of the work of the Commission was left by its British member, Major Charles E. Yate. It appears that historical, geographic and ethnographic

considerations did not play any significant role in the process of demarcation. The British believed that 'in principle all territory which at that time was actually in the possession of the Amir of Afghanistan should belong to Afghanistan'. Charles E. Yate, *Northern Afghanistan or Letters from the Afghan Boundary Commission*, Lahore: Al-Biruni, 1976, p.379. See also Hope Verity Fitzhardinge, 'The Establishment of the North-West Frontier of Afghanistan, 1884–1888', Ph.D. Thesis, Australian National University, Canberra, 1968. Thus, the interests and grievances of the peoples of Afghanistan and small independent principalities to the north of the Hindu Kush were sacrificed for the sake of maintaining the *status quo* between the two colonial powers.

57.   The non-Pashtun population, as well as Pashtun clans who opposed the Mohammadzai rule, either stayed aloof or even welcomed the British during the First Anglo-Afghan war. Dupree, *Afghanistan*, pp.378, 382. Cf. also the notes of an officer in the Indus Army on the march in February 1839: 'We every day received numerous letters from the various chiefs of Bilochestan and of Afghanistan, all professing their joy at our approach, and all entertaining hopes of the reward that might be promised for co-operating with us in furtherance of the object of the expedition.' Lala Munshi Mohana, *Life of the Amir Dost Mohammed Khan, of Kabul: With His Political Proceedings towards the English, Russian, and Persian Governments, Including the Victory and Disasters of the British Army in Afghanistan*, Vol. II, London: Longman, Brown, Green, and Longmans, 1846, pp.183–4.

58.   The capacity of the Afghan state to exert social control over the populace depended on its ability to control tribal strongmen. The success of centralisation efforts of Durrani monarchs in the nineteenth century hinged on their personal qualities and statesmanship, the resources at their disposal and the peculiarities of current inter-tribal and inter-ethnic struggle in the country. However, the single most crucial factor that affected the balance between the central government and tribes was foreign intervention. Ludwig Adamec has made a sweeping but plausible generalisation that 'prior to Abdur Rahman's reign [1880–1901], Afghans sought outside support to rule over Afghanistan'. Ludwig W. Adamec, *Afghanistan, 1900–1923*, Berkeley and Los Angeles: University of California Press, 1967, p.3. During the 1870s, the plans to partition Afghanistan were prepared in London, and only the return of the Liberals to power prevented them from becoming a reality. Gregorian, *The Emergence of Modern Afghanistan*, p.116. Not surprisingly, even such strong Mohammadzai leaders as Dost Mohammad and Sher Ali were literally obsessed with the idea of gaining British recognition of the legitimacy of their dynastic rule.

59.   Rawlinson, *England and Russia in the East*, p.355.

60.   In 1843, Sind was occupied and then, following two swift but brutal campaigns, Punjab was subjugated by 1849. Kashmir, the richest province of the Durrani Empire under Ahmad Shah, was detached from Punjab as a separate entity and was irretrievably lost to Afghanistan. Baluchistan and North-West Frontier topped the list of Ahmad Shah's original empire taken by the British, in 1859 and 1895 respectively.

61.   See Fletcher, *Afghanistan*, pp.119–21.

62.   On 11 March 1839, Tsar Nicholas I set up a Special Committee to explore 'the successful activities of the competitors of the Russian Empire in Afghanistan' and prevent 'the strengthening of power and influence of the Englishmen over the

entire population of Central Asia'. Khalfin, *Rossiia i khanstva Srednei Azii*, p.275. The Committee's recommendations resulted in the ill-fated military expedition against Khiva later that year. The next attempt was not to be made until four decades later.

63. Christine Noelle, *State and Tribe in Nineteenth-Century Afghanistan: The Reign of Amir Dost Muhammad Khan (1826–1863)*, Richmond: Curzon Press, 1997, pp.288–9.

64. Dost Mohammad was survived by 16 sons born to five mothers.

65. *Shams ul-Nahar* was founded by Said Jamaluddin al-Afghani and was published from 1875 to 1879. Al-Afghani, who served briefly as advisor to Mohammad Azam Khan, authored a programme of reforms that influenced and was partially implemented by Sher Ali. Kh. Nazarov, *Said Jamaladdin Afgani i ego obshchestvenno-politicheskaia shkola*, Dushanbe: Donish, 1993, pp.22–3. For a discussion on al-Afghani's activities in Afghanistan, see Nikki R. Keddie, *Sayyid Jamal ad-din 'al-Afghani': A Political Biography*, Berkeley: University of California Press, 1972, pp.37–57.

66. Angus Hamilton, referring to Sher Ali's reign in particular, wrote that 'the gravest confusion prevailed in every department of political, military and civil administration, while the supremacy of the Amir of Kabul received no definite recognition from the Sirdars who were ruling over the several tribes which together made up the state... the Sirdars, jealous, ambitious and turbulent, governed in their respective districts each after his own fashion. The controlling authority of the Amir of Kabul was not infrequently defied; and as no community of interests existed between Kabul and the khanates there was no enduring form of government'. Angus Hamilton, *Afghanistan*, London: William Heinemann, 1906, p.269.

67. In Spring 1878, a Russian diplomatic mission headed by Major-General N. Stoletov was sent from Russian Turkestan to Kabul, without the knowledge of the Amir. A draft agreement of alliance between Russia and Afghanistan was brought to Sher Ali, but never endorsed. The entire expedition was little more than a demonstration of strength to the British before the Congress of Berlin (July 1878). The statement that 'by 1878 there was no question but that Afghanistan had fallen under Russian influence' (Gerald Morgan, *Anglo-Russian Rivalry in Central Asia: 1810–1895*, London: Frank Cass, 1981, p.176) is an exaggeration.

68. In the adroit phrasing of Suhash Chakravarty, 'the official debate no longer concerned itself with the desirability of a firm stand against Russia. Instead its primary interests lay in the problems of where, by whom and how the Russians were to be checkmated'. Chakravarty, *From Khyber to Oxus*, p.129.

69. As Fraser-Tytler has put it, 'While the British and Indian Governments were arguing over the dismembered corpse of the Afghan Kingdom, the one man who could fulfil the requirements of a desperately difficult situation was moving southwards into Afghanistan... Sardar Abdur Rahman... was just the type of man for the task in hand.' Fraser-Tytler, *Afghanistan*, pp.150–1.

70. Duprée, *Afghanistan*, p.410.

71. Khan, *The Life of Abdur Rahman*, Vol. II, p.80.

72. Gregorian, *The Emergence of Modern Afghanistan*, p.130.

73. Duprée, *Afghanistan*, p.417.

74. Kakar, *Government and Society in Afghanistan*, pp.8–10.

75. Between 1884 and 1886 alone, 18,000 Ghilzai families were resettled to Afghan Turkestan from the south. Khashimbekov, *Uzbeki Severnogo Afganistana*, p.10.

See also Nancy Tapper's chapter in R. Tapper (ed.), *The Conflict of Tribe and State in Iran and Afghanistan*. Abdur Rahman's idea was to dilute recalcitrant Uzbeks in sensitive frontier areas with loyal Pashtun tribes: 'It is proper that as the king is an Afghan, his tribesmen, the Afghans should guard the frontier.' Quoted in Kakar, *Government and Society in Afghanistan*, p.132. Following the conquest of Hazarajat, thousands of Hazaras were scattered all over the country during the 1890s. N. Tapper, *Bartered Brides*, p.27.

76. Although Abdur Rahman was sometimes referred to as the 'Justinian of Afghanistan' by sycophant contemporaries (see Rob Hager, 'State, Tribe and Empire in Afghan Inter-Polity Relations', in R. Tapper (ed.), *The Conflict of Tribe and State in Iran and Afghanistan*, p.117ff), he never accomplished codification of the Afghan law on the lines of the Roman Emperor's *Corpus Iuris Civilis*. Abdur Rahman was simply in a position to expand the reach of a centralised law-enforcement system based as much on traditional sources of jurisprudence (*Adat* and *Shari'at*), as on his idiosyncratic interpretation of legal issues.

77. The factory imparted 'to the position of Afghanistan... for the first time in its history some element of security'; it was capable of producing each week 'two guns, one hundred and seventy-five rifles and a varying quantity of small arms ammunition'. Hamilton, *Afghanistan*, p.320.

78. The stable northern frontier was established in its present form in 1895 by an Anglo-Russian agreement; both sides 'were not greatly concerned with the Amir's views on the subject'. Fletcher, *Afghanistan*, p.162. The eastern, western and southern borders of Afghanistan were finally demarcated between 1894 and 1903 by the British. Percy Sykes, *A History of Afghanistan*, Vol. II, London: Macmillan, 1940, pp.201–14.

79. Khan, *The Life of Abdur Rahman*, p.164.

80. Adamec, *Afghanistan, 1900–1923*, pp.22–3.

81. 'During the course of twenty-one years, 'Abd al-Rahman Khan probably had as many as 100,000 persons judiciously executed, whilst hundreds of thousands more perished from hunger, forced migrations, epidemics, or died as a result of the numerous campaigns which the Amir conducted... The fear that the Amir's atrocities engendered was a shadow which fell across the lives of everyone in Afghanistan.' Lee, *The 'Ancient Supremacy'*, p.xxvi.

82. Shahrani, 'State Building and Social Fragmentation in Afghanistan: A Historical Perspective', in Ali Banuazizi and Myron Weiner (eds), *The State, Religion, and Ethnic Politics: Afghanistan, Iran, and Pakistan*, Syracuse: Syracuse University Press, 1986, p.39.

83. Kakar, a Pashtun nationalist, has coyly remarked that 'the Tajiks paid more revenue than the Pashtuns did'. Kakar, *Government and Society in Afghanistan*, p.73. The truth is, the Durrani did not pay taxes at all, the border tribes paid very occasionally and whenever Ghilzais and other in-land tribes were taxed it was their Tajik, Hazara, Baluch and Turkic *hamsaya* who carried the burden. Cf. Yurii Gankovsky's conclusion: 'The Durrani tribe to which the shah himself belonged, was put in a privileged position. It was exempted from land tax, taxes on cattle, orchards and vineyards, and chimney duty; apart from a small tax on mills... it did not have to pay anything. This largely applied to other Afghan tribes... In some cases Afghan tribes were obliged to pay the Durrani shahs a definite tribute, but as a rule it was of a purely symbolic character.' Yurii Gankovsky, 'The Durrani Empire', in

Afghanistan: Past and Present, Moscow: USSR Academy of Sciences, 1982, p.91. Slavery amongst non-Pashtun groups increased dramatically under Abdur Rahman, especially affecting Hazara. It has been estimated that in the second half of the 1890s slaves accounted for five to ten per cent of Afghanistan's population. Romodin, 'Rabstvo i nekotorye drugie formy zavisimosti v pozdnefeodalnom Afganistane', in O.G. Bolshakov and E.I. Kychanov (eds), *Rabstvo v stranakh Vostoka v srednie veka*, Moscow: Nauka, 1986, p.455.

84. Jonathan Lee has ample grounds to argue that 'the focus of European attention from 1747 onwards had been concentrated, more or less exclusively, on the rise of Afghan power in Qandahar and, later, Kabul. Even today, historical works on Afghanistan still reflect this bias (e.g., Duprée 1978). The reason for this is not difficult to pinpoint. In the nineteenth century, the rivalry between Britain and Russia, known inappropriately by the Kiplingesque sobriquet, "The Great Game", resulted in British sponsorship of "Afghanistan" – or perhaps, more accurately, the Amirs of that country – as a buffer between the Tsarist empire and British India... There is strong evidence that British ignorance of Central Asian history and the traditional alignments beyond the Hindu Kush, was manipulated both by the Sadozai and Barakzai Amirs in order to extend their power up to the Amu Darya or even Bukhara.' Lee, *The 'Ancient Supremacy'*, pp.74, 76.

85. Khashimbekov, *Uzbeki severnogo Afganistana*, p.11.

86. N.L. Luzhetskaia, *Ocherki istorii Vostochnogo Gindukusha vo vtoroi polovine XIXv*, Moscow: Nauka, 1986, pp.133–4.

87. Lee, *The 'Ancient Supremacy'*, p.532.

88. Kakar, *Government and Society in Afghanistan*, pp.126–7.

89. 'Although "Afghan" is officially promoted as applying to all citizens of the Afghan state, in the north of the country it is often used for "Pashtun" even by the Pashtu-speakers themselves... To the Durrani tribespeople... "Durrani", "Pashtun" and "Afghan" are practically synonymous, and they use these words interchangeably to identify Durrani as opposed to all other groups, including non-Durrani Pashtu-speakers.' N. Tapper, *Bartered Brides*, p.39.

90. Lee, *The 'Ancient Supremacy'*, pp.530–1.

Chapter 2: National Awakening and Nationalism

1. The takeover by Abdur Rahman's eldest son was a remarkably non-violent action: 'Habibullah, though by no means a weak ruler, was a far less dominating personality than his father, and it is a tribute to the discipline which the latter had impressed upon his subjects that the succession passed without bloodshed.' Fraser-Tytler, *Afghanistan*, p.177. In fact, it has so far proved to be the only instance of a peaceful transfer of power in Afghanistan – monarchical, republican, communist or Islamic.

2. 'A profoundly pious Muslim... he [Nasrullah Khan] advocated Islamic perspectives in domestic and foreign policy, a perspective that made him popular among the ulama... The prince had established connections with virtually all of the religious leaders in Afghanistan and across the border in the North-West Frontier Province of British India.' Senzil Nawid, 'The State, the Clergy, and British Imperial Policy in Afghanistan During the 19th and Early 20th Centuries', *International Journal of Middle East Studies*, 29(4), 1997, p.596.

3. In order to secure stability of his rule, Habibullah Khan combined harsh reprisals

with skilful diplomacy. Thus, he maintained the much-feared secret police and internal espionage networks. At the same time, he made concessions to powerful tribal chiefs, and appointed Nasrullah Khan as the army commander, eventually proclaiming him heir to the throne, to the detriment of his own sons, in order to placate the religious establishment. Masson and Romodin, *Istoriia Afganistana*, Vol. II, p.312. The Amir was eventually successful in securing if not the allegiance, at least the quiescence, of his siblings. Ravan Farhadi, while acting as the Secretary of the Cabinet of Afghanistan between 1964 and 1970, had access to a collection of letters sent by Sardar Nasrullah Khan to his elder brother, in which the former respectfully put forth some ideas on the improvement of the functioning of the government and humbly asked the Amir's permission for marriage and the naming of his newborn sons.

4.   Perhaps the best description of Habibullah's personality has been left by A.C. Jewett, an American engineer who supervised the construction of the first hydropower station in Afghanistan between 1911 and 1919. Most of the time, he is far from flattering: 'His Majesty, the Amir... is the best of the bunch, and if he didn't have such a poisonous lot about him he could accomplish something. He's vain to the last degree, arrogant, and despotic, but he could not be otherwise... He hasn't done a tap of work this year; what time he is not in the haram [sic] is spent motoring, hunting, and golfing.' Yet, in hindsight, Jewett has concluded: 'His majesty Habibullah Khan was the fairest and most capable Afghan I have met. He had a forceful personality, a large fund of general knowledge, and a fine retentive memory. He governed not as he wished but as he could, in a constant atmosphere of intrigue and conspiracy. If he had had a few good advisers and some strong and loyal men about him, he could have done more.' Marjorie Jewett Bell (ed.), *An American Engineer in Afghanistan: From the Letters and Notes of A.C. Jewett*, Minneapolis: University of Minnesota Press, 1948, pp.193, 207, 327.

5.   In his coronation speech on 3 October 1901, Habibullah Khan solemnly swore 'to keep Afghanistan intact, to repel foreign aggression and to promote reforms'. Sykes, *A History of Afghanistan*, Vol. II, p.216. In April 1903, he launched a modest but systematic programme of modernisation, based on industrialisation and secular education, reactive and defensive in nature: 'We need to move forwards gradually, in order not to lag behind our neighbours and to prevent the triumph of our enemies.' D. Ia. Ochildiev, *Ocherki bor'by afganskogo naroda za natsionalnuiu nezavisimost' i vnutrennie reformy (1900–1914gg)*, Tashkent: Fan, 1967, pp.18–19.

6.   Al-Afghani 'has come to symbolise the first generation of those in the Islamic world who engaged in the dialogue with Europe over the reason for the decline of the Islamic world and the formulas for its reemergence.' Cyril E. Black et al, *The Modernization of Inner Asia*, Armonk, NY: M.E. Sharpe, 1991, p.146. The best analysis of al-Afghani's political, economic and philosophical legacy can be found in Elie Kedourie, *Afghani and 'Abduh: An Essay on Religious Unbelief and Political Activism in Modern Islam*, London: Frank Cass, 1966.

7.   This group emerged in 1906 in Kabul under the name of *Jami'at-e serri-ye melli*, or 'Secret National Society', with the aim of 'replacing the absolutist regime with the constitutional one, achieving independence of Afghanistan, and spreading modern civilisation and culture in the country'. Mir Gholam Mohammad, Gubar, *Afganistan na puti istorii*, Moscow: Nauka, 1987, p.43. In 1907, its membership did not exceed 50 people, whereas the Istanbul organisation of the 'Young Turks'

alone numbered more than 3,000. Abdulhai Habibi, *Jonbesh-e mashruteyat dar Afghanestan*, Kabul: Komita-ye dawlati-ye tab'-u nashr-e Jomhuri-ye Afghanestan, 1985, pp.23–54; G.Z. Aliev, *Turtsiia v period pravleniia mladoturok*, Moscow: Nauka, 1972, p.91.

8.   The Young Afghans comprised a handful of Afghan *literati*; several Indian Muslims who had been employed as teachers, medics and other professionals by the Amir; and a group of pages at the royal court, mostly sons of influential Pashtun and non-Pashtun chiefs whom Abdur Rahman had kept as hostages. The latter category was of particular importance: 'From amongst these royal pages there came famous civilian and military leaders who subsequently played a significant role in the occurrences of the period of reign of Amanullah.' Habibi, *Jonbesh-e mashruteyat dar Afghanestan*, p.51.

9.   Quoted in I. Akhmedkhodzhaev, 'K voprosu o stanovlenii obshchestvennoi mycli i burzhuaznoi istoriografii v Afganistane v nachale XX veka', in *Tashkentskii universitet. Trudy. Novaia seriia. Vypusk 690*, Tashkent: Izdatelstvo TGU, 1983, p.12.

10.   When in Istanbul, Mahmud Tarzi frequented al-Afghani's house. Tarzi reminisced later: 'These seven months of interlocution are worth seventy years of travelling. The contents of our conversations dealt with the issues of science, politics, philosophy, economics and so on, that could have made topics for entire volumes.' Quoted in Nazarov, *Said Jamaladdin Afgani i ego obshchestvenno-politicheskaia shkola*, Dushanbe: Donish, 1993, p.242.

11.   Habibi, *Jonbesh-e mashruteyat dar Afghanestan*, p.104. For a detailed analysis of Tarzi's published articles, see Ravan Farhadi, *Maqalat-e Mahmud-e Tarzi*, Kabul: no publisher, 1973.

12.   Tarzi for a long time teetered on the brink of disgrace, promoting concepts not necessarily in line with Habibullah Khan's convictions. The Amir on several occasions even threatened to kill the recalcitrant editor 'if he continued to harp on internal reforms, threats which the editor ignored'. Duprée, *Afghanistan*, p.440.

13.   A detailed review of Tarzi's socio-political credo can be found in Vartan Gregorian, 'Mahmud Tarzi and Saraj-ol-Akhbar: Ideology of Nationalism and Modernisation in Afghanistan', *The Middle East Journal*, 21(3), Summer 1967, pp.345–68. The foregoing discussion is largely based on this seminal article and Gregorian, *The Emergence of Modern Afghanistan*, pp.163–180.

14.   Gregorian, *The Emergence of Modern Afghanistan*, p.184.

15.   It has been argued that 'Tarzi and the Young Afghans were... well ahead of their times, and their vision of a modern worldview was only tenuously adopted a century later'. Black et al, *The Modernisation of Inner Asia*, p.139. Indeed, while Tarzi's planned reforms in many ways emulated earlier modernisers, putting a special emphasis on education, patriotism, defensive modernisation and economic development, the starting level was much lower in Afghanistan. Turkey had been exposed to European influences for centuries. Iran had been seriously affected by capitalist development and the regime of capitulations, and, later on, by the revolutionary movement in Russia. The Young Afghans simply could not appeal to wide masses of people and had to concentrate their efforts on the royal family. It is noteworthy that Tarzi was never able to propose the creation of an advisory council of some sort attached to the Amir.

16.   Amanullah Khan received an honorary title of Ain-ud-Dawlah ('Eye of the State')

from his father. At the same time, unlike his uncle and elder half-brother, he had no formal administrative assignment, which, however, did not harm his reputation as a bright and ambitious prince.

17.   Duprée, *Afghanistan*, p.430.

18.   Ulya Hazrat reached the position of chief queen some time in 1905. In a contemporary's characterisation, 'She is a woman of ungovernable passions, wilful, domineering, and capricious – an odd mixture of the termagant and the shrew. She has killed with her own hands three of her slaves who had become *enciente* [pregnant] through their intercourse with the Amir'. Hamilton, *Afghanistan*, pp.362, 366.

19.   On the early history of the Musahiban family, their fall-out with Amir Dost Mohammad and Sultan Mohammad's collaboration with the Sikhs, see Olaf Caroe, *The Pathans*, pp.307–15.

20.   L.B. Poullada, *Reform and Rebellion in Afghanistan*, p.36.

21.   Ulya Janab appears to have been quite a remarkable person: educated in a convent in British India, she was 'a woman of education, charm and accomplishment'. She may have played a role in introducing Habibullah to such pastimes as photography, piano music and singing. For a while she was Amir's favourite wife; yet 'she is no admirer of the Afghan ruler, his people, or the state; and it was the chance expression of this aversion which brought about her displacement'. Hamilton, *Afghanistan*, p.362. This 'displacement' caused a great deal of animosity between Nadir Khan and the Amir.

22.   Rubin, *The Fragmentation of Afghanistan*, pp.309–10.

23.   Enayatullah Khan, who lacked in energy and personal magnetism, 'was fat (a very unusual trait in Afghanistan)'. Fletcher, *Afghanistan*, p.176. He remained relatively marginalised as far as Afghan politics was concerned. In a situation where every male member of the royal family functioned as part of the state machine, the Amir put him in charge of a relatively unimportant sphere, namely armaments workshops, and the wages and pensions chamber. S. Shokhumorov, 'Arkhiv Inaiatulla-khana kak istochnik po istorii Afganistana', *Narody Azii i Afriki*, No. 1, 1978, pp.114–20.

24.   Many Western journalists and scholars who focused on the persona of Amanullah have been quite eloquent in praising his agile mind and vast quantities of the 'personal charm and dignity inherent in his family'. Mary Bradley Watkins, *Afghanistan: Land in Transition*, Princeton: D. van Nostrand, 1963, p.58. Analysts embracing a directly opposite viewpoint on Amanullah have stressed the 'intemperate reforming zeal... of a young man of limited ability, determined to drag his country into the twentieth century no matter how loud its protests'. John C. Griffiths, *Afghanistan: Key to a Continent*, Boulder: Westview Press, 1981, p.31.

25.   L.B. Poullada, *Reform and Rebellion in Afghanistan*, p.39.

26.   This liberal wing of Afghan reformists came to prominence in the wake of the harsh reprisals against radical constitutionalists from the Secret National Society which organised an unsuccessful attempt on Amir Habibullah's life in March 1909. The etymology of the word *Mashruta*, widely used throughout the Middle East in relation to the issues of constitutionalism, deserves a special comment. Contrary to the popular interpretation, it was not derived from Arabic *shart* ('condition'). In fact, it goes back to the French word *Chartre* – a nomen for the Royal Edict of French monarchy in 1830, which introduced certain constitutional traits to that country.

27. Ghobar, *Afghanestan dar masir-e ta'rikh*, p.826.

28. 'During the remaining days of Amir Habibullah Khan's reign, Sardar Mohammad Nadir Khan and members of his family, all men of great ability and exceptional administrative capacity, did their best for the advancement of their motherland. It was chiefly through their efforts that progressive measures were adopted by H.M. Amir Habibullah Khan.' Mohammad Ali, *Progressive Afghanistan*, Lahore: Punjab Educational Electric Press, 1933, p.75.

29. George N. Curzon, *Persia and the Persian Question*, Vol. I, p.4.

30. Intelligence gathered by Russians in Afghanistan during 1911–1912 pointed to dozens of 'Germano-Turkish agents who tried to suggest to the people of Afghanistan an idea that unless their government concludes a sacred union with Turkey and Germany against England and Russia, Afghanistan will perish'. Ochildiev, *Mladoafganskoe dvizhenie (1900–1920)*, Tashkent: Uzbekistan, 1985, p.81. For a comprehensive account of Germany's 'active diplomacy' in Afghanistan and in the region on the whole on the eve and during the course of the First World War, see Hopkirk, *On Secret Service East of Constantinople: Like Hidden Fire: The Plot to Bring Down the British Empire*, New York: Kodansha International, 1994.

31. During a hearing at the special Indo-Afghan Commission organised by Russia's Ministry of Finance which took place on 5 October 1905, it was said that 'the Russian prestige amongst Asians has been utterly destroyed by the defeats in the Far East. The Russian arms have lost its reputation of invincibility... This development has also caused a change in the behaviour of Habibullah, the Amir of Afghanistan, who had been inimical [to England] hitherto'. 'Iz "Protokolov komissii po izucheniiu Afganistana i Indii" za 1905 god.' *Vostok*, No. 3, 1989, p.99. The publication by Tarzi of a translation of the Turkish book *War between Russia and Japan* in 1910 had great impact on the minds of the Amir and his coterie, suggesting to them that Europeans were not invincible.

32. Habibullah's order to Nasrullah concerning the despatch of 24 able Afghan officers as envoys to England, France, Germany, Russia, Persia, China, Japan, Turkey, Egypt and the USA precipitated a particularly furious reaction in Calcutta. Hamilton, *Afghanistan*, p.452.

33. It is noteworthy that *Siraj al-Akhbar* was regularly banned in British India – Tarzi's mixture of modernisation, nationalism and pan-Islamism proved to be too explosive in the eyes of colonial administration. Black et al, *The Modernisation of Inner Asia*, p.184.

34. For a detailed account on the delimitation in Sistan, see Sykes, *A History of Afghanistan*, Vol. II, pp.208–14.

35. Gregorian has identified the conclusion of the St. Petersburg Convention as the single most important factor to mould the nationalist-reformist policies in Afghanistan: 'It reinforced the position of those who called for a program aimed at strengthening Afghanistan's military, economic and political position. At the same time, it reinforced the fears of the Afghan ruling elite about the serious consequences of foreign investment and concessions, and so had the effect of slowing the pace and distorting the character of that program.' Gregorian, *The Emergence of Modern Afghanistan*, p.212.

36. Dr Abdul Ghani, an Indian Muslim, did spend nine years in Cambridge, and it was in England that Nasrullah Khan solicited his services. He was appointed as the director of the Habibiyya college. The only written reference to him as a

British agent is in Abdul Hai Habibi's book, *Jonbesh-e mashruteyat dar Afghanestan*, pp.64–7, but even Habibi is extremely cautious, calling it a 'rumour' and arguing that had he indeed been a 'mole', Amanullah Khan would never have released him from prison and included him in the delegation to negotiate with the British at Rawalpindi in 1919. Even Soviet historians who suspected British involvement behind *every* occurence in Afghanistan refrained from propounding a conspiracy theory in this instance.

37. Once again, so far it has been impossible to prove British involvement in conspiratorial activities against Habibullah Khan. An attempt on the Amir's life was made in 1909 by a group of radicals who were not linked to Dr Ghani. Apparently, a handful of *gholambachas* Army officers and intellectuals supported Amir Abdur Rahman's widow (and Dost Mohammad's granddaughter), Bibi Halima, in her intrigue to place her feeble-minded son, Mohammad Omar Khan, on the throne. Radical reformers believed they would have freedom of action under a weak ruler. One of them, Mohammad Osman Khan Parwani, said to Habibullah during the tribunal: 'We did not want to kill you. We wanted to reform Afghanistan.' Habibi, *Jonbesh-e mashruteyat dar Afghanestan*, p.53. Eighty-five plotters were executed, but the Amir cracked down on all liberal groupings regardless of their involvement, sending droves to jail. Ochildiev, *Ocherki bor'by afganskogo naroda*, pp.68–9.

38. Tate, *The Kingdom of Afghanistan*, p.1.

39. Religious figures and reformers, 'Old' and 'Young Afghans' united temporarily under the banner of the War Party, being convinced that 'since the British were occupied in war, it was a God-sent opportunity to win back captured Afghan areas'. Raja Anwar, *The Tragedy of Afghanistan: A First-hand Account*, London and New York: Verso, 1989, p.17. The bulk of the population supported the Ottoman cause as defence of the caliphate: 'Outside the capital, public opinion was unanimously pro-war.' Nawid, 'The State, the Clergy, and British Imperial Policy', p.601.

40. A.C. Jewett wrote in his diary that in June 1915 the Amir confronted thousands of armed Pashtuns at the Great Mosque in Kabul who demanded *jihad* against the British and said: 'Show me a place in the Koran where the faithful are advised to make war on friends... O my people! The British are my friends. I, the light of the Nation and Faith, decree that no subject of mine shall bear arms against them.' Jewett then added: 'Probably only Allah will know whether he was really loyal to the British or to the six hundred thousand dollars' subsidy that they paid him annually.' Bell, *An American Engineer in Afghanistan*, p.257.

41. Duprée, *Afghanistan*, p.434.

42. Adamec, 'Germany, Third Power in Afghanistan's Foreign Relations', in G. Grassmuck and L.W. Adamec with F.H. Irwin (eds), *Afghanistan: Some New Approaches*, p.210.

43. The developments in Russia on the eve of the Bolshevik coup were monitored with great attention by the Afghan leadership. Thus, the issue of *Siraj ul-Akhbar* published on 13 October 1917 was almost completely dedicated to analysis of Russia's domestic and foreign policy. Masson and Romodin, *Istoriia Afganistana*, Vol. II, p.349. Generally, throughout the First World War the reformists' attitude towards Russia remained hostile, which was reflected in the paper's clichéd wording: *Rus-e manhus*, or 'Russia the Malevolent'.

44.   In the summer of 1918, a British expeditionary corps operating out of Khorasan occupied the Transcaspian *oblast* of Russian Turkestan and concluded an agreement with the White Russians whereby the whole of Turkestan was to become a British protectorate and enjoy the same degree of autonomy as the African colonies of Britain, Transvaal and the Orange Province. A. Babakhodzhaev, *Ocherki po istorii sovetsko-afganskikh otnoshenii*, Tashkent: Fan, 1970, p.15.

45.   Habibullah, still entertaining the hope of achieving sovereignty as a reward for his pro-British stance during the First World War, ignored overtures from the Bolshevik regime, which recognised the independence of Afghanistan in the Brest-Litovsk Treaty with Germany in March 1918 and expressed readiness to exchange diplomatic representations in June 1918. Moreover, he rendered assistance to the Amir of Bukhara, Said Alim-Khan, to contain the Soviet onslaught. Romodin, 'U istokov sovetsko-afganskikh otnoshenii', in *Afganistan: ekonomika, politika, istoriia*, Moscow: Nauka, 1984, p.36.

46.   On the eve of the First World War, Indian revolutionaries 'succeeded in establishing a network that extended from the Punjab to Kabul, Rangoon, and Singapore'. Gregorian, *The Emergence of Modern Afghanistan*, p.221. On 1 December 1915, their leader, Mahendra Pratap, announced the creation of a provisional government of India in Kabul. Pratap became its President, Mohammad Barakatullah was appointed as the Prime Minister and Obaidullah Sindhi received the post of the Minister of Interior. They actively fomented anti-British sentiments in the region and were involved with the activities of the Turko-German mission in Afghanistan. See P.I. Khoteev, 'Novye dannye o "Zagovore shelkovykh pisem"', in *Afganistan: ekonomika, politika, istoriia*, Moscow: Nauka, 1984, pp.104–8. See also Sykes, *A History of Afghanistan*, Vol. II, pp.258–62. Shortly after the Bolshevik Revolution, Barakatullah said in an interview with *Izvestiia*: 'I am neither communist nor socialist... for the time being, my political program is expulsion of the British from Asia. I am the uncompromising enemy of capitalism in Asia represented mainly by the British. In this I solidarise with the communists, in this respect we are your natural allies.' Romodin, 'U istokov sovetsko-afganskikh otnoshenii', p.37.

47.   Whilst Lord Chelmsford, the Viceroy, was inclined to seek a suitable compromise, his superiors in London remained stubborn and generally showed lack of awareness of the changed situation. Thus, the Secretary of State for India asked Lord Chelmsford whether the King should bestow the Order of the Garter on Habibullah or whether 'an autographed letter was sufficient reward for the Amir'. Adamec, *Afghanistan, 1900–1923*, p.105.

48.   Eventually, even Habibullah's patience ran out. On 2 February 1919 he sent a letter to the Viceroy where he insisted on sending an Afghan delegate to the Versailles Peace Conference as befitted a sovereign state. Habibullah stressed that he expected the Conference to issue a document recognising 'absolute liberty, freedom of action and permanent independence of the High State of Afghanistan'. N.A. Khalfin, *Zaria svobody nad Kabulom*, Moscow: Nauka, 1985, p.77.

49.   In January 1918, Tarzi published a fiery editorial headlined 'Independence of the High Afghan Sovereign State', where he proclaimed that 'the Afghan state has been, is and will be independent'. Gubar, *Afganistan na puti istorii*, p.69. That issue of his newspaper was banned by the Amir. In later years, when asked why he abandoned *Siraj al-Akhbar*, Mahmud Tarzi would reply: 'I had achieved my goal. Afghan independence of British control was near.' Duprée, *Afghanistan*, p.440.

50.   Early Soviet sources squarely blamed the British for the Amir's demise: 'Lazy, languid, immersed into the harem pleasures of the basest sort, he, of course, fell an easy prey to the English plot.' V.A. Gurko-Kriazhin, *Istoricheskie sud'by Afganistana*, Moscow: Gosizdat, 1922, pp.71–2. Afghan authors suspected a conspiracy conceived by 'the Kremlin rulers annoyed by the British dealings with Habibullah'. Abdur Rahman Ala Najib, *Afghanestan dar gozargah-e atash wa khun*, Peshawar: Haj Nayyer Hosaini, 1991, p.120. However, Arnold Fletcher's position appears to be the most logical and convincing: 'As suspects the British may be eliminated because they had so much to lose and so little to gain from the murder; the Communists would have had a motive but not the opportunity.' Fletcher, *Afghanistan*, p.184. Habibullah was most likely assassinated as a result of a factional struggle at the Afghan court, and it is surprising that he managed to survive that long given that the first attempt at his life was made at a very tender age, to be followed by half a dozen more. Gray, *At the Court of the Amir*, p.37.

51.   George N. Molesworth, *Afghanistan 1919: An Account of Operations in the Third Afghan War*, Bombay: Asia Publishing House, 1962, p.22.

52.   As many as six people, Habibullah's two brothers and four sons, could have laid realistic claims to the throne. Donald Wilber (ed.), *Afghanistan*, New Haven: Human Relations Area Files, 1956, p.74.

53.   Nasrullah Khan died in prison in 1921. Kabul at the time was flooded with rumours that he had been 'helped' out of this world by people in the employ of his nephew, Amir Amanullah.

54.   For a detailed analysis of the composition of Amanullah's first government, see M. Davliatov, 'M.G.M. Gubar o progressivnykh obshchestvennykh dvizheniiakh v Afganistane v nachale XXv', in *Afganistan: istoriia, ekonomika, kultura*, Moscow: Nauka, 1989, pp.35–7.

55.   Gubar, *Afganistan na puti istorii*, pp.72, 76.

56.   This interpretation of events was widely held by intellectuals contemporary to Amanullah's succession, and they passed on their views to the subsequent generations.

57.   The assessments of Habibullah Khan as a statesman range from the denigrating 'slow-witted despot who defected to the camp of the anti-national forces of his country' (Ochildiev, *Mladoafganskoe dvizhenie*, p.59) to the flattering 'great moderniser of Afghanistan' (Watkins, *Afghanistan*, p.56). An interesting testimony has been left by an Afghan historian who wrote *after* Habibullah's death: 'Under him there emerged: love for enlightenment, patriotism, compassion for universal Moslem interests, self-preservation of freedom, love for mutual unity and alliance, development of the warrior's spirit for the sake of strengthening of the independent Afghan state, observance of laws and principles of equality.' Burkhan-ud-Din-khan-i-Kushkaki, *Kattagan i Badakhshan*, p.2.

Chapter 3: Independence and Radical Modernisation

1.   The main strength of the Musahiban family lay in their influence amongst southern Pashtuns – the Mangals, Ahmadzais, Jadrans, Jajis, Wazirs and several others. It was Mohammad Nadir Khan, not Amanullah, who in April 1919 managed to persuade the majority of tribes south of the Khyber Pass to forego their internecine squabbles and unite to fight for Afghanistan's independence. See Marshal Shah

Wali, *Moi vospominaniia*, Moscow: OGIZ, 1960, pp.21–4.

2. Shah Wali married Samarat us-Siraj, a full sister of Amanullah. Shah Mahmud married Qamar ul-Banat, Amanullah's half-sister.

3. Amanullah habitually referred to the Turks as 'elder brothers and guides'. Gregorian, *The Emergence of Modern Afghanistan*, p.258; Amin Saikal, 'Kemalism: Its Influence on Iran and Afghanistan', *International Journal of Turkish Studies*, 2(2), 1982, pp.25–32.

4. The limited, almost utopian nature of Amanullah's project has been well captured by Richard Newell: 'He envisioned modernisation primarily as educational, social and cultural change. He emphasised new attitudes, ideas, knowledge, and styles of behaviour. Modernisation was seen more as a problem of persuasion than a process of institution building.' Newell, *The Politics of Afghanistan*, Ithaca and London: Cornell University Press, 1972, p.54.

5. This article of the Manifesto was an exercise in double-talk: Amanullah was aware of who was behind the impending assassination of Amir Habibullah, although, perhaps, he was not the actual instigator of the plot. The investigation into the royal murder was superficial, the real culprits from the Mohammadzai nobility were rewarded with high government positions, and the scapegoats hastily executed by Amanullah included his personal adversaries. See Sayyed Mahdi Farrokh, *Ta'rikh-e siyassi-ye Afghanestan*, reprint, Qom: no publisher, 1993, pp.422–36.

6. Masson and Romodin, *Istoriia Afganistana*, Vol. II, p.373.

7. Amanullah immediately promoted all officers, increased soldiers' pay, lowered taxes, abolished forced labour (*begari*) and even allowed 'kangaroo courts' to get rid of the most corrupt officials of the old regime. Aleksandr N. Kheifets, *Sovetskaia Rossiia i sopredelnye strany Vostoka, 1918–1920*, Moscow: Nauka, 1964, pp.269–70; Sykes, *A History of Afghanistan*, Vol. II, p.267.

8. In his letter to the Viceroy of India, dated 3 March 1919, Amanullah officially proclaimed the independence of Afghanistan and requested Britain to negotiate a new inter-state treaty based on equality. In his reply that followed 43 days later, Lord Chelmsford 'refrained from making any reference to independence and alluded to the mourning over the death of the late amir as an excuse for not discussing the treaty suggested by Amanullah'. Ghaus, *The Fall of Afghanistan*, p.31.

9. The high-handed treatment of members of the Pashtun aristocracy and the Ulama, and calls for reforms and modernisation, had already begun to disaffect traditionalist strongmen vis-à-vis Amanullah. On 25 April 1919, for example, the notables of Kandahar refused to read the *khutbah* in the name of the King. However, 'Amanullah immediately regained the support of the traditionalist ulama and tribal leaders, as well as that of the army, by declaring a jihad against the British in pursuit of his goal of achieving Afghan national independence.' Shahrani, 'State Building and Social Fragmentation in Afghanistan', p.46.

10. General Saleh Mohammad Khan, Commander-in-Chief and Commander of the Khyber Front, was defeated by the British on 17 May near Jalalabad but the city held. Forces under General Abdul Quddus Khan, Commander of the Kandahar Front, remained largely static. It was General Nadir Khan, 'the only commander they [Afghans] had with any real knowledge, or initiative' (Molesworth, *Afghanistan 1919*, p.112), who managed to inflict a series of humiliating defeats upon the British on their territory. His success should be ascribed to the fact that he had solicited

cooperation of militant Afghan tribes using his personal authority: 'Units of the Masud, Ahmedzai, Kabulhel, Waziri and other tribes – numerous, with their own arms – came and swore to fight selflessly.' N.A. Khalfin, 'The Struggle of the Peoples of Afghanistan for Independence and Against the British Colonialists', in *Afghanistan: Past and Present*, Moscow: USSR Academy of Sciences, 1982, p.117.

11. Afghan and Soviet historians alike claimed that the British had sustained an overall miltary defeat and thus 'the leading English political figures decided to seek ways to stop the war'. Kheifets, *Sovetskaia Rossiia i sopredelnye strany Vostoka*, p.278; also see Najib, *Afghanestan dar gozargah-e atash wa khun*, p.141. British authors, naturally, maintained quite the opposite: the 'vanquished Afghan nation' was left alone only because 'the British Government had no desire whatsoever to add to their commitments by continuing a fight which would in all probability lead to the disintegration of Afghanistan and the disappearance of the buffer between India and Russia'. Fletcher, *Afghanistan*, p.194; Fraser-Tytler, *Afghanistan*, p.196. Whatever the interpretations of the results of the conflict, its major ramification was clear to everybody: complete sovereignty could no longer be withheld from the Afghans. The question remained, on what conditions would they acquire it?

12. A. Kh. Babakhodzhaev has gone so far as to argue that the entire round of peace negotiations at Rawalpindi (26 July–8 August 1919) was little more than a ploy to buy time for the British troops to regroup: 'Through peace talks, the English tried to lull the Afghan Supreme Command's vigilance, preparing to stab Afghanistan in the back. British forces were to be relocated from the Transcaucasus and Iranian Azerbaijan... to Kushka. From there, the English planned to descend suddenly on Herat, thus launching an attack on central districts of Afghanistan from the North-West.' A. Kh. Babakhodzhaev, *Proval angliiskoi antisovetskoi politiki v Srednei Azii i na Srednem Vostoke v period priznaniia Sovetskogo gosudarstva de-fakto i de-iure (1921–1924gg)*, Tashkent: Izdatelstvo AN UzSSR, 1957, pp.51–2.

13. Leon Poullada has noted that from the outset of Amanullah's rule his policies 'were characterised by openly expressed anti-British bias. One very knowledgeable informant assured me that Amanullah in fact distrusted and disliked Bolsheviki yet went out of his way to show them public favour simply to taunt the British.' L.B. Poullada, *Reform and Rebellion in Afghanistan*, p.244.

14. In 1919 and 1920, Amanullah seriously pondered the possibility of transferring the Caliphate to Afghanistan from Turkey, which was allegedly succumbing to the will of the Great Powers of Europe, and assuming the duties of the Caliph. In a letter to the British authorities, the Amir stated that 'no Muslim can tolerate any interference in the affairs of the Caliphate no more than he can witness his Caliph submitted to any control. A combination of such sort is not compatible with the pride and dignity of Afghanistan'. Gregorian, *The Emergence of Modern Afghanistan*, p.235. Particularly in the wake of the Anglo-Afghan War, Amanullah 'seemed to many Muslims in Asia as the most popular candidate for that position'. Abdul Quadir Amiryar, 'Soviet Influence, Penetration, Domination and Invasion of Afghanistan', Ph.D. Thesis, George Washington University, Washington, DC, 1989, p.67.

15. In Poullada's colourful phrasing, 'the die-hards in the imperial structure both in India and England wanted to see the upstart young king of Afghanistan, who had dared to challenge British power, eat dirt'. L.B. Poullada, *Reform and Rebellion in Afghanistan*, pp.241–2.

16. In a supplementary letter to the Treaty, the British acknowledged Afghanistan as being officially free and independent in its internal and external affairs and rescinded all previous treaties. Yet, Article V of the new instrument preserved the Indo-Afghan frontier in the configuration set under Abdur Rahman and Habibullah, thus upholding the Durand Agreement of 1893. Additionally, the British banned importation of war materials to Afghanistan through India, confiscated Afghan government arrears in Indian banks, cancelled the annual subsidy to the Amir and imposed a six-month probationary period before the final inter-state agreement would be signed. Sykes, *A History of Afghanistan*, Vol. II, pp.284, 358–9. Sir A.H. Grant, Head of the British delegation at Rawalpindi, wrote that 'our policy throughout has been to give Afghanistan the liberty she now regards as essential, in the confident belief that money-hunger and need for guidance will before long bring her back to us for help and advice in practice, an infinitely better solution than the old agreement.' Adamec, *Afghanistan, 1900–1923*, p.129.

17. Duprée, *Afghanistan*, p.446.

18. Ghaus has referred to the renewed aggressive activities of the British in the tribal zone as the 'modified forward policy', noting that 'It seems reasonable to assume that the British, preoccupied as always with the defense of India, wanted to transform the tribal belt into a controlled buffer zone between India and Afghanistan and position themselves more advantageously in the area, since the "irresponsible" ruler in Kabul had proved himself untrustworthy and hostile to British interests.' Ghaus, *The Fall of Afghanistan*, p.36.

19. James Spain has made a poignant observation concerning the status of territories Kabul laid claims on: 'In passing, it is well to note that Afghan sovereignty in one form or another continued to be recognised in the border area until a surprisingly late date. The Baluch districts of Pishin and Sibi, the Kurram Valley between Parachinar and Thal, and the Khyber itself were "assigned" to the British only in 1879 under the Treaty of Gandamak... While all of the present tribal agencies were separated from Afghanistan by the Durand Agreement, none of them except Kurram was ever formally proclaimed British territory... There is also no doubt that in the social and cultural spheres, the tribes remained closer to Kabul than to Delhi right up to 1947.' James Spain, *The Pathan Borderland*, The Hague: Mouton, 1963, p.231.

20. Article II of the Kabul Treaty confirmed the provisions of earlier documents concerning territorial arrangements between the parties. However, on the insistence of the Afghan side, Article XI implicitly recognised its vested interests in the trans-border tribal areas. The full text of the Treaty is in Sykes, *A History of Afghanistan*, Vol. II, pp.364–9.

21. The train that carried Afghan negotiators across Indian territory to the Mussoorie Conference in April 1920 was refuelled and watered at remote by-stations in order to avoid 'hundreds of cheering Indian nationalists' – a highly combustible element, undoubtedly inspired by Amanullah's example. Duprée, *Afghanistan*, p.444.

22. In addition to objective policy discrepancies, subjective psychological factors and personal animosities played a significant part in moulding the British position on many issues. The selection in 1922 of Sir Francis Humphrys as the first British Minister to Afghanistan was, in hindsight, a mistake: 'He simply could not adapt or bend to the currents of fierce nationalism, independence, and modernisation

that were sweeping through Kabul during Amanullah's reign. He saw Amanullah as a comic-opera king and a fool... Humphrys' total lack of sympathy for Amanullah and his policies had an important effect in the progressive deterioration of Anglo-Afghan relations.' L.B. Poullada, *Reform and Rebellion in Afghanistan*, pp.251–2.

23.   It took the USA 14 years from the de facto recognition in 1921 to sign the first consular agreement with Afghanistan.

24.   Information disclosed by Ambassador Najibullah Khan to Ravan Farhadi during a private conversation in Washington, DC, in 1963.

25.   In summer 1921, the US authorities were informed in relation to the Wali diplomatic mission that the British government: 'does not look with favour on the activities of this mission or on their endeavours to conclude agreements with other governments. We consider Afghanistan, though ostensibly independent, as still within our sphere of political influence, and are anxious to discourage any proceedings which imply that we are not concerned in the foreign relations of that country.' Leon B. Poullada and Leila D.J. Poullada, *The Kingdom of Afghanistan and the United States: 1828–1973*, Lincoln: The Centre for Afghanistan Studies at the University of Nebraska in Omaha and Dageford Publishing, 1995, pp.37–8.

26.   Technical problems also contributed to the difficult choices of the nascent diplomatic service of Afghanistan: there were few specialists with the knowledge of Western languages, funding for missions was scarce, and communications were extremely slow.

27.   Persia became Iran in 1935.

28.   Nicosia, '"Drang Nach Osten" Continued', pp.240, 252.

29.   Adamec, 'Germany, Third Power in Afghanistan's Foreign Relations', p.221.

30.   M. Nazarshoev, *Partiinaia organizatsiia Pamira v bor'be za sotsializm i kommunizm*, Dushanbe: Irfon, 1970, pp.19–21.

31.   Soviet rule was established in the Pamir region of the former General-Governorship of Turkestan in November 1918. However, it remained extremely fragile and was effectively liquidated in July 1919, when four Austro-Hungarian POWs killed a handful of Bolshevik activists in Khorog. There existed a possibility that all of Badakhshan would secede to Afghanistan. The restraint shown by Kabul in this matter was appreciated by Soviet authorities in Tashkent, which constantly praised 'friendly Afghanistan'. Nazarshoev, *Partiinaia organizatsiia Pamira*, pp.19–29.

32.   Soviet Russia was the first country to recognise Afghanistan's unlimited sovereignty. In an official letter dated 7 April 1919, Amanullah informed Lenin of his accession to the throne and expressed readiness to establish friendly relations. The letter proceeded to say: 'since you, Your Majesty, my great and gentle friend – the President of the High Russian state – together with your comrades – friends of the humankind – have assumed a noble and honourable task of taking care of peace and well-being of people, and have promulgated the principle of freedom and equality of countries and nations throughout the world, I am happy for the first time, on behalf of the Afghan people striving for progress, to despatch to you this friendly communication of the free and independent Afghanistan.' *Dokumenty vneshnei politiki SSSR*, Vol. II, Moscow: Gospolitizdat, 1960, p.175. The Bolshevik leader's reply, made in an equally florid and bombastic manner on 27 May 1919, hailed Amanullah's reign, called for the immediate exchange of diplomatic missions and pledged support 'to the independent Afghan nation which heroically defends its freedom from foreign enslavers'. Leonid B. Teplinskii, *Istoriia sovetsko-*

afganskikh otnoshenii, 1919–1987, Moscow: Mysl, 1988, p.38.

33. While the Bolsheviks had not mastered the art of diplomatic casuistry to its full extent, they tended to make rather revealing statements concerning their real plans in Asia. In the middle of 1919, Trotsky put forward the plan of re-orienting Bolshevik proselytism from the West to the East: 'If in the West we manoeuvre, observe caution, and compromise in order to avert a large-scale intervention, then in the East, in Asia, we should conduct a swift and active policy and prepare an attack on India through Afghanistan, Punjab and Bengal.' Vladimir Medvedev, 'Nechaiannaia revoliutsiia. Bukhara, 1920g', *Druzhba narodov*, No. 1, 1992, p.155.

34. Mikhail I. Volodarskii, *Sovety i ikh iuzhnye sosedi Iran i Afganistan (1917–1933)*, London: Overseas Publications Interchange, 1985, p.163.

35. Teplinskii, *Istoriia sovetsko-afganskikh otnoshenii*, p.39.

36. Cited in A. Saikal, *The Rise and Fall of the Shah*, Princeton: Princeton University Press, 1980, p.19.

37. *Dokumenty vneshnei politiki SSSR*, Vol. IV, Moscow: Gospolitizdat, 1961, pp.166–7.

38. The British closely monitored the progress of Afghan-Soviet negotiations, mostly through reading Russian diplomatic cables. Soon they discovered that the Soviet government tried to avoid confrontation with Britain at all costs and was interested at that juncture only in the establishment of friendly relations with Afghanistan. Still, 'the viceroy of India was so alarmed that he appealed to London to settle the Afghanistan question with Moscow. He suggested that Britain conclude an agreement with the Soviet Union designed to prevent Afghanistan from playing off one European power against the other. In this agreement Britain would share with the Soviet Union equal influence in Afghanistan.' Adamec, *Afghanistan's Foreign Affairs to the Mid-Twentieth Century: Relations with the USSR, Germany, and Britain*, Tucson: University of Arizona Press, 1974, p.57. However, the new edition of the Anglo-Russian imperialist agreements of 1895 and 1907 proved to be impossible in the post-First World War world.

39. For a detailed analysis of the Treaty, see Aleksandr N. Kheifets, *Sovetskaia diplomatiia i narody Vostoka, 1921–1927*, Moscow: Nauka, 1968, pp.70–2.

40. The Bolshevik government spared no efforts to win the indigenous population of border areas to its side, promising security and tangible material benefits. In the early 1920s, Mir Ahmed Yar, the future Khan-e Baluch XIII and then an officer in British Military Intelligence, reported to his superiors in India that many poor Baluchis 'would draw a very impressive picture of Russia, saying: "Russia is virtually a bliss,' surplus in food to such a degree that we can burn the grains as a fuel; and they impart free education to our children; and we have no housing problems, etc., etc." It was thus natural for simple-minded folks to fall into the trap spread out through a forceful propaganda machinery of the Russians.' Mir Ahmed Yar Khan Baluch, *Inside Baluchistan*, Karachi: Royal Book Company, 1975, pp.112–13. In a similar vein, as early as March 1920 the Red Army supremo in Turkestan, M.V. Frunze, reported to Lenin that if there were a poll in the disputed Pende and Serakhs zones, local Turkmens would vote in favour of Moscow and, moreover, 'we have all grounds to believe that the Turkmens of Bukhara, Afghanistan and Persia will be drawn to us'. Kheifets, *Sovetskaia Rossiia i sopredelnye strany Vostoka*, p.298. At the end of the day, the Soviet Union retained all territories to which Afghanistan may have laid claim, and the entire Article IX was pronounced null and void by both sides in 1946.

41. For the text of the Treaty between Great Britain and Afghanistan Establishing Friendly and Commercial Relations, see Adamec, *Afghanistan, 1900–1923*, pp.183–8. Arnold Fletcher has characterised the speedy conclusion of the Treaty after 11 months of painstaking talks as a 'surprise'. Fletcher, *Afghanistan*, p.199.

42. Adamec, *Afghanistan's Foreign Affairs to the Mid-Twentieth Century*, p.110. In Soviet studies, Humphrys was invariably portrayed as the insidious mastermind behind subversive activities of British 'secret services'. Leonid Teplinskii has alleged that in 1922 his agents killed five Soviet diplomats and several diplomatic couriers, made an unsuccessful attempt on the Consul-General, N.A. Ravich, and generally 'tried to compromise Soviet representatives and provoke Afghanistan to sever relations with the RSFSR; spread rumours that allegedly Soviet Russia intends to establish Soviet power in Afghanistan; planted forged documents exposing imaginary conspiracies of Amir Amanullah against Soviet Russia, thus hoping to stir Moscow's distrust to the Afghan government and weaken Soviet-Afghan cooperation'. Teplinskii, *Istoriia sovetsko-afganskikh otnoshenii*, p.72.

43. Cf. the reminiscences of the Khan of Kalat, then in the employ of the Government of British India: 'My second report concerned Amir Amanullah Khan of Afghanistan. I apprised the British Government that he... was receiving aid from Soviet Russia... I made it clear in my report that given more time, these pro-Russian leanings of the Afghan ruler would seriously undermine the British position in the Indian subcontinent, and that the infiltration of Communism into this area would jeopardise the prestige of British rule in India.' Mir Ahmed Yar Khan Baluch, *Inside Baluchistan*, p.113.

44. It is highly illuminating that in September 1921 Amanullah showed readiness to break with the Russians and repudiate the Afghan-Soviet treaty if Britain showed flexibility and acceded to rather moderate demands of Afghanistan. Adamec, *Afghanistan, 1900–1923*, p.165.

45. 'One commentator referred to the Soviet behaviour in the wake of signing the 1921 Treaty as a "direct swindle" which caused the Afghan government's "disgust and indignation".' Mikhail Volodarsky, *The Soviet Union and Its Southern Neigbours: Iran and Afghanistan, 1917–1933*, Ilford: Frank Cass, 1994, p.130.

46. Aleksandr N. Kheifets, 'Uzy dobrososedstva i bratstva nerastorzhimy', *Aziia i Afrika segodnia*, No. 2, 1981, p.19.

47. Teplinskii, *SSSR i Afganistan, 1919–1981*, Moscow: Nauka, Glav. red. vostochnoi lit-ry, 1982, pp.74–5.

48. The Soviets occupied the island, inhabited predominantly by Tajik and Uzbek refugees from Eastern Bukhara, in December 1925. Apparently, the Red Army had suspicions that the island's main village, Darqad, was a base for Muslim guerrillas. Amanullah treated this act as a potential *casus belli* and moved regular troops to the north. Subsequently, the Kremlin had to apologise and back off, inventing a ridiculous story that 'the actions of Soviet border guards on the island of Urta Toghai were undertaken without Moscow's knowledge'. Kheifets, *Sovetskaia diplomatiia i narody Vostoka*, p.274. The island was officially returned to Afghanistan on 15 August 1926.

49. The process of incorporation of Central Asia into the Soviet fold culminated in 1924 with the so-called 'national delimitation' and creation of national republics to replace old state entities. For a concise outline of the Sovietisation of Central Asia, see Steven Sabol, 'The Creation of Soviet Central Asia: The 1924 National

Delimitation', *Central Asian Survey*, 14(2), 1995, pp.225–41.

50. See Martha B. Olcott, 'The Basmachi or Freemen's Revolt in Turkestan, 1918–24', *Soviet Studies*, 33(3), July 1981, pp.352–69.

51. Throughout 1925, Amanullah constantly remonstrated with the Soviet government with regard to the aggressive action of the latter. On 25 December that year, he addressed people during the Friday prayer, warning them 'that hostilities might break out any time and Afghans should be prepared to fight rather than let themselves be destroyed piecemeal.' Adamec, *Afghanistan's Foreign Affairs to the Mid-Twentieth Century*, p.110.

52. Mohammad Ali ebn-e Mohammad Sayyed Baljowani, *Ta'rikh-e nafe'*, Dushanbe: Irfon, 1994, p.92.

53. Audrey Shalinsky has maintained that between 1914 and 1931 the *cumulative* loss of population in Central Asia amounted to 1.23 million people – those who perished during the 1916 revolt, were killed by the Bolsheviks, starved to death, died of infectious diseases and migrated abroad. Audrey C. Shalinsky, *Long Years of Exile: Central Asian Refugees in Afghanistan and Pakistan*, Lanham: University Press of America, 1994, p.19. Some of the migrants went to Chinese Turkestan. Kamol Abdoullaev has provided a more concrete figure: as of 1926, the year when the Soviet-Afghan border was sealed, 479,855 Central Asian émigrés resided in Afghanistan. Kamol Abdoullaev, 'Central Asian Emigres in Afghanistan: First Wave 1920–1931', *Central Asia Monitor*, No. 5, 1994, p.18.

54. Amanullah gave Amir Alim Khan a monthly pension of 16,500 rupees and a villa in the southern part of Kabul. Medvedev, 'Nechaiannaia revoliutsiia', p.173. However, in compliance with the Afghan-Soviet Treaty of 1921, the deposed monarch of Bukhara was not allowed to indulge in active anti-Soviet operations. Moreover, he was eventually sent into honourable exile in Jalalabad, where he and a handful of his courtiers shocked local officials by licentious behaviour, alcoholism and narcotics abuse. Fitrat, *Dawrai hukmronii amir Olimkhon*, pp.54–5.

55. Refugees (*muhajirs*) from the Tajik city of Uroteppa, for example, told their stunned hosts in Afghanistan that in the winter of 1925 the public bath in that city was heated for the whole month with the burning of Qur'ans and other religious books. Abduqodir Holiqzoda, *Ta'rikhi siyosii Tojikon*, Dushanbe: self-published, 1994, p.78.

56. Khalilullah Khalili, an Afghan historian and eyewitness, has described the situation in Afghanistan in 1921 as follows: 'People were of the opinion that the government of Afghanistan had been deceived by the promises of the Soviet Union and had forgotten its lofty religious and political duty to support its Muslim neighbours and brothers, and believed that the unconditioned cooperation of its government with the Soviet state was against its religious and political interests and against supreme interests of the entire world of Islam. Those religious leaders who had political conscience were very worried by this and were looking for counter-measures.' Khalili, *'Ayyori az Khorasan*, pp.92–3.

57. Poullada and Poullada, *The Kingdom of Afghanistan and the United States*, p.42.

58. The blueprint for future Anglo-Afghan relations was authored by Humphrys and endorsed by the British government in 1924. Its main provisions included: no attempt to regain control of Afghan foreign relations was to be made; no territorial concessions or permanent subsidy were to be offered to Afghanistan; the Amir was to sever all relations with the trans-border Pashtun tribes; and the Bolshevik

threat was not to be a serious subject for negotiation for the time being. Adamec, *Afghanistan's Foreign Affairs to the Mid-Twentieth Century*, pp.96–7.

59.   The turning point in the Soviet-Afghan relationship as far as the Bolshevik subjugation was concerned should be dated to summer 1922. In early July, Mohammad Nadir Khan, who had been seconded by Amanullah to command all troops in the north of the country, sent a harsh message to the Kremlin: 'If the hostile activities of the Bolsheviks against Bukhara do not cease, the government of Afghanistan will be forced to annex Bukhara. This is the only means to help a Muslim state situated in the centre of Asia against the Bolshevist plotting.' Volodarskii, *Sovety i ikh iuzhnye sosedi Iran i Afganistan*, p.178. However, a month later the bulk of the Basmachi were destroyed by the Red Army; one of their ablest leaders, Enver Pasha, was killed and it had become painfully clear to Amanullah that Britain, Turkey and Persia would not rush to help combat communism in Central Asia. On 25 July 1922, he published a manifesto ordering all Afghan subjects to quit the ranks of the Islamic fighters in Central Asia or be deprived of Afghan citizenship and have their property confiscated. Kabul extended official guarantees of non-interference in the developments in Bukhara. Moreover, throughout 1923, Afghan authorities disarmed and extradited a number of Basmachi units. The Kremlin was satisfied: 'By the end of 1923, the Bukhara question had practically lost all significance in Soviet-Afghan relations. The armed resistance of the local reactionary forces and the last *basmachi* gangs had been quashed in Bukhara once and for all.' Teplinskii, *SSSR i Afganistan*, p.52.

60.   Medvedev, 'Basmachi – obrechennoe voinstvo', *Druzhba narodov*, No. 8, 1992, pp.126–7.

61.   According to Chapter III of the Pact, both parties undertook 'on their respective territories, to forbid and render inactive groups and individuals operating to the detriment of the other Contracting Party, or undermining government principles of the other Contracting Party, or conspiring against the state integrity of the other Contracting Party, or recruiting or raising armed formations against the other Contracting Party'. *Monasebat-e Afghanestan wa Ettehad-e Shurawi dar salha-ye 1919–1969*, Kabul: Wezarat-e omur-e khareja-ye Afghanestan [1970], p.27.

62.   Poullada has come to the following conclusion concerning Amanullah's policies vis-à-vis Soviet Russia: 'The USSR can hardly be blamed for acting in what it considered its own best interests and following the traditional models of diplomacy of the great powers of that day. We may ascribe a certain amount of opprobrium to its deliberately deceptive rhetoric about its "benevolent" intentions toward its own Muslims and surrounding Muslim states. But such dissimulation would have never fooled Abdur Rahman and it certainly did not deceive Ataturk or Reza Shah, both of whom were subjected to similar pressures and wiles. Given the long history of Russian tactics toward Afghanistan, an Afghan ruler, of all people, should have been able to see through such Soviet maneuvres and adjust his policies accordingly.' L.B. Poullada, *Reform and Rebellion in Afghanistan*, pp.231–2.

63.   For an exhaustive discussion of the Deobandi Islamic tradition, see Barbara D. Metcalf, *Islamic Revival in British India: Deoband, 1860–1900*, Princeton: Princeton University Press, 1982.

64.   The foregoing discussion is largely based on three sources: Ghobar, *Afghanestan dar masir-e ta'rikh*, pp.789–820; L.B. Poullada, *Reform and Rebellion in Afghanistan*, pp.66–159; Korgun, *Afganistan v 20–30e gody XXv. Stranitsy politicheskoi istorii*,

Moscow: Nauka, 1979, pp.15–65.

65. Nazif Shahrani, assessing Amanullah's legislative work, has summarised it by concluding that the laws adopted prior to 1924 'curtailed or eliminated the privileges of the Muhammadzai sardars, the feudal interests of some Pashtun khans, the ulama, and especially the judges of the Shari'a courts... for the first time the constitution and some of these laws legally acknowledged the fact that citizens had rights in relations to the government, and that they had equal rights without discrimination.' Shahrani, 'State Building and Social Fragmentation in Afghanistan', p.47.

66. Amanullah was the first Afghan ruler to introduce paper money: in July 1920, the Treasury bills exchangeable for gold were issued. G. Georgiev, 'Iz istorii denezhnogo obrashcheniia v Afganistane v 20-e gody XXv', in *Afganistan: istoriia, ekonomika, kultura*, Moscow: Nauka, 1989, p.166. Interestingly, the high quality and precious metal content in the new Afghan coins made them a preferred currency in the NWFP compared to the British currency. Spain, *The Pathan Borderland*, p.231.

67. The first telegraph line from Kabul to Kandahar was built in 1924, but already in 1929 the length of telegraph lines exceeded 2,000 kilometres. The first radio station was launched in Kabul in 1925; three years later there were 1,000 radio sets inside the country. The first regular air route Kabul-Termez-Tashkent was opened in 1927, and in the same year Afghanistan joined the International Postal Union. *Afganistan*, Moscow: Nauka, 1964, pp.120–7.

68. It is interesting that in 1990 the Najibullah regime turned to the experience of Amanullah, praising the latter's agricultural policies, especially those aimed at setting up small-scale food-processing enterprises, such as creameries, oil mills, cheese dairies, raisin workshops, tanneries, and so on. *Payam*, 29 Asad 1369 Solar Hijrah.

69. *Mulk* in Afghanistan was extremely limited, and usually consisted of urban vegetable gardens and small suburban plots. Amalendu Guha, 'The Economy of Afghanistan During Amanullah's Reign, 1919–1929', *International Studies*, 9(2), 1967, p.171.

70. An excellent account of land and land relations in Afghanistan in the first half of the twentieth century can be found in A.D. Davydov, 'O selskoi obshchine i ee khoziaistvennom znachenii v Afganistane', in *Voprosy ekonomiki Afganistana*, Moscow: Izdatelstvo vostochnoi literatury, 1963, pp.57–124.

71. Masson and Romodin, *Istoriia Afganistana*, Vol. II, p.331.

72. *Nezamnama-ye forush-e amlak-e sarkari*, Kabul, 1302AH.

73. Guha, 'The Economy of Afghanistan', p.171. One *jarib* (0.42 hectares) of irrigated land was usually sold for ten afghanis – cf. the annual rate of land tax per *jarib* at the time was between four and 20 afghanis.

74. The Amir planned to introduce compulsory education for children of both sexes between the ages of six and 11, but this task proved to be beyond the means of the Afghan state. By 1927, the total enrolment in the Afghan primary schools may have stood at 51,000, and in the secondary and vocational schools at 3,000. Hasan Kakar, 'Trends in Modern Afghan History', in Louis Duprée and Linette Albert (eds), *Afghanistan in the 1970s*, New York: Praeger Publishers, 1974, p.24. This figure undoubtedly constituted an impressive achievement compared with the preceding epoch, but was nowhere near enough to provide Afghanistan's

modernisation drive with the required pool of reasonably educated people.

75. Prior to 1929, some 300 Afghan students went abroad for continuous education, mostly in France, Italy, Germany and the USSR. Sh. Imomov, 'Iz istorii obshchestvennoi mysli Afganistana', in *Afganistan: ekonomika, politika, istoriia*, Moscow: Nauka, 1984, p.150.

76. B.-R. Logashova, 'Etnokulturnaia situatsiia v Afganistane', *Rasy i narody*, No. 16, 1986, p.127.

77. Newell, *The Politics of Afghanistan*, p.55.

78. In July 1923, the *Loya Jirgah*, or the Grand Assembly of influential people of Afghanistan, pronounced that 'Amanullah's marriage code... that encouraged monogamy, taxed polygaminous marriages, and required marriage certificates, was declared inconsistent with Islamic law. At the same time the assembly recommended punishment for the ill-treatment of women.' Adamec, *Afghanistan's Foreign Affairs to the Mid-Twentieth Century*, p.83.

79. In a dramatic gesture, the Queen tore off her veil in front of several hundred participants in the *Loya Jirgah* in October 1928. Fraser-Tytler, *Afghanistan*, p.213.

80. In Poullada's words: 'the removal of the veil seems to have been encouraged but not legally ordered or enforced. Queen Soraya's unveiling act on the palace steps no doubt offended the more traditional, but it must be noted that few felt forced to imitate her example. The fact is that during Amanullah's reign nearly all women who traditionally wore the veil continued to do so.' L.B. Poullada, 'Political Modernisation in Afghanistan', in Grassmuck and Adamec with Irwin (eds), *Afghanistan: Some New Approaches*, p.135.

81. One of the first dignitaries to be fined for violation of the new dress code was the exiled Amir of Bukhara. Korgun, *Intelligentsiia v politicheskoi zhizni Afganistana*, p.37.

82. Amongst Pashtuns, brideprice traditionally was the equivalent of 100 sheep. N. Tapper, *Bartered Brides*, p.142. Eric Newby has described a typical marital arrangement of a lower middle-class Tajik, who had to part with 9,000 afghanis in money and two horses, five cows and 40 sheep in kind to secure a bride, and invite some 300 people to the wedding banquet. Eric Newby, *A Short Walk in the Hindu Kush*, London and Sydney: Pan Books, 1974, pp.139–40. The fact that Newby's observations took place in the mid 1950s testifies to the persistence of traditional ways, despite numerous government edicts and regulations.

83. In 1924, an attempt was made to bring medical practice under state control. All doctors were to pass examinations to obtain the licence, and the activities of traditional healers, *hakims* and *tabibs*, were curbed to an extent. Gregorian, *The Emergence of Modern Afghanistan*, p.246.

84. Ochildiev, *Mladoafganskoe dvizhenie*, p.20.

85. Asta Olesen has made an astute observation that Amanullah's policy in religious matters, as was the case under Habibullah Khan as well, 'had in fact been the exact opposite of institutional secularisation. What had taken place was the integration of religious institutions within the state bureaucracy and the consequent subordination of religious authority to the political. This process of *polity-dominance*, which took the outward form of Islamisation, was primarily aimed at undermining the religious autonomy.' Olesen, *Islam and Politics in Afghanistan*, p.128. It was in the *symbolic* realm that traditional elements of the Afghan society felt most threatened by the Amir's endeavours.

86. ` Amanullah signed a 30-year agreement with the French government which gave exclusive rights for systematic archaeological exploration to Delegation Archeologique Française en Afghanistan (DAFA). Nancy Hatch Duprée, 'Archaeology and the Arts in the Creation of a National Consciousness', in Duprée and Albert (eds), *Afghanistan in the 1970s*, p.205.

87. The very first issue of *Aman-e Afghan* proclaimed that amongst its main objectives were: cultivation of love for science and knowledge in Afghanistan; objective coverage of world politics and events in Islamic countries in particular; and dissemination of free-thinking, and 'rendering sincere assistance to the leaders of Afghanistan in their activities'. No fewer than 50 laws and other legislative documents were published by the newspaper during the Amanullah period, making it the only reliable source of vital information for local officials throughout the country. Imomov, 'Iz istorii obshchestvennoi mysli Afganistana', pp.148–9.

88. Altogether, 23 periodicals were published in Afghanistan in the 1920s. Korgun, *Intelligentsiia v politicheskoi zhizni Afganistana*, p.33.

89. Rubin, *The Fragmentation of Afghanistan*, p.56.

90. Mohammad Ali, *Progressive Afghanistan*, pp.11–12.

91. Adamec, *Afghanistan's Foreign Affairs to the Mid-Twentieth Century*, p.86.

92. Fletcher, *Afghanistan*, p.207.

93. Sykes, *A History of Afghanistan*, Vol. II, p.299.

94. L.B. Poullada, 'Political Modernisation in Afghanistan', p.124.

95. One of their leaders, Ghulam Mohiuddin Arti – a true patriot who had donated 300,000 afghani to purchase military equipment from abroad – berated Amanullah during a *Loya Jirgah* session: 'Until your sinful ministers are tried and hanged, no reforms will be possible in this country.' Korgun, *Intelligentsiia v politicheskoi zhizni Afganistana*, p.38.

96. 'Corruption was rampant in all departments, civil as well as military. Most of the officials were inexperienced, incompetent and self-conceited and had secured their jobs by favouritism, bribery or nepotism... Posts of all sorts were sold openly and nobody was ashamed or afraid of receiving or offering bribes – the highest officials of the King and even of the Queen not excepted.' Ali, *Progressive Afghanistan*, p.9.

97. L.B. Poullada, *Reform and Rebellion in Afghanistan*, p.93.

98. When in 1922 the state budget (*booja*) was introduced, even Cabinet ministers could not understand its basic principles. Ordinary peasants perceived *booja* as the abstract epitome of evil and blamed it for the poor harvests. Rhea Talley Stewart, *Fire in Afghanistan, 1914–1929: Faith, Hope and the British Empire*, New York: Doubleday, 1973, p.269.

99. 'Although the educational reforms and those related to the status of women would for a long while have no practical effect on the Khost tribesmen, they could agree with the religious leaders in objecting to them as violating deep-rooted customs, which were generally assumed to be sanctioned by Islam. And the conscription system to the army was enough of an offence from the central power to cause rebellion. So there was ample basis for an alliance between religious and tribal leaders.' Olesen, *Islam and Politics in Afghanistan*, pp.137–8.

100. The cost of the rebellion was put at £5,000,000, or two years' revenue of the state. Sykes, *A History of Afghanistan*, Vol. II, p.298. The Soviet interpretation of the uprising was as follows: 'In 1924 an anti-government mutiny was incited in Afghanistan by reactionary forces with active support of the British imperialism.

The mutineers demanded abolition of the progressive laws and reforms adopted by the government of Amanullah Khan and insisted on the reorientation of Afghanistan to England in its foreign policy. The British provided the mutineers with arms and money. At the same time, England tried to prevent the lawful Afghan government from strengthening its armed forces.' Teplinskii, *SSSR i Afganistan*, p.57. Not unexpectedly, the Soviets ascribed the salvation of Amanullah's 'anti-imperialist' regime to themselves: 'The situation was rather threatening at one point, since the rebels had managed to advance deep into the country and were at 80 miles from the capital. The situation was saved by the arrival of our combat aeroplanes which had flown eagle-wise over the Hindukush and destroyed the rebels. These apparata with pilots stayed in the Amir's service.' Kheifets, *Sovetskaia diplomatiia i narody Vostoka*, p.273. In reality, when the regular army crumbled, Amanullah had to summon tribal levies from the Mohmand, Shinwari, Afridi, and Hazaras who had perennial feuds with the Mangal. Through exploiting inter-tribal friction and the traditional diplomacy of buying certain chieftains off, Amanullah finally quashed the rebellion in January 1925.

101. L.B. Poullada, *Reform and Rebellion in Afghanistan*; Gregorian, *The Emergence of Modern Afghanistan*; Ghobar, *Afghanestan dar masir-e ta'rikh*.

102. Korgun, *Intelligentsiia v politicheskoi zhizni Afganistana*.

103. Adamec, *Afghanistan, 1900–1923*.

104. As Hasan Kakar has rightfully observed, it was due to the unconditional support of the Young Afghans 'that the first phase of the reforms was implemented amid public enthusiasm and without opposition'. Kakar, 'Trends in Modern Afghan History', p.29.

105. In one of his articles in *Aman-e Afghan*, Tarzi extolled the virtues of law-based gradualism and social tranquillity as the prerequisites for the success of the reforms: 'The laws are developed not for the benefit of *khans* and *maliks*, officials and princes, but to allow the most oppressed and impoverished strata of the society to lead a quiet and happy life… [If this happens] the *khan*, the landlord and the mullah will live in tranquillity, peace will reign in the society and the necessary conditions for the country's progress will be created.' Imomov, 'Iz istorii obshchestvennoi mysli Afganistana', p.149.

106. Both Sher Ahmad Khan and Mohammad Nadir Khan were descendants of Sultan Ahmad Khan Tela'i. Mahmud Tarzi once said about representatives of this extended family that 'These people aim at the throne'. Communication between Abdul Wahab Tarzi, the elder son of Mahmud Tarzi, and Ravan Farhadi, Geneva, 1983.

107. Sherzad was imprisoned by the Communists between 1978 and 1979, sought asylum in Switzerland in 1980, and died in Lausanne in 1994.

108. By 1928, the whole constellation of bright Young Afghans had been removed from official positions, including Mohammad Wali Khan, Abdul Hadi Dawi, Abdurrahman Khan Lodi, Mohiuddin Arti and Mir Gholam Mohammad Ghobar. Many middle-ranked officers in the army and civil service had been dismissed, too. 'Now Amanullah was surrounded by sycophants and careerists, many of whom were open opponents of the reforms. In the Amir's coterie there emerged an atmosphere of intrigues, mistrust and mutual animosity.' M. Davliatov, 'M.G.M. Gubar o progressivnykh obshchestvennykh dvizheniiakh v Afganistane v nachale XXv', p.36.

109. Gregorian, *The Emergence of Modern Afghanistan*, p.245.

110. The crunch came in 1924, when Nadir Khan unsuccessfully reasoned with Amanullah that the army was not prepared to put down the Khost rebellion and that Amanullah should negotiate with the insurgents. Ali, *Progressive Afghanistan*, p.77.

111. William K. Fraser-Tytler, who knew Amanullah rather well, has left the following florid description of the Afghan monarch: 'An abrupt, impulsive, and at the same time a weak character. Weak that is to say in his inability to choose good advisors and in the influence in state affairs which he allowed to such evil counsellors as the notorious Charkhi family of Logar, while he banished or disregarded the notable Musahiban family; impulsive in that he was governed not by any reason or understanding of the requirements of his country, but by sudden decisions based on imperfect knowledge, which caused him to embark on projects often quite unsuitable or beyond the power of his servants to carry through. To these fatal weaknesses must be added an absurd conceit and arrogance of disposition.' Fraser-Tytler, *Afghanistan*, p.201. Of course, this is not a view shared by a number of prominent Afghan historians, most notably Ghobar and M.M.S. Farhang, who considered that Nadir Khan had always had an eye on the Afghan throne during Amanullah's reign.

112. Gregorian, *The Emergence of Modern Afghanistan*, p.256.

113. Ataturk emphasised the instrumentality of the armed forces several times. One of his remarks addressed to Amanullah was: 'Do not engage yourself in reforms threatening the interests of the nobility and of the clergy unless and until you have a strong army.' Ali Mohammad Khan, Amanullah's chief interpreter present at the meeting, recounted this episode to Ravan Farhadi in 1974 in Kabul.

114. Adamec, *Afghanistan's Foreign Affairs to the Mid-Twentieth Century*, p.128.

115. Successful negotiations with Germany proved to be of special significance: in addition to numerous supplies contracts, Amanullah managed to secure a credit of four million marks to finance his programmes – the only foreign credit of this kind that Afghanistan received before the Second World War. Adamec, 'Germany, Third Power in Afghanistan's Foreign Relations', p.230.

116. Ravan Farhadi's conversation with Ali Mohammad Khan in Kabul, 1974.

117. In a pamphlet circulated amongst the Shinwaris in late 1928, the local religious figures proclaimed that 'Before his [Amanullah's] return from Europe... he was introducing these reforms, which are against Shariat, secretly and politically, on account of which our Ulema were making enquiries about them... But after his return from Europe, he introduced his evil reforms publicly and as the population of Afghanistan generally belong to the Hanafi sect they have made up their minds to dethrone him and murder him.' Quoted in Stewart, *Fire in Afghanistan*, p.432.

118. For a penetrating analysis of the perceived incompatibility of Amanullah's behaviour during his voyage with the traditional Pashtun norms of dignity (*namus*), see Olesen, *Islam and Politics in Afghanistan*, p.146.

119. George McMunn, *Afghanistan: From Darius to Amanullah*, London: G. Bell and Sons Ltd., 1929, p.329.

120. It was said in Kabul that fake photographs showing Queen Soraya nude had been prepared and disseminated in tribal areas by British Intelligence agents.

121. Stewart, *Fire in Afghanistan*, pp.433–4.

122. A detailed account of Habibullah Kalakani's deeds is provided in the next chapter.

In 1928, he was a highwayman of some renown, whose gang had swollen from 24 to nearly 2,000 over the period of four years. Muhammad, *Memoir of the Coup*, pp.24, 26. At the time of the Shinwari uprising, Bacha had vast areas populated by Tajiks around the town of Charikar under his control. There is no evidence to support the supposition that anti-Amanullah rebellions in the East and Habibullah's bandit forays were coordinated; the claim that Bacha, a Tajik of humble origin, was the recognised leader of anti-Amanullah opposition which included, among others, the Mahsuds and other frontier tribes (Amiryar, 'Soviet Influence, Penetration, Domination and Invasion', p.74) is incorrect.

123. Anne Baker, *Wings over Kabul: The First Airlift*, London: William Kimber, 1975, p.40.

124. Habibullah Kalakani obviously took advantage of the fact that the bulk of the government forces was engaged in Jalalabad, and very few soldiers remained to garrison Kabul. On 11 December 1928, only 18 well-armed cadets of the military college offered successful resistance to some 300 bandits who intended to plunder the Arg. Ghobar, *Afghanestan dar masir-e ta'rikh*, p.822.

125. Gregorian, *The Emergence of Modern Afghanistan*, p.265.

126. Muhammad, *Memoir of the Coup*, pp.32–3. 'But the good Inayatullah was not the man to sit on that throne of uneasiness even in the way of peaceful succession. Stout, amiable, lethargic, not even, so far as was known, wise in council, the situation was far beyond his control or the group of king-making sirdars who hoped to save the dynasty and secure continuity.' McMunn, *Afghanistan*, p.333.

127. Fraser-Tytler, *Afghanistan*, p.217.

128. Grigorii Agabekov, *OGPU: The Russian Secret Terror*, Westport: Hyperion Press, 1975 [1931], p.167.

129. This perception was moulded by missives from the Soviet Ambassador in Kabul, Leonid Stark, who, reporting on his meeting with Amanullah on 29 November 1928, wrote that the King 'immediately and in a rather categorical form declared that the rebellion had been inspired by the British and was aimed directly at him'. *Dokumenty vneshnei politiki SSSR*, Vol. XI, Moscow: Gosizdat, 1957, p.591.

130. Such views prevailed in the OGPU, which was locked in a bitter inter-departmental rivalry with the People's Commissariat of Foreign Affairs (NKID), which tended to support Amanullah's cause for pragmatic reasons. Stewart, *Fire in Afghanistan*, pp.560–1.

131. As late as summer 1929, confidential documents of the Central Asian Bureau of the Communist Party wrote about Bacha as a 'socially close element', the leader of a peasant movement, who had dealt a blow to the power of mullahs and landed aristocracy. Volodarskii, *Sovety i ikh iuzhnye sosedi Iran i Afganistan*, pp.190–1.

132. Adamec, *Afghanistan's Foreign Affairs to the Mid-Twentieth Century*, p.150.

133. The Politburo voted in principle to render support to Amanullah against all other contenders in late December 1928. Stalin apparently listened neither to the OGPU nor to the NKID experts, but was guided by his own, not fully understood, calculations in this decision. Volodarskii, *Sovety i ikh iuzhnye sosedi Iran i Afganistan*, p.156. On 20 December 1928, *Pravda* published an article portraying the rebellion in Afghanistan as 'the fruit of labour of English Colonel Lawrence, the notorious Lawrence of Arabia'.

134. Baker, *Wings over Kabul*, pp.168–9.

135. One of the Soviet officers attached to Charkhi reminisced with a touch of sorrow:

'I must say, our boys can shoot very well indeed, and in one week we could have reached Kabul, had Amanullah held the ground in Kandahar.' The 'boys' killed 8,000 Afghans during the campaign, having lost just a handful of Red Army soldiers. G.S. Agabekov, *Ch.K. za rabotoi*, Berlin: Strela, 1931, pp.281–2.

136. This agreement was never put on paper and existed as a sort of informal under-standing between the two parties in regard to their activities in Afghanistan.

137. An Afghan pilot who flew Tarzi from Kandahar to Herat and then to Iran reminisced that the ideologue of Afghan nationalism wept and recited a Pashto verse:

> Da sta py mina py shpo shpo zy karidylai yem
> Os di preg dy ma che Ingriz dyrta ghundylai yem.
> From love for you [Motherland] I have suffered every night
> Now allow me to leave to the British

Habibi, *Jonbesh-e mashruteyat dar Afghanestan*, p.107.

Chapter 4: The Nadiri Dynasty

1. Contemporary Tajik scholars, both in Tajikistan and Afghanistan, tend to interpret Habibullah's rule almost exclusively from the positions of ethnic struggle: 'Tajik peasants and craftsmen... rose against the Afghan [Pashtun] domination. This is why this uprising had the essence of the national liberation movement... The oppression of Tajiks by Afghans [Pashtuns] nearly reached its end. The victory of Tajik rebels increased the Tajiks' national consciousness. After several centuries, they again acquired their ancient rights.' Sa'di, *Mukhtasari ta'rikhi siyosii Tojikoni Afghoniston*, p.49. There is no evidence whatsoever that Habibullah viewed his mission in these terms. For him belonging with the supra-ethnic Islamic community, the *'Umma*, remained the predominant form of identification. In criticising Amanullah, he accused the deposed king of a lack of faith and righteousness, never invoking the argument of Pashtun supremacy.

2. Faiz Mohammad was especially dismissive in characterising 'Bacha-ye Saqao' and his followers: 'These wild filthy Kuhistanis and Kohdamanis... savage bandits, who had never seen wheat bread in their lives, covering themselves with Islamic slogans, committed atrocities that human brain refused to comprehend.' Faiz Mohammad, *Kniga upominanii o miatezhe*, Moscow: Mysl, 1988, pp.54, 57. Mohammad Ali described Bacha as a 'foul-minded tyrant... quite indifferent to murder and totally incapable of pity or remorse'. Mohammad Ali, *Progressive Afghanistan*, p.46. For Mir Gholam Mohammad Ghobar's views, see his *Afghanistan in the Course of History*, Vol. II, trans. Sharief A. Fayez, Virginia: All Prints Inc, 2001, Chapter 1.

3. Amanullah's long-time favourite, acting Prime Minister Mohammad Wali Khan, the Kabul Region Military Commander Mahmud Sami, and Kabul's Mayor Ali Ahmad Khan, were but a few figures who maintained secret ties with Habibullah. A.I. Shkirando, 'Novye dannye ob afganskom letopistse Faiz Muhammade i ego sochineniiakh', in *Afganistan: ekonomika, politika, istoriia*, Moscow: Nauka, 1984, p.167.

4. The following account is based on Khalili's book: *'Ayyori az Khorasan*.

5. In February 1929, Habibullah asked an experienced man of letters to teach him how to read and write in Persian. The teaching process never took off the ground

owing to Habibullah's becoming 'too busy and worried about the events in the country'. (Information related to Rawan Farhadi by his father.)

6. Sir Francis Humphrys thus analysed the reasons for Amanullah's demise: 'It would be a mistake to suppose that the primary cause of King Amanullah's downfall is to be found in the resolutions which he formed during the European tour. He has admitted to me that ever since he came to the throne he has been impelled by an uncontrollable desire to bring about the complete modernisation of his country during his own lifetime… The fact that the king was inveighing against undoubted national defects when he criticised the gross superstitions of the people, their unchivalrous attitude towards women, and the exaggerated powers of the fanatical priesthood only served to enhance the melancholy effect which was produced by his impracticable programme.' Quoted in Anne Baker, *Wings over Kabul*, pp.43, 45.

7. Olivier Roy has commented extensively on the fact that Habibullah was heavily involved with the activities of the Naqshbandi Sufi order and, possibly, was the *murid* of Shams ul-Haqq Mujaddidi Kuhistani. There is no doubt that his entrance into Kabul was sanctioned by the Mujaddidi family – the most influential hereditary Islamic leaders in Afghanistan. 'As always the fundamentalist *'ulama* wished to see on the throne a sovereign who would re-establish the *shari'at* and who would undo the modernist reforms of Amanullah. Popular support for Bacha had the same foundation: it was first and foremost a cultural revolt, rather than a political or economic one.' O. Roy, *Islam and Resistance in Afghanistan*, pp.65–7.

8. Korgun, *Afganistan v 20–30e gody XXv*, p.67.

9. Ghobar, *Afghanestan dar masir-e ta'rikh*, pp.827–8.

10. In the first week following Habibullah's capture of Kabul on 17 January 1929, his forces committed numerous atrocities, including ransacking the houses of 191 well-known reformist figures of the Amanullah regime and imprisoning their inhabitants. For a detailed account, see McChesney, *Kabul under Seige*, pp.55–61.

11. The Young Afghans took the brunt of the reprisals. Their erstwhile leader, Abdur Rahman Lodi, was arrested; the editor of the *Aman-e Afghan* newspaper, Gholam Nabi Jalalabadi, was killed alongside several comrades, and dozens more fled to India where they started a pro-Amanullah publication, *Afghanistan*, in Lahore. The only paper sanctioned by Habibullah was *Habib ul-Islam*, which was the mouthpiece of the new regime and promoted ultra-reactionary views. It referred to the Afghans who had been sent to the West for education as follows: 'During their stay in Europe these people ate ham and bacon. This food penetrated their blood vessels and blackened their tissues and veins.' Quoted in *Izvestiia*, 12 May 1929.

12. Adamec, 'Germany, Third Power in Afghanistan's Foreign Relations', p.235.

13. Muhammad, *Memoir of the Coup*, p.133.

14. Taxation of agricultural production was the main source of revenues for Amanullah's government. Between 1919 and 1929, land tax rates increased four-fold and livestock tax rates five-fold. Guha, 'The Economy of Afghanistan', p.175. The situation had reached the point where up to 45 per cent of the value of produce was exacted from the peasants in taxes. Korgun, 'The First Stage of Afghanistan's Independent Development', *Afghanistan: Past and Present*, Moscow: USSR Academy of Sciences, 1982, p.146.

15. Over a period of seven months in 1929, the residents of Kabul alone were 'persuaded' to part with 12,000,000 afghanis to shoulder the burden of maintaining

tribal levies in Habibullah's army. Muhammad, *Memoir of the Coup*, p.146.

16. G. Georgiev, 'Iz istorii denezhnogo obrashcheniia v Afganistane v 20-e gody XXv', in *Afghanistan: istoriia, ekonomika, kultura*, Moscow: Nauka, 1989, pp.169–71.

17. L.B. Poullada, *Reform and Rebellion in Afghanistan*, p.191.

18. The Musahiban brothers took an active part in hammering out a Pashtun tribal force to overthrow Habibullah. Shah Wali worked with the Mangals, Shah Mahmud was despatched to incite the Jajis, Mohammad Hashim conducted sensitive negotiations with tribal chiefs in the Eastern Province, while Mohammad Nadir stayed with the Jadrans. Ikbal Ali Shah, *Modern Afghanistan*, London: Low, 1939, p.184. The coalition which started to evolve in March 1929 was in a position to challenge Habibullah's forces in earnest only six months later. The crucial development was the infusion of several thousand Wazir and Mahsud warriors from beyond the Durand Line, which occurred with British encouragement in September 1929. *Istoriia Afganistana s drevneishikh vremen do nashikh dnei*, Moscow: Mysl, 1982, p.240.

19. The agreement between Habibullah and Nadir Khan was recorded in the margin of a printed copy of the Qur'an, which signified the sanctity and inviolability of the document.

20. During a six-hour conversation with Humphrys on 9 February 1929, Nadir's brother, Shah Mahmud, made it clear that the Musahiban family, as well as the bulk of Pashtun tribes, would strenuously object to Amanullah's return to the throne, but that a compromise might be achieved 'in favour of an Afghan nobleman who was generally approved by tribes and provided that he was not a member of Amanullah's family'. Baker, *Wings over Kabul*, p.168. In May 1929, the Barakzai sardars, Nadir Khan included, were considering the figure of Amanullah's nephew, Asadullah Khan, as a possible successor. McMunn, *Afghanistan*, p.337.

21. Korgun has argued that the Young Afghans who 'had come close to understanding the demands of the people's masses and reflecting the common national interests, went farther than superficial reformist radicalism of Amanullah. In the eyes of Nadir, their opposition to the regime was more dangerous than dynastic claims of the ex-King.' Korgun, *Intelligentsiia v politicheskoi zhizni Afganistana*, p.44. Immediately upon assuming the throne, Nadir cracked down on the reformists with a severity greater than Habibullah's. In 1930, three prominent members of the original movement were ruthlessly executed: Abdur Rahman Khan Lodi, Taj Mohammad Paghmani and Faiz Mohammad Barutsaz. Mir Gholam Mohammad Ghobar and many others were incarcerated. Even those who had emigrated but continued active political life were not safe: Mohiuddin Khan Arti was assassinated in Peshawar several years later. See Ghobar, *Afghanistan in the Course of History*, Vol. II.

22. William K. Fraser-Tytler, who first met Nadir and his brothers in Kabul in 1922, wrote that 'they were outstanding... for courtesy, good breeding, and a certain indefinable air of authority which distinguished them among their fellow subjects of the Amir. They were men of a ruling race, and, owing perhaps to their early experiences abroad, were also men of the world who did not allow their political outlook to interfere with their personal relationships.' Fraser-Tytler, *Afghanistan*, p.223.

23. Nancy Peabody Newell and Richard S. Newell, *The Struggle for Afghanistan*, Ithaca and London: Cornell University Press, 1981, p.38; Adamec, 'Germany, Third Power in Afghanistan's Foreign Relations', p.240.

24. Cf. the following statements of the British and Soviet officials. Sir Austen Chamberlain, Foreign Secretary, 30 January 1929: 'His Majesty's government have no intention of interfering in the internal affairs of Afghanistan by supporting or assisting any of the parties at present contending for power in that country. They earnestly desire the establishment of a strong Central Government, and they will be prepared, when the Government is established, to show their friendship for the Afghan people by giving such assistance as they can in the reconstruction and development of the country.' Baker, *Wings over Kabul*, pp.166–7. M.M. Litvinov, Acting People's Commissar for Foreign Affairs, 4 December 1929: 'Remaining faithful to the fundamental principles of our policy, we refrained from any kind of interference into the acute internal struggle in that country, and from supporting one grouping against another, making certain at the same time that such interference would not transpire from other countries adjacent to Afghanistan.' Teplinskii, *Istoriia sovetsko-afganskikh otnoshenii*, p.107.

25. It is very revealing that in the worst traditions of distorting or even concealing objective information for the sake of Marxist political correctness, the Soviet Ambassador, Leonid Stark, did not even *mention* the activities of Nadir Khan to his superiors in Moscow until October 1929. Volodarskii, *Sovety i ikh iuzhnye sosedi Iran i Afganistan*, p.194.

26. British displeasure with Soviet involvement was expressed in the mildest possible form: 'Britain decided to drop the idea of giving the Soviets a hands-off warning as Britain was not prepared to use force if the warning was disregarded.' Ludwig W. Adamec, *Afghanistan's Foreign Affairs to the Mid-Twentieth Century: Relations with the USSR, Germany, and Britain*, Tucson: University of Arizona Press, 1974, p.161.

27. Grigorii Agabekov, a high-ranking officer of the OGPU, reproduced the argumentation of the Deputy People's Commissar for Foreign Relations (in charge of Asia), L.M. Karakhan: 'Do you know why I prefer to deal with Nadir Khan rather than Bacha-ye Saqao? Bacha-ye Saqao is a Tajik, he has fellow-countrymen in Turkestan. He may attempt to attack our frontiers. On the contrary, Nadir Khan is a Pashtun, and will send his forces to the border with India.' *Tojikiston*, 24 July 1992.

28. 'He was a patriot who wanted his country to be independent, and it was felt in London and Delhi that Nadir would steer the same middle course in dealing with his two neighbours that had been maintained by Afghan rulers since the days of Abdur Rahman.' Adamec, *Afghanistan's Foreign Affairs to the Mid-Twentieth Century*, p.175.

29. Gregorian, *The Emergence of Modern Afghanistan*, p.297.

30. Shahrani, 'State Building and Social Fragmentation in Afghanistan, p.52.

31. Gregorian, *The Emergence of Modern Afghanistan*, p.293.

32. Korgun, *Afganistan v 20-30e gody XXv*, p.115.

33. Ghaus, *The Fall of Afghanistan*, p.48.

34. Nadir created the Society of Islamic Scholars (*Jamiat ul-Ulama*) in 1929 and the 45-strong Assembly of Nobles (*Majles-e A'yan*) in 1931 – temporary consultative organs, embodying representatives of the religious and tribal elites respectively. Wilber (ed.), *Afghanistan*, p.79. Mohammad Siddiq, the leader of the Mojaddidi clan, was appointed as the Ambassador to Egypt, and a number of other prominent mullahs received appointments in the state agencies. Fletcher, *Afghanistan*, p.227.

For at least two years Nadir remained dependent on tribal force to stay in power: the massive rebellion of Kuhdaman Tajiks in June 1930 was suppressed only due to the arrival of 25,000 trans-border Pashtun warriors. *Istoriia Afganistana*, p.242.

35.   'The power and influence of Pashtun tribal groups... were ensured through exemption from military conscription and taxation. Many rural aristocrats were also elected to, or selected for, the two houses of parliament. Their participation in what turned out to be a rubber-stamp parliament served two purposes. It gave the local khans the satisfaction of sharing government power, but it also helped the centralisation of the government by keeping the local leaders in Kabul for more than seven months of each year under the watchful eye of the police. The government also tried to recruit the sons of these local leaders into schools to ensure more long-term support by the rural aristocracy.' Shahrani, 'State Building and Social Fragmentation in Afghanistan', pp.52–3.

36.   Duprée has given the following summary of the new legislation: 'The 1931 Constitution, in essence, established the kingship in the line of Mohammad Nadir Shah, created a façade of parliamentary government while leaving control in the hands of the royal family, kept the judiciary primarily under the religious leaders, created a semi-socialist economic framework with the principle of free enterprise accepted, and guaranteed theoretical individual equality.' Duprée, *Afghanistan*, p.471.

37.   By 1933, Nadir Shah had created a formidable regular army of 40,000. Watkins, *Afghanistan*, p.59.

38.   In October 1929, *Afghanistan*, a newspaper of Afghan liberal emigrants in Lahore, wrote: 'The experience of Afghanistan and other nations definitely points to the fact the unlimited supreme power is harmful. For Afghanistan absolutism is totally unacceptable... The Afghan people has many times rebelled against its despots, the kings, but, unfortunately, having escaped from the hands of one, it was readying its neck for the knife of another. Educated and rational Afghans must declare: "We don't need an unlimited monarch, we want to rule our country ourselves, through our deputies and manage our affairs the way we want".' A.I. Shkirando, 'Gazeta "Afganistan" kak organ afganskoi oppozitsii v 1929g', in *Afganistan: Istoriia, ekonomika, kultura*, Moscow: Nauka, 1989, p.265.

39.   When, on 8 November 1933, Nadir Shah was assassinated, Amanullah made the following comment from his residence in Rome: 'Today's event is the result of the agitation caused by Nadir's policy amongst the Afghans. This policy has been leading to numerous murders, incarcerations, and so on. The slaughter of the intelligentsia has sown terror.' Korgun, *Intelligentsiia v politicheskoi zhizni Afganistana*, p.46.

40.   It has been calculated that under the Musahiban dynasty the ethnic composition of the senior officer positions remained stable at 70 per cent Pashtuns, 20 per cent Tajiks and 10 per cent others. Logashova, 'Etnokulturnaia situatsiia v Afganistane', p.135.

41.   Rubin, *The Fragmentation of Afghanistan*, p.59.

42.   Fraser-Tytler, *Afghanistan*, p.238.

43.   Spain, *The Pathan Borderland*, pp.165–8.

44.   Nadir's restraint, not unnaturally, caused bitterness in Moscow: 'The King lived up to the expectations placed on him by British imperialism... feudal and reactionary elements once again rendered assistance to imperialism in colonies and semi-colonies.' *Pravda*, 8 August 1930.

45. Teplinskii, *SSSR i Afganistan*, p.87.

46. Afghan mujahideen never seemed to forgive Nadir for this: 'This act of Nadir the Butcher... destroyed the Islamic movement of Central Asia forever. It was totally unexpected by the Russians, and came really handy to them. It was the greatest service that Nadir the Traitor rendered to the Russians.' Najib, *Afghanestan dar gozargah-e atash wa khun*, p.173.

47. In March 1931, the last Basmachi commander, Ibrahim Bek, who had been Habibullah's ally two years previously, was forced to cross the Amu with a handful of followers. He surrendered to the Soviet authorities, was tried and executed in August 1932. Medvedev, 'Basmachi – obrechennoe voinstvo', p.157.

48. Volodarskii, *Sovety i ikh iuzhnye sosedi Iran i Afganistan*, p.197.

49. Turkish experts were too easily identifiable with Amanullah's reforms, and Nadir Shah never restored them to eminent positions. Adamec, *Afghanistan's Foreign Affairs to the Mid-Twentieth Century*, p.189.

50. Adamec, 'Germany, Third Power in Afghanistan's Foreign Relations', p.251.

51. Poullada and Poullada, *The Kingdom of Afghanistan and the United States*, p.41.

52. Gregorian, *The Emergence of Modern Afghanistan*, p.337.

53. For a detailed account of the trial of Nadir Shah's assassin and his colleagues, see Ghobar, *Afghanistan in the Course of History*, Vol. II, pp.134–45.

54. Mohammad Aziz, technically the most senior amongst the siblings, was excessively shy, lacked dynamism and ambition and generally avoided politics. Nadir Shah thus enjoyed all the privileges accorded by the informal code of the Pashtun family to the clan leader.

55. The fact that Zahir Shah was devoid of real power for 20 years while Mohammad Hashim and Shah Mahmud managed the affairs of state conformed with the requirements of a traditionalist society: 'When a young man's father dies (or is killed), his paternal uncle or uncles replace his father in the culturally defined father-son rights and obligations. So rule by the uncles was most logical, and gave the King time to study his nation, his role, and his responsibilities, and to assess his political future.' Duprée, *Afghanistan*, p.477.

56. Maxwell J. Fry, *The Afghan Economy*, Leiden: E.J. Brill, 1974, p.83.

57. *Istoriia Afganistana*, p.245.

58. Korgun, *Afganistan v 20-30e gody XXv*, p.141.

59. *Noveishaia istoriia stran zarubezhnogo Vostoka*, Vyp. 2, Moscow: Izdatelstvo Moskovskogo universiteta, 1955, p.187.

60. Gregorian, *The Emergence of Modern Afghanistan*, p.363.

61. The first Communist President of Afghanistan, Nur Mohammad Taraki, was Zabuli's co-patrimonialist and protégé. Zabuli employed Taraki as a clerk in one of his trading companies in Bombay in the 1940s, and in 1978 donated some of his substantial wealth to Taraki's regime as a gesture of solidarity.

62. 'The laissez-faire economic policy of the government resulted in unprecedented commercial and industrial growth during the 1930s and brought about a radical change in the political economy of the Afghan state: the major source of government revenues shifted from direct taxation, which had made up two-thirds of the national revenue during Amanullah's rule, to indirect taxes and customs duties, with less than one-third of the revenues coming from land and livestock taxes.' Shahrani, 'State Building and Social Fragmentation in Afghanistan', pp.54–5.

63. In 1932, Afghanistan's Ambassador in Moscow, Mohammad Aziz, received strict

instructions 'not to discuss any treaties with the USSR, including the Trade Agreement'. Volodarskii, *Sovety i ikh iuzhnye sosedi Iran i Afganistan*, p.197. Although the conditions offered by the Kremlin in relation to trade with Afghanistan were extremely favourable to the latter, Mohammad Hashim suspected ulterior motives behind Moscow's diplomatic initiative, and the Trade Agreement was not signed until 1936. Teplinskii, *Istoriia sovetsko-afganskikh otnoshenii*, p.127.

64. Fletcher, *Afghanistan*, p.228.

65. Yapp, *The Near East Since the First World War*, London and New York: Longman, 1991, p.163.

66. The British and Soviet ambassadors presented relevant démarches on 9 and 11 October 1941 respectively.

67. Altogether, some 200 Axis citizens who were not diplomatic staff had to leave Afghanistan. Teplinskii, *SSSR i Afganistan*, p.108.

68. Yapp, *The Near East Since the First World War*, p.182.

69. A. Saikal, *The Rise and Fall of the Shah*, p.35.

70. Information obtained by Rawan Farhadi in private conversations with the members of the delegation. Apparently, Aini was particularly stultified by the presence of a Russian security officer in the meeting.

71. One of the most prominent figures during this period was Mohammad Qul Mohmand who became the Governor of Mazar and Maimana in 1932 and arduously promoted the influx of Pashtun settlers to Afghan Turkestan.

72. Pazhwak's eulogy of the Pashtuns as the authentic population of 'Ariana' possessing exceptional qualities can be found in Rahman Pazhwak, *Pakhtunistan: A New State in Central Asia*, London: The Royal Afghan Embassy, 1960.

73. Pashtu was made an official language in Afghanistan in 1936. Shortly afterwards, all civil servants were required to undertake a course of study in the language, upon completion of which a ten per cent increase in salary could be expected. *Area Handbook for Afghanistan*, Washington: The American University, 1969, p.79.

74. 'This reform was accompanied by the forced assimilation of the non-Afghan ethnic groups, which had been already deprived of the possibility to develop their ancient cultures. They were forcibly enrolled as "Afghans" and were denied the very right of being called Uzbeks, Tajiks, Turkmens, Hazaras.' *Noveishaia istoriia stran zarubezhnogo-Vostoka*, p.186.

75. Under Daoud, a clear dichotomy began to evolve in the Afghan army: offspring of Pashtun aristocratic clans were channelled to traditional arms of service, such as infantry, which guaranteed them quick promotion and direct control over enlisted personnel, whereas commissions in signals and engineering units were regarded as less prestigious and, consequently, had a higher percentage of non-Pashtuns receiving them. Korgun, *Intelligentsiia v politicheskoi zhizni Afganistana*, pp.10–11.

76. Poullada and Poullada, *The Kingdom of Afghanistan and the United States*, pp.90–1.

77. Gregorian, *The Emergence of Modern Afghanistan*, p.387.

78. The programme of *Wikh-i Zalmayan*, adopted by its 20 members in Kabul on 28 April 1947, included the following items: introduction of constitutional monarchy; protection of independence and territorial integrity of Afghanistan; upholding of freedom of speech and public associations; support for the struggle for Pashtunistan; fight against corruption; development of sciences and education; establishment of harmony between the government and the people; and promotion

of the Pashtu language and culture. *Afganistan: problemy voiny i mira*, Moscow: IVRAN, 1996, p.103.

79.   Korgun, *Intelligentsiia v politicheskoi zhizni Afganistana*, p.90.

80.   *Watan*'s Editor-in-Chief was Dari-speaking historian and former Deputy Mayor of Kabul, Mir Mohammad Siddiq Farhang. Amongst the organisation's prominent members were the Premier's advisor, Abdul Husain; poets Sarwar Juya and Ali Ahmad Naimi; writers Abdul Khalim 'Atefi and Abdul Hashim Mozhda – all Tajiks – and General Fateh Mohammad, a Hazara.

81.   'Stanovlenie demokraticheskoi obshchestvennoi mysli i demokraticheskikh dvizhenii', in *Afganistan: problemy voiny i mira*, Moscow: IVRAN, 1996, p.108.

82.   Guha, 'The Rise of Capitalistic Enterprises in Afghanistan, 1929–45', *The Indian Economic and Social History Review*, 1(2), October–December 1963, p.165.

83.   R.T. Akhramovich, 'K kharakteristike etapov obshchestvennoi evoliutsii Afganistana posle vtoroi mirovoi voiny', *Narody Azii i Afriki*, No. 3, 1967, p.52.

84.   Duprée, *Afghanistan*, p.494.

85.   Korgun, *Intelligentsiia v politicheskoi zhizni Afganistana*, pp.92–3.

86.   Bhabani Sen Gupta, *Afghanistan: Politics, Economics and Society*, London: Frances Pinter, 1986, p.13.

Chapter 5: The Cold War and the Rise of a Rentier State

1.   Commenting on the changes in government structure after 1953, Duprée observed: 'In this modified oligarchy, the prime minister, supported by the army, still holds ultimate power, but he seldom makes decisions without consultations.' Duprée, 'A Suggested Pakistan-Afghanistan-Iran Federation', *The Middle East Journal*, 17(4), Autumn 1963, p.390. While Zahir Shah was quickly excluded from the policy deliberation process, he was in a position to continue to keep a close watch on political developments in the country. The King would regularly invite members of the intelligentsia to his palace in order to exchange views and make forecasts for the future.

2.   A rentier state is characterised by an economy which relies on substantial *external* rent, and a situation where the *government* is the principal recipient of the external rent in the economy. See Hazem Beblawi, 'The Rentier State in the Arab World', in Giacomo Luciani (ed.), *The Arab State*, London: Routledge, 1990, pp.85–8.

3.   It has been argued that 'the Cold War began on March 4, 1946. On that day 15 Soviet armoured brigades began to pour into the northwestern Iranian province of Azerbaijan, and to deploy along the Turkish and Iraqi frontiers and toward central Iran.' Robert Rossow Jr, 'The Battle of Azerbaijan, 1946', *The Middle East Journal*, 10(1), Winter 1956, p.17.

4.   The Kremlin's fears were obviously not without foundation. An influential London-based journal, *Contemporary Review*, wrote in April 1949: 'Afghanistan, which traditionally served as a political buffer between India and Russia, may acquire significance akin to that of the states situated on the fringes of the "Iron Curtain" in Europe.' *Contemporary Review*, No. 4, 1949. Assistant Secretary of State for Near Eastern, South Asian and African Affairs, George C. McGhee, in his memorandum to Secretary of State, Dean Acheson, dated 7 June 1950, called for increased help to Afghanistan: 'Experience has shown that countries in such close proximity to the USSR orbit need the stiffening and confidence provided

by the United States economic assistance.' Rajendra K. Jain (ed.), *US-South Asian Relations, 1947–1982*, Vol. 1, New Delhi: Radiant Publishers, 1983, pp.133–4.

5. Teplinskii, *SSSR i Afganistan*, p.122. Subsequently, over the period from 1953 to 1958, a series of agreements provided for the large-scale geological survey of northern Afghanistan conducted by Soviet, Czechoslovak and Romanian experts.

6. Teplinskii, *Istoriia sovetsko-afganskikh otnoshenii*, p.153.

7. Mohammad Khalid Ma'aroof, *Afghanistan in World Politics. (A Study of Afghan-US Relations)*, Delhi: Gian Publishing House, 1987, p.50.

8. Poullada and Poullada, *The Kingdom of Afghanistan and the United States*, p.133.

9. In October 1952, Afghanistan's Foreign Minister, Ali Mohammad Khan emphasised that 'the Government and people of Afghanistan have always had a desire to maintain good relations with the Government and people of the Soviet Union subject to the preservation of their respective rights and independence.' Teplinskii, *Istoriia sovetsko-afganskikh otnoshenii*, p.154.

10. Fletcher, *Afghanistan*, p.251.

11. S.M.M. Qureshi, 'Pakhtunistan: The Frontier Dispute between Afghanistan and Pakistan', *Pacific Affairs*, 39(1–2), Spring–Summer 1966, p.105.

12. This point was related to Amin Saikal by Sayyed Qassim Reshtya in interview in Geneva in 1990.

13. Hasan Ali Shah Jafri, *Indo-Afghan Relations (1947–67)*, New Delhi: Sterling Publishers, 1976, p.68.

14. Griffiths, *Afghanistan*, pp.65–6.

15. Quoted in Poullada and Poullada, *The Kingdom of Afghanistan and the United States*, pp.101–2.

16. *Jawaharlal Nehru's Speeches, 1949–1953*, Delhi: The Publications Division, Ministry of Information and Broadcasting, Government of India, 1954, p.146.

17. See, for instance, the National Security Council Report to President Truman, 8 August 1951 (NSC 114/1), quoted in Jain, *US-South Asian Relations*, p.182.

18. Ghaus, *The Fall of Afghanistan*, p.78.

19. *Afganistan*, Moscow: Nauka, 1964, p.217.

20. Duprée viewed subjective factors as far outweighing possible material benefits for both countries: 'Regardless of political stability, the difficulty of accommodating two kings in a federation cannot be dismissed lightly and seems to preclude political federation at this time. In all probability, neither the Shahinshah nor the Padishah would abdicate in favour of the other, and national pride would rally to each monarch's support, no matter what the public sentiment might be concerning the continued existence of a kinghead at the national level.' Duprée, 'A Suggested Pakistan-Afghanistan-Iran Federation', p.390.

21. In the aftermath of the Bandung Conference in 1955, Mohammad Daoud announced that his country 'does not want to join any military grouping. Afghanistan wants to live, that is why it needs peace. Afghanistan regards neutrality as the best way towards peace, and the nation's tranquillity and blooming. This policy has not been conducted just recently, it has become the traditional policy of our country.' *Pravda*, 26 February 1956.

22. American strategists at the time were convinced that providing military aid to Afghanistan would be senseless, 'on the grounds that no amount could make it defendable against a determined Soviet attack'. Shaheen F. Dil, 'The Cabal in Kabul: Great-Power Interaction in Afghanistan', *American Political Science Review*,

71(2), June 1977, p.468.

23. Commenting on the thriving military cooperation between the USA and Pakistan, the Afghan press lamented bitterly in December 1953 that if 'Pakistan beefs up its army with Americans' help or give them bases in return for armaments, these actions will contradict the process of strengthening peace and security in the Near East'. Quoted in Teplinskii, *Istoriia sovetsko-afganskikh otnoshenii*, p.160.

24. Ma'aroof, *Afghanistan in World Politics*, p.51.

25. 'The Afghans were not only disappointed again by this refusal, but were outraged by Dulles's flagrant breach of diplomatic practice in revealing their confidential request to their rival, Pakistan. *One month later*, in January 1955, Daoud accepted the long-standing offer of military aid, which Afghanistan had previously rejected.' Poullada and Poullada, *The Kingdom of Afghanistan and the United States*, p.149.

26. It has been argued that the new Soviet strategy of gaining a foothold in Afghanistan was based on two main premises: (a) to penetrate the Afghan economy by diverting its trade from free-world markets; by granting large-scale credits at uneconomically low, nominal interest rates of two per cent or less; and by insinuating direct Soviet participation into Afghan economic planning and policy formulation; and (b) to increase Afghan dependency on the Soviet economy through a rising volume of bilateral trade; through increased transit trade via the USSR; through increasing Afghan debt obligations; and through complex monetary and barter arrangements. Noorzoy, 'Soviet Economic Interests in Afghanistan', p.44.

27. See Teplinskii, *Istoriia sovetsko-afganskikh otnoshenii*, p.171; Rezun, *Intrigue and War in Southwest Asia*, p.39. A comprehensive review of the provision of economic aid by the USSR as a political act can be found in Paul Dibb, *The Soviet Union: The Incomplete Superpower*, Basingstoke: Macmillan Press, 1988, pp.232–39.

28. 'It's my strong feeling that the capital which we've invested in Afghanistan hasn't been wasted. We have earned the Afghans' trust and friendship, and it hasn't fallen into the Americans' trap; it hasn't been caught on the hook baited with American money... The amount of money we spent in gratuitous assistance to Afghanistan is a drop in the ocean compared to the price we would have had to pay in order to counter the threat of an American military base on Afghan territory.' Nikita S. Khrushchev, *Khrushchev Remembers*, Boston: Little, Brown and Company, 1970, p.508.

29. Following the initial mammoth loan of US$100 million offered in 1955, the Soviet Union continued to pump funds to Afghanistan. Its total commitments by 1961 had exceeded US$217 million in credits and grants, exclusive of military aid which was growing exponentially. The US Technical Assistance Programme launched in 1956 as a countermeasure barely reached a third of what the Soviets were spending by the early 1960s. Manzur Zaidi, 'Afghanistan: Case Study in Competitive Peaceful Co-Existence', *Pakistan Horizon*, 15(2), 1962, p.98.

30. During his speech to the Supreme Soviet in December 1955, the Soviet Premier Nikolai Bulganin declared that 'We think the demands of Afghanistan to give the population of bordering Pashtunistan an opportunity of freely expressing their will are justified and grounded. The people of the region have the same right to national self-determination as any other people. There can be no justification for the stand of those who do not want to reckon and disregard the lawful national interests of the people of Pashtunistan.' Ghaus, *The Fall of Afghanistan*, p.85.

31. While right from the outset the Indian leadership described relations with

Afghanistan as 'exceedingly cordial', 'it was only after a considerable lapse of time since India's independence that any fruitful efforts were being made, to strengthen in actual life the "close bonds" between them.' Jafri, *Indo-Afghan Relations*, pp.90–1. The two countries became especially close around 1962, when Afghanistan voiced solidarity with India in its conflict with China, and India supported, 'at least indirectly', the Pashtunistan claim of Kabul. 'Pakistan. Relations with Afghanistan', *The Round Table*, 52, December 1961–September 1962, p.83.

32. In 1956, the Soviet bloc countries disbursed the first US$25 million grant for the refurbishment of the Afghan armed forces. By 1961, from a motley assortment of ill-equipped illiterate recruits, the Afghan army had been transformed into a formidable 60,000-strong force with dozens of MiG-17 fighters, 24 IL-28 bombers, 134 tanks and 152 artillery pieces. 'The Foreign Policy of Afghanistan', *Pakistan Horizon*, 17(1), 1964, p.53.

33. Gupta, *Afghanistan*, p.12.

34. Newell, 'Afghanistan: The Dangers of Cold War Generosity', p.173.

35. It has been alleged that a substantial proportion of the newly arrived Soviet military-technical personnel 'were experienced members of GRU – the military intelligence branch.' M. Siddiq Wahidi-Wardak, 'Events Leading Up to the Soviet Invasion of Afghanistan', in Ewan W. Anderson and Nancy Hatch Duprée (eds), *The Cultural Basis of Afghan Nationalism*, London and New York: Pinter Publishers, 1990, p.93.

36. R. Tursunov, 'Pomoshch' sovetskikh sredneaziatskikh respublik Afganistanu', *Narody Azii i Afriki*, No. 6, 1972, p.128.

37. G.I. Kukhtina, 'K voprosu o podgotovke natsionalnykh tekhnicheskikh kadrov v Afganistane (1919–1961)', in N.M. Gurevich (ed.), *Voprosy ekonomiki Afganistana*, Moscow: Izdatelstvo vostochnoi literatury, 1963, p.154.

38. *Area Handbook for Afghanistan*, p.138.

39. Soviet aid went chiefly to fundamental and high profile projects, crucial to the strengthening of a state-run economy such as the Jalalabad agricultural complex, the Naghlu hydro-power station and the Herat-Kandahar motorway. This approach won praise from other countries in the region: 'On the whole, American economic projects tend to contrast with those of the Soviet in that they are less tangible and have a lesser immediate impact on the life of the people. On the other hand of greater utility and perceptibility to the common man has been Soviet aid, such as that for public transport, a hundred-bed hospital and asphalted streets in the city of Kabul.' 'Recent Developments in Afghanistan', *Pakistan Horizon*, 19(3), 1966, p.259.

40. Between 1950 and 1960, the trade turnover between the two countries grew 14-fold. In 1963, the Soviet Union accounted for 23.8 per cent of all Afghan exports and 42.8 per cent of all imports. A. Babakhodzhaev, *Ocherki po istorii sovetsko-afganskikh otnoshenii*, p.114.

41. The volume of Afghan transit through the USSR increased by 77 per cent between 1959 and 1961. V.G. Kukhtin, 'Problema tranzita v ekonomike i politike Afganistana', in N.M. Gurevich (ed.), *Voprosy ekonomiki Afganistana*, Moscow: Izdatelstvo vostochnoi literatury, 1963, p.54.

42. In 1961, due to the blockade imposed by Pakistan, Afghanistan could not export its harvest of fresh fruit to India – traditional market for this produce. The Soviet Union bought 2,500 tonnes of grapes and 1,300 tonnes of pomegranates in

Afghanistan and airlifted them to Tashkent. Iu. M. Golovin, *SSSR i Afganistan*, Moscow: Izdatelstvo vostochnoi literatury, 1962, p.66.

43.   Fry, *The Afghan Economy*, p.73.

44.   As of 1 January 1978, Afghanistan had received international loans, credits and aid to the tune of $2,860 million. The USSR had given 54 per cent of this sum, whereas the US share had not exceeded 15 per cent. *Afganistan: problemy voiny i mira*, Moscow: IVRAN, 1996, p.15.

45.   Adeed I. Dawisha, *Egypt in the Arab World: The Elements of Foreign Policy*, London: Macmillan Press, 1976, p.86.

46.   Kirk J. Beattie, *Egypt During the Nasser Years: Ideology, Politics, and Civil Society*, Boulder: Westview Press, 1994, p.155.

47.   Daoud's proposed reform, which was to take 25 years, envisaged limitation of land holdings and redistribution of surplus amongst landless peasantry. According to a Russian economist, Georgii P. Ezhov, who in the 1960s and 1970s worked as an advisor in the Ministry of Planning of Afghanistan, Zahir Shah categorically refused to endorse these measures, and the ensuing tension between the King and the Prime Minister was one of the main reasons for the latter's resignation in 1963. (Interviews in Moscow, March 1992.)

48.   John Waterbury, *The Egypt of Nasser and Sadat: The Political Economy of Two Regimes*, Princeton: Princeton University Press, 1983, p.307.

49.   Harley H. Hinrichs, 'Certainty as Criterion: Taxation of Foreign Investment in Afghanistan', *National Tax Journal*, 15(2), 1962, p.148.

50.   Newell, 'The Prospects for State Building in Afghanistan', in Banuazizi and Weiner (eds), *The State, Religion, and Ethnic Politics*, p.113.

51.   See Teplinskii, *Istoriia sovetsko-afganskikh otnoshenii*, pp.163–6.

52.   In Welles Hangen's words, 'Long experience in dealing with the Russians has given the Afghans considerably more acumen than such other neutrals as India and the Arab countries. The Afghans have little love for the Russians but they understand Russian bargaining tactics... For his part, Daoud understood Soviet methods better than Western democratic principles. Because of his affinity for things Russian, he was often mistakenly regarded as pro-Soviet. Western diplomats celebrated his overthrow in March 1963 with "Farewell to Daoud" parties.' Welles Hangen, 'Afghanistan', *Yale Review*, 56(1), October 1966, pp.73–4.

53.   People close to Daoud later suggested that he had been impressed by the fact that when Nasser suppressed Egyptian communists after 1955, Khrushchev did not react angrily and continued all-round aid to the Young Officers' regime. Daoud tolerated leftist elements in the establishment, because, after all, they were people trained in the ways of modernity – still a rare commodity in Afghanistan at the time. He thought he could keep them under control and dispose of them if need be. Information provided by Rawan Farhadi.

54.   That this strategy was successful and the US position of indifference vis-à-vis Afghanistan was beginning to change became clear in 1957, when the National Security Council came up with the following reassessment: 'The United States should try to resolve the Afghan dispute with Pakistan and encourage Afghanistan to minimise its reliance upon the Communist bloc for military training and equipment to look to the United States and other free world sources for military training and assistance.' Poullada and Poullada, *The Kingdom of Afghanistan and the United States*, p.152.

55. See Duprée, *Afghanistan*, p.513.
56. In 1954, 80 per cent of Afghan exports and 79 per cent of Afghan imports proceeded through Pakistan. Kukhtin, 'Problema tranzita v ekonomike i politike Afganistana', p.36.
57. George L. Montagno, 'The Pak-Afghan Detente', *Asian Survey*, 3(12), 1963, p.616.
58. See Khurshid Hasan, 'Pakistan-Afghanistan Relations', *Asian Survey*, 2(7), 1962, p.17.
59. *Area Handbook for Afghanistan*, p.331.
60. The only visit of the Shah of Iran to Kabul was for this purpose in September 1961. The Afghan King never visited Tehran, and even on the occasion of the '2500th anniversary of the Iranian monarchy' in 1971, Afghanistan was represented by Zahir Shah's daughter, Princess Belqis.
61. It was calculated that if the transit route through Pakistan had not reopened by the summer of 1963 when the new fruit crop was ready, the annual increase in Afghanistan's debt to the Soviet Union due to the enormous air tariffs would have exceeded the entire return on the year's fruit crop. Hangen, 'Afghanistan', p.65.
62. Still, the agreement on the Afghan-Iranian transport corridor was signed between the two countries on 1 February 1962.
63. Poullada and Poullada, *The Kingdom of Afghanistan and the United States*, p.115.
64. Daoud tendered his resignation shortly after Zahir Shah's visit to the USA in 1963.
65. The King networked primarily with the two members of the 'inner cabinet': his uncle Shah Wali Khan – Mohammad Nadir's last surviving brother, known as the 'Conqueror of Kabul' since the days of Habibullah Kalakani's rule, and Abdul Wali – Shah Wali's son, the King's son-in-law and a senior military officer. The first was immensely popular amongst the tribes and common people; the second had excellent ties within the army. Patrick J. Reardon, 'Modernisation and Reform. The Contemporary Endeavour', in Grassmuck and Adamec with Irwin (eds), *Afghanistan: Some New Approaches*, p.166.
66. Zahir Shah and Mohammad Daoud, despite their different views on life and politics, were men of integrity and honoured their agreement. The King recalled in 1976 that when in 1964 rumours began to spread in Kabul alleging Daoud's involvement into anti-government activities, 'he directly confronted Sardar Da'ud with these rumours; they were immediately and emphatically denied. Sardar Da'ud had told him that it was not in his character to become a plotter. If he had anything to say for the good of the nation, it was his right and duty to go down to the *Loyah Jirgah* and say it openly. If necessary, he would go out into the streets and speak his mind.' Ralph H. Magnus, 'Muhammad Zahir Khan, Former King of Afghanistan', *The Middle East Journal*, 30(1), Winter 1976, p.79.
67. These ideas were outlined in a series of letters addressed by Daoud to Zahir Shah in late 1962. One of them stated that 'the King is a symbol of unity, national dignity and integrity of the state... He is not responsible to anyone... The monarchy is neutral in relation to political parties and does not interfere into administrative management... The government elected by the people's representatives bears responsibility for the conduct of domestic and foreign policy and determination of the socio-political course.' Korgun, *Intelligentsiia v politicheskoi zhizni Afganistana*, p.105.
68. Black et al, *The Modernization of Inner Asia*, p.192.

69. The increase in industrial output under Daoud can be gauged from the following table:

Industrial Commodity	1956–57	1962–63
Electricity, *kWt/hr*	35.6	158
Coal, *thou. tonnes*	28.9	85
Cement, *thou. tonnes*	0	59.6
Cotton Fabrics, *mln. metres*	15.4	36.8
Soap, *mln. pieces*	1.1	2.6
Matches, *mln. boxes*	2.4	6.5
China, *thou. units*	0	220

70. E.R. Mahmudov, 'Afganistan. Osnovnye etapy evoliutsii gosudarstvennoi politiki v oblasti industrializatsii', in *Afganistan: ekonomika, istoriia, kultura*, Moscow: Nauka, 1989, p.142.

71. Rubin, *The Fragmentation of Afghanistan*, p.62.

72. Wolfram Eberhard, 'Afghanistan's Young Elite', *Asian Survey*, 1(12), February 1962, p.3.

73. Between 1939 and 1951, the provinces of Mazar-e Sharif and Qattagan alone received 6,000 families of Pashtun settlers. Viktor G. Korgun, 'K voprosu o roli kochevnikov v Afganistane noveishego vremeni', in *Arabskie strany, Turtsiia, Iran, Afganistan. Istoriia, ekonomika*, Moscow: Nauka, 1973, p.95.

74. *Istoriia Afganistana*, p.268.

75. Rubin, *The Fragmentation of Afghanistan*, p.70.

76. 'Both the Soviets and the United States appear to have chosen certain sectors of the Afghan economy on which to concentrate. Although the overall picture is one of competition, the individual projects are in many cases complementary. Both are now involved in irrigation and transportation, but while the Americans tend to choose long-range undertakings, the Soviets are more project-oriented. The Soviets are so far uncontested in aid to industry; the Americans maintain a similar position in terms of educational programmes.' Zaidi, 'Afghanistan: Case Study', p.101.

77. Anatoly Dobrynin, *In Confidence: Moscow's Ambassador to America's Six Cold War Presidents (1962–1986)*, New York: Times Books, 1995, p.434. Dobrynin was friends with Mohammad Hashim Maiwandwal, the Afghan Ambassador in Washington between 1958 and 1963.

78. *Istoriia Afganistana*, p.275.

79. Gupta, *Afghanistan*, p.12.

80. Ghaus, *The Fall of Afghanistan*, p.88.

81. Reardon, 'Modernisation and Reform', p.163.

82. Duprée, *Afghanistan*, p.556.

Chapter 6: Experiment with Democracy, 1963–1973

1. A revealing article describing the processes unleashed by Daoud's policies was published in the official newspaper, *Kabul Times*, on 19 March 1963. It read in particular: 'Old social fabrics are broken, community rules are replaced by individualistic behaviours, revolt of the young against the old sets in... As the pace of development gains momentum and because of increased economic activity people gravitate to the cities... Neither facilities nor trade of towns can cope with

the great influx of population and mass migration. Unemployment, delinquency, poverty and mass unrest, bad housing becomes menacing problem of the day… Economic development calls for some basic social changes.' Quoted in Roman T. Akhramovich, *Outline History of Afghanistan After the Second World War*, Moscow: Nauka, 1966, p.151.

2.   Mohammad Yusuf was born in Kabul in 1917 and received his secondary education at the German-sponsored *Nejat* school. Later he received a Ph.D. in physics in Germany and became a professor at Kabul University. He first entered public service in 1949, when he became Deputy Minister of Education. Adamec, *Historical Dictionary of Afghanistan*, Metuchen and London: Scarecrow Press, 1991, pp.166–7.

3.   Reardon, 'Modernisation and Reform', p.161.

4.   Full text of the statement can be found in Duprée, 'The Decade of Daoud Ends', *AUFS Reports Service: South Asia Series*, 7(7), 1963, pp.24–7.

5.   Roman T. Akhramovich, 'K kharakteristike etapov obshchestvennoi evoliutsii Afganistana posle vtoroi mirovoi voiny', pp.56–7.

6.   For example, he had to continue to show respect and offer hospitality to the erstwhile champion of the Pashtunistan cause, Khan Abdul Ghaffar Khan, who was wanted by Pakistani authorities for subversive activities.

7.   The then Chairman of the Presidium of the Supreme Soviet of the USSR, Leonid Brezhnev, visited Kabul in October 1963 and signed a package of economic and military agreements, including the strategically important document concerning development of gas fields in northern Afghanistan. The joint communiqué published after this visit emphasised that 'both parties are deeply satisfied with the state of Soviet-Afghan relations and will not allow any harm to be done to them.' Teplinskii, *Istoriia sovetsko-afganskikh otnoshenii*, p.209.

8.   Ghaus, *The Fall of Afghanistan*, p.100.

9.   In June 1963, the King said in a remarkably frank interview: 'We don't want to achieve American standards of living or Russian standards of living in this country. We realise it is impossible. But we do want to raise our standards as rapidly as possible. To this end, the entire government is dedicated. We know that across the Amu Darya and the Ab-i-Panja, only 40 metres wide in many places, we can see the results of Soviet development in Tajikistan SSR and Uzbekistan SSR. Our Afghan Uzbeks and Tajiks will not wait forever. We must begin to improve their lot – and the lot of all our countrymen – now, not next year, but now.' Duprée, 'An Informal Talk with King Mohammad Zahir of Afghanistan', *AUFS Reports Service: South Asia Series*, 7(9), 1963, p.7.

10.   See Duprée, 'A Suggested Pakistan-Afghanistan-Iran Federation', pp.395–6.

11.   Montagno, 'The Pak-Afghan Detente', p.617.

12.   George C. McGhee, 'The Strategic Importance of Iran, Afghanistan and Pakistan to the United States', in Hafeez Malik (ed.), *Soviet-American Relations with Pakistan, Iran and Afghanistan*, London: Macmillan, 1987, p.32.

13.   Akhramovich, 'K kharakteristike etapov obshchestvennoi evoliutsii', p.41.

14.   Dilip Mukerjee, 'Afghanistan under Daud: Relations with Neighbouring States', *Asian Survey*, 15(4), April 1975, p.309. Prime Minister Yusuf felt the change in attitude during his official visit to Moscow in April 1965, when the Soviet side indicated that it was not amenable to mentioning 'Pashtunistan' in the joint communiqué.

15.   S.M. Burke and Lawrence Ziring, *Pakistan's Foreign Policy: An Historical Analysis*,

Karachi: Oxford University Press, 1990, p.299.

16.   Syed Iqbal Ahmad, *Balochistan: Its Strategic Importance*, Karachi: Royal Book Company, 1992, p.213.

17.   Zubeida Hasan, 'Pakistan-USSR Relations', *Pakistan Horizon*, 21(2), 1968, p.151. Khrushchev's ire was sparked by an incident with a US U-2 spy aircraft shot down over Soviet territory on 1 May 1960. It had taken off from an airbase in Peshawar.

18.   Rezun, *Intrigue and War in Southwest Asia*, p.61.

19.   Burke and Ziring, *Pakistan's Foreign Policy*, pp.349–50.

20.   On 6 September 1965, the Afghan Cabinet 'in an extraordinary session, without taking any position, simply described the situation as a matter of anxiety and concern to the people and Government of Afghanistan. Pakistan claimed that she had been assured of full sympathies from the Afghan side. On the other hand, the Indian Government... maintained that Afghanistan was keeping strictly neutral.' Jafri, *Indo-Afghan Relations*, p.85.

21.   'Recent Developments in Afghanistan', *Pakistan Horizon*, 19(3), 1966, p.263.

22.   Alvin Z. Rubinstein, *Soviet Policy toward Turkey, Iran and Afghanistan: The Dynamics of Influence*, New York: Praeger, 1982, p.139.

23.   Akhramovich, 'K kharakteristike etapov obshchestvennoi evoliutsii', p.140.

24.   Duprée, 'Afghanistan: 1966', *AUFS Reports Service: South Asia Series*, 10(4), 1966, p.21.

25.   In the course of this visit, the Afghan and Pakistani leaders held a series of informal discussions tête-à-tête on a range of sensitive issues. One day, on the way to Taxila Museum, Ayub Khan complained to the Afghan King about the seditious activities of Khan Abdul Ghaffar Khan and his son, Abdul Wali Khan: 'They want the kingship for themselves and do not care about Afghanistan or Pakistan.'

26.   For details, see A. Saikal, *The Rise and Fall of the Shah*, pp.171–6.

27.   Duprée, 'A Suggested Pakistan-Afghanistan-Iran Federation', p.399.

28.   Newell, 'Afghanistan: The Dangers of Cold War Generosity', p.174.

29.   Burke and Ziring, *Pakistan's Foreign Policy*, p.307.

30.   Agha Shahi, 'Pakistan's Relations with the United States', in Malik (ed.), *Soviet-American Relations with Pakistan, Iran and Afghanistan*, p.164.

31.   For the text of the Tashkent Declaration, see *Asian Recorder*, Vol. XII, No. 5, 1966, p.6896.

32.   Burke and Ziring, *Pakistan's Foreign Policy*, p.352. Babrak Karmal was a particularly vocal critic of RCD in the Parliament, labelling it as an instrument of 'American imperialism'.

33.   The Prime Minister of Afghanistan, Mohammad Hashim Maiwandwal, sent a telegram to Kosygin on 3 January 1966 saying that 'by promoting negotiations between Field Marshal Mohammad Ayub Khan and His Excellency Lal Bahadur Shastri... Your Excellency is bound to render a great service to the cause of the preservation of peace and maintenance of tranquillity in the region.' *Monasebat-e Afghanestan wa Ettehad-e Shurawi dar salha-ye 1919–1969*, Kabul: Ministry of Foreign Affairs of Afghanistan, No Date, Document 149, p.206.

34.   Hasan, 'Pakistan-USSR Relations', p.152.

35.   Yuri V. Gankovsky, Railya Muqeemjanova, Vyacheslav Belokrenitsky and Vladimir Moskalenko, 'Soviet Relations with Pakistan', in Malik (ed.), *Soviet-American Relations with Pakistan, Iran and Afghanistan*, p.193.

36. *World Military Expenditures and Arms Transfers, 1970–1979*, ACDA Publication 112, Washington, DC: Arms Control and Disarmament Agency, March 1982, p.130.

37. Quoted in Burke and Ziring, *Pakistan's Foreign Policy*, p.366.

38. Abdul G. Noorani, *India: The Superpowers and the Neighbours*, New Delhi: South Asian Publishers, 1985, p.166.

39. Amongst heads of main Soviet agencies involved in the foreign policy decision making (the CPSU Central Committee, the Ministry of Foreign Affairs, the Ministry of Defence, and intelligence community), Alexei N. Kosygin stood alone as a pragmatic and relatively independent leader. In a characterisation given by a high-placed GRU officer, Kosygin 'was not inclined to cooperate with the Central Committee. He was on his own. A lonely and somewhat tragic figure. Apparently, he understood our faults and shortcomings of our situation generally and those in our Middle Eastern policy in particular, but, being a highly restrained man, he preferred to be cautious.' Alexei Vasiliev, *Rossiia na Blizhnem i Srednem Vostoke: ot messianstva k pragmatizmu*, Moscow: Nauka, 1993, p.239. Until the mid 1970s, Kosygin remained a chief 'expert' in the Kremlin on questions related to the Middle East and South Asia. He was behind the Tashkent Conference and an equally successful conciliation between Damascus and Cairo in 1966. As a career Soviet diplomat reminisced, 'he always had an opinion of his own, and defended it. He was a very alert man, and performed brilliantly during negotiations. He was able to cope quickly with the material that was totally new to him. I have never seen people of such calibre afterwards.' Vasiliev, *Rossiia na Blizhnem i Srednem Vostoke*, p.246.

40. *Monasebat-e Afghanestan wa Ettehad-e Shurawi*, Document 184, p.279.

41. Morris McCain, 'Thinking South: Soviet Strategic Interests in Iran, Afghanistan, and Pakistan', in Malik (ed.), *Soviet-American Relations with Pakistan, Iran and Afghanistan*, pp.43–4.

42. Rubinstein, *Soviet Policy toward Turkey, Iran and Afghanistan*, p.143.

43. Duprée, 'The Decade of Daoud Ends', pp.13, 21.

44. There is an unconfirmed report that in March 1963 Daoud did try to solicit the army's support against the King, but the generals preferred to side with Zahir Shah. Hammond, *Red Flag over Afghanistan*, p.29. Given the fact that Daoud, an army man himself, was an architect of modern Afghan armed forces, and a good percentage of middle and upper ranks in the officer corps owed him personal allegiance, this is hardly credible. 'It is more than likely that his influence in the armed services could have enabled him to stage a coup even then, as it did a decade later. However, in a remarkable gesture of self-denial, he stepped down from office... and there slowly began Afghanistan's second experiment in democracy.' Griffiths, *Afghanistan*, p.161.

45. Duprée, *Afghanistan*, pp.569–70.

46. As early as autumn 1964, there were renewed allegations that Daoud was contemplating a military coup. Magnus, 'The Constitution of 1964: A Decade of Political Experimentation', in Duprée and Albert (eds), *Afghanistan in the 1970s*, p.79.

47. Take, for instance, his much-quoted pronouncement made in June 1963: 'The present Royal Family has held power in its hands for 35 years because it had no choice. Its contributions have been great, but now it is the time to give the rule to

the people.' Duprée, 'An Informal Talk with King Mohammad Zahir', p.3.

48. Abdul Wali had opposed Daoud during family meetings on issues of high politics even when the latter was in the zenith of power. Abdul Wali 'felt entitled to play a vital role in the destiny of Afghanistan as his cousins had done.' Hasan Kakar, 'The Fall of the Afghan Monarchy in 1973', *International Journal of Middle East Studies*, 9(2), 1978, p.213.

49. Reshtia (1913–1998) had a reputation as a writer, historian and diplomat. His appointments under Daoud included President of the Department of Press and Ambassadorships in Prague and Cairo. Adamec, *Historical Dictionary of Afghanistan*, p.204.

50. For Sayed Qassem Reshtia's account of the decade of 'experiment with democracy', see Reshtia's political memoirs: *Khatirat-e siyasi Sayed Qassem Reshtia, 1311 to 1371 [1932–1992]*, Virginia: American Speedy Press, 1997, pp.150–383.

51. Magnus, 'The Constitution of 1964', p.55. Daoud's admiration for revolutionary reformers like Nasser of Egypt was well known amongst Afghans. After 1973, Daoud developed friendly personal ties with Presidents Sadat of Egypt and Qaddafi of Libya.

52. Akhramovich, *Outline History of Afghanistan*, p.171.

53. *Area Handbook for Afghanistan*, p.180.

54. Newell, *The Politics of Afghanistan*, p.99.

55. Reardon, 'Modernisation and Reform', p.174.

56. The typical argument against the exclusionist article in the Constitution was that Afghanistan, suffering from an acute shortage of qualified manpower, could ill afford to let talented peripheral members of royalty become lost to government service. Duprée, 'Constitutional Development and Cultural Change. Part III: The 1964 Afghan Constitution (Articles 1–56)', *AUFS Reports Service: South Asia Series*, 9(3), 1965, p.18.

57. A full text of the 1964 Afghan Constitution can be found in Akhramovich, 'K kharakteristike etapov obshchestvennoi evoliutsii', pp.145–71.

58. Duprée, *Afghanistan*, p.568.

59. Duprée, 'Constitutional Development and Cultural Change. Part VIII: The Future of Constitutional Law in Afghanistan and Pakistan, *AUFS Reports Service: South Asia Series*, 9(10), 1965, p.7.

60. Mohammad Hashim Kamali, *Law in Afghanistan*, Leiden: E.J. Brill, 1985, p.24.

61. Olesen, *Islam and Politics in Afghanistan*, p.208.

62. Magnus, 'The Constitution of 1964', p.58.

63. Article 35 was not present in the original draft of the Constitution. It was pushed through at the last moment by Abdul Majid Zabuli and other pro-Pashtunists in the *Loya Jirgah*.

64. N.A. Dvoriankov, 'Literaturnyi iazyk i dialekty pashto v Afganistane', *Narody Azii i Afriki*, No. 2, 1964, p.146.

65. A.S. Gerasimova, 'Zhurnal "Kabul" v 1966–1969 godakh', *Narody Azii i Afriki*, No. 1, 1971, p.170.

66. Logashova, 'Etnokulturnaia situatsiia v Afganistane', p.135.

67. Korgun, *Intelligentsiia v politicheskoi zhizni Afganistana*, pp.10–11. Practically all cadets in the Military High School (*Harbi Shwonzai*) – an establishment which trained officers for command duties – were Pashtuns.

68. Duprée, 'Constitutional Development and Cultural Change. Part III', p.18.

69. Etemadi did so on the grounds that the wording of Article 24 would make Mohammad Daoud and Mohammad Naim uneasy.

70. Duprée, 'Afghanistan and the Unpaved Road to Democracy', *Journal of the Royal Central Asian Society*, 56(3), October 1969, p.273.

71. William R. Polk, 'The Nature of Modernisation: The Middle East and North Africa', *Foreign Affairs*, 44(1), October 1965, p.106.

72. Articles 25–40 guaranteed fundamental personal freedoms (speech, religion, assembly, organisation, travel, choice of work, inviolability of home, no discrimination, no forced labour, no arbitrary arrest and punishment) and rights to free education and medical protection.

73. The first permanent Cabinet to be formed under the new Constitution on 25 October 1965 consisted of the Prime Minister, Deputy Prime Minister, 14 Ministers and the President of the Department of Tribal Affairs, who carried ministerial rank.

74. *Area Handbook for Afghanistan*, p.186.

75. Duprée, 'Constitutional Development and Cultural Change. Part IV: The 1964 Afghan Constitution (Articles 57–128)', *AUFS Reports Service: South Asia Series*, 9(4), 1965, p.19. A sociologist, Dr Abdul Hakim Ziayee, was appointed by the King as Chief Justice. However, there were several Hanafi *'ulama* amongst top-ranking justices, such as Mawlawi Abdul Basir and Ubaydullah Safi. The cooperation between university-trained and traditional-Islamic jurists unfolded rather smoothly.

76. Ironically, in the 1980s, the Marxist leaders of Afghanistan revived the *Jirgah* practice again, claiming that it was only natural for them 'to turn to our people's long-standing traditions. The easiest and most simple way for the masses to accept revolutionary democracy is through the prism of historically established forms. This leads to the next coil of the dialectical spiral of development and makes it possible to build the new on the basis of traditions.' Mahmoud Baryalai, 'National Traditions Serve the Revolution', *World Marxist Review*, No. 4, April 1986, p.89.

77. Kamali, *Law in Afghanistan*, pp.44–5.

78. Kamali, *Law in Afghanistan*, p.228.

79. Magnus, 'The Constitution of 1964', p.61.

80. Duprée, *Afghanistan*, pp.589–90.

81. Duprée, 'Afghanistan Continues Its Experiment in Democracy', *AUFS Reports Service: South Asia Series*, 15(3), 1971, p.8.

82. Magnus, 'The Constitution of 1964', p.59.

83. Polk, 'The Nature of Modernisation', p.106.

84. M. Ishaq Negargar, 'Afghanistan and the Nightmare of Communism', in S.B. Majrooh and S.M.Y. Elmi (eds), *The Sovietisation of Afghanistan*, Peshawar: Afghan Information Centre, No Date, pp.10–11.

85. Shahrani, 'Afghanistan: State and Society in Retrospect', in Ewan W. Anderson and Nancy Hatch Duprée (eds), *The Cultural Basis of Afghan Nationalism*, London and New York: Pinter Publishers, 1990, p.47.

86. Wahidi-Wardak, 'Events Leading Up to the Soviet Invasion of Afghanistan', p.95.

87. Gennadii Krugliakov, 'Afganskii izlom', *Kazakhstanskaia Pravda*, 5 December 1997, p.3.

88. Bradsher, *Afghanistan and the Soviet Union*, p.27.

89. Mukerjee, 'Afghanistan under Daud', p.302.

90. Proximity to Zahir Shah played an important role in the amount of influence a person could amass. The career of Mohammad Ibrahim Kandahari, a self-educated astrologer to the King, may be illustrative. In the late 1950s, Kandahari, a Popalzai Durrani, was appointed president of the Government Press, the largest publishing conglomerate in the country, which printed all state-owned and private newspapers and magazines and, despite his well-known incompetence and corrupt personality, he was retained in that position until 1973. The Government Press functioned under the aegis of the Ministry of Information and Culture, but Kandahari, being the King's and Queen's favourite, acted as prime wheeler and dealer in the entire ministry, censored private newspapers, insulted Cabinet members, and ran the Government Press as his own company; yet none of the successive King's ministers could dismiss him. Another person whose influence stemmed from his special relationship with the monarch was Zahir Shah's Special Attendant, Mohammad Rahim, also known as Gholambacha. Put in charge of organising the King's social activities, Mohammad Rahim eventually became Zahir Shah's frequent social companion and confidant, and started to carry more weight in political affairs than his position could have warranted under different circumstances. He was connected with many senior public servants who sought his favours to ingratiate themselves with the King.

91. See Duprée, 'Parliament Versus the Executive in Afghanistan: 1969–1971', *AUFS Reports Service: South Asia Series*, 15(5), 1971, pp.10–11.

92. Kakar, 'The Fall of the Afghan Monarchy', p.213.

93. A member of the influential Ziayee family, Abdul Razaq was the great-grandson of Amir Abdur Rahman Khan by a Hazara mother, and a half-brother of Dr Abdul Hakim Ziayee, who served as Minister of Planning (1966–1967) until the King appointed him Chief Justice and Head of the Supreme Court in mid 1967 in fulfilment of the new Constitution's provision for an 'independent judiciary'. His other half-brother, Abdul Azim Ziayee, was a Professor of Physics at Kabul University, whose wife, Shafiqa Ziayee acted as a Minister Without Portfolio (1969–1972).

94. Duprée, 'Parliament Versus the Executive in Afghanistan', p.1.

95. Representatives of the illegal Marxist People's Democratic Party of Afghanistan (PDPA) won four seats in the *Wolosi Jirgah* in the 1965 elections. Apart from Karmal, Anahita Ratebzad, Noor Ahmad Noor and Fezanulhaq Fezan were elected to the legislature.

96. Arnold, *Afghanistan's Two-Party Communism: Parcham and Khalq*, Stanford: Hoover Institution Press, 1983, p.43.

97. Kakar, 'The Fall of the Afghan Monarchy', p.200.

98. 'An effective speaker, Maiwandwal won the day. The students hoisted him on their shoulders and triumphantly paraded through the campus. They thought *they* had won the day.' Duprée, 'Afghanistan: 1966', p.8.

99. More often, however, it was referred to as Hezb-e Mosawat (the Equality Party, after the newspaper *Mosawat*), or Hezb-e Maiwandwal (Maiwandwal's Party).

100. Akhramovich, 'K kharakteristike etapov obshchestvennoi evoliutsii', p.122.

101. Korgun, *Intelligentsiia v politicheskoi zhizni Afganistana*, p.130.

102. Mohmand later became a member of the Revolutionary Council under the Communist regime (1980–1988).

103. Duprée, 'Afghanistan Continues Its Experiment in Democracy', pp.8–11.

104. As a contemporary observer wrote: 'No adequate libel laws exist, and the free press constantly libels more important public figures... Such attacks often result in government inaction and defeat the real purpose of free speech and a free press – especially as the accusers are not held responsible for their statements and, by their criticisms, whether true or false, can prevent necessary executive action from being taken.' Duprée, 'Afghanistan: 1968. Part III: Problems of a Free Press', *AUFS Reports Service: South Asia Series*, 12(6), 1968, p.9.

105. In Hasan Kakar's words, 'a situation was created in which the backward-looking traditional elements of the old order rather than the forward-looking elements of the middle class, came into the forefront of national politics. Parliamentary life fell into the hands of those who did not really understand it. Most often, the Jirga lacked a quorum, because many of the members either stormed government departments for personal matters or did not take interest in parliamentary affairs.' Kakar, 'The Fall of the Afghan Monarchy', p.201.

106. Duprée, 'Parliament Versus the Executive in Afghanistan', p.6.

107. Marvin G. Weinbaum, 'The Legislator as Intermediary: Integration of the Centre and Periphery in Afghanistan', in Albert F. Eldridge (ed.), *Legislatures in Plural Societies: The Search for Cohesion In National Development*, Durham: Duke University Press, 1977, pp.113–14.

108. Typical criticism of Zahir Shah focused on his aloofness and indifference: 'The king lacked the qualities of an effective leader. He was more interested in open-air sports and cultural pursuits than in day to day problems of his country.' Kamali, *Law in Afghanistan*, p.52.

109. Fry, *The Afghan Economy*, p.72.

110. Mehrunnisa Ali, 'The Attitude of the New Afghan Regime Towards its Neighbours', *Pakistan Horizon*, 27(3), 1974, p.45.

111. Griffiths, *Afghanistan*, p.154.

112. Poullada, 'The Road to Crisis 1919–1980 – American Failures, Afghan Errors and Soviet Successes', in Rosanne Klass (ed.), *Afghanistan: The Great Game Revisited*, New York: Freedom House, 1987, p.53.

113. In the late 1960s, land tax rates remained the same as 40 years previously and made up only two per cent of state revenues. When Pashtun nomad deputies in *Wolosi Jirgah* mulled abolition of all livestock taxes, Maiwandwal wrote: 'The deputies must realise that governments do not subsist on air, and if this source of direct taxation is annulled, the government will be induced to raise indirect taxes to compensate the losses. This will lead to a greater damage to the economy than the deputies can imagine.' V.V. Basov, 'Voprosy sotsialno-ekonomicheskogo razvitiia Afganistana', *Narody Azii i Afriki*, No. 3, 1971, p.159. All the same, in February 1966, collection of livestock taxes was 'suspended at the Parliament's request'.

114. Rubin, *The Fragmentation of Afghanistan*, p.77.

115. As a Kabul University professor observed later: 'Having learned the new ideas about time, history and rapid development, the educated became impatient... the myth of revolution became the magical solution for all evil. In this respect, Marxism-Leninism presented the most attractive prospect: it was magic with a scientific and rational appearance, a rational dream doomed to become true.' Quoted in George Arney, *Afghanistan*, London: Mandarin, 1990, p.53.

116. Korgun, *Intelligentsiia v politicheskoi zhizni Afganistana*, p.93.

117. Arnold, *Afghanistan's Two-Party Communism*, p.21.

118. Col.-General V.A. Merimskii, 'Voina v Afganistane: zapiski chastnika.' *Novaia I noveishaia istoriia*, No. 3, May–June 1995, p.95.

119. Arnold, *Afghanistan's Two-Party Communism*, p.21.

120. Bradsher, *Afghanistan and the Soviet Union*, p.39.

121. Fred Halliday, 'Revolution in Afghanistan', *New Left Review*, No. 112, November–December 1978, p.22.

122. David Gai and Vladimir Snegirev, 'Vtorzhenie', Part I, *Znamia*, No. 3, March 1991, p.197.

123. For a discussion of the Soviet role in the evolution of *Parcham* and *Khalq*, see Arnold, *The Fateful Pebble: Afghanistan's Role in the Fall of the Soviet Empire*, Novato: Presidio Press, 1993, p.50.

124. Vasiliev, *Rossiia na Blizhnem i Srednem Vostoke*, p.262.

125. Gai and Snegirev, 'Vtorzhenie', Part I, p.199.

126. Two decades later the Afghan Mujahideen castigated 'the repulsive Zahir Shah who had reached an understanding with the Russians in regards to putting Afghanistan's nation into the bottomless pit of Communism.' Hajj Nayez Hosaini, *Afghanestan daz gogazgah-e Atash Wa Khun*, Peshawar: No Publisher, 1991, p.272.

127. Shahrani, 'Afghanistan: State and Society in Retrospect', p.60.

128. Taher Badakhshi was jailed in 1978 by the PDPA regime and quietly executed in October 1979 on orders from Hafizullah Amin.

129. Amiryar, 'Soviet Influence, Penetration, Domination and Invasion of Afghanistan', p.135.

130. Korgun, *Intelligentsiia v politicheskoi zhizni Afganistana*, p.147.

131. V.N. Spolnikov, *Afganistan: islamskaia kontrrevoliutsiia*, Moscow: Nauka, 1987, p.18.

132. M. Hassan Kakar, *Afghanistan: The Soviet Invasion and the Afghan Response, 1979–1982*, Berkeley: University of California Press, 1997, p.88.

133. Tahir Amin, *Afghanistan Crisis: Implications and Options for Muslim World, Iran, and Pakistan*, Islamabad: Institute of Policy Studies, 1982, p.69.

134. Hosaini, *Afghanestan daz gogazgah-e*, p.280.

135. Amin Saikal and William Maley, *Regime Change in Afghanistan: Foreign Interventions and the Politics of Legitimacy*, Boulder: Westview Press, 1991, p.23.

136. These ties may have been facilitated through personal affinity: Ghulam Jilani Bakhtari, Karmal's nephew, was a staunch admirer of Daoud; conversely, Sayyid Abdul Ilah, Daoud's adopted son, had been influenced by the *Parcham* ideology while studying at Kabul University.

137. Twenty years later Sayed Qassem Reshtia lamented: 'While the leftist groups enjoyed virtual liberty of action, not only in paralysing the government and infiltrating freely into educational institutions, factories and even the army, the government was busy restricting their adversaries, the rightist groups, which were the only forces able to fight them. These were composed of religious and other moderate elements who wanted for themselves the same liberty that was accorded to the left.' Sayed Qassem Reshtia, 'Social Reforms in Afghanistan in Relation to Neighbouring Countries: Interference and Peace', in Ewan W. Anderson and Nancy Hatch Duprée (eds), *The Cultural Basis of Afghan Nationalism*, London and New York: Pinter Publishers, 1990, p.57.

138. The PDPA factions in the period between 1969 and 1973 had somewhat different targets in their propaganda campaigns: 'While the Khalq was concentrating on raising the consciousness of the masses, Parchamite efforts, under the direction

of Mir Akbar Khyber, sought to attract a following within the officer corps. As the Parchamite network spread, and as dissatisfaction with Zahir Shah grew, not only within the armed forces, but also within the royal family... it was only a short step to an alliance between Daoud, Parcham and the military.' Beverley Male, *Revolutionary Afghanistan: A Reappraisal*, London and Canberra: Croom Helm, 1982, pp.52–3.

139.   Kamal Matinuddin, *Power Struggle in the Hindukush: Afghanistan (1978–1991)*, Lahore: Wajidalis, 1991, p.24.

140.   Danilo Zolo, *Democracy and Complexity: A Realist Approach*, Cambridge: Polity Press, 1992, p.120.

141.   See Alfred Stepan, 'Democratic Opposition and Democratisation Theory', *Government and Opposition*, 32(4), 1997, pp.657–663.

Chapter 7: Daoud's Republicanism

1.   Hisham Sharabi, *Neopatriarchy: A Theory of Distorted Change in Arab Society*, New York: Oxford University Press, 1988, p.60.

2.   Rubin, *The Fragmentation of Afghanistan*, p.77.

3.   Stephan Haggard and Robert R. Kaufman, 'The Political Economy of Democratic Transitions', *Comparative Politics*, 29(3), April 1997, p.279.

4.   Arney, *Afghanistan*, p.66.

5.   Halliday, 'Revolution in Afghanistan', p.20.

6.   Duprée, 'A Note on Afghanistan: 1974', *AUFS Reports Service: South Asia Series*, 18(8), 1974, p.1; also Marvin Brant, 'Recent Economic Development', in Duprée and Albert (eds), *Afghanistan in the 1970s*, p.112.

7.   For a comprehensive coverage of the Helmand River problem, see A.H.H. Abidi, 'Irano-Afghan Dispute over the Helmand Waters', *International Studies*, 16(3), July–September 1977, pp.357–77.

8.   In fact, Shafiq reconfirmed the concessions already agreed upon by the government of Noor Ahmad Etemadi, which did not differ much from an even earlier version of a compromise suggested by Daoud and Mohammad Naim to the Shah of Iran (and rejected) in 1954.

9.   Abidi, 'Irano-Afghan Dispute over the Helmand Waters', p.372. Coming from Maiwandwal, who had been in favour of such settlement while Premier, this criticism was merely an exercise in gaining political capital.

10.   *Asian Recorder*, 18(27), 24–30 June 1972, p.10849. Most analysts have identified the inflexible Pakistani stance on the Pashtunistan issue as the major hurdle in the relationship between the two countries: 'Pakistani unwillingness to recognise the unquestionable desire for self-identity in the Pushtun areas of Pakistan has made it impossible for Afghan governments to point to any progress through diplomatic channels. This has played into the hands of the Afghan extremists, making it more difficult for Afghan leaders to impose moderation and restraint on the more strident advocates of the Pushtun cause'. Poullada, 'Pushtunistan: Afghan Domestic Politics and Relations with Pakistan', in Ainslie T. Embree (ed.), *Pakistan's Western Borderlands: The Transformation of a Political Order*, New Delhi: Vikas Publishing House, 1977, p.150.

11.   Shaheen F. Dil, 'The Cabal in Kabul: Great-Power Interaction in Afghanistan', p.470.

12. Mukerjee, 'Afghanistan under Daud', p.309.

13. Pazhwak was an old friend of Karmal and Bakhtari.

14. Gai and Snegirev, 'Vtorzhenie', Part I, p.197.

15. Korgun, *Intelligentsiia v politicheskoi zhizni Afganistana*, p.165.

16. Quoted in Gupta, *Afghanistan*, p.18.

17. Duprée, 'A Note on Afghanistan: 1974', p.3.

18. Control over strategic points in Kabul was secured by a force of 65 officers and 240 men. Only 23 men, mainly military, and Daoud's closest confidants, were cognisant of the takeover plan in full detail; the others simply carried out their orders. Kakar, 'The Fall of the Afghan Monarchy', p.214. According to Arnold, only three of the key military officers involved had no leftist inclinations. Arnold, *Afghanistan: The Soviet Invasion in Perspective*, p.57. Quite a few of them had studied in Soviet military academies: Col. Faiz Mohammad, Col. Khalilullah, Col. Pacha Gul Wafadar, and Abdul Hamid Mohtat. Pacha Gul Wafadar (a Pashtun and the only *Khalqi* amongst the predominantly *Parchami* plotters) had a Russian wife.

19. N.A. Dvoriankov, 'Pervyi god', *Aziia i Afrika segodnia*, No. 7, 1974, p.2.

20. Cf. the words of Abdur Razaq Ziayee to a gathering of Daoud's supporters *circa* 1966: 'If Daoud returns to politics a new genuine *monarchy* will be founded, even if he does this under the name of President' (Ravan Farhadi).

21. Duprée, 'A New Decade of Daoud?', *AUFS Reports Service: South Asia Series*, 17(4), 1973, p.8.

22. Ibid. p.9.

23. A. Saikal, *The Rise and Fall of the Shah*, p.172.

24. Arnold, *Afghanistan's Two-Party Communism: Parcham and Khalq*, p.44.

25. Zia Majid was a Mohammadzai, and a one-time protégé of General Abdul Wali. His closeness to the King's son-in-law and Commander of the Kabul garrison was of great importance to the plotters.

26. Arney, *Afghanistan*, p.71.

27. See, for instance, Mohammad Alam Faizzad, *Jirgaha-ye bozorg-e melli-ye Afghanestan (Loya Jirgaha) wa Jirgaha-ye namnehad taht-e tasallot-e kamunestha wa rusha*, Lahore: No Publisher, 1368YH, p.301.

28. Cf. Ghaus: 'I am… convinced, after years of association with Daoud and his colleagues, that the coup of July 17, 1973, was definitely not a Russian initiative. It was an Afghan venture in pursuit of purely Afghan aims.' Ghaus, *The Fall of Afghanistan*, p.107.

29. The King also continued to collect revenues from his land possessions in Afghanistan. In return for Daoud's prudent attitude, Zahir Shah refrained from any criticism of the new regime, using the standard formula that 'he didn't want to embarrass the present government of Afghanistan'. Magnus, 'Muhammad Zahir Khan, Former King of Afghanistan', p.80.

30. Ravan Farhadi has estimated the number of Islamists arrested in Kabul under Daoud – mainly professors, students, civil servants and army officers – at 250.

31. Rubin, 'Human Rights in Afghanistan', in Klass (ed.), *Afghanistan*, p.336.

32. Spolnikov, *Afganistan*, p.24.

33. Anthony Hyman, *Afghanistan Under Soviet Domination, 1964–81*, London: Macmillan, 1982, pp.67–8.

34. Amin, *Afghanistan Crisis*, p.70.

35.   O. Roy, *Islam and Resistance in Afghanistan*, p.78.

36.   In early 1973, Maiwandwal embarked on a tour abroad where he used every opportunity to stress his newly acquired sympathy for socialism. The news of the coup found him in Baghdad, and he welcomed it enthusiastically.

37.   In October 1973, a six-page photostat of the protocols of Maiwandwal's interrogation was published in Kabul, in which he confessed to arranging a conspiracy against Daoud's regime. *Asian Recorder*, 19(37), 1973, p.11587. The authenticity of this confession was probably of the same order as that of the testimonies given by indicted Soviet officials during Stalin's purges.

38.   Informed Afghans believed that the killer was a police officer named Samad Azhar.

39.   Duprée, 'A Note on Afghanistan: 1974', p.5.

40.   See Mehrunnisa Ali, 'The Attitude of the New Afghan Regime Towards its Neighbours', pp.52–5.

41.   Henry Kissinger, *The White House Years*, London: Weidenfeld and Nicolson and Michael Joseph, 1979, p.1259.

42.   Saikal, *The Rise and Fall of the Shah*, p.144.

43.   Stanley Wolpert, *Zulfi Bhutto of Pakistan: His Life and Times*, New York: Oxford University Press, 1993, p.210.

44.   Duprée, 'A New Decade of Daoud?', p.8. At the time, experts in Afghanistan were of the opinion that the first segment of Daoud's broadcast statement had been drafted by Babrak Karmal, while its second part dealing with foreign policy was redolent of Mohammad Naim's style.

45.   Korgun, *Intelligentsiia v politicheskoi zhizni Afganistana*, p.168.

46.   G.P. Ezhov, 'Nekotorye tendentsii mirnogo razvitiia Afganistana k 70-80m godam', in *Afganistan: problemy voiny i mira*, Moscow: IVRAN, 1996, p.14.

47.   Kamali, *Law in Afghanistan*, p.241.

48.   The friction between *Parchamis* and Daoud's personal clients in the new Cabinet became palpable almost immediately. For a while, Mohammad Hassan Sharq, Deputy Prime Minister, acted as a moderating element between the two groups, but his position gradually became precarious, and he was sent as Ambassador to Tokyo. Figures like Abdul Qadir, the Interior Minister, Dr Abdullah Omar, the Minister of Health, Ahmad Ali Khorram, the Minister of Planning, and Wahid Abdullah, Deputy Foreign Minister, had their own agendas and grew increasingly independent of Daoud, who proved incapable of overcoming discord at the very top of the government hierarchy. During the last year of Daoud's presidency, several members of the Cabinet tendered their resignation but were invariably asked to stay on. Dr Abdullah Omar confessed to Ravan Farhadi in a prison cell shortly after the anti-Daoud coup of 1978 that 'in the last months of his life Sardar Daoud had lost his mind and was very silent and withdrawn.'

49.   Nassim Jawad, *Afghanistan: A Nation of Minorities*, London: Minority Rights Group, 1990, p.16.

50.   Duprée, 'Afghanistan 1977: Does Trade Plus Aid Guarantee Development?', *AUFS Reports Service: South Asia Series*, 21(3), 1977, pp.10–11.

51.   As of 1977, the total committed and uncommitted Soviet credit to Afghanistan had reached US$1,265 billion, compared to America's US$470 million. Noorzoy, 'Long-Term Soviet Economic Interests and Policies in Afghanistan', in Klass (ed.), *Afghanistan*, p.77.

52.   Daoud's first visit abroad as President of the Republic of Afghanistan took place

in June 1974, when he went to Moscow. He endorsed Brezhnev's Collective Security system in Asia – something Zahir Shah had refused to do despite pressure from the Kremlin.

53.   *Pravda*, 11 December 1975.

54.   M. Pokrovskii, 'Dorogoi kulturnogo progressa', *Aziia i Afrika segodnia*, No. 7, 1974, p.7.

55.   Vladimir Kuzichkin, *Inside the KGB: My Life in Soviet Espionage*, New York: Pantheon Books, 1990, p.232.

56.   During the first three years of Daoud's presidency, the volume of bilateral trade between Afghanistan and the USSR trebled. Ezhov, 'Nekotorye tendentsii mirnogo razvitiia Afganistana', p.15.

57.   Mehrunissa Ali, 'The Attitude of the New Afghan Regime towards its Neighbours', p.67. Using their usual strategy for enticing Third World clients, the Soviets sold military hardware at bargain basement prices but charged exorbitant fees for spare parts and maintenance later on.

58.   Newell and Newell, *The Struggle for Afghanistan*, p.49.

59.   Arnold, *Afghanistan The Soviet Invasion in Perspective*, p.63.

60.   Cited in Hammond, *Red Flag over Afghanistan*, p.37.

61.   Jonathan Steele, *The Limits of Soviet Power: The Kremlin's Foreign Policy – Brezhnev to Chernenko*, Harmondsworth: Penguin Books, 1985, p.122.

62.   Grants from Saudi Arabia included US$500 million for hydroelectric works, the United Arab Emirates pledged US$8.5 million for a sugar factory, and regional lending institutions, such as the OPEC Special Fund and the Islamic Bank for Development, also did not stay aloof. David Chaffetz, 'Afghanistan in Turmoil', *International Affairs*, 56(1), 1980, p.19.

63.   Zubeida Mustafa, 'Pakistan-Afghanistan Relations and Central Asian Politics (1973–1978)', *Pakistan Horizon*, 31(4), 1978, p.26.

64.   Saikal, *The Rise and Fall of the Shah*, p.174; Gupta, *Afghanistan*, p.23.

65.   Iran's commitment was US$1,141 million, twice the Soviet figure. Duprée, 'Afghanistan 1977', p.10.

66.   Despite initial enthusiasm, Total did not complete its contractual obligations. High-ranking officials in the Daoud administration believed that 'a combination of Soviet machinations and bureaucratic corruption was responsible'. John F. Shroder, Jr and Abdul Tawab Assifi, 'Afghan Resources and Soviet Exploitation', in Klass (ed.), *Afghanistan*, p.115. In 1976, Ravan Farhadi received regular reports from the interpreting service pointing to the fact that negotiations with partners from beyond the Soviet bloc were deliberately frustrated by the 'Afghan experts in the Ministries of Planning, Communications, Agriculture, Irrigation, and Industry who were given to communist ideology, had attachment to the Soviet Union, and opposed the West'. Skilfully using poor interdepartmental coordination, bureaucratic red tape and often ridiculous 'technical' considerations, they were instrumental in the failure of several international projects including a French-sponsored railroad station and a cartography survey financed by Kuwait.

67.   Ghaus, *The Fall of Afghanistan*, p.156.

68.   Kissinger's views in late 1973 appeared to be as follows: 'The officers close to Daoud were pro-Soviet; we probably had not yet seen the last of Afghan upheavals. Afghan irredentism against neighbouring Pakistan and Iran, even if not Soviet-inspired, would serve Soviet designs. It would weaken Pakistan and Iran and give

Moscow a corridor to the Indian Ocean. The United States should strengthen Pakistan, which found itself in dire peril... I knew there was no chance of Congressional approval of a serious effort to strengthen Pakistan... The best we could do... was to strengthen Iran to back up Pakistan. Thus the Shah's role as protector of his neighbours was impelled in part by our internal disarray.' Henry Kissinger, *Years of Upheaval*, London: Weidenfeld and Nicolson and Michael Joseph, 1982, p.687. After his visit to Kabul on 1 November 1974, he demonstrated more awareness of Afghanistan's vulnerable position in the region. Nevertheless, US diplomacy remained remarkably inactive. Michael Austrian, then Head of the Afghan Desk at the US State Department, has recollected that there was hardly a single senior US official interested in Afghanistan at the time, and that it took several months and direct intervention by the President to have the cooking oil shipped to Afghanistan. Interview with Michael Austrian, Canberra, 21 June 1998.

69. Zbigniew Brzezinski, *Power and Principle*, New York: Farrar Straus Giroux, 1985, p.356.

70. Following numerous defaults on the part of Iran, Daoud sent Mohammad Naim to Tehran in May 1977 in order to clarify the situation with the Shah's aid programme. Naim returned 'with the feeling that the Iranians, in their first burst of optimistic enthusiasm, had simply overestimated their long-term capabilities. At one point, the Afghans offered to forego all Iranian assistance, which the proud Iranians, bent on somehow achieving the Shah's dream of a "Great Civilisation", could not accept.' Duprée, 'Afghanistan 1977', p.4.

71. For details, see Saikal, *The Rise and Fall of the Shah*, p.200; Amiryar, 'Soviet Influence, Penetration, Domination and Invasion of Afghanistan', p.185.

72. Moscow was promptly informed about the highly sensitive parleys between Daoud and Sadat by Jalalar who had been included in the Afghan delegation as the Minister of Trade.

73. See Saikal, *The Rise and Fall of the Shah*, pp.167–9, 176.

74. Ghaus, *The Fall of Afghanistan*, p.180.

75. Daoud made his first public anti-communist speech in Herat in 1977 immediately after his return from Iran: 'We do not want imported ideologies!'

76. Arnold, *Afghanistan's Two-Party Communism*, p.51.

77. Korgun, *Intelligentsiia v politicheskoi zhizni Afganistana*, p.180.

78. Chaffetz, 'Afghanistan in Turmoil', p.20.

79. See Richard Pipes, 'Detente: Moscow's View', in Erik P. Hoffmann and Frederic J. Fleron, Jr (eds), *The Conduct of Soviet Foreign Policy*, New York: Aldine Publishing Company, 1980, pp.384–5.

80. For a penetrating review of the Soviet perspective on Bhutto and Zia ul-Haq, see A.A. Rodionov, 'Zapiski posla SSSR v Pakistane v 1971–1974gg', *Novaia i noveishaia istoriia*, No. 1, 1997, pp.122–42, and No. 2, 1997, pp.113–25.

81. The formal *Parchami-Khalqi* reunification was achieved during the PDPA conference on 3 July 1977, which elected a new 30-strong Central Committee. Nur Mohammad Taraki became General Secretary, and Babrak Karmal was appointed Secretary of the Committee. Participants in the conference put forth the slogan 'liquidating the dictatorship of Daoud.' P. Demchenko, 'Afganistan: na strazhe interesov naroda', *Kommunist*, No. 5, 1980, p.74. On *Parcham*'s insistence, Hafizullah Amin was not included in any of the top organs of the PDPA.

82. In a pamphlet entitled 'The Nights of Kabul', published in Peshawar in November

1995, a former police officer (and clandestine *Parchami*) named Omarzai recalled that he had been ordered to arrest Hafizullah Amin at his house on the night of 26–27 April. Amin pleaded to be allowed to stay at home until 7 o'clock in the morning, and Omarzai did not object. Before dawn Amin managed to send a signal for immediate action to the *Khalqi* plotters in the army: this was done by Amin's son, who was not barred from leaving the house.

83.   Male, *Revolutionary Afghanistan*, p.61. Amin was echoed by Taraki on the matter of timing: Taraki told journalists at a press conference in September 1979 that 'When the revolution took place President Carter and Comrade Brezhnev were equally surprised.' Steele, *The Limits of Soviet Power*, p.122.

84.   Several *Parchami* prisoners intimated this to Ravan Farhadi in Pol-e Charkhi jail, located just outside Kabul, during the rule of the *Khalqis* from mid 1978 until the Soviet invasion of Afghanistan in late 1979.

85.   See Arnold, *The Fateful Pebble: Afghanistan's Role in the Fall of the Soviet Empire*, pp.52–5; Zalmay Khalilzad, *The Return of the Great Game: Superpower Rivalry and Domestic Turmoil in Afghanistan, Iran, Pakistan, and Turkey*, Santa Monica: Caifornia Seminar on International Security and Foreign Policy, 1980, p.48.

86.   Kornienko, 'The Afghan Endeavour: Perplexities of the Military Incursion and Withdrawal', *Journal of South Asian and Middle Eastern Studies*, 17(2), Winter 1994, pp.2–3.

87.   For example, it has been alleged that Soviet pilots may have been flying Afghan jets which attacked government installations in Kabul, simply because their bombing appeared unusually accurate. Hannah Negaran, 'The Afghan Coup of April 1978: Revolution and International Security', *Orbis*, 23(1), Spring 1979, p.101.

88.   Gai and Snegirev, 'Vtorzhenie', Part I, p.198. Apparently, Soviet advisors attached to the 4th and 15th Armoured Brigades, which played a crucial role in the takeover, did not have a clue as to what was happening and were seized by panic when tanks began to leave the regimental parks.

89.   Peter W. Rodman, *More Precious than Peace: The Cold War and the Struggle for the Third World*, New York: C. Scribner's Sons, 1994, p.204.

90.   Stephen T. Hosmer and Thomas W. Wolfe, *Soviet Policy and Practice toward Third World Countries*, Lexington: Lexington Books, 1983, p.111.

91.   Maley, 'The Dynamics of Regime Transition in Afghanistan', *Central Asian Survey*, 16(2), 1997, p.169.

92.   A. Saikal, 'Afghanistan: Culture and Ideology under Pre-1978 Governments', *Central Asian Survey*, 11(1), 1992, p.113.

93.   Matinuddin, *Power Struggle in the Hindu Kush*, p.41.

94.   Halliday, 'Revolution in Afghanistan', p.30.

95.   By 1978, there may have been as many as 3,000 PDPA members in the armed forces. Gai and Snegirev, 'Vtorzhenie', Part I, p.198. Needless to say, the majority of them had at best a very vague understanding of the classical tenets of Marxism, which by no means affected their desire to change the state of affairs in the country.

Chapter 8: Communist Rule, the Soviet Invasion and Resistance

1.   William Maley and Fazel Haq Saikal, *Political Order in Post-Communist Afghanistan*, Boulder: Lynne Rienner Publishers, 1992, p.15.

2.   Formulae used by the PDPA leaders in their first programmatic statement on

foreign policy, 9 May 1978. See Teplinskii, *Istoriia sovetsko–afganskikh otnoshenii*, p.263.

3.   Mark Urban, *War in Afghanistan*, London: Macmillan, 1990, p.12.

4.   Quoted in Odd Arne Westad, 'Prelude to Invasion: The Soviet Union and the Afghan Communists, 1978–1979', *The International History Review*, 16(1), February 1994, p.51.

5.   Ravan Farhadi ,who was arrested on 27 May 1978 and held in Pol-e Charkhi prison until 20 January 1980, has left a vivid description of the real alignment of forces in the first period of the 'revolution': 'Initially they brought me to the Ministry of Interior. Here I found out that the newly appointed Minister of Interior, Nur Ahmad Nur [a *Parchami*], is only a nominal head of this establishment, and in fact cannot even enter the Ministry's premises at night-time. His driver doesn't have the permit to drive after the curfew. All security arrangements are in the hands of the *Khalqis*. They accept only government orders which are signed by Mohammad Aslam Watanjar. The *Khalqis* in security organs do absolutely what they please.'

6.   See Male, *Revolutionary Afghanistan*, pp.134–8.

7.   Paul Overby, *Holy Blood: An Inside View of the Afghan War*, Westport: Praeger, 1993, p.58.

8.   *Demokraticheskaia Respublika Afganistan*, Moscow: Nauka, 1981, p.84.

9.   Many peasants were convinced that assuming ownership of land which has already been in somebody else's possession was *haram*, that is, not permissible by Islam.

10.   *Haqiqat-e enqelab-e sawr*, 21 February 1986.

11.   Gai and Snegirev, 'Vtorzhenie', Part I, p.202.

12.   Spolnikov, *Afganistan*, pp.43, 111.

13.   Tahir Amin, *Afghanistan in Crisis: Implications and Options for Muslim World, Iran, and Pakistan*, Islamabad: Institute of Policy Studies, 1982, p.74.

14.   A.A. Liakhovskii and V.M. Zabrodin, *Tainy afganskoi voiny*, Moscow: Planeta, 1991, p.20.

15.   Arundhati Roy, *The Soviet Intervention in Afghanistan: Causes, Consequences, and India's Response*, New Delhi: Associated Publishing House, 1987, p.21.

16.   Teplinskii, *Istoriia sovetsko–afganskikh otnoshenii*, p.266.

17.   Arnold, *Afghanistan's Two-Party Communism: Parcham and Khalq*, p.95.

18.   Duprée, *Afghanistan*, pp.776–7.

19.   Dokumenty sovetskogo rukovodstva o polozhenii v Afganistane. 1979–1980', p.92.

20.   'Memorandum of Conversation Between Brezhnev and Taraki, March 20, 1979 (Moscow)', *Journal of South Asian and Middle Eastern Studies*, 17(2), Winter 1994, p.39.

21.   These requests included, *inter alia*, the following proposals (1979):

14 April	Send 15–20 combat helicopters with crews.
16 June	Send several armoured battalions to protect government installations, communication lines and airfields.
11 July	Deploy several commando battalions to guard Kabul.
19 July	Send two divisions to Afghanistan.
20 July	Send a paratroop division.
24 July	Deploy 3 brigades in Kabul.
21 August	Send 1,500–2,000 paratroopers to Kabul. Man all anti-aircraft defences with Soviet personnel.
2 October	Send a special forces battalion for Amin's personal protection.

> 2 December   Deploy a reinforced regiment in Badakhshan.
> 4 December   Send Soviet militia units to northern Afghanistan.
> 12 December   Station Soviet garrisons throughout northern Afghanistan and along major highways.
> *Komsomolskaia pravda*, 27 December 1990.

22. B.V. Gromov, *Ogranichennyi kontingent*, Moscow: Progress, 1994, p.73.

23. Liakhovskii and Zabrodin, *Tainy afganskoi voiny*, p.42.

24. Hyman, *Afghanistan under Soviet Domination, 1964–83*, London: Macmillan, 1984, pp.109–10.

25. Kakar, *Afghanistan*, p.63.

26. Gai and Snegirev, 'Vtorzhenie', Part I, p.206.

27. The events of 14 September 1979 in Kabul still await proper exploration. The dominant interpretation is that Taraki, finally heeding advice from Moscow, decided to get rid of Amin through assassination, but the latter survived and struck back. Newell and Newell, *The Struggle for Afghanistan*, pp.88–9. However, top-secret Soviet documents, including KGB reports, argue in favour of the version that the shoot-out at the presidential palace on that day was staged by Amin himself. 'Dokumenty sovetskogo rukovodstva o polozhenii v Afganistane. 1979–1980', pp.93, 96.

28. Quoted in Joseph J. Collins, *The Soviet Invasion of Afghanistan: A Study in the Use of Force in Soviet Foreign Policy*, Lexington: DC Heath and Company, 1986, p.67.

29. Taraki's assassination was carried out by three officers of the Presidential Guard on direct orders from Amin. See Liakhovskii and Zabrodin, *Tainy afganskoi voiny*, pp.53–4.

30. Andrei Gromyko, in a private conversation with his son in 1989, emphasised Brezhnev's role in policy deliberations concerning Afghanistan: 'It was up to the wish of the General Secretary of the CPSU CC who was and who was not invited to the [Politburo] meetings dealing with Afghanistan... I would like to note that Brezhnev was simply devastated by Taraki's murder.' Quoted in Igor Beliaev, 'Tak my voshli v Afganistan', in Iu.V. Aksiutin (ed.), *L.I. Brezhnev: Materialy k biografii*, Moscow: Politizdat, 1991, p.309. Undoubtedly, the emotional stress adversely affected the already impaired judgement of the ageing Soviet leader.

31. 'Abstract from the Minutes N172 of the meeting of the Political Bureau of the Central Committee of the Communist Party of the Soviet Union, October 31, 1979', *Journal of South Asian and Middle Eastern Studies*, 17(2), Winter 1994, p.55.

32. John Fullerton, *The Soviet Occupation of Afghanistan*, Hong Kong: Far Eastern Economic Review, 1983, p.35.

33. Matinuddin, *Power Struggle in the Hindu Kush*, p.56.

34. Gerard Chaliand, *Report from Afghanistan*, Harmondsworth: Penguin Books, 1982, p.62.

35. *Krasnaia zvezda*, 18 November 1989.

36. Amin felt so beleaguered that he actually pleaded for a Soviet special forces battalion to be sent to Kabul to guarantee his physical security. See 'Abstract from the Minutes N176 of the Politburo of the CPSU's Central Committee, to Brezhnev, Andropov, Gromyko, Suslov and Ustinov, December 6, 1979', *Journal of South Asian and Middle Eastern Studies*, 17(2), Winter 1994, p.59. A 500-strong GRU detachment was indeed despatched to Afghanistan and played a crucial role in *eliminating* Amin and his supporters.

37. See A. Saikal and Maley, *Regime Change in Afghanistan*, pp.44–5. For an inside senior *Parchami* military officer's account of the state of the military, Amin's fear of the Soviets replacing him with Karmal, rumours in Kabul that Amin was essentially a CIA agent and was ready to forge an alliance with the USA and the Soviet invasion, see General Mohammad Nabi Azimi, *Urdo wa siyasat dar seh dahe-i akheer-e Afghanistan, [dar du juld]*, Peshawar: Sabah Ketabkhana, 1376, pp.207–324.

38. Gai and Snegirev, 'Vtorzhenie', Part I, p.195.

39. Urban, *War in Afghanistan*, p.42.

40. Yossef Bodansky, 'Soviet Military Involvement in Afghanistan', in Klass (ed.), *Afghanistan*, p.239.

41. Gai and Snegirev, 'Vtorzhenie', Part II, p.224.

42. Merimskii, 'Voina v Afganistane: zapiski uchastnika', p.95.

43. These were: Karmal, Nur Ahmad Nur, Anahita Ratebzad and Mohammad Aslam Watanjar. The first three were despatched as ambassadors during June–July 1978 in the first wave of the purge unleashed by the *Khalqis*, to Prague, Washington and Belgrade respectively. By mid 1979, all had left their diplomatic posts and assembled in Moscow. Watanjar joined them later, after having been extracted from Kabul in September 1979 by the Soviets. Karmal, Nur and Ratebzad belonged to the *Parcham* faction, while Watanjar was a *Khalqi* and an ardent supporter of Taraki.

44. *Komsomolskaia pravda*, 27 January 1993. According to the group commander, Valentin Shergin, 'Babrak trusted us more than he could trust any Afghan.'

45. For a detailed account of Amin's death, see 'Kak ubivali H. Amina', *Argumenty i fakty*, No. 44, November 1990, p.3. Ravan Farhadi, who was incarcerated in Pol-e Charkhi at the time, has recollected that when Soviet troops entered the prison they told those inmates who knew Russian that they had come to overthrow Hafizullah Amin and put Babrak Karmal in his place. Clearly they had been given very explicit orders concerning their mission in Kabul.

46. Georgii Kornienko has argued that 'it was not by chance that the final decision [to invade] was made by the end of December 12, 1979, after Moscow learned the same day the decision of the NATO council to deploy in Europe American medium range missiles.' Kornienko, 'The Afghan Endeavour', p.8.

47. Gabriella Grasselli, *British and American Responses to the Soviet Invasion of Afghanistan*, Aldershot: Dartmouth Publishing Company, 1996, p.57.

48. Burke and Ziring, *Pakistan's Foreign Policy*, p.444.

49. Hammond, *Red Flag over Afghanistan*, p.119.

50. Apparently, President Carter signed the first directive on clandestine aid to opponents of the *Khalqi* regime on 3 July 1979. According to the author of the directive, Zbigniew Brzezinski, 'I explained that, in my view, this aid would bring a military intervention by the Soviets... We did not push the Russians into intervening, but we knowingly increased the probability that they would... The effect was to draw the Russians into the Afghan trap.' *Canberra Times*, 15 January 1998.

51. Asger Christensen, *Aiding Afghanistan: The Background and Prospects for Reconstruction in a Fragmented Society*, Copenhagen: NIAS Books, 1995, pp.96, 105.

52. In February 1980, according to Soviet estimates, 70 per cent of PDPA members were involved in acute factional struggles. Merimskii, 'Voina v Afganistane', p.97.

In 1982, the continuous disputes between *Khalq* and *Parcham* adherents took particularly violent forms, leaving scores of dead and wounded; Soviet troops often had to be summoned in order to stop bloodshed and violence. Fullerton, *The Soviet Occupation of Afghanistan*, pp.135–6.

53. By 1986, the Mujahideen controlled 77 per cent of Afghanistan's territory, as compared to 70 per cent in December 1979. Classified Afghanistan Dossier of the Institute of Oriental Studies of the Russian Academy of Sciences (IVRAN). Folder AF:POO.

54. See Teplinskii, *Istoriia sovetsko-afganskikh otnoshenii*, pp.280–3.

55. For a detailed discussion, see A. Saikal, 'The Regional Politics of the Afghan Crisis', in Saikal and Maley (eds), *The Soviet Withdrawal from Afghanistan*, Cambridge: Cambridge University Press, 1989, pp.52–8; Milan Hauner, 'The Soviet Geostrategic Dilemma', in Hauner and Canfield (eds), *Afghanistan and the Soviet Union*, pp.160–94.

56. Jimmy Carter, *Keeping Faith: Memoirs of a President*, London: Collins, 1982, pp.471–2.

57. Grasselli, *British and American Responses*, p.175. Individual members of the US Congress knew next to nothing about developments on the ground in Afghanistan and the growing resistance to the Soviet-backed regime. The situation changed only in 1982 after a fact-finding mission sponsored by the Congress returned from Pakistan. Personal observation of Ravan Farhadi.

58. In early 1981, the Zia regime accepted Reagan's offer of US$3.2 billion in economic and military aid, which made it the fourth largest recipient of US security assistance, behind Israel, Egypt and Turkey. Syed Rifat Hussain, 'Pakistan-American Relations in Soviet Perspective: An Evaluation', in Leo E. Rose and Kamal Matinuddin (eds), *Beyond Afghanistan: The Emerging US-Pakistan Relations*, Berkeley: Institute of East Asian Studies, University of California, 1989, p.317.

59. Liakhovskii and Zabrodin, *Tainy afganskoi voiny*, p.213.

60. 'Kakuiu pomoshch' urezat'?', *Za rubezhom*, No. 8, 1991, p.10.

61. Gromov, *Ogranichennyi kontingent*, p.231.

62. Najibullah, a *Parchami*, had to dedicate a lot of energy to combatting Karmal, who had retained several government positions, including a seat at the Revolutionary Council, and his coterie. Karmal departed for Moscow on 4 May 1987.

63. In 1986, the regime could field only around 50,000 soldiers. Zalmay Khalilzad, 'Moscow's Afghan War', *Problems of Communism*, 35, January–February 1986, p.7.

64. For a comparative study of the Afghanistan and Vietnam Wars, see Douglas A. Borer, *Superpowers Defeated: Vietnam and Afghanistan Compared*, London: Frank Cass, 1999.

65. In the year leading up to November 1987, the Soviets lost 300 military aircraft costing US$2.5 billion, to sophisticated air defence weapons that the rebels were now using. Tom Rogers, *The Soviet Withdrawal from Afghanistan: Analysis and Chronology*, Westport: Greenwood Press, 1992, p.92.

66. For an interesting discussion of the evolution of Gorbachev's thinking vis-à-vis Afghanistan, see Robert A. Jones, *The Soviet Concept of 'Limited Sovereignty' from Lenin to Gorbachev: The Brezhnev Doctrine*, Basingstoke: Macmillan, 1990, pp.191–2.

67. *Materialy XXVII s'ezda KPSS*, Moscow: Izdatelstvo politicheskoi literatury, 1987, p.69.

68. The then Soviet Chief of General Staff, Marshal Sergei Akhromeev, noted with acidity that in Afghanistan 'the adventurous action went horribly wrong, somebody had to be blamed for this, a guilty party needed to be found, so the army was made a "scapegoat".' S. Akhromeev and G. Kornienko, *Glazami marshala i diplomata*, Moscow: Mezhdunarodnye otnosheniia, 1992, p.168. Open criticism of the invasion did not appear in the Soviet press until 1989, and Najibullah referred to it as a 'wrong decision' only in 1990. *Izvestiia*, 23 July 1990.

69. For a detailed discussion on this point, see Sarah E. Mendelson, *Changing Course: Ideas, Politics, and the Soviet Withdrawal from Afghanistan*, Princeton: Princeton University Press, 1998.

70. Two retired US diplomats appear to have played an important role in facilitating semi-official dialogue between Moscow and Washington on the issue of Afghanistan during the early Gorbachev period: Robert Neumann (former US Ambassador to Kabul), and Tom Gouttiere. They visited Moscow several times and held talks with a number of Soviet political figures and members of the *Parchami* leadership. Personal communication of Robert Neumann to Ravan Farhadi.

71. For an inside account of the negotiations, see Diego Cordovez and Selig S. Harrison, *Out of Afghanistan: The Inside Story of the Soviet Withdrawal*, New York: Oxford University Press, 1995.

72. *Pravda*, 16 April 1988.

73. Amiryar, 'Soviet Influence, Penetration, Domination and Invasion of Afghanistan', pp.321–2.

74. In January 1988, Najibullah summarised the essence of the policy of 'national reconciliation' in the following way: 'Our party has never and will never give up power. However, taking into account political realities existing in Afghanistan, and giving priority to the national interests for the sake of a speedy attainment of peace on our land, it is giving up the monopoly on power. Abandonment of the monopoly on power and abandonment of power are two different things. It is the Party which acts as the initiator of a ruling coalition at all levels of government.' Classified Afghanistan Dossier of the IVRAN. Folder AF:A05.

75. In late 1988, officially the armed forces of the Republic of Afghanistan included:
    the Army 132,000 (50 per cent strength)
    the Sarandoy 100,000 (60 per cent strength)
    Ministry of State Security 70,000 (70.5 per cent strength)
    Presidential Guard 11,500 (full strength)
    Liakhovskii and Zabrodin, *Tainy afganskoi voiny*, p.166.
    The rivalry between the *Parchami*-controlled KHAD and the Sarandoi, which between 1980 and 1988 was under the jurisdiction of Major-General Sayyid Mohammad Golabzoi, a *Khalqi*, was a reflection of the fundamental split in the PDPA. Eyewitnesses reported that officers of the two services who were being trained in Tashkent in 1980 often attacked each other while on leave. Soviet hosts had to alter the roster of leaves so that these officers would not go out into the city at the same time.

76. Vasiliev, *Rossiia na Blizhnem i Srednem Vostoke*, p.294. The value of war materiel left by the Soviets to Najibullah was estimated at US$1 billion. Rogers, *The Soviet Withdrawal from Afghanistan*, p.55.

77. *Izvestiia*, 23 May 1992. In 1989, Najibullah received 2.5 billion roubles worth of military hardware, and in 1990, 1.4 billion. Russian sources quote the following

figures concerning the armaments 'inherited' by Najibullah: 1,200 tanks; 550 APCs; 2,000 artillery systems of the 76-mm calibre and higher; 30 jet fighters; 80 assault planes; and 55 helicopters. *Izvestiia*, 20 August 1998.

78. A UN document published in 1993 suggested that there were as many as ten million mines and items of unexploded ordnance dotting Afghanistan. Kabul and its environs were amongst the most affected territories, with some 19 square kilometres classified as 'high priority areas for clearance'. Maley, 'Mine Action in Afghanistan', *Refuge*, 17(4), October 1998, p.13.

79. On the divergent points of view between the US administration and Pakistani government, as well as friction between Zia and Premier Junejo on the Afghan issue, see Rodney W. Jones, 'Beyond Afghanistan: US-Pakistan Security Relations', in Rose and Matinuddin (eds), *Beyond Afghanistan*, pp.45–7.

80. Rodman, *More Precious than Peace*, pp.353–5. The USA perceived that a successful conclusion to the Soviet military involvement in Afghanistan would provide a major boost to Gorbachev's reformist policies at home and abroad, which had been consistently attacked by the CPSU hardliners after January 1987.

81. Hussain, 'Pakistan-American Relations in Soviet Perspective', pp.325–6.

82. A spokesman for the Mujahideen's Afghan Interim Government (AIG) thus commented on the results of the talks: 'From the point of view of Moscow and Kabul, national reconciliation in Afghanistan means that the mujahideen should share power with Najibullah and the PDPA. We shall never consent to this. The Soviet Union must stop its support to the regime in Kabul, and then we will prevail quickly.' *Sovetskaia Rossiia*, 13 January 1990.

83. *Krasnaia zvezda*, 22 August 1991.

84. The Hazara account for approximately 15 per cent of Afghanistan's population. However, during the years of anti-Soviet resistance, leaders of this ethnic community consistently claimed that their share in the country's population exceeded one-third, and even published maps of the imagined homeland of the Hazara ('Garjistan') which encompassed the greater part of Afghanistan.

85. Urban, *War in Afghanistan*, p.270.

86. According to Ijaz Gilani, as of 1989, 'a third of Pakistanis agree with the thesis that America would continue to fuel the Afghan conflict to serve its own interests... after a decade of generous assistance to the Afghan *jihad* against the Soviets, Americans are viewed in Pakistan as not significantly less threatening to the Muslim world than the Soviets.' Ijaz S. Gilani, 'Afghanistan Conflict and Prospects for the Future', in Rose and Matinuddin (eds), *Beyond Afghanistan*, p.280.

87. Burke and Ziring, *Pakistan's Foreign Policy,* p.472.

88. In 1989, Soviet sources evaluated the number of people under arms subordinated to Hekmatyar at 30,500 united in 855 groups. Gromov, *Ogranichennyi kontingent*, p.224. The total number of Mujahideen at the time was believed to be in the region of 85,000. Hekmatyar's international high profile was also partly due to the fact that some Afghan intellectuals living abroad, particularly in the USA, Europe and Australia, were his supporters. By the end of 1990, however, the majority of them had become disillusioned with him.

89. Christensen, *Aiding Afghanistan*, p.87.

90. Rodman, *More Precious than Peace*, pp.354–5.

91. Niccolò Machiavelli, *The Prince*, Harmondsworth: Penguin, 1972, p.99.

92. Joel S. Migdal, *Strong Societies and Weak States: State-Society Relations and State*

Capabilities in the Third World, Princeton: Princeton University Press, 1988, p.223.

93. See Azimi, *Urdo wa siyasat dar seh dahe-i akheer-e Afghanistan*, Vol. 2, Chapter 3.

94. *Za rubezhom*, No. 9, 1991, p.7.

95. A thorough analysis of Najibullah's 'limited liberalisation' can be found in Rubin, *The Fragmentation of Afghanistan*, pp.166–71.

96. *Pravda*, 29 June 1990. Slogans of coalition-building and diversifying support for the regime were constantly present in the PDPA political lexicon after the ascendancy of Babrak Karmal, partly due to the insistence of party advisors from Moscow. In 1980, a broad umbrella organisation called *Jabha-ye melli-ye Padarwatan* (the National Patriotic Front) came into existence, intended to rally non-party members behind the government. The Soviets touted the establishment of the NPF as a smashing success: 'the National Patriotic Front has become the most formidable socio-political organisation... having united 800,000 people on patriotic and democratic grounds.' M.A. Babakhojaev, 'NDPA – krupneishaia i samaia vliiatelnaia sila afganskogo obshchestva', in *Respublika Afganistan: opyt i tendentsii razvitiia*, Tashkent: Fan, 1990, p.11. In reality, the NPF was simply an artificial assembly of state-controlled and state-sanctioned institutions; in 1982, Karmal had already admitted that this was a stillborn idea, and that the NPF enjoyed absolutely no authority amongst the people. V. Plastun, 'NDPA: voprosy edinstva i soiuznikov na sovremennom etape revoliutsii', *Spetsialnyi bulleten' IV AN SSSR*, No. 2 (246), 1987, p.132.

97. *Izvestiia*, 21 January 1992.

98. *Izvestiia*, 9 February 1992.

99. In March 1992, a renowned field commander, Ismail Khan, took over Herat without a fight, having reached an accommodation with Najibullah's civil and military officials who thus retained their posts in the new administration.

100. 'Najibullah's "Heroes" Harass Kabul's People', *AFGHANews*, 6(1), 1 January 1990, p.1. Dostum was born in 1955 in the village of Khojadukuh of the Sheberghan district of Jawzjan province. He worked at the Sheberghan oil rigs, joined the PDPA after April 1978 and formed a militia unit in his patrimony which was subsequently transferred to KHAD jurisdiction. His military education was limited to a regimental school of junior officers. He spent three months in Tashkent attending KGB-run security officers' courses.

101. Khashimbekov, *Uzbeki severnogo Afganistana*, p.38.

102. See T.A. Davis, 'Communists Hit Back', *Asia-Pacific Defence Reporter*, April–May 1993, p.7.

103. Amongst high-profile defectors were Vice-President General Mohammad Rafi, Defence Minister Aslam Watanjar, Minister of the Interior Rasul Paktin and General Manokai Mangal. Practically the entire corps of the military police (*Sarandoy*) joined forces with Hekmatyar.

104. Rubin, *The Fragmentation of Afghanistan*, p.271.

105. See Azimi, *Urdo wa siyasat dar seh dahe-i akheer-e Afghanistan*, Vol. 2, Chapter 8.

106. Fred Halliday and Zahir Tanin, 'The Communist Regime in Afghanistan 1978–1992: Institutions and Conflicts', *Europe-Asia Studies*, 50(8), 1998, p.1377.

Chapter 9: Mujahideen Islamic Rule, Taliban Extremism and US Intervention

This chapter draws partly on material in Amin Saikal, 'The Rabbani Government, 1992–

1996', in William Maley (ed.), *Fundamentalism Reborn? Afghanistan and the Taliban*, London: Hurst & Company, 1998, pp.29–42.

1.   Anwar-ul-Haq Ahady, 'The Decline of the Pashtuns in Afghanistan', *Asian Survey*, 35(7), July 1995, p.626.

2.   For a detailed discussion, see O. Roy, 'Afghanistan: Back to Tribalism or on to Lebanon?', *Third World Quarterly*, 11(4), October 1989, pp.70–82; A. Saikal and Maley, *Regime Change in Afghanistan*, pp.118–34.

3.   Iu. Gankovskii, 'Afganistan: v boi vstupaiut taliby', *Rossiia i musulmanskii mir*, No. 9 (39), 1995, p.79.

4.   For an excellent review of Pakistan's strategic objectives in the region, see Dietrich Reetz, 'Pakistan and the Central Asian Hinterland Option: The Race for Regional Security and Development', *Journal of South Asian and Middle Eastern Studies*, 17(1), Fall 1993, pp.28–56.

5.   Rubin, *The Fragmentation of Afghanistan*, p.199.

6.   O. Roy, *Islam and Resistance in Afghanistan*, p.123.

7.   *Segodnia*, 15 March 1993.

8.   Eden Naby, 'Ethnic Factors in Afghanistan's Future', in Bo Huldt and Erland Jansson (eds), *The Tragedy of Afghanistan: The Social, Cultural and Political Impact of the Soviet Invasion*, London: Croom Helm, 1988, p.69.

9.   Quoted in Spolnikov, *Afganistan*, p.63.

10.   O. Roy, *Afghanistan: From Holy War to Civil War*, pp.112–13.

11.   *Pravda*, 25 June 1990.

12.   See A. Saikal, 'The UN and Afghanistan: A Case of Failed Peacemaking Intervention', *International Peacekeeping*, 3(1), Spring 1996, pp.19–34.

13.   On elite settlements more generally, see Michael G. Burton and John Higley, 'Elite Settlements', *American Sociological Review*, 52(3), June 1987, pp.295–307.

14.   For the text of the Agreement, see *Situation of Human Rights in Afghanistan*, New York: United Nations, A/47/656, 17 November 1992, Appendix I. The involvement of Nawaz Sharif and the Pakistani Foreign Ministry was active and overt; however, as it subsequently became clear, it was the ISI that effectively determined Pakistan's Afghan policy – the policy which was clandestine in nature and that ran contrary to this Agreement.

15.   This term (and the institution which it denotes) was a novelty in Afghan political life. However, it was widely used in medieval political treatises in Arabic and can be found in the parlance of present-day activists of the 'Muslim Brotherhood'.

16.   *Komsomolskaia pravda*, 12 November 1991.

17.   *Afghan Peace Accord*, New York: United Nations, S/25435, 19 March 1993.

18.   Sergei Strokan and Ruslan Budrin, 'Afganistan: strana nakanune raskola?', *Rossiia i musulmanskii mir*, No. 3, 1994, p.55.

19.   *Izvestiia*, 21 September 1994.

20.   *Izvestiia*, 26 May 1994. Dostum also had an office in Turkey, and visited European countries frequently.

21.   'A Tank, a Tank, My Kingdom for a Tank', *The Economist*, 26 February 1994, p.33.

22.   *Russkaia mysl'*, 19 January 1994.

23.   A. Saikal, 'Afghanistan's Ethnic Conflict', *Survival*, 40(2), Summer 1998, p.118.

24.   For a full discussion, see Nasri Haqshinas, *Tahwulat-e siyasi-e jihad-e Afghanistan*, Vol. 3, New Delhi: Jayyed Press, 1377.

25. One can gauge from the Pakistani publications of the period that political leaders of that country were convinced that Rabbani and Massoud were Pakistan's sworn enemies. In line with this premise the ISI did its best to beef up Hekmatyar's strength. The CIA, probably by inertia, unequivocally supported activities of the Pakistani secret service in this respect.

26. For background material, see O. Roy, *Islam and Resistance in Afghanistan*, pp.69–138; Naby, 'The Afghan Resistance Movement', in Magnus (ed.), *Afghan Alternatives: Issues, Options, and Policies*, New Brunswick: Transaction Books, 1985, pp.59–81; O. Roy, *Afghanistan*; *Afghan Resistance: Achievements and Problems*, Peshawar: Jam'iat-e Islami Afghanistan, 1986.

27. *Izvestiia*, 28 April 1992.

28. In late 1991, the discrepancy in political viewpoints between Massoud and the Mujahideen leaders in Peshawar was so acute as to encourage President Nabiev of Tajikistan to make the following statement: 'If you try bring a fundamentalist solution to Afghanistan then you would be responsible for the break-up of Afghanistan, because our Tajiks would not live in that kind of Afghanistan. Even Ahmed Shah Masud, who is an important commander, and a Tajik, will not accept an extreme rightist government. He will be persuaded to create an independent Tajik enclave in Afghanistan.' Reetz, 'Pakistan and the Central Asian Hinterland Option', p.49.

29. See Rubin, *The Fragmentation of Afghanistan*, p.239.

30. In the apt description of Ahmed Rashid, 'Hekmatyar had failed not only to conquer the capital but also to unite the Ghilzai Pushtuns against the Tajik dominated regime of President Burhanuddin Rabbani. The majority of Pushtuns loathed Hekmatyar as much as they disliked Rabbani. Thus for much of 1994, Pakistan's Afghan policy was stranded like a beached whale, directionless and without powerful surrogates in Afghanistan.' Rashid, 'Pakistan and the Taliban', in Maley (ed.), *Fundamentalism Reborn?*, p.74.

31. For an analysis of the imperatives underlying Islamabad's policy towards Afghanistan in the 1980s and 1990s, see Abdul Rasul Amin, *Afghanestan az kham-o pech-e khatarnak-e ta'rikh migozarad*, Peshawar: WUFA, 1996, pp.21–33.

32. Mirza Aslam Beg, 'Balance of Power Paradigm and Pakistan's Security Problems', in Tarik Jan et al, *Foreign Policy Debate: The Years Ahead*, Islamabad: Institute of Policy Studies, 1993, pp.128–9.

33. Rashid, 'Afghanistan: Apocalypse Now', *The Herald*, October 1995.

34. A.D. Davydov, 'Dvizhenie "Taliban" i problemy dostizheniia mira', in *Afganistan: problemy voiny i mira*, Moscow: IVRAN, 1996, p.159. It is interesting that the ISI did not sever its communication lines with Hekmatyar until early 1995, when the Taliban moved against his headquarters in Char Asyab and had to endure a flurry of complaints on his part about the sudden change in his fortunes.

35. For a detailed discussion, see 'Introduction: Interpreting the Taliban', in Willam Maley (ed.), *Fundamentalism Reborn?*

36. 'Babar Admits Training Taliban in 1994', *Electronic Document posted on 8 September 1998 to afghanistan@hypermail.com*

37. Gankovskii, 'Afganistan', p.80.

38. *Vek*, 28 September 1995.

39. For a full discussion of the Taliban and their rise to power, see Rashid, *Taliban*, especially Parts 1 and 2.

40.   Quoted in *Vechernii Dushanbe*, 14 August 1998.

41.   Arkady Dubnov, 'Kabul: The Fate of Carthago?', *New Times*, December 1996, p.55.

42.   A. Saikal, 'Afghanistan, Terrorism, and American and Australian Responses', *Australian Journal of International Affairs*, 56(1), April 2002, p.25.

43.   The demonstrations were triggered partly by the Rabbani administration's accusations that the fall of Herat to the Taliban had been organised by Pakistan. In the words of Rabbani's spokesperson, Abdul Aziz Murad, 'Herat was captured not by the Taliban, but rather by foreign armed formations paid by the ISI.' *Segodnia*, 7 September 1995.

44.   For details, see Maley, *The Afghanistan Wars*, Chapter 9.

45.   Ishtiaq Ahmed, 'Options in Afghanistan', *The Nation*, 5 November 1996; Edward Barnes, 'Friends of the *Taliban*', *Time*, 4 November 1996.

46.   For subsequent Pakistani setbacks, see Christopher Thomas, 'Taliban Rout Ends Islamabad's Dream', *The Australian*, 4 June 1997; M. Ilyas Khan, 'War Without End', *The Herald*, June 1997.

47.   *Obshchaia gazeta*, 19 August 1998.

48.   Zalmay Khalilzad, 'Afghanistan: Time to Re-Engage', *The Washington Post*, 7 October 1996.

49.   For a discussion of the power game over the gas and oil resources of Central Asia and their possible export through Afghanistan, see Rashid, 'Power Play, and "Pipe dreams"', *Far Eastern Economic Review*, 10 April 1997, pp.22–8.

50.   For a detailed account, see John K. Cooley, *Unholy Wars: Afghanistan, America and International Terrorism*, London: Pluto Press, 1999, especially Chapter 5.

51.   For details, see Maley, *The Afghanistan Wars*, Chapters 10 and 11; Rohan Gunaratna, *Inside Al Qaeda: Global Network of Terror*, London: Hurst & Company, 2002, especially Chapters 1 and 2.

52.   John Jennings, 'The *Taliban* and Foggy Bottom', *Washington Times*, 25 October 1996.

53.   *Reuters*, 18 November 1997.

54.   A. Saikal, 'The Role of Outside Actors in Afghanistan', *The Middle East Policy*, 7(4), October 2000, pp.50–7.

55.   For the comments of Iran's Supreme Leader, Ayatullah Khamenei, on the issue, see *Kayhan Havai*, 16 October 1996.

56.   See O.N. Mehrotra, 'The Troubled CIS', in Sreedhar (ed.), *Taliban and the Afghan Turmoil: The Role of USA, Pakistan, Iran and China*, New Delhi: Himalayan Books, 1997.

57.   Present-day Pakistani geostrategists often speak about the necessity of an active policy in Afghanistan as the means to secure 'strategic depth' vis-à-vis India, 'still considered the prime threat'. Citha D. Maass, 'The Afghanistan Conflict: External Involvement', *Central Asian Survey*, 18(1), 1999, p.70.

58.   *Russkii telegraf*, 10 September 1998. One Iranian diplomat from the consulate in Mazar-e Sharif managed to escape having pretended to be dead. Once in Tehran, he maintained that the man who had ordered the Taliban to execute his colleagues spoke Urdu.

59.   *Vremia*, 29 July 1998. Some interesting information about the size and nature of Uzbekistan's assistance to Dostum (including the alleged shipment of 5,000 tanks) can be found in Stuart Horsman, 'Uzbekistan's Involvement in the Tajik Civil

War 1992–1997: Domestic Considerations', *Central Asian Survey*, 18(1), 1999, pp.38–40.

60.   Arkady Dubnov, 'To Find the Last Enemy…', *New Times*, June 1997, p.45.

61.   *Biznes i politika*, No. 33, August 1998, p.1.

62.   *Vremia*, 20 August 1998.

63.   Following the seizure of Mazar-e Sharif, the Taliban systematically and deliberately killed thousands of Hazara civilians between 8 and 11 August 1998. According to an Amnesty International report, 'Foreign governments bankrolling or giving military support to the Taleban bear some responsibility for failing to rein in the Taleban's worst excesses.' 'Afghanistan: Thousands of Civilians Killed Following Taleban Takeover of Mazar-e Sharif', News Service, 171/98, 3 September 1998, electronic publication distributed through the Afghan News Service. On 27 August 1998, the UN Security Council passed a resolution condemning the Taliban for the atrocities committed in Mazar-e Sharif.

Conclusion

1.   A. Saikal, 'Afghanistan After the Loya Jirga', *Survival*, 44(3), Autumn 2002, p.48.

Bibliography

'A Tank, a Tank, My Kingdom for a Tank', *The Economist*, 26 February 1994

Abdoullaev, K., 'Central Asian Emigres in Afghanistan: First Wave 1920–1931', *Central Asia Monitor*, No. 5, 1994

Abidi, A.H.H., 'Irano-Afghan Dispute over the Helmand Waters', *International Studies*, 16(3), July–September 1977

'Abstract from the Minutes N172 of the meeting of the Political Bureau of the Central Committee of the Communist Party of the Soviet Union, October 31, 1979', *Journal of South Asian and Middle Eastern Studies*, 17(2), Winter 1994

'Abstract from the Minutes N176 of the Politburo of the CPSU's Central Committee, to Brezhnev, Andropov, Gromyko, Suslov and Ustinov, December 6, 1979', *Journal of South Asian and Middle Eastern* Studies, 17(2), Winter 1994

Adamec, L.W., *Afghanistan, 1900–1923*, Berkeley and Los Angeles: University of California Press, 1967

Adamec, L.W., 'Germany, Third Power in Afghanistan's Foreign Relations', in G. Grassmuck and L.W. Adamec with F.H. Irwin (eds), *Afghanistan: Some New Approaches*, Ann Arbor: Center for Near Eastern and North African Studies, University of Michigan, 1969

Adamec, L.W., *Afghanistan's Foreign Affairs to the Mid-Twentieth Century: Relations with the USSR, Germany, and Britain*, Tucson: The University of Arizona Press, 1974

Adamec, L.W., *Historical Dictionary of Afghanistan*, Metuchen and London: Scarecrow Press, 1991

Afganistan, Moscow: Nauka, 1964

Afganistan: problemy voiny i mira, Moscow: IVRAN, 1996

Afghan Peace Accord, New York: United Nations, S/25435, 19 March 1993

Afghan Resistance: Achievements and Problems, Peshawar: Jam'iat-e Islami Afghanistan, 1986

'Afghanistan: Thousands of Civilians Killed Following Taleban Takeover of Mazar-e Sharif', *News Service 171/98 AI INDEX: ASA! 1/07/98 3 SEPTEMBER 1998*. Electronic publication distributed through the Afghan News Service

Agabekov, G.S., *Ch.K. za rabotoi*, Berlin: Strela, 1931

Agabekov, G., *OGPU: The Russian Secret Terror*, Westport: Hyperion Press, 1975 [1931]

Ahady, A.H., 'The Decline of the Pashtuns in Afghanistan', *Asian Survey*, 35(7), July 1995

Ahmad, S.I., *Balochistan: Its Strategic Importance*, Karachi: Royal Book Company, 1992

Ahmed, A.S., *Pukhtun Economy and Society*, London: Routledge & Kegan Paul, 1980

Ahmed, I., 'Options in Afghanistan', *The Nation*, 5 November 1996

Akhmedkhodzhaev, I., 'K voprosu o stanovlenii obshchestvennoi mysli i burzhuaznoi istoriografii v Afganistane v nachale XX veka', in *Tashkentskii universitet. Trudy. Novaia seriia. Vypusk 690*, Tashkent: Izdatelstvo TGU, 1983

Akhramovich, R.T., *Outline History of Afghanistan After the Second World War*, Moscow: Nauka, 1966

Akhramovich, R.T., 'K kharakteristike etapov obshchestvennoi evoliutsii Afganistana posle vtoroi mirovoi voiny', *Narody Azii i Afriki*, No. 3, 1967

Akhromeev, S., and G. Kornienko, *Glazami marshala i diplomata*, Moscow: Mezhdunarodnye otnosheniia, 1992

Ali, M., *Progressive Afghanistan*, Lahore: Punjab Educational Electric Press, 1933.

Ali, M., 'The Attitude of the New Afghan Regime Towards its Neighbours', *Pakistan Horizon*, 27(3), 1974

Aliev, G.Z., *Turtsiia vperiodpravleniia mladoturok*, Moscow: Nauka, 1972

Allah, N., *History of the Afghans*, London: S. Gupta, 1965

Amin, A.R., *Afghanestan az kham-o pech-e khatarnak-e ta'rikh migozarad*, Peshawar: WUFA, 1996

Amin, T., *Afghanistan Crisis: Implications and Options for Muslim World, Iran, and Pakistan*, Islamabad: Institute of Policy Studies, 1982

Anderson, J.W., 'Khan and Khel: Dialectics of Pakhtun Tribalism', in R. Tapper (ed.), *The Conflict of Tribe and State in Iran and Afghanistan*, London and Canberra: Croom Helm, 1983

Anwar, R., *The Tragedy of Afghanistan: A First-hand Account*, London and New York: Verso, 1989

Area Handbook for Afghanistan, Washington: The American University, 1969

Arney, G., *Afghanistan*, London: Mandarin, 1990

Arniryar, A.Q., Soviet Influence, Penetration, Domination and Invasion of Afghanistan, Ph.D. Thesis, George Washington University, Washington, DC, 1989

Arnold, A., *Afghanistan: The Soviet Invasion in Perspective*, Stanford: Hoover Institution Press, 1981

Arnold, A., *Afghanistan's Two-Party Communism: Parcham and Khalq*, Stanford: Hoover Institution Press, 1983

Arnold, A., *The Fateful Pebble: Afghanistan's Role in the Fall of the Soviet Empire*, Noato: Presidio, 1993

Arunova, M.R., 'Iz istorii pervykh russkikh posolstv na territorii Afganistana', in *Afganistan: ekonomika, politika, istoriia*, Moscow: Nauka, 1984

Azimi, M.N., *Urdo wa siyasat dar seh dahe-i akheer-e Afghanistan [dor dujuld]*, Peshawar: Sabah Ketabkhana, 1376

Babaeva, A.K., 'Turkmeny severo-zapadnogo Afganistana: k voprosu o rasselenii turkmenskikh piemen', in *Afganistan: ekonomika, politika, istoriia*, Moscow: Nauka, 1984

Babakhodzhaev, A. Kh., *Proval angliiskoi antisovetskoi politiki v Srednei Azii i na Srednem Vostoke v period priznaniia Sovetskogo gosudarstva de-fakto i de-iure (1921–1924gg.)*, Tashkent: Izdatelstvo AN UzSSR, 1957

Babakhodzhaev, A., *Ocherkipo istorii sovetsko-afganskikh otnoshenii*, Tashkent: Fan, 1970

Babakhojaev, M.A., *Bor'ba Afganistana za nezavisimost': 1838–1842*, Moscow: Nauka, 1960

Babakhojaev, M.A., 'NDPA – krupneishaia i samaia vliiatelnaia sila afganskogo obschestva', in *Respublika Afganistan: opyti tendentsii razvitiia*, Tashkent: Fan, 1990

Baker, A., *Wings over Kabul: The First Airlift*, London: William Kimber, 1975

Baljowani, M.A.M.S., *Ta'rikh-e nafe'*, Dushanbe: Irfon, 1994

Baluch, M.A.Y.K., *Inside Baluchistan*, Karachi: Royal Book Company, 1975

Barnes, E., 'Friends of the *Taliban*', *Time*, 4 November 1996

Baryalai, M., 'National Traditions Serve the Revolution', *World Marxist Review*, No. 4, April 1986

Basov, V.V., 'Voprosy sotsiahio-ekonomicheskogo razvitiia Afganistana', *Narody Azii i Afriki*, No. 3, 1971

Beattie, K.J., *Egypt during the Nasser Years: Ideology, Politics, and Civil Society*, Boulder: Westview Press, 1994

Becker, S., *Russia's Protectorates in Central Asia: Bukhara and Khiva, 1865–1924*, Cambridge, MA: Harvard University Press, 1968

Beg, M.A., 'Balance of Power Paradigm and Pakistan's Security Problems', in T. Jan et al., *Foreign Policy Debate: The Years Ahead*, Islamabad: Institute of Policy Studies, 1993

Beliaev, I., 'Tak my voshli v Afganistan', in I.V. Aksiutin (ed.), *LI. Brezhnev: Materialy k biografii*, Moscow: Politizdat, 1991

Bell, M.J. (ed.), *An American Engineer in Afghanistan: From the Letters and Notes of A.C. Jewett*, Minneapolis: University of Minnesota Press, 1948

Biznes i politika, No. 33, August 1998

Black, C.E. et al., *The Modernization of Inner Asia*, Armonk, NY: M.E. Sharpe, 1991

Bodansky, Y., 'Soviet Military Involvement in Afghanistan', in R. Klass (ed.), *Afghanistan: The Great Game Revisited*, New York: Freedom House, 1987

Bokiev, O., *Zavoevanie i prisoedinenie Severnogo Tadzhikistana, Pamira i Gornogo Badakhashan k Rossii*, Dushanbe: Won, 1994

Borer, D.A., *Superpowers Defeated: Vietnam and Afghanistan Compared*, London: Frank Cass, 1999

Bradsher, H.S., *Afghanistan and the Soviet Union*, Durham: Duke University Press, 1983

Brant, M., 'Recent Economic Development', in L. Duprée and L. Albert (eds), *Afghanistan in the 1970s*, New York: Praeger Publishers, 1974

Braudel, F., *The Mediterranean and the Mediterranean World in the Age of Philip II*, Vol. I, trans. Sian Reynolds, London: Collins, 1972

Brzezinski, Z., *Power and Principle*, New York: Farrar Straus Giroux, 1985

Burke, S.M. and L. Ziring, *Pakistan's Foreign Policy: An Historical Analysis*, Karachi: Oxford University Press, 1990

Burkhan-ud-Din-khan-i-Kushkeki, *Kattagan i Badakhshan*, Tashkent: Gosudarstvennoe izdatelstvo, 1926

Burton, M.G. and J. Higley, 'Elite Settlements', *American Sociological Review*, 52(3), June 1987

Caroe, O., *The Pathans: 550BC–AD1957*, Karachi: Oxford University Press, 1980

Carter, J., *Keeping Faith: Memoirs of a President*, London: Collins, 1982

Chaffetz, D., 'Afghanistan in Turmoil', *International Affairs*, 56(1), 1980

Chakravarty, S., *From Khyber to Oxus: A Study in Imperial Expansion*, Delhi: Orient Longman, 1976

Chaliand, G., *Report from Afghanistan*, Harmondsworth: Penguin Books, 1982

Christensen, A., *Aiding Afghanistan: The Background and Prospects for Reconstruction in a Fragmented Society*, Copenhagen: NIAS Books, 1995

Classified Afghanistan Dossier of the Institute of Oriental Studies of the Russian Academy of Sciences (IVRAN), Folder AF:POO

Classified Afghanistan Dossier of the IVRAN, Folder AF:A05

Cohen, R., 'State Origins: A Reappraisal', in H.J.M. Claessen and P. Skalnik (eds), *The Early State*, The Hague: Mouton Publishers, 1978

Collins, J.J., *The Soviet Invasion of Afghanistan: A Study in the Use of Force in Soviet Foreign Policy*, Lexington: DC Heath and Company, 1986

Cooley, J.K., *Unholy Wars: Afghanistan, America and International Terrorism*, London: Pluto Press, 1999

Cordovez, D. and S.S. Harrison, *Out of Afghanistan: The Inside Story of the Soviet Withdrawal*, New York: Oxford University Press, 1995

Crummey, R.O., *The Formation of Muscovy, 1304–1613*, London & New York: Longman, 1987

Curzon, G.N., *Persia and the Persian Question*, Vol. I, reprint, London: Frank Cass, 1996

Curzon, G.N., *Russia in Central Asia in 1889 and the Anglo-Russian Question*, reprint, London: Frank Cass, 1967

d'Encausse, H.C., 'Systematic Conquest, 1865 to 1884', in E. Allworth (ed.), *Central Asia: A Century of Russian Rule*, New York and London: Columbia University Press, 1967

Davis, T.A., 'Communists Hit Back', *Asia-Pacific Defence Reporter*, April–May 1993

Davliatov, M., 'M.G.M. Gubar o progressivnykh obshchestvennykh dvizheniiakh v Afganistane v nachale XXv', in *Afganistan: istoriia, ekonomika, kultura*, Moscow: Nauka, 1989

Davydov, A.D., 'O selskoi obshchine i ee khoziaistvennom znachenii v Afganistane', in *Voprosy ekonomiki Afganistana*, Moscow: Izdatelstvo vostochnoi literatury, 1963

Davydov, A.D., 'Dvizhenie 'Taliban' iproblemy dostizheniiamira', in *Afganistan: problemy voiny i mira*, Moscow: IVRAN, 1996

Dawisha, A.I., *Egypt in the Arab World: The Elements of Foreign Policy*, London: Macmillan, 1976

Demchenko, P., 'Afganistan: na strazhe interesov naroda', *Kommunist*, No. 5, 1980

Demokraticheskaia Respublika Afganistan, Moscow: Nauka, 1981

Dibb, P., *The Soviet Union: The Incomplete Superpower*, Basingstoke: Macmillan, 1988

Dil, S.F., 'The Cabal in Kabul: Great-Power Interaction in Afghanistan', *American Political Science Review*, 71(2), June 1977

Dobrynin, A., *In Confidence: Moscow's Ambassador to America's Six Cold War Presidents (1962–1986)*, New York: Times Books, 1995

'Dokumenty sovetskogo rukovodstva o polozhenii v Afganistane. 1979–1980', *Novaia i noveishaia istoriia*, No. 3, May–June 1996

Dokumenty vneshnei politiki SSSR, Vol. II, Moscow: Gospolitizdat, 1960

Dokumenty vneshnei politiki SSSR, Vol. IV, Moscow: Gospolitizdat, 1961

Dokumenty vneshnei politiki SSSR, Vol. XI, Moscow: Gosizdat, 1957

Donish, A.M., *Risola yo mukhtasare az ta'rikhi saltanati khonadoni manghitiya*, Dushanbe: Sarwat, 1992

Dubnov, A., 'Kabul: The Fate of Carthago?', *New Times*, December 1996.

Dubnov, A., 'To Find the Last Enemy', *New Times*, June 1997

Duprée, L., 'The Decade of Daoud Ends', *AUFS Reports Service: South Asia Series*, 7(7), 1963

Duprée, L., 'An Informal Talk with King Mohammad Zahir of Afghanistan', *AUFS Reports Service: South Asia Series*, 7(9), 1963

Duprée, L., 'A Suggested Pakistan–Afghanistan–Iran Federation', *The Middle East Journal*, 17(4), Autumn 1963

Duprée, L., 'Constitutional Development and Cultural Change. Part III: The 1964 Afghan Constitution (Articles 1–56)', *AUFS Reports Service: South Asia Series*, 9(3), 1965

Duprée, L., 'Constitutional Development and Cultural Change. Part IV: The 1964 Afghan Constitution (Articles 57–128)', *AUFS Reports Service: South Asia Series*, 9(4), 1965

Duprée, L., 'Constitutional Development and Cultural Change. Part VIII: The Future of Constitutional Law in Afghanistan and Pakistan', *AUFS Reports Service: South Asia Series*, 9(10), 1965

Duprée, L., 'Afghanistan: 1966', *AUFS Reports Service: South Asia Series*, 10(4), 1966

Duprée, L., 'Afghanistan: 1968. Part III: Problems of a Free Press', *AUFS Reports Service: South Asia Series*, 12(6), 1968

Duprée, L., 'Afghanistan and the Unpaved Road to Democracy', *Journal of the Royal Central Asian Society*, 56(3), October 1969

Duprée, L., 'Afghanistan Continues its Experiment in Democracy', *AUFS Reports Service: South Asia Series*, 15(3), 1971

Duprée, L., 'Parliament Versus the Executive in Afghanistan: 1969–1971', *AUFS Reports Service: South Asia Series*, 15(5), 1971

Duprée, L., 'A New Decade of Daoud?', *AUFS Reports Service: South Asia Series*, 17(4), 1973

Duprée, L., 'A Note on Afghanistan: 1974', *AUFS Reports Service: South Asia Series*, 18(8), 1974

Duprée, L., 'Afghanistan 1977: Does Trade Plus Aid Guarantee Development?', *AUFS Reports Service: South Asia Series*, 21(3), 1977

Duprée, L., *Afghanistan*, Princeton: Princeton University Press, 1980

Duprée, L. and L. Albert (eds), *Afghanistan in the 1970s*, New York: Praeger Publishers, 1974

Dvoriankov, N.A., 'Literaturnyi iazyk i dialekty pashto v Afganistane', *Narody Azii i Afriki*, No. 2, 1964

Dvoriankov, N.A., 'Pervyi god', *Aziia iAfrika segodnia*, No. 7, 1974

Eberhard, W., 'Afghanistan's Young Elite', *Asian Survey*, 1(12), February 1962

Edwardes, Michael, *Playing the Great Game: A Victorian Cold War*, London: Hamilton, 1975

Eickelman, D.F., *The Middle East: An Anthropological Approach*, Englewood Cliffs: Prentice Hall, 1989

Eisenstadt, S.N., *Traditional Patrimonialism and Modern Neo-Patrimonialism*, Beverly Hills: Sage, 1973

el Alami, D.S. and D. Hinchcliffe, *Islamic Marriage and Divorce Laws of the Arab World*, London: Kluwer Law International, 1996

el Saadawi, N., *The Hidden Face of Eve: Women in the Arab World*, Boston: Beacon Press, 1982

Elphinstone, M., *An Account of the Kingdom of Caubul*, Vols I and II, Karachi: Oxford University Press, 1972

Ezhov, G.P., 'Nekotorye tendentsii mirnogo razvitiia Afganistana k 70–80m godam', in *Afganistan: problemy voiny i mira*, Moscow: IVRAN, 1996

Faizzad, M.A., *Jirgaha-ye bozorg-e melli-ye Afghanestan (Loya Jirgaha) wa Jirgaha-ye namnehad taht-e tasallot-e kamunestha wa rusha*, Lahore: No Publisher, 1368YH

Farhadi, R., *Maqalat-e Mahmud-e Tarzi*, Kabul: No Publisher, 1973

Farrokh, S.M., *Ta'rikh-e siyassi-ye Afghanestan*, reprint, Qom: No Publisher, 1993

Fazal-ur-Rehman, 'Power Struggle in Afghanistan', *Strategic Studies*, 16(4), 1994

Fitrat, *Davrai hukmronii Amir Olimkhon*, Dushanbe: Palatai davlatii kitobho, 1991

Fitzhardinge, H.V., The Establishment of the North-West Frontier of Afghanistan, 1884–1888, Ph.D. Thesis, Australian National University, Canberra, 1968

Fletcher, A., *Afghanistan: Highway of Conquest*, Ithaca, NY: Cornell University Press, 1965

Fraser-Tytler, W.K., *Afghanistan: A Study of Political Developments in Central and Southern Asia*, London: Oxford University Press, 1967

Fullerton, J., *The Soviet Occupation of Afghanistan*, Hon Kong: Far Eastern Economic Review, 1983

Furnas, J.C., *The Americans: A Social History of the United States, 1587–1914*, New York: Putnam, 1969

Fry, M.J., *The Afghan Economy*, Leiden: E.J. Brill, 1974

Gai, D. and V. Snegirev, 'Vtorzhenie', Part I, *Znamia*, No. 3, March 1991.

Gai, D.and V. Snegirev, 'Vtorzhenie', Part II, *Znamia*, No. 4, April 1991

Gankovskii, I., 'Afganistan: v boi vstupaiut taliby', *Rossiia i musulmanskii mir*, No. 9 (39), 1995

Gankovsky, Y.V., Railya Muqeemjanova, Vyacheslav Belokrenitsky and Vladimir Moskalenko, 'Soviet Relations with Pakistan', in H. Malik (ed.), *Soviet-American Relations with Pakistan, Iran and Afghanistan*, London: Macmillan, 1987

Gankovsky, Y., 'The Durrani Empire', in *Afghanistan: Past and Present*, Moscow: USSR Academy of Sciences, 1982

Gellner, E., *Postmodernism, Reason and Religion*, London and New York: Routledge, 1993

Georgiev, G., 'Iz istorii denezhnogo obrashcheniia v Afganistane v 20–e gody XXv', in *Afganistan: istoriia, ekonomika, kultura*, Moscow: Nauka, 1989

Gerasimova, A.S., 'Zhurnal "Kabul" v 1966–1969 godakh', *Narody Azii iAfriki*, No. 1, 1971

Ghaus, A.S., *The Fall of Afghanistan: An Insider's Account*, Washington: Pergamon-Brassey's International Defense Publishers, 1988

Ghobar, M.G.M., *Afghanestan dar masir-e ta'rikh*, Kabul: Markaz-e nashr-e inqelab, 1366

Ghobar, M.G.M., *Afghanistan in the Course of History*, Vol. II, trans. Sharief A. Fayez, Virginia: All Prints Inc, 2001

Giddens, A, *Central Problems in Social Theory: Action, Structure and Contradiction in Social Analysis*, London: Macmillan, 1979

Gilani, I.S., 'Afghanistan Conflict and Prospects for the Future', in L.E. Rose and K. Matinuddin (eds), *Beyond Afghanistan: The Emerging US-Pakistan Relations*, Berkeley: Institute of East Asian Studies, University of California, 1989

Golovin, I.M., *SSSR i Afganistan*, Moscow: Izdatelstvo vostochnoi literatury, 1962

Grasselli, G., *British and American Responses to the Soviet Invasion of Afghanistan*, Aldershot: Dartmouth Publishing Company, 1996

Gray, J.A., *At the Court of the Amir: A Narrative*, London: Darf Publishers, 1987

Gregorian, V., 'Mahmud Tarzi and Saraj-ol-Akhbar: Ideology of Nationalism and Modernisation in Afghanistan', *The Middle East Journal*, 21(3), Summer 1967

Gregorian, V., *The Emergence of Modern Afghanistan: Politics of Reform and Modernization, 1880–1946*, Stanford: Stanford University Press, 1969

Griffiths, J.C., *Afghanistan: Key to a Continent*, Boulder: Westview Press, 1981

Gromov, B.V., *Ogranichennyi kontingent*, Moscow: Progress, 1994

Gubar, M.G.M., *Afganistan an puti istorii*, Moscow: Nauka, 1987

Guha, A., 'The Rise of Capitalistic Enterprises in Afghanistan, 1929–45', *The Indian Economic and Social History Review*, 1(2), October–December 1963

Guha, A., 'The Economy of Afghanistan During Amanullah's Reign, 1919–1929', *International Studies*, 9(2), 1967

Gunaratna, R., *Inside Al Qaeda: Global Network of Terror*, London: Hurst & Company, 2002

Gupta, B.S., *Afghanistan: Politics, Economics and Society*, London: Frances Pinter, 1986

Gurko-Kriazhin, V.A., *Istoricheskie sud'by Afganistana*, Moscow: Gosizdat, 1922

Habibi, A., *Jonbesh-e mashruteyat dar Afghanestan*, Kabul: Komita-ye dawlati-ye tab'-u nashr-e Jomhuri-ye Afghanestan, 1363 YH

Hager, R., 'State, Tribe and Empire in Afghan Inter-Polity Relations', in R. Tapper (ed.), *The Conflict of Tribe and State in Iran and Afghanistan*, London and Canberra: Croom Helm, 1983

Haggard, S. and R.R. Kaufman, 'The Political Economy of Democratic Transitions', *Comparative Politics*, 29(3), April 1997

Halliday, F., 'Revolution in Afghanistan', *New Left Review*, No. 112, November–December 1978

Halliday, F. and Z. Tanin, 'The Communist Regime in Afghanistan 1978–1992: Institutions and Conflicts', *Europe-Asia Studies*, 50(8), 1998

Hamilton, A., *Afghanistan*, London: William Heinemann, 1906

Hammond, T.T., *Red Flag over Afghanistan: The Communist Coup, the Soviet Invasion, and the Consequences*, Boulder: Westview Press, 1984

Hangen, W., 'Afghanistan', *Yale Review*, 56(1), October 1966

Haqiqat-e enqelab-e sawr, 21 February 1986

Haqshinas, N., *Tahwulat-e siyasi-e jihad-e Afghanistan*, Vols 1-3, New Delhi: Jayyed Press, 1377

Hasan, K., 'Pakistan-Afghanistan Relations', *Asian Survey*, 2(7), 1962

Hasan, Z., 'Pakistan-USSR Relations', *Pakistan Horizon*, 21(2), 1968

Hauner, M., 'The Soviet Geostrategic Dilemma', in M. Hauner and R.L. Canfield (eds), *Afghanistan and the Soviet Union: Collision and Transformation*, Boulder: Westview Press, 1989

Hinrichs, H.H., 'Certainty as Criterion: Taxation of Foreign Investment in Afghanistan', *National Tax Journal*, 15(2), 1962

Holiqzoda, A., *Ta'rikhi siyosii Tojikon*, Dushanbe: Self-published, 1994

Hopkirk, P., *The Great Game: The Struggle for Empire in Central Asia*, New York: Kodansha International, 1992

Hopkirk, P., *On Secret Service East of Constantinople: Like Hidden Fire: The Plot to Bring Down the British Empire*, New York: Kodansha International, 1994

Horsman, S., 'Uzbekistan's Involvement in the Tajik Civil War 1992–1997: Domestic Considerations', *Central Asian Survey*, 18(1), 1999

Hosaini, H.N., *Afghanestan daz gogazgah-e Atash Wa Khun*, Peshawar: No Publisher, 1991

Hosmer, S.T. and T.W. Wolfe, *Soviet Policy and Practice toward Third World Countries*, Lexington: Lexington Books, 1983

Hudud, al-'Alam, *'The Regions of the World': A Persian Geography 372 AH–982 AD*, Oxford: Oxford University Press, 1937

Hussain, S.R., 'Pakistan-American Relations in Soviet Perspective: An Evaluation', in L.E. Rose and K. Matinuddin (eds), *Beyond Afghanistan: The Emerging US-Pakistan Relations*, Berkeley: Institute of East Asian Studies, University of California, 1989

Hyman, A., *Afghanistan under Soviet Domination, 1964–81*, London: Macmillan, 1982

Hyman, A., *Afghanistan under Soviet Domination, 1964–83*, London: Macmillan, 1984

Imomov, S., 'Iz istorii obshchestvennoi mysli Afganistana', in *Afganistan: ekonomika, politika, istoriia*, Moscow: Nauka, 1984

Istoriia Afganistana s drevneishikh vremen do nashikh dnei, Moscow: Mysl, 1982

'Iz "Protokolov komissii po izucheniiu Afganistana i Indii" za 1905 god', *Vostok*, No. 3, 1989

Jafri, H.A.S., *Indo-Afghan Relations (1947–67)*, New Delhi: Sterling Publishers, 1976

Jain, R.K. (ed.), *US-South Asian Relations, 1947–1982*, Vol. 1, New Delhi: Radiant Publishers, 1983

Jawad, N., *Afghanistan: A Nation of Minorities*, London: Minority Rights Group, 1990

Jawaharlal Nehru's Speeches, 1949–1953, Delhi: The Publications Division, Ministry of Information and Broadcasting, Government of India, 1954

Jennings, J., 'The *Taliban* and Foggy Bottom', *The Washington Times*, 25 October 1996

Jones, R.A., *The Soviet Concept of 'Limited Sovereignty' from Lenin to Gorbachev: The Brezhnev Doctrine*, Houndmills: Macmillan, 1990

Jones, R.W., 'Beyond Afghanistan: US-Pakistan Security Relations', in L.E. Rose and K. Matinuddin (eds), *Beyond Afghanistan: The Emerging US-Pakistan Relations*, Berkeley: Institute of East Asian Studies, University of California, 1989

'Kak ubivali H. Amina', *Argumenty i fakty*, No. 44, November 1990

Kakar, H., 'Trends in Modern Afghan History', in L. Duprée and L. Albert (eds), *Afghanistan in the 1970s*, New York: Praeger Publishers, 1974

Kakar, H., 'The Fall of the Afghan Monarchy in 1973', *International Journal of Middle East Studies*, 9(2), 1978

Kakar, H.K., *Government and Society in Afghanistan: The Reign of Amir 'Abd al-Rahman Khan*, Austin and London: University of Texas Press, 1979

Kakar, M.H., *Afghanistan: The Soviet Invasion and the Afghan Response, 1979–1982*, Berkeley: University of California Press, 1997

Kamali, M.H., *Law in Afghanistan*, Leiden: E.J. Brill, 1985

Kartha, T., 'The Diffusion of Light Weapons in Pakistan', *Small Wars and Insurgencies*, 8(1), Spring 1997

Keddie, N.R., *Sayyid Jamal ad-din 'al-Afghani': A Political Biography*, Berkeley: University of California Press, 1972

Kedourie, E., *Afghani and 'Abduh: An Essay on Religious Unbelief and Political Activism in Modern Islam*, London: Frank Cass, 1966

Khalfin, N.A., *Prisoedinenie Srednei Azii k Rossii*, Moscow: Nauka, 1965.

Khalfin, N.A., *Rossiia i khanstva Srednei Azii*, Moscow: Nauka, 1974

Khalfin, N.A., *Zaria svobody nad Kabulom*, Moscow: Nauka, 1985

Khalfin, N., 'The Struggle of the Peoples of Afghanistan for Independence and against the British Colonialists', in *Afghanistan: Past and Present*, Moscow: USSR Academy of Sciences, 1982

Khalili, K., *'Ayyari az Khorasan. Amir Habibullah khadem-e din-e rasulullah*, Peshawar: No Publisher, 1984

Khalilzad, Z., *The Return of the Great Game: Superpower Rivalry and Domestic Turmoil in Afghanistan, Iran, Pakistan, and Turkey*, Santa Monica: California Seminar on International Security and Foreign Policy, 1980

Khalilzad, Z., 'Moscow's Afghan War', *Problems of Communism*, 35, January–February 1986

Khalilzad, Z., 'Afghanistan: Time to Re-Engage', *The Washington Post*, 1 October 1996

Khan, I., 'Afghanistan: A Geopolitical Study', *Central Asian Survey*, 17(2), 1998

Khan, M.I., 'War Without End', *The Herald*, June 1997

Khan, M.M.S.M., *The Life of Abdur Rahman, Amir of Afghanistan*, Vol. II, London: John Murray, 1900

Khashimbekov, Kh., *Uzbeki severnogo Afganistana*, Moscow: IVRAN, 1994

Kheifets, A.N., *Sovetskaia Rossiia i sopredelnye strany Vostoka, 1918–1920*, Moscow: Nauka, 1964

Kheifets, A.N., *Sovetskaia diplomatiia i narody Vostoka, 1921–1927*, Moscow: Nauka, 1968

Kheifets, A.N., 'Uzy dobrososedstva i bratstva nerastorzhimy', *Aziia i Afrika segodnia*, No. 2, 1981

Khoteev, P.I., 'Novye dannye o "Zagovore shelkovykh pisem"', in *Afganistan: ekonomika, politika, istoriia*, Moscow: Nauka, 1984

Khrushchev, N.S., *Khrushchev Remembers*, Boston: Little, Brown and Company, 1970

Kiseleva, L.N., *Iazyk Dari Afganistana*, Moscow: Nauka, 1985

Kissinger, H., *The White House Years*, London: Weidenfeld & Nicolson and Michael Joseph, 1979

Kissinger, H., *Years of Upheaval*, London: Weidenfeld & Nicolson and Michael Joseph, 1982

Klass, R. (ed.), *Afghanistan: The Great Game Revisited*, New York: Freedom House, 1987

Kohzad, A.A., 'Men and Events in Afghanistan through the 18th and 19th Century', *Afghanistan*, 11(4), October–December 1956

Kollmann, N.S., *Kinship and Politics: The Making of the Muscovite Political System, 1345–1547*, Stanford: Stanford University Press, 1987

Korgun, V.G., 'K voprosu o roli kochevnikov v Afganistane noveishego vremeni', in *Arabskie strany, Turtsiia, Iran, Afganistan. Istoriia, ekonomika*, Moscow: Nauka, 1973

Korgun, V.G., *Afganistan v 20–30e gody XX v. Stranitsy politicheskoi istorii*, Moscow: Nauka, 1979

Korgun, V., 'The First Stage of Afghanistan's Independent Development', *Afghanistan: Past and Present*, Moscow: USSR Academy of Sciences, 1982

Korgun, V.G., *Intelligentsiia v politicheskoi zhizni Afganistana*, Moscow: Nauka, 1983

Kornienko, G.M., 'Kak prinimalis' resheniia o vvode sovetskikh voisk v Afganistan i ikh vyvode', *Novaia i noveishaia istoriia*, No. 3, May–June 1993

Kornienko, G.M., 'The Afghan Endeavour: Perplexities of the Military Incursion and Withdrawal', *Journal of South Asian and Middle Eastern Studies*, 17(2), Winter 1994

Krugliakov, G., 'Afganskii izlom', *Kazakhstanskaia pravda*, 5 December 1997

Kukhtin, V.G., 'Problema tranzita v ekonomike i politike Afganistana', in N.M. Gurevich (ed.), *Voprosy ekonomiki Afganistana*, Moscow: Izdatelstvo vostochnoi literatury, 1963

Kukhtina, G.I., 'K voprosu o podgotovke natsionalnykh tekhnicheskikh kadrov v Afganistane (1919–1961)', in N.M. Gurevich (ed.), *Voprosy ekonomiki Afganistana*, Moscow: Izdatelstvo vostochnoi literatury, 1963

Kuzichkin, V., *Inside the KGB: My Life in Soviet Espionage*, New York: Pantheon Books, 1990

Lee, J.L., *The 'Ancient Supremacy': Bukhara, Afghanistan and the Battle for Balkh, 1731–1901*, Leiden, New York, Koln: E.J. Brill, 1996

Liakhovskii, A.A. and V.M. Zabrodin, *Tainy afganskoi voiny*, Moscow: Planeta, 1991

Logashova, B.-R., 'Etnokulturnaia situatsiia v Afganistane', *Rosy i narody*, No. 16, 1986

Luciani, G. (ed.), *The Arab State*, London: Routledge, 1990

Luzhetskaia, N.L., *Ocherki istorii Vostochnogo Gindukusha vo vtoroi polovine XIX*, Moscow: Nauka, 1986

Ma'aroof, M.K., *Afghanistan in World Politics (A Study of Afghan-US Relations)*, Delhi: Gian Publishing House, 1987

Maass, C.D., 'The Afghanistan Conflict: External Involvement', *Central Asian Survey*, 18(1), 1999

Machiavelli, N., *The Prince*, Harmondsworth: Penguin, 1972

Magnus, R., 'The Constitution of 1964: A Decade of Political Experimentation', in L. Duprée and L. Albert (eds), *Afghanistan in the 1970s*, New York: Praeger Publishers, 1974

Magnus, R.H., 'Muhammad Zahir Khan, Former King of Afghanistan', *The Middle East Journal*, 30(1), Winter 1976

Mahmudov, E.R., 'Afganistan. Osnovnye etapy evoliutsii gosudarstvennoi politiki v oblasti industrializatsii', in *Afganistan: ekonomika, istoriia, kultura*, Moscow: Nauka, 1989

Male, B., *Revolutionary Afghanistan: A Reappraisal*, London and Canberra: Croom Helm, 1982

Maley, W., 'Afghanistan Observed', *Australian Journal of International Affairs*, 51(2), 1997

Maley, W., 'The Dynamics of Regime Transition in Afghanistan', *Central Asian Survey*, 16(2), 1997

Maley, W., 'Introduction: Interpreting the Taliban', in W. Maley (ed.), *Fundamentalism Reborn? Afghanistan and the Taliban*, London: Hurst & Company, 1998

Maley, W., 'Mine Action in Afghanistan', *Refuge*, 17(4), October 1998

Maley, W., *The Afghanistan Wars*, London: Palgrave Macmillan, 2002

Maley, W. and F.H. Saikal, *Political Order in Post-Communist Afghanistan*, Boulder: Lynne Rienner Publishers, 1992

Marvin, C., *The Russian Advance Towards India*, London: Sampson Low, Marston, Searle, & Rivington, 1882

Marx, K., *Notes on Indian History (664–1858)*, Moscow: Foreign Languages Publishing House, 1956

Masson, V.M. and V.A. Romodin, *Istoriia Afganistana*, Vol. I, Moscow: Nauka, 1964

Masson, V.M. and V.A. Romodin, *Istoriia Afganistana*, Vol. II, Moscow: Nauka, 1965

Materialy XXVIIs'ezda KPSS, Moscow: Izdatelstvo politicheskoi literatury, 1987

Matinuddin, K., *Power Struggle in the Hindu Kush: Afghanistan (1978–1991)*, Lahore: Wajidalis, 1991

McCain, M., 'Thinking South: Soviet Strategic Interests in Iran, Afghanistan, and Pakistan', in H. Malik (ed.), *Soviet-American Relations with Pakistan, Iran and Afghanistan*, London: Macmillan, 1987

McChesney, R.D., *Kabul under Seige: Fayz Muhammad's Account of the 1929 Uprising*, Princeton: Markus Wiener Publishers, 1999

McGhee, G.C., 'The Strategic Importance of Iran, Afghanistan and Pakistan to the United States', in H. Malik (ed.), *Soviet-American Relations with Pakistan, Iran and Afghanistan*, London: Macmillan, 1987

McMunn, G., *Afghanistan: From Darius to Amanullah*, London: G. Bell and Sons, 1929

Medvedev, V., 'Nechaiannaia revoliutsiia. Bukhara, 1920g', *Druzhba narodov*, No. 1, 1992

Medvedev, V., 'Basmachi – obrechennoe voinstvo', *Druzhba narodov*, No. 8, 1992

Mehrotra, O.N., 'The Troubled CIS', in Sreedhar (ed.), *Taliban and the Afghan Turmoil: The Role of USA, Pakistan, Iran and China*, New Delhi: Himalayan Books, 1997

'Memorandum of Conversation Between Brezhnev and Taraki, March 20, 1979 (Moscow)', *Journal of South Asian and Middle Eastern Studies*, 17(2), Winter 1994

Mendelson, S.E., *Changing Course: Ideas, Politics, and the Soviet Withdrawal from Afghanistan*, Princeton: Princeton University Press, 1998

Merimskii, V.A., 'Voina v Afganistane: zapiski uchastnika', *Novaia i noveishaia istoriia*, No. 3, May–June 1995

Metcalf, B.D., *Islamic Revival in British India: Deoband, 1860–1900*, Princeton: Princeton University Press, 1982

Migdal, J.S., *Strong Societies and Weak States: State-Society Relations and State Capabilities in the Third World*, Princeton: Princeton University Press, 1988

Moghadam, V.M., 'Patriarchy and the Politics of Gender in Modernizing Societies: Iran, Pakistan and Afghanistan', *South Asia Bulletin*, 13(1–2), 1993

Mohammad, F., *Kniga upominanii o miatezhe*, Moscow: My si, 1988

Mohana, L.M., *Life of the Amir Dost Mohammed Khan, of Kabul: With His Political Proceedings towards the English, Russian, and Persian Governments, Including the Victory and Disasters of the British Army in Afghanistan*, Vol. II, London: Longman, Brown, Green, and Longmans, 1846

Molesworth, G.N., *Afghanistan 1919: An Account of Operations in the Third Afghan War*, Bombay: Asia Publishing House, 1962

Monasebat-e Afghanestan wa Ettehad-e Shurawi dar salha-ye 1919–1969, Kabul: Wezarat-e omur-ekhareja-ye Afghanestan [1970]

Monasebat-e Afghanestan wa Ettehad-e Shurawi dar salha-ye 1919–1969, Kabul: Ministry of Foreign Affairs of Afghanistan, [n.d.], Document 149

Montagno, G.L., 'The Pak-Afghan Detente', *Asian Survey*, 3(12), 1963

Morgan, G., *Anglo-Russian Rivalry in Central Asia: 1810–1895*, London: Frank Cass, 1981

Mote, V.L., 'Afghanistan and the Transport Infrastructures of Turkestan', in M. Hauner and R.L. Canfield (eds), *Afghanistan and the Soviet Union*, Boulder: Westview Press, 1989

Muhammad, F., *Memoir of the Coup*, trans. from Russian by R.D. McChesney, unpublished manuscript, April 1996

Mukerjee, D., 'Afghanistan under Daoud: Relations with Neighbouring States', *Asian Survey*, 15(4), April 1975

Mundy, Martha, *Domestic Government: Kinship, Community and Polity in North Yemen*, London and New York: I.B.Tauris, 1995

Mustafa, Z., 'Pakistan-Afghanistan Relations and Central Asian Politics (1973–1978)', *Pakistan Horizon*, 31(4), 1978

Naby, E., 'The Afghan Resistance Movement', in R.H. Magnus (ed.), *Afghan Alternatives: Issues, Options, and Policies*, New Brunswick: Transaction Books, 1985

Naby, E., 'Ethnic Factors in Afghanistan's Future', in B. Huldt and E. Jansson (eds), *The Tragedy of Afghanistan: The Social, Cultural and Political Impact of the Soviet Invasion*, London: Croom Helm, 1988

Najib, A.R.A., *Afghanestan dar gozargah-e atash wa khun*, Peshawar: Haj Nayyer Hosaini, 1991

'Najibullah's "Heroes" Harass Kabul's People', *AFGHANews*, 6(1), 1 January 1990

National Security Council Report to President Truman, 8 August 1951 (NSC 114/1)

Nawid, S., 'The State, the Clergy, and British Imperial Policy in Afghanistan During the 19th and Early 20th Centuries', *International Journal of Middle East Studies*, 29(4), 1997

Nazarov, Kh., *Said Jamaladdin Afgani i ego obshchestvenno-politicheskaia shkola*, Dushanbe: Donish, 1993

Nazarshoev, M., *Partiinaia organizatsiia Pamira v bor'be za sotsializm i kommunizm*, Dushanbe: Irfon, 1970

Negaran, H., 'The Afghan Coup of April 1978: Revolution and International Security', *Orbis*, 23(1), Spring 1979

Negargar, M.I., 'Afghanistan and the Nightmare of Communism', in S.B. Majrooh and S.M.Y. Elmi (eds), *The Sovietisation of Afghanistan*, Peshawar: Afghan Information Centre, No Date

Newby, E., A *Short Walk in the Hindu Kush*, London and Sydney: Pan Books, 1974

Newell, N.P. and R.S. Newell, *The Struggle for Afghanistan*, Ithaca and London: Cornell University Press, 1981

Newell, R.S., "The Prospects for State Building in Afghanistan', in A. Banuazizi and M. Weiner (eds), 'The Foreign Policy of Afghanistan', *Pakistan Horizon*, 17(1), 1964

Newell, R.S., 'Afghanistan: The Dangers of Cold War Generosity', *The Middle East Journal*, 23(2), Spring 1969

Newell, R.S., *The Politics of Afghanistan*, Ithaca and London: Cornell University Press, 1972

Nezamnama-ye forush-e amlak-e sarkari, Kabul, 1302AH

Nicosia, F.R., '"Drang Nach Osten" Continued: Germany and Afghanistan during the Weimar Republic', *Journal of Contemporary History*, 32(2), April 1997

Noelle, C., *State and Tribe in Nineteenth-Century Afghanistan: The Reign of Amir Dost Muhammad Khan (1826–1863)*, Richmond: Curzon Press, 1997

Noorani, A.G., *India: The Superpowers and the Neighbours*, New Delhi: South Asian Publishers, 1985

Noorzoy, M.S., 'Soviet Economic Interests in Afghanistan', *Problems of Communism*, 36(3), May–June 1987

Noorzoy, M.S., 'Long-Term Soviet Economic Interests and Policies in Afghanistan', in R. Klass (ed.), *Afghanistan: The Great Game Revisited*, New York: Freedom House, 1987

Norris, J.A., *The First Afghan War, 1838–1842*, Cambridge: Cambridge University Press, 1967

Noveishaia istoriia stran zarubezhnogo Vostoka, Vol. 2, Moscow: Izdatelstvo Moskovskogo universiteta, 1955

Ochildiev, D.I., *Ocherki bor'by afganskogo naroda za natsionalnuiu nezavisimost' i vnutrennie reformy, (1900–1914gg)*, Tashkent: Fan, 1967

Ochildiev, D.I., *Mladoafganskoe dvizhenie (1900–1920)*, Tashkent: Uzbekistan, 1985

Olcott, M.B., 'The Basmachi or Freemen's Revolt in Turkestan, 1918–24', *Soviet Studies*, 33(3), July 1981

Olesen, A., *Islam and Politics in Afghanistan*, Richmond: Curzon Press, 1995

Overby, P., *Holy Blood: An Inside View of the Afghan War*, Westport: Praeger, 1993

'Pakistan. Relations with Afghanistan', *The Round Table*, 52, December 1961–September 1962

Pazhwak, R., *Pakhtunistan: A New State in Central Asia*, London: The Royal Afghan Embassy, 1960

Pipes, R., 'Detente: Moscow's View', in E.P. Hoffmann and F.J. Fleron, Jr (eds), *The Conduct of Soviet Foreign Policy*, New York: Aldine Publishing Company, 1980

Plastun, V., 'NDPA: voprosy edinstva i soiuznikov na sovremennom etape revoliutsii', *Spetsialnyi bulleten' IVAN SSSR*, No. 2 (246), 1987

Pokrovskii, M., 'Dorogoi kulturnogo progressa', *Aziia i Afrika segodnia*, No. 7, 1974

Polk, W.R., 'The Nature of Modernisation. The Middle East and North Africa', *Foreign Affairs*, 44(1), October 1965

Poullada, L.B., 'Political Modernisation in Afghanistan: The Amanullah Reforms', in G. Grassmuck and L.W. Adamec with F.H. Irwin (eds), *Afghanistan: Some New Approaches*, Ann Arbor: Center for Near Eastern and North African Studies, University of Michigan, 1969

Poullada, L., *Reform and Rebellion in Afghanistan, 1919–1929: King Amanullah's Failure to Modernize a Tribal Society*, Ithaca, NY: Cornell University Press, 1973

Poullada, L.B., 'Pushtunistan: Afghan Domestic Politics and Relations with Pakistan', in A.T. Embree (ed.), *Pakistan's Western Borderlands: The Transformation of a Political Order*, New Delhi: Vikas Publishing House, 1977

Poullada, L.B., 'The Road to Crisis 1919–1980 – American Failures, Afghan Errors and Soviet Successes', in R. Klass (ed.), *Afghanistan: The Great Game Revisited*, New York: Freedom House, 1987

Poullada, L.B. and L.D.J. Poullada, *The Kingdom of Afghanistan and the United States: 1828–1973*, Lincoln: Center for Afghanistan Studies at the University of Nebraska in Omaha and Dageford Publishing, 1995

Quddus, S.A., *Afghanistan and Pakistan: A Geopolitical Study*, Lahore: Ferozsons Ltd, 1982

Quddus, S.A., *The Pathans*, Lahore: Ferozsons, 1987

Qureshi, S.M.M., 'Pakhtunistan: The Frontier Dispute between Afghanistan and Pakistan', *Pacific Affairs*, 39(1–2), Spring–Summer 1966

Rashid, A, 'Afghanistan: Apocalypse Now', *The Herald*, October 1995

Rashid, A., 'Power Play, and "Pipe Dreams"', *Far Eastern Economic Review*, 10 April 1997

Rashid, A., 'Pakistan and the Taliban', in W. Maley (ed.), *Fundamentalism Reborn? Afghanistan and the Taliban*, London: Hurst and Company, 1998

Rashid, A., *Taliban: Militant Islam, Oil and Fundamentalism in Central Asia*, London: I.B.Tauris, 2000

Rawlinson, Sir H., *England and Russia in the East*, reprint, New York: Praeger Publishers, 1970

Reardon, P.J., 'Modernisation and Reform: The Contemporary Endeavour', in G. Grassmuck and L.W. Adamec with F.H. Irwin (eds), *Afghanistan: Some New Approaches*, Ann Arbor: Center for Near Eastern and North African Studies, University of Michigan, 1969

'Recent Developments in Afghanistan', *Pakistan Horizon*, 19(3), 1966

Reetz, D., 'Pakistan and the Central Asian Hinterland Option: The Race for Regional Security and Development', *Journal of South Asian and Middle Eastern Studies*, 17(1), Fall 1993

Reisner, I., 'Specific Features of the Development of Feudalism among the Afghans', in *Afghanistan: Past and Present*, Moscow: USSR Academy of Sciences, 1982

Reisner, I.M., *Afghanistan*, Moscow: Gosizdat, 1929

Reshtia, S.Q., 'Social Reforms in Afghanistan in Relation to Neighbouring Countries: Interference and Peace', in E.W. Anderson and N.H. Duprée (eds), *The Cultural Basis of Afghan Nationalism*, London and New York: Pinter Publishers, 1990

Reshtia, S.Q., *Khatirat-e siyasi Sayed Qassem Reshtia, 1311 to 1371 [1932–1992]*, Virginia: American Speedy Press, 1997

Rezun, M., *Intrigue and War in Southwest Asia: The Struggle for Supremacy from Central Asia to Iraq*, New York: Praeger, 1992

Roberts, J.M., *History of the World*, London: Hutchinson, 1976

Rodionov, A.A., 'Zapiski posla SSSR v Pakistane v 1971–1974gg', *Novaia i noveishaia istoriia*, Nos 1 and 2, 1997

Rodman, P.W., *More Precious than Peace: The Cold War and the Struggle for the Third World*, New York: C. Scribner's Sons, 1994

Rogers, T., *The Soviet Withdrawal from Afghanistan: Analysis and Chronology*, Westport: Greenwood Press, 1992

Romodin, V.A., 'U istokov sovetsko-afganskikh otnoshenii', in *Afganistan: ekonomika, politika, istoriia*, Moscow: Nauka, 1984

Romodin, V.A., *Afganistan vo vtoroi polovine XIX - nachale Xv. Ofitsialnaia istoriia i istoriograftia*, Moscow: Nauka, 1990

Rossow, R. Jr, 'The Battle of Azerbaijan, 1946', *The Middle East Journal*, 10(1), Winter 1956

Roy, A., *The Soviet Intervention in Afghanistan: Causes, Consequences, and India's Response*, New Delhi: Associated Publishing House, 1987

Roy, O., *Islam and Resistance in Afghanistan*, Cambridge: Cambridge University Press, 1986

Roy, O., 'Afghanistan: Back to Tribalism or on to Lebanon?', *Third World Quarterly*, 11(4), October 1989, pp. 70–82

Roy, O., *Afghanistan: From Holy War to Civil War*, Princeton: The Darwin Press, 1995

Rubin, B.R., 'Human Rights in Afghanistan', in R. Klass (ed.), *Afghanistan: The Great Game Revisited*, New York: Freedom House, 1987

Rubin, B.R., *The Fragmentation of Afghanistan: State Formation and Collapse in the International System*, New Haven: Yale University Press, 1995

Rubin, B.R., 'Women and Pipelines: Afghanistan's Proxy Wars', *International Affairs*, 73(2), 1997

Rubinstein, A.Z., *Soviet Policy toward Turkey, Iran and Afghanistan: The Dynamics of Influence*, New York: Praeger, 1982

Rule, J.B., *Theories of Civil Violence*, Berkeley: University of California Press, 1988

Sa'di, S., *Mukhtasari ta'rikhi siyosii Tojikoni Afghanistan*, Dushanbe: Oli Somon, 1995

Sabol, S., 'The Creation of Soviet Central Asia: The 1924 National Delimitation', *Central Asian Survey*, 14(2), 1995

Saikal, A., *The Rise and Fall of the Shah*, Princeton: Princeton University Press, 1980

Saikal, A., 'Kemalism: Its Influence on Iran and Afghanistan', *International Journal of Turkish Studies*, 2(2), 1982

Saikal, A., 'The Regional Politics of the Afghan Crisis', in A. Saikal and W. Maley (eds), *The Soviet Withdrawal from Afghanistan*, Cambridge: Cambridge University Press, 1989

Saikal, A., 'Afghanistan: Culture and Ideology under Pre-1978 Governments', *Central Asian Survey*, 11(1), 1992

Saikal, A., 'The UN and Afghanistan: A Case of Failed Peacemaking Intervention', *International Peacekeeping*, 3(1), Spring 1996

Saikal, A, 'Afghanistan's Ethnic Conflict', *Survival*, 40(2), Summer 1998

Saikal, A., 'The Role of Outside Actors in Afghanistan', *Middle East Policy*, 7(4), October 2000

Saikal, A., 'Afghanistan, Terrorism, and American and Australian Responses', *Australian Journal of International Affairs*, 56(1), April 2002

Saikal, A. and W. Maley, *Regime Change in Afghanistan: Foreign Interventions and the Politics of Legitimacy*, Boulder: Westview Press, 1991

Shah, I.A., *Modern Afghanistan*, London: Low, 1939

Shahi, A., 'Pakistan's Relations with the United States', in H. Malik (ed.), *Soviet-American Relations with Pakistan, Iran and Afghanistan*, London: Macmillan, 1987

Shahrani, M.N., 'State Building and Social Fragmentation in Afghanistan: A Historical Perspective', in A. Banuazizi and M. Weiner (eds), *The State, Religion, and Ethnic Politics: Afghanistan, Iran, and Pakistan*, Syracuse: Syracuse University Press, 1986

Shahrani, M.N., 'Afghanistan: State and Society in Retrospect', in E.W. Anderson and N.H. Duprée (eds), *The Cultural Basis of Afghan Nationalism*, London and New York: Pinter Publishers, 1990

Shahrani, M.N., The Future of the State and the Structure of Community Governance in Afghanistan', in W. Maley (ed.), *Fundamentalism Reborn? Afghanistan and the Taliban*, London: Hurst & Co., 1998

Shalinsky, A.C., *Long Years of Exile: Central Asian Refugees in Afghanistan and Pakistan*, Lanham: University Press of America, 1994

Sharabi, H., *Neopatriarchy: A Theory of Distorted Change in Arab Society*, New York: Oxford University Press, 1988

Shkirando, A.I, 'Novye dannye ob afganskom letopistse Faiz Muhammade i ego sochineniiakh', in *Afganistan: ekonomika, politika, istoriia*, Moscow: Nauka, 1984

Shkirando, A.I., 'Gazeta "Afganistan" kak organ afganskoi oppozitsii v 1929g', in *Afganistan: Istoriia, ekonomika, kultura*, Moscow: Nauka, 1989

Shokhumorov, S., 'Arkhiv Inaiatulla-khana kak istochnik po istorii Afganistana', *Narody Azii i Afriki*, No. 1, 1978

Shroder, J.F., Jr and A.T. Assifi, 'Afghan Resources and Soviet Exploitation', in R. Klass (ed.), *Afghanistan: The Great Game Revisited*, New York: Freedom House, 1987

Situation of Human Rights in Afghanistan, New York: United Nations, A/47/656, 17 November 1992

Smith, A.D., *The Ethnic Revival*, Cambridge: Cambridge University Press, 1981

Smith, Dennis, *The Rise of Historical Sociology*, Philadelphia: Temple University Press, 1991

Spain, J., *The Pathan Borderland*, The Hague: Mouton, 1963

Spolnikov, V.N., *Afganistan: islamskaia kontrrevoliutsiia*, Moscow: Nauka, 1987

'Stanovlenie demokraticheskoi obshchestvennoi mysli i demokraticheskikh dvizhenii', in *Afganistan: problemy voiny i mira*, Moscow: IVRAN, 1996

Steele, J., *The Limits of Soviet Power: The Kremlin's Foreign Policy – Brezhnev to Chernenko*, Harmondsworth: Penguin Books, 1985

Stepan, A., 'Democratic Opposition and Democratisation Theory', *Government and Opposition*, 32(4), 1997

Stewart, R.T., *Fire in Afghanistan, 1914–1929: Faith, Hope and the British Empire*, New York: Doubleday, 1973

Strokan, S. and R. Budrin, 'Afganistan: strana nakanune raskola?', *Rossiia i musulmanskii mir*, No. 3, 1994

Sykes, P., *A History of Afghanistan*, Vol. II, London: Macmillan, 1940

Tapper, N. and R. Tapper, 'Marriage Preferences and Ethnic Relations among Durrani Pashtuns of Afghan Turkestan', *Folk*, 24, 1982

Tapper, N., *Bartered Brides: Politics, Gender and Marriage in an Afghan Tribal Society*, Cambridge: Cambridge University Press, 1991

Tapper, R. (ed.), *The Conflict of Tribe and State in Iran and Afghanistan*, New York: St. Martin's Press, 1983

Tate, G.P., *The Kingdom of Afghanistan: A Historical Sketch*, Karachi: Indus Publications, 1973

Temirkhanov, L., *Vostochnye pushtuny v novoe vremia*, Moscow: Nauka, 1984

Teplinskii, L.B., *SSSR i Afganistan, 1919–1981*, Moscow: Nauka, Glav. red. vostochnoi lit-ry, 1982

Teplinskii, L.B., *Istoriia sovetsko-afganskikh otnoshenii, 1919–1987*, Moscow: Mysl, 1988

The Life of Abdur Rahman, Amir of Afghanistan, Vol. II, London: John Murray, 1900

The State, Religion, and Ethnic Politics: Afghanistan, Iran, and Pakistan, Syracuse: Syracuse University Press, 1986

Thomas, C, 'Taliban Rout Ends Islamabad's Dream', *The Australian*, 4 June 1997

Tilly, C., 'Town and Country in Revolution', in J.W. Lewis (ed.), *Peasant Rebellion and Communist Revolution in Asia*, Stanford: Stanford University Press, 1974

Tursunov, R., 'Pomoshch' sovetskikh sredneaziatskikh respublik Afganistanu', *Narody Azii i Afriki*, No. 6, 1972

Uberoi, J.P.S., Social Organisation of the Tajiks of Andarab Valley, Afghanistan, Ph.D. Thesis, Australian National University, Canberra, 1964

Urban, M., *War in Afghanistan*, London: Macmillan, 1990

Vasiliev, A., *Rossiia na Blizhnem i Srednem Vostoke: ot messianstva k pragmatizmu*, Moscow: Nauka, 1993

Verrier, A., *Francis Younghusband and the Great Game*, London: Jonathan Cape, 1991

Volodarskii, M.I., *Sovety i ikh iuzhnye sosedi Iran i Afganistan (1917–1933)*, London: Overseas Publications Interchange, 1985

Wahidi-Wardak, M.S., 'Events Leading Up to the Soviet Invasion of Afghanistan', in E.W. Anderson and N.H. Duprée (eds), *The Cultural Basis of Afghan Nationalism*, London and New York: Pinter Publishers, 1990

Wali, M.S., *Moi vospominaniia*, Moscow: OGIZ, 1960

Waterbury, J., *The Egypt of Nasser and Sadat: The Political Economy of Two Regimes*, Princeton: Princeton University Press, 1983

Watkins, M.B., *Afghanistan: Land in Transition*, Princeton: D. van Nostrand, 1963

Weinbaum, M.G., 'The Legislator as Intermediary: Integration of the Centre and Periphery in Afghanistan', in A.F. Eldridge (ed.), *Legislatures in Plural Societies: The Search for Cohesion in National Development*, Durham: Duke University Press, 1977

Westad, O.A., 'Prelude to Invasion: The Soviet Union and the Afghan Communists, 1978–1979', *The International History Review*, 16(1), February 1994

Wilber, D. (ed.), *Afghanistan*, New Haven: Human Relations Area Files, 1956

Wolpert, S., *Zulfi Bhutto of Pakistan: His Life and Times*, New York: Oxford University Press, 1993

World Military Expenditures and Arms Transfers, 1970–1979, ACDA Publication 112, Washington, DC: Arms Control and Disarmament Agency, March 1982

Yapp, Malcolm E., 'A Little Game: Afghanistan Since 1918', *South Asian Review*, 8(4), 1975

Yapp, M.E., *The Near East Since the First World War*, London and New York: Longman, 1991

Yate, C.E., *Northern Afghanistan or Letters from the Afghan Boundary Commission*, Lahore: Al-Biruni, 1976

Zaidi, M., 'Afghanistan: Case Study in Competitive Peaceful Co-Existence', *Pakistan Horizon*, 15(2), 1962

Zolo, Da., *Democracy and Complexity: A Realist Approach*, Cambridge: Polity Press, 1992

Index